William Truran, J. A Phillips, W. H. Dorman

The Iron Manufacture of Great Britain

William Truran, J. A Phillips, W. H. Dorman

The Iron Manufacture of Great Britain

ISBN/EAN: 9783337177270

Printed in Europe, USA, Canada, Australia, Japan

Cover: Foto ©ninafisch / pixelio.de

More available books at **www.hansebooks.com**

THE

IRON MANUFACTURE

OF

GREAT BRITAIN,

THEORETICALLY AND PRACTICALLY CONSIDERED;

INCLUDING

DESCRIPTIVE DETAILS OF THE ORES, FUELS, AND FLUXES EMPLOYED,
THE PRELIMINARY OPERATION OF CALCINATION,
THE BLAST, REFINING, AND PUDDLING FURNACES, ENGINES AND MACHINERY,
AND THE VARIOUS PROCESSES IN UNION,
ETC. ETC.

BY W. TRURAN, C.E.,

FORMERLY ENGINEER AT THE DOWLAIS IRON-WORKS UNDER THE LATE SIR JOHN GUEST, BART.,
SUBSEQUENTLY AT THE HIRWAIN AND FOREST WORKS, UNDER MR CRAWSHAY.

REVISED FROM THE MANUSCRIPT OF THE LATE MR. TRURAN

BY J. ARTHUR PHILLIPS,

AUTHOR OF "A MANUAL OF METALLURGY," "RECORDS OF MINING," ETC. ETC., AND

WILLIAM H. DORMAN, C.E.

THIRD EDITION,
REPRINTED FROM THE SECOND.

LONDON:
E. AND F. N. SPON, 16, BUCKLERSBURY.
1865.

[*The right of Translation is reserved.*]

PREFACE TO THE FIRST EDITION.

Among the manufactures of Great Britain, that of iron has recently risen to a magnitude which entitles it to rank as the most important, both as regards the value of the products, and the direct bearing they have on the progress of civilisation and commerce. Iron is a metal comparatively unknown in uncivilised districts, and it is worthy of remark that the production and consumption of this metal in proportion to the population is highest in nations excelling in commerce and the mechanic arts, and declining as we descend the scale of civilisation, until, arriving at the lowest degree of intelligence displayed by the human race, it is entirely wanting. The ores of iron are extensively disseminated throughout the globe, but their conversion in large quantities into metallic iron is limited to a few of the more advanced European nations and the Anglo-Saxon population of America. The presence of apparently inexhaustible supplies of ores, obtained with the greatest facility, and yielding irons of the finest description, immediately contiguous to vast deposits of mineral fuel peculiarly adapted for their reduction, has resulted in an extraordinary development of this manufacture in Great Britain. At the present day, the annual production of three of the principal districts of the United Kingdom, viz. South Wales, South Staffordshire, and Scotland, considerably exceeds the collective production of all other nations. The importance of this branch of metallurgical industry to the commercial prosperity of the kingdom may be inferred from the circumstance, that, while the home consumption in foundries and manufactories absorbs one-half of the production, the quantity exported is scarcely inferior to the gross produce of all other nations, a fact which shows a high state of mechanical science and the attainment of a degree of perfection far beyond that common in other countries. The production of crude iron during the year (1854) exceeded $3\frac{1}{4}$ millions of tons; and the production of malleable iron amounted to nearly 2 millions of tons; value in the manufactured form, at current prices, 25 millions; the number of operatives employed in the manufacture, including those engaged in the operations of quarrying and mining the ore, was 238,000; and in giving motion to the various machines, and blowing the various furnaces, 2120 steam-engines of an aggregate power of 242,000 horses were employed.

On a manufacture of such magnitude and importance there exists no special treatise beyond the one entitled "Mushet's Papers on Iron and Steel," originally published more than half a century ago, when the annual production scarcely reached 100,000 tons, and these are confined to a consideration of the then known facts relating to the production of crude iron. In later years papers on subjects connected with the manufacture have appeared in various journals, but their scientific value is considerably lessened either through their antique bearings, or the theoretical views and evident bias of the writers in favour of particular processes and patented inventions. This paucity of reliable information on the principles involved in the various processes of the manufacture, has principally arisen from the disinclination to communicate their experience so generally manifested by parties practically acquainted with the subject, but partially, also, from the inability of those otherwise competent and disposed to undertake the task to illustrate their work by the requisite drawings. In submitting the following pages, the author deems an apology unnecessary—the general want of a comprehensive work on the subject is too well known to require comment; the facts and observations put forward are founded on the results of nearly seventeen years of practice, and comprise, in addition to descriptive details of the furnaces and machines employed, and the various operations incidental to the manufacture of iron in a large way, theoretical analyses of the causes contributing to the economical production of the various qualities of crude and malleable iron from different descriptions of ores under dissimilar modes of treatment—the object being the dissemination of correct information on the points of greatest importance.

The remarks on the hot-blast system, and the conclusions drawn relative to the effect so commonly ascribed to the application of this invention being due to causes other than the mere heating, though given after mature consideration, and an attentive examination of the results produced on different furnaces, are at variance with received opinions on this subject, and may lead the reader to the inference that their purpose is other than to convey correct ideas on a very important department of the manufacture. In arriving, however, at just conclusions it will be remembered that while the surprising economy of the hot-blast in certain districts previously using very large quantities of coal is freely admitted, the reason given by writers generally of its superiority, "that the heated blast is better fitted for supporting combustion," is altogether untenable. It does not account for the heat yielded by the combustion of a given quantity of coal in the stove grates being so much superior to that developed by a similar quantity consumed in the furnace; it does not account for the inability of the heated blast to economise fuel in heavily-burdened charcoal furnaces; it is insufficient to account for the variation in the results obtained with different coals in similarly formed furnaces, and the dissimilar effects observed with the same fuel in differently shaped furnaces; neither does it explain the reason why the beneficial effects of heated air on combustion should be confined to blast furnaces, nor for the cold blast being for a limited period superior to the hot when introduced into hot-blast furnaces.

The remarks on the withdrawal of the gases from blast furnaces and their subsequent combustion may also lead to similar misapprehension, and the inference be drawn that the author deprecates innovation; but on this subject, which has recently been extensively agitated, it may be well to state that the withdrawal of heat or gases from a furnace, either at a low level by natural draught, or from a high level by mechanical means, unless attended by a corresponding disturbance in the smelting operations, implies a superabundance and previous waste; the utilization of which, by the erection and adaptation of secondary apparatus, may be profitable, but the legitimate mode of operating, by which a greater economy may be attained, is to adapt the quantity of fuel and form of the furnace to the requirements of the smelting process. If this be done, waste heat or other products capable of utilization will not be evolved, and the advantages of superior economy be attained without having recourse to the large outlay of capital incidental to all plans for economising superfluous products.

On other points, also, in which his views differ from the opinions generally advanced by writers on iron, the author has been guided by deductions drawn from practical observation, and however novel may appear the conclusions, he believes they are substantially correct, and

PREFACE TO THE FIRST EDITION.

in the elimination of the principles regulating the economy of the several processes entitled to greater consideration than mere speculative theories unsupported by practice.

The historical portion of the subject has been omitted. The author's acknowledgments are due to Mr. P. L. Simmonds, and other gentlemen, for much valuable matter bearing on this portion; its able treatment by Mr. Scrivenor in his "History of the Iron Trade;" and the generally little interest taken in it by many manufacturers and parties practically engaged, has been considered a sufficient reason for confining the work to its present limits.

July, 1855.

PREFACE TO THE SECOND EDITION.

In preparing the present work for the press we have done little more than arrange and systematize the papers and drawings of the late Mr. Truran. At the time of his death, which took place in Australia, he had nearly completed the second edition of his Metallurgy of Iron, or, to speak more correctly, re-written the volume, and increased the number of explanatory illustrations from twenty-three to eighty-four.

These papers having, on their arrival in England, been placed in our hands with a view to their publication, we have endeavoured to lay them before the public as nearly as possible in accordance with the expressed views of the author.

The great experience of Mr. Truran as an Iron Metallurgist, and the untiring industry with which, during many years, he collected notes and sketches of every kind of apparatus connected with the manufacture, is a sufficient guarantee for the perfect accuracy of the smallest practical details, while as an able draughtsman he has left behind him a series of beautifully-executed drawings of the furnaces and machinery he describes. These drawings, which have been carefully reproduced by Mr. Newbery, give a greatly increased value to the present over the former edition; and it is not too much to say that this work now forms the most complete and practical treatise on the Metallurgy of Iron to be found in the English language.

With respect to the opinions held by the author relative to the subject of waste heat, and the advantageous application of the unconsumed gases issuing from the blast furnace, we may remark that the experience of the last few years does not appear to entirely bear out the conclusions to which he had arrived.

It must, however, be remembered that Mr. Truran was essentially a practical man, and that the great value of his work is rather as a record of the exact state of this industry at the time at which he wrote, than as a scientific treatise affording information explanatory of the physical and chemical agencies which play such an important part in this branch of our manufactures.

With some of his observations of a theoretical nature we cannot ourselves entirely agree, but there can be no doubt that his remarks on the influence exerted by the area of the tunnel-head on the working and yield of furnaces are of much practical importance, and that the attention of ironmasters cannot be too carefully directed to this subject.

London, August, 1862.

CONTENTS.

IRON ORES.

	PAGE
Materials used in iron-making	1
Classes of iron ores	ib.
Analysis of argillaceous ores of South Wales	ib.
Staffordshire, North Wales, and Derbyshire	3
Yorkshire and Scotland	4
Carbonaceous ores of Scotland	5
North Staffordshire and South Wales	6
Calcareous ores of Dean Forest	7
Siliceous ores of Lancashire and Somersetshire, Cornwall and North Wales	9
Northamptonshire	10

SECTION I.
FUEL AND FLUX.

Analysis of South Wales coal	11
Staffordshire Derbyshire, Newcastle, Yorkshire, and Scotch coal	12
Analysis of limestone flux	13

SECTION II.
CALCINATION OF ORES.

Calcining kiln used in South Wales	15
Calcining in heaps in Staffordshire, Scotland, and South Wales	ib.
Merits of the two systems compared as relates to argillaceous ores	16
Calcining the black band ore of Scotland	17
The red and brown hematites	18
Process of calcining in kilns in Wales	20
Effect of calcining on various kinds of ironstone as regards loss of weight	21
Preparation of fuel	ib.
Preparation of flux	ib.

SECTION III.
BLAST FURNACES.

	PAGE
Erection of blast furnaces, foundations and external form	22
Material	23
Details of construction	ib.
Stack and lining	24
Bottom	25
Hearth	ib.
Boshes and body	26
Tunnel-head	27
Method of bricklaying	ib.
Binding	ib.
Drying and preparations for blowing-in and furnace fittings	28
Conveyance of blast to the furnace, blast valves, blast pipes	29
Tunnel-head paving	31
Cupola furnaces	ib.
Apparatus for lifting materials, inclined plane, water-balance lift, pneumatic lift	33
Blast heating-stoves	37

SECTION IV.
BLAST FURNACE OPERATIONS.

Blowing-in	40
Evils of forcing the furnace	41
Theory of the blast furnace	43
Chemical composition of the products of the furnace	45
Analyses of the gaseous column at various heights in the furnace	ib.
Composition of cinders	52
Composition of iron and accompanying cinder	55
Composition of various English and foreign pig-irons	60
Smelting	64

CONTENTS

SECTION V.

OBSERVATIONS ON THE WORKING OF BLAST FURNACES.

	PAGE
Charging	66
Scaffolds	68
Tuyeres, dark and bright	69
Blowing into the cinders	71
Tuyers blowing into the breast	ib.
Production of pig-iron	72
Quality of pig-iron referred to the ironstone from which it was produced	ib.
Argillaceous and carbonaceous ore	73
Calcareous and siliceous ore	74
Burden in Wales, Staffordshire, and Scotland compared	76
Proportions the materials bear to each other, to capacity of furnace, to blast, &c., in Welsh, Staffordshire, and Scotch furnaces, compared	77
Also in Welsh furnaces, working on various burdens	79

SECTION VI.

PRODUCE AND QUANTITY OF METAL.

Production of metal, cinder, and gases, compared with capacity of furnace, blast, bulk of materials, &c., in lais and Hirwain furnaces	83
Yield of ironstone of different kinds	88
Loss of metal in cinders through derangement of the furnace	90
Yield of ironstone on mixed burden	91
Yield of coal, and circumstances affecting it	92
Effect of water in the furnace on the yield of fuel	94
Effect of caustic lime as a flux	95
Value of raw coal for smelting	96
Large yield of fuel with carbonaceous ores	ib.
Effect of a hot blast on the yield of fuel	97
Yield of limestone	98
Proportionate to the amount of silica in the burden	ib.
Evils of an excess of limestone	99
Consumption of blast compared with that of fuel	100
Quality of metal	103
Effect upon the quality of weak coal and coke	104
Of other defects in the fuel	105
Of raw bituminous coal	106
Of small coal	107
Of limestone in different conditions	109
Of water on the blast furnace	110
Rate of production	111
Dependent on the kind of ore	112
On the quality of the fuel	113
On the season of the year	114

SECTION VII.

DENSITY OF BLAST.

Circumstances governing the density of the blast	115
Dependent on the breadth of the hearth	116
Necessity for maintaining a considerable pressure	117
Proper number of tuyeres discussed	118
Form and construction of tuyere and nose pipe	121

SECTION VIII.

INTERNAL OF FURNACES.

Reason for the slow progress of improvement in the construction of the furnace	124
Form of hearth	125
Dimensions of hearth	126
Form of boshes	127
Wear of boshes	129
Diameter of furnace and form of upper part	131
Diameter of throat	132
Advantage of a wide throat	134
Furnace parallel from the boshes to the throat	136
Height of furnace	137

SECTION IX.

QUALITY AND FUSIBILITY OF THE CRUDE IRON DEPENDENT ON THE STRUCTURE AND COMPOSITION OF THE ORE.

Effect of the density of the ore on the quality of the metal	139
As exemplified in different ores	140

SECTION X.

HOT BLAST.

Value of the hot blast to the manufacture of iron discussed	142
Heating blast stoves by hot furnace gases	144
Value of water blocks	146

SECTION XI.

FURNACE GASES.

Value of furnace gases as a heating agent	147
Instances of the attempted utilization of furnace tunnel-head gases	149
Modes of collecting the gases	151
Injurious effects on the working of the furnace of some methods of collecting the gases	153
Saving to be effected by the utilization of the gases	154

SECTION XII.

THE ECONOMY OF HEATED AIR AND THE INFLUENCE EXERTED BY THE FORM OF FURNACE ON THE CONSUMPTION OF COAL.

Examination of the reasons alleged for the superiority of a hot blast	156
Effect of a small comparative consumption of coal on the make of the furnace	157

	PAGE
Injurious effect of a hot blast on some kinds of ore	158
Carbonaceous ore under a heated blast	159
Effect of a heated blast on the consumption of fuel	ib.
Relation of quantity of blast to coal consumed, various examples	161
Probability of great consumption of fuel in furnace throat	162
Supported by reasoning	163
By effect of changing from a hot to a cold blast	165
By effect of hot blast on charcoal furnaces	168
Proposed remedy, enlarging the furnace throat	169
Apparent neglect of scientific men, in their researches into the utilization of the furnace waste gases, of the causes which impart value to them	171

SECTION XIII.

THE USE OF RAW COAL IN BLAST FURNACES.

Of the different coal used in the blast furnace	173
Raw coal in the blast furnace	174
In narrow-topped furnaces	175
At the Dowlais and other works	177
Anthracite in the blast furnace	178
Improved form of furnace suggested for anthracite	179
Value of the improved form	180

SECTION XIV.

BLOWING ENGINES.

Importance of sound construction in a blast engine	182
High-pressure blowing engines	183
Horizontal blowing engines	185
Wind valves and passages	186
Performance of various blowing engines	189
Dimensions of parts	191
Consumption of stores	192

SECTION XV.

REFINING.

The finery furnace	193
Process	194
Tuyere pipes	195
Theory of refining	196
Make and consumption of fuel and blast	197
Raw coal in the finery	198
Anthracite	199
Carbonaceous ore	ib.
Hot blast	200
Lime	201
Proportion of carbon in refined metal	202
Yield of refined iron as compared with quantity of pigs charged	203

SECTION XVI.

BOILING AND PUDDLING PIG-IRON.

	PAGE
The "boiling" furnace	205
Process of "boiling"	208
Make	209
Boiling direct from the blast furnace	210
Double furnaces	ib.
Puddling	ib.
Effect on the process of the presence of certain foreign substances	211
Grey iron in the puddling furnace	ib.
Puddling with steam	212
Iron and sand bottoms	213
Air and water boshes	214
Yields of iron and fuel	215
Gas furnaces	216
Area of "take up" and fire-grate	ib.
Make	217

SECTION XVII.

HAMMERS AND SQUEEZERS.

Forge hammer	218
Reciprocating squeezer	219
Revolving squeezers	221

SECTION XVIII.

PUDDLING ROLLS.

Puddling rolls	223
Dimensions of parts	225

SECTION XIX.

HEATING AND BALLING.

Balling furnace	226
Make, loss, and consumption of fuel	227
Piling	ib.
Mill hammer	231
Rolling mill	ib.
Modes of rolling bars	ib.
Rolling guide iron	233
Speed of mills	234
Reversing mills	235
Finishing ends of bars	ib
Working up crop ends	237
Plate rolling	238
Flue dampers	239
Boilers heated by furnace flue	ib.

SECTION XX.

Power absorbed by the various processes of iron-making . 241

SECTION XXI.

VARIOUS QUALITIES OF WROUGHT AND CAST-IRON.

Formation of fibre 243

Attempted improvement of the quality of iron by the incorporation of foreign substances in it . . . 245
Repeated remelting 246
Difference between wrought and cast-iron . . . 247
Property of welding 248
Method of manufacturing wrought-iron direct from the ore 249

DESCRIPTION OF PLATES.

PLATE I.

Kiln for calcining ore at Dowlais iron-works, South Wales.
Fig. 1. Front elevation.
 „ 2. Longitudinal section.
 „ 3. Transverse section.
 „ 4, 5. Plan, partly in section.

PLATE II.

Kiln for calcining ore, with coal and ore trams running on railway overhead, and tipping direct into kiln, in use in some of the South Wales iron-works.
Fig. 6. Front elevation.
 „ 7. Longitudinal section.
 „ 8. Transverse section.
 „ 9, 10. Plan, partly in section.

PLATE III.

Figs. 11, 12. Plan and section of brick kilns at Dowlais iron-works. Four are grouped together around a central stack.
Fig. 13. Longitudinal section of ore-roasting kiln.
 „ 14. Transverse section.
 „ 15. Sectional plan.
 „ 16. Elevation.

PLATE IV.

Ordinary double coke oven.
Figs. 17, 18. Elevations.
 „ 19, 20. Sections.
 „ 21. Sectional plan.
 „ 22—24. Details of iron-work of damper.
 „ 25—27. „ doors.

PLATE V.

Figs. 28, 29. Sections of coke oven on Cox's patent, with flue returning over the oven crown, in use at Ebbw Vale iron-works and elsewhere.

Fig. 30. Sectional plan.
 „ 31. Section of group of coke ovens as constructed in the north of England with central stack.
Fig. 32. Sectional plan.
 „ 33. Elevation of part of group.

PLATE VI.

Figs. 34—36. Plan, section and elevation of common circular or elliptical oven.
Fig. 37. Section of part of double row of square coke ovens.
Fig. 38. Cross section.
 „ 39. Sectional plan.
 „ 40. Elevation.

PLATES VII. to XII.

Figs. 41 to 81. Outlines of the interior of blast furnaces at home and abroad.
Fig. 66 should be " Yniscedwyn."
 „ 67 „ " Ystalyfera new furnace."

PLATE XIII.

Fig. 82. Section of blast furnace.
 „ 83. Foreign blast furnace with channels for abstracting the gases at the boshes.
Fig. 84. Blast furnace with cylindrical body, suggested by Mr. Truran.

PLATE XIV.

Figs. 85—87. Vertical section and plan of hearth of blast furnace at Plymouth iron-works.
Fig. 86. Plan of hearth of blast furnace at Rhymney iron-works.

PLATE XV.

Large blast furnace at Dowlais iron-works, 18 feet diameter at the boshes.

Fig. 88. Vertical section through back tuyere-house and cinder-fall, showing blast pipe, tuyeres, damplate, and other details.
Fig. 89. Half plan, through hearth.
„ 90. Vertical section through bottom showing the peculiar form of the fire-bricks of which it is composed.

PLATE XVI.

Large 18-feet blast furnace—Dowlais iron-works.
Fig. 91. Horizontal section through boshes at the level of the top of hearth, showing castings with which the furnace is bound together.
Fig. 92. Horizontal section through hearth at level of tuyeres, showing tuyeres and pipes in position.
Fig. 93. Vertical section before the hearth and boshes are put in, with mould by which the in-walls are built.
Fig. 94. Front view of cinder-fall.

PLATE XVII.

Large 18-feet blast furnace at Dowlais iron-works.
Figs. 95, 96. Elevation and plan.

PLATE XVIII.

Cupola furnace at Dowlais iron-works.
Figs. 97, 98, 99. Front elevation, vertical section and sectional plan of hearth.
Fig. 100. Sectional plan of hearth of cupola furnace at Sirhowy iron-works.

PLATE XIX.

Figs. 101, 102. Vertical section, and sectional plan through hearth of blast furnace at Tredegar iron-works.
Figs. 103, 104. Hearth of Aberamman furnace, vertical section and plan, showing tuyere openings both in sides and breast.
Fig. 105. Vertical section of hearth of Ystalyfera furnace, showing three tuyere openings on each side and one in breast.

PLATE XX.

Blast furnace at Coltness iron-works.
Figs. 106, 107, 108. Elevation, vertical section and plan.

PLATE XXI.

Fig. 109. Vertical section of blast furnace at Cwm Afon iron-works.
Figs. 110, 111. Vertical section and plan of hearth of blast furnaces, Oldbury iron-works.

PLATE XXII.

Fig. 112. Vertical section of blast furnace at Towlaw iron-works.
Fig. 113. Vertical section of blast furnace at Stockton-upon-Tees.

PLATE XXIII.

Water-balance lift for pits and for raising materials to furnace top—employed frequently in South Wales.
Fig. 114. View of framing at top of lift, with chain wheel and brake, showing tram arrived at the top, and ready to be wheeled off on to the charging plates.
Fig. 115. Side view of top and bottom of lift, showing tram wheeled on to the platform and ready to be hoisted.
Fig. 116. Vertical section of bucket with escape valve.
„ 117. Plan of platform on bucket.
„ 118. View of inclined plane furnace-lift, worked by a steam-engine—much used in Staffordshire.

PLATE XXIV.

Fig. 119. Vertical section of pneumatic furnace-lift in use at Corbyn's Hall furnace and elsewhere.
Figs. 120, 121, 122. Sectional plan of pneumatic tube, air-pipes and well, plan of platform and guides. Sketch of top pulley for counterbalancing chain.
Fig. 123. Section of valve chest with three passages, placed on blast pipes of hot-blast furnaces to direct the blast either through the stoves or at once into the furnaces at pleasure.
Fig. 124. Section of hot-blast stove placed between furnaces at Ystalyfera, heated by hot gases abstracted from the furnace.

PLATE XXV.

Fig. 125. Section of blast stove with V-pipes, horizontal pipes being built in with fire-brick.
Fig. 126. Section of blast stove with V-pipes at Pen-y-darran iron works.
Figs. 127, 128. Sketches of stove-pipe junctions, one with ordinary faucet, the other with separate removable socket.
Fig. 129. Cross section of blast stove at Dowlais iron-works, with U-pipes.

PLATE XXVI.

Figs. 130, 131. Longitudinal section and sectional plan of blast stove at Dowlais iron-works (outlet at right side of furnace door, is in error).

PLATE XXVII.

Figs. 132, 133, 134. Longitudinal section, transverse section, and part of sectional plan of blast-stove used at Ebbw Vale iron-works, Wales, heated by waste gases from the tunnel head.

PLATE XXVIII.

Figs. 135, 136. Vertical section and sectional plan of blast-stove, with upright pipes—used in Staffordshire.
Fig. 137. Sectional plan of divided horizontal pipes, in which vertical pipes stand.
Fig. 138. Vertical section of blast stove, with tall pipes, and arch over fire.

PLATE XXIX.

Figs. 139—144. Various methods of collecting gases from furnaces.

PLATE XXX.

Figs. 145, 146. Mode of collecting the furnace gases in use at Brymbo iron-works—Danby's patent.
Figs. 147, 148. Foundry cupola at Rhymney iron works.
„ 150, 151, 152, 153. Details of blast furnaces, construction, bottom-frame, doors, and loose curb, for charging holes at furnace-top.

PLATE XXXI.

Details of the construction of blast-furnace blast valves.
Figs. 154, 155. Sections of valve-box.
„ 156, 157. View and section of valve for slide valve, with spindle and plain handle.
Figs. 158, 159, 160. Sections of throttle valve.
„ 161, 162, 163, 164. Slide valve, with rack and pinion, vertical and horizontal sections, view of slide face, side elevation of box.
Figs. 165, 166. Vertical and horizontal sections of spindle valve, with screw.
Figs. 167, 168. Vertical and horizontal section of valve, with circular slide.

PLATE XXXII.

Details of the construction of blast furnaces. Tuyere-pipes.
Fig. 169. Section of telescopic tuyere-pipe for conveying the blast from the main to the tuyere, at Dowlais iron-works.
Figs. 170, 171, 172. Three views of ball and socket joint of tuyere-pipe.
Fig. 173. Nozzle-pipe.
„ 174, 175. Side and end views of tuyere-pipes at Ebbw Vale iron-works.
Figs. 176, 177. Side and end views of compound nozzle-pipe—Aberdare iron-works.
Fig. 178. Nozzle-pipe.
„ 179. Cast-iron tuyere-pipe for hot blast—Dowlais iron-works.

PLATE XXXIII.

Details of the construction of blast furnaces.
Figs. 180, 181. Section and end view of cast-iron water tuyere.
Fig. 182. Tuyere-pipe with leather bag for conveying cold blast—Plymouth iron-works.
Fig. 183. Wrought-iron tuyere-pipe for hot blast—Dowlais iron-works.
Figs. 184, 185. Section and end view of cast-iron water tuyeres.
Figs. 186, 187, 188. Section, end view and plan of cast-iron dry tuyeres.

Figs. 189, 190. Front view and section of water tuyere-block—Aberdare iron-works.
Fig. 191. Water block—Aberdare iron-works.
„ 192, 193. Front view and section of water block.

PLATE XXXIV.

Figs. 194, 195, 196. Elevation plan and cross section of water block below tuyere—Dowlais iron-works.
Figs. 197, 198, 199. Sectional elevation, plan, and cross section of water tymp—Langloan iron-works.
Figs. 200, 201. Section and side view of cast-iron tuyere-pipe with flange-joint, movable only in one plane.
Fig. 202. Water tuyere-block—Ystalyfera iron-works.
„ 203, 204. Side view and end view of compound tuyere-pipe for two tuyeres.
Fig. 205, 206. Front and side view of tymp and damplate.

PLATE XXXV.

Figs. 207, 208. Side and end view of charging barrow.
„ 209, 210. Side and end view of charging train.
„ 211, 212. Side and end view of coke barrow.
„ 213. Filling pike for coke.

PLATE XXXVI.

Fig. 213. Plan of cinder fall, showing on one side of the cinder-plate the cinder gutters and tubs and tramway leading to the cinder tip, and, on the other side, metal gutter and pig bed.
Fig. 214. Vertical section of cinder fall through metal gutter, with cinder flowing into movable tub.
Fig. 215. Cinder crane; where cinder is allowed to flow into holes in the ground instead of tubs, the cinder pig is lifted by means of an iron bar cast into it and subsequently removed.
Figs. 216, 217. Cast-iron pig mould.
„ 218, 219. Sections of cast-iron gutters.
„ 220. A. B. C.—Tools used by moulder.

PLATE XXXVII.

Figs. 221, 222. Side and end view of cinder tub with loose sides.
Fig. 223. A similar tub, with sides removed and cinder pig, ready to be tipped off.
Fig. 224. A—L.—Furnace-keeper's tools.
„ 225. Cinder tub, with wrought-iron sides made to lift off.

PLATE XXXVIII.

Fig. 226. General view of large high-pressure blowing engine at Dowlais iron-works.

PLATE XXXIX.

Fig. 227. Large blowing engine Dowlais iron-works—Section of blowing cylinder and passages.
Figs. 228, 229. Seatings of single and double air valves.

PLATE XL.

Large blowing engine—Dowlais iron-works.
Fig. 230. Sectional part plan of blast cylinder, showing air valves.
Fig. 231. Part plan of top of blast cylinder and air-valve seats.
Fig. 232. Section of edge of blast piston with junk ring for hemp packing.
Fig. 233. Section of rib of piston.
„ 234. Junk-ring bolt.
„ 235. Section of edge of blast piston with leather packing.
Fig. 236. Part section of air valve for blast cylinder cover.
„ 237. Hind pressure gauge.

PLATE XLI.

Fig. 238. Vertical transverse section of double refinery—Dowlais iron-works.
Fig. 239. Section of blast valve-box with three separate valves for three tuyeres.
Fig. 240. Tuyere-pipe with ball joint.

PLATE XLII.

Double refinery—Dowlais iron-works.
Fig. 241. Sectional plan of refinery, with dovetailed joints to pig mould and two tuyeres on each side.
Fig. 242. Elevation of part of finery fire and section of pig mould.
Fig. 243. Pig mould jointed with clips.
„ 244, 245. Longitudinal and transverse sections of blast valve-box for three tuyeres with single valve.

PLATE XLIII.

Large double refinery—Dowlais iron-works.
Fig. 246. Longitudinal section of finery fire.
„ 247. Pig-mould blocks, with double-rabbeted joints.
„ 248. Section of pig mould.
„ 249, 250, 251. Pig of refined metal on cart commonly used to remove it.
Figs. 252, 253. Two-handed sledge for breaking refined metal.
Fig. 245. Spanner for the same purpose.
„ 255, 256. Hot-water tuyere for finery.
„ 257, 258. Scraper.

PLATE XLIV.

Furnace for boiling pig-iron, as usually constructed in the South Wales iron-works.
Fig. 259. Sectional plan through body of furnace.
„ 260. Vertical longitudinal section through centre of furnace and stack.
Figs. 261, 262. Front and back elevations.

PLATE XLV.

Double puddling furnace for refined iron.
Figs. 263, 264. Sectional plan and longitudinal section.
„ 265. Side elevation.
„ 266, 267. Tub for cinder.

PLATE XLVI.

Double boiling furnace, with air bosbes.
Figs. 268, 269. Sectional plan and longitudinal section.
„ 270. Cross section through stack.

PLATE XLVII.

Puddling furnace for refined plate metal at Dowlais iron-works.
Figs. 271, 272. Longitudinal section and sectional plan.
„ 273. Cross section through body of furnace, looking toward stack.
Fig. 274. Back elevation, stack frame.

PLATE XLVIII.

Puddling furnace—Dowlais iron-works.
Fig. 275. Side elevation.
„ 276, 277. Plan and end views of top of stack, showing damper.
Fig. 278. Sectional plan of stack.
„ 279. Section of stack, with damper at the bottom.
„ 280, 281. View and section of working door.
„ 282. View of charging door.

PLATE XLIX.

Puddling furnace, with flue damper—Plymouth iron-works.
Figs. 283, 284. Sectional plan and longitudinal section.
„ 285. Back elevation.
„ 286, 287, 288. Plan, side view, and section of cooling bosh for puddlers' tools.

PLATE L.

Puddling furnace, Cyfarthfa iron-works.
Figs. 289, 290. Sectional plan and longitudinal section.
„ 291, 292. Elevation and plan of carriage for conveying puddle balls to squeezer, or shingling hammer.
Figs. 293 to 297. Puddlers' tools.

PLATE LI.

Figs. 298, 299, 300. Longitudinal sections of puddling furnaces, with iron bosbes.
Fig. 300. With boiler in flue.

PLATE LII.

Figs. 301, 302. Transverse section and plan of part of puddling forge—Dowlais iron-works—showing arrangement of furnaces, coal and iron tramways, races, &c.

DESCRIPTION OF PLATES.   xvii

PLATE LIII.

Forge train—Cyfarthfa iron-works.
Fig. 303. Elevation of train complete from crab on driving shaft to squeezer-crank.
Fig. 304. Elevation of squeezer.
„ 305. Bed-plate of squeezer and part of bed-plate of train.
Figs. 306, 307. Side and front view of fast half of coupling crab.
Figs. 308, 309. Side and front view of rolls' pinion.
„ 310. Clip for keeping rolls' coupling up to their place.
„ 311, 312. Side and front view of loose half of coupling-crab.

PLATE LIV.

Forge train—Cyfarthfa iron-works. Details of rolls' standards.
Fig. 313. Front elevation of rolls' standards, showing chocks, brasses, roll-necks, and setting screws.
Fig. 314. Plan of standard.
„ 315, 316, 317. Horizontal sections of standard.
„ 318, 319. Front view and sectional plan of pinion housing.

PLATE LV.

Forge train—Cyfarthfa iron-works. Details of squeezer.
Figs. 320, 321. Side view and sectional plan of squeezer-arm.
Fig. 322. View of top gudgeon.
„ 323. Squeezer-crank.
„ 324, 325. Elevation and horizontal section of standards for squeezer-crank.
Fig. 326. Section of standards for squeezer-arm, showing gudgeon, &c.
Fig. 327. Side elevation of squeezer-arm standard.
„ 328. Horizontal section of the same through brass bearing.
Figs. 329, 330. Side view and cross section of anvil of squeezer.

PLATE LVI.

Forge train—Cyfarthfa iron-works. Details of rolls and squeezer.
Figs. 331, 332. Side and end view of roughing-roll.
„ 333, 334, 335. Side view and two end views of connecting spindle.
Figs. 336—339. Section, side view, and two end views of pinion on roll end, with crab for driving squeezer.
„ 340, 341. Butt-ends of squeezer connecting-rod.
„ 342, 343. Side and end view of coupling-box.
„ 344, 345. End of squeezer-anvil.
„ 346, 347. Section of rolls, showing loose guides and guides cottered down to rest.
Fig. 348. Cinder plate to go between rolls to keep the cinders out of the bearings.

PLATE LVII.

Forge trains—Dowlais iron-works.
Fig. 349. Complete elevation of train from engine fly-wheel to squeezer-crank, with pinions in separate housings and connecting spindle.
Fig. 350. Similar train, but without connecting spindle, and with pinions on roll ends.
Figs. 351, 352. Plan and cross section of bed-plate for Fig. 349.

PLATE LVIII.

Forge trains—Dowlais iron-works. Details of housings.
Fig. 353. Elevation of rolls, housing complete, with chocks, bearings, roll-necks, &c.
Figs. 354, 355, 356. Horizontal sections of housing.
„ 357. Top plan of housing.
„ 358, 359. Elevation and sectional plan of pinion housing.

PLATE LIX.

Forge trains—Dowlais iron-works. Details of rolls.
Figs. 360, 361. Side and end view of roughing-roll.
„ 362, 363. Side and end view of pinion.
„ 364. Spindle.
„ 365, 366. Side and end views of coupling-box for spindles and roll flutes.
Figs. 367, 368, 369. Side and two end views of coupling-crabs.
Figs. 370—372 and 373—376. Rests and guides for finishing rolls.

PLATE LX.

Forge trains—Dowlais iron-works. Details of rolls and squeezer.
Figs. 377, 378, 379. Side and end views and plan of foreplate for roughing-rolls.
Fig. 380. Cross section through finishing-rolls, showing rests and guides.
Fig. 381. Cross section through roughing-rolls, showing foreplate and rest.
Fig. 382. Cross section through gudgeon of squeezer.
„ 383, 384. Side and end view of squeezer-crank.
„ 385, 386. Butt-end of the squeezer connecting-rod.

PLATE LXI.

Forge train—Dowlais iron-works. Details of double squeezer.
Figs. 387, 388. Elevation and sectional plan of double squeezer.
Figs. 389, 390. Sections of squeezer-arm through gudgeon, and through hammer.
Fig. 391. End view of squeezer arm, showing gudgeon.

PLATE LXII.

Forge hammer—Dowlais iron-works.

c

Fig. 392. Sectional elevation.
„ 393. Plan of bed-plate.
„ 394. Cross section of harness block, and end view of helve.
Fig. 395. Section of cam-ring, shaft, and bearing block.
„ 396. Plan of cam-shaft bearing block.
„ 397. Plan of harness block.
„ 398. Shingling tongs.

PLATE LXIII.

Forge hammer—Dowlais Iron-works. Details of hammer.
Figs. 399, 400. Sections of anvil and block.
„ 401. Plan of anvil and block.
„ 402. Elevation of anvil block, showing sectional helve supported on "jack."
Fig. 403. Cross section of cam-ring.
„ 404. Plan of helve.
„ 405. Side view of helve head.
„ 406, 407. Elevation and section of driving wheels.
„ 408. Elevation of eccentric squeezer.

PLATE LXIV.

Mill hammer—Dowlais Iron-works.
Fig. 409. Sectional elevation.
„ 410. Plan of helve and driving gear.
„ 411. Section of anvil block.
„ 412. End view of helve and part of harness blocks.
„ 413. Plan of anvil block.
„ 414. View of nose of helve.

PLATE LXV.

Heating furnace at Forest and Cyfarthfa iron-works.
Figs. 415, 416. Longitudinal section and sectional plan.
„ 417, 418, 419. Side and end views, and plan of cart for carrying piles to the rolls.
Fig. 420. Balling furnace tongs.

PLATE LXVI.

Heating furnace at Dowlais iron-works.
Figs. 421, 422. Longitudinal section and sectional plan.
„ 423, 424. Side and end view of piling tables.
„ 425. Rest.

PLATE LXVII.

Smaller heating furnace—Dowlais Iron-works.
Figs. 426, 427. Longitudinal section and sectional plan.
„ 428, 429. Elevation and plan of pile carriage.
„ 430—433. Balling furnace tools.

PLATE LXVIII.

Twelve-inch merchant train—Dowlais iron-works.
Fig. 434. Front elevation.
„ 435. Elevation of rolls standard.
„ 436, 437, 438. Sections of standard.
„ 439. Plan of standard.

PLATE LXIX.

Details of 12-inch merchant train—Dowlais iron-works.
Fig. 440. Side view.
„ 441. End view of pinion.
„ 442. Section of chock and brass.
„ 443. Rolls spindle.
„ 444. Side view of crab, showing part of engine shaft.
„ 445, 446, 447. Front view, side view, and back view of loose crab.
Figs. 448, 449. Side and end elevation and sectional plan of standard.

PLATE LXX.

Details of merchant train—Dowlais iron-works.
Figs. 451, 452. Side and end view of roll.
„ 453, 454. Side and end view of connecting spindle, between pinions and rolls.
Fig. 455. Top chock for rolls where two only are used.
„ 456, 457, 458. Plan, side and end view of fore-plate.
„ 459, 460, 461. Side and end views, and plan of rest.
„ 462, 463. Side and end view of coupling-box.
„ 464, 465. Side and end view of guides.
„ 466. Cross section of bed-plate.

PLATE LXXI.

Guide train—Dowlais iron-works.
Fig. 467. Elevation of 8-inch guide train.
„ 468. Section of bed-plate.
„ 469, 470. Elevation and sectional plan of pinion standard.

PLATE LXXII.

Details of guide train—Dowlais iron-works.
Figs. 475, 476. Side view of connecting spindle between pinion and rolls.
Figs. 477, 478. Sections of coupling-boxes.
„ 476. Side view of pinion.
„ 471, 472, 473, 474. Side elevation, end elevation, sectional plan, and plan of rolls' housing.
Fig. 480. End view of spindle.

PLATE LXXIII.

Details of guide train—Dowlais iron-works.
Figs. 481, 482, 483. Front elevation, side elevation, and section of rolls' housing and rolls.
Fig. 484. Side view of crab.
„ 485. Side view of roll.
„ 486. Gauge for screwing down rolls.
„ 487, 488, 489. Guides for square iron.
„ 490, 491, 492. Plan, side view and cross section of guides.
Figs. 493, 494. Plan and end view of fore-plate.

PLATE LXXIV.

Slitting mill—Dowlais iron-works.
Fig. 495. General view of slitting mill.
„ 496, 497. Side view and front view of slitting mill in detail.

Figs. 498, 499. Plan and sectional plan of slitting mill.
„ 500, 501. Side and end view of connecting spindle.

PLATE LXXXV.

Details of slitting mill—Dowlais iron-works.
Figs. 502, 503. Cross and longitudinal sections.
„ 504. Sectional plan.
„ 505, 506. End view and sectional plan of pinion standards.
Figs. 507, 508. Side and end views of coupling-box.
„ 510. Crab.
„ 511. End and side views of pinion.

PLATE LXXXVI.

Details of implements used at Rolls.
Figs. 512, 513. Elevation and section plan of housings of plate mill.
Figs. 514—527. Hooks, tongs, &c., used in rolling bars.

PLATE LXXXVII.

Saw for cutting rail ends—Dowlais iron-works.
Fig. 528. General view of a saw.
„ 529. Cross section of saw, showing lever for moving saw bench.
Fig. 530. Cross section of saw, showing stop for holding bar.
Fig. 531. Sectional front view of saw.
„ 532. Details of stop.
„ 533. Cross section of saw bench.

PLATE LXXXVIII.

Details of saw—Dowlais iron-works.
Figs. 534, 535, 536. Plan, elevation and section of saw bench, showing screw stop for adjusting length of rails.
Fig. 537. Section of saw frame, showing spindle and cooling boxes generally.
Fig. 531. Eccentric shears, elevation of gearing.
„ 539. Details of disconnecting gear.
„ 540. End view of crab.

PLATE LXXXIX.

Shears driven by power. Shears for mill bars.
Fig. 545. Sectional elevation.
„ 546. Sectional plan of shear castings.
„ 547. Part cross section of shears.
„ 548. End of shear bar.

Figs. 549, 550. Sectional elevation and end view of shears for puddled bars.
Figs. 551, 552. Elevation and plan of framing for shears.
„ 553. Shears crank.
„ 554. Knife for cutting bars. Eccentric shears.
„ 552. Cross section.
„ 553. Plan of frame.
„ 554. Sectional plan of shears.

PLATE LXXX.

Rail straightening press—Cyfarthfa iron-works.
Figs. 555, 556, 557. Front elevations and side elevation of rail straightening press.
Figs. 558, 559. Sectional plans.
„ 560, 561 561. Details of connecting-rod and die block.

PLATE LXXXI.

Rail straightening press—Dowlais iron-works.
Figs. 562, 563. Front and side elevation of rail straightening press.
Fig. 564. Die block.
„ 565. Sectional plan of press, horizontal section of frame and die blocks.
Fig. 567. Section of guide for die block.
„ 568. Details of roller for carrying bars.
„ 569. Main shafting.

PLATE LXXXII.

Heavy gearing between engine and trains.
Figs. 586, 587. Plan and elevation of gearing.
„ 588. Section of eye of fly-wheel.
„ 589. Section at driving wheel arm.
„ 590. Detail of fly-wheel.

PLATE LXXXIII.

Heavy gearing between engine and mills.
Figs. 582, 583. Sectional elevation and plan of gearing.
„ 584. Section of eye of fly-wheel.
„ 585. Detail of rim of fly-wheel.

PLATE LXXXIV.

Independent rail-straightening machine driven by a band—Dowlais iron-works.
Figs. 570, 571. Front and side elevation.
„ 572, 573. Side view and plan of bar straightening block.
Figs. 574—581. Tools used in rail straightening.

MANUFACTURE OF IRON.

FOR the production of pig or crude iron three materials are required—iron ore—coal, coke, or charcoal, as fuel—and limestone or some other suitable substance, as flux. Before entering upon a description of smelting operations we purpose giving a brief notice of the qualities and general composition of the principal ores, fuels, and fluxes, used in this manufacture.

IRON ORES.

The ores from which crude iron is smelted in Great Britain may be divided into four great classes: the argillaceous ores of the coal formations having clay, but sometimes silica, as the chief impurity: the carbonaceous ores of the same formation, distinguished by their large per-centage of carbon: the calcareous ores, principally obtained from the limestone of the coal measures, having lime as their chief earthy admixture; and the siliceous ores, having silica as their predominating earth. This last class is subdivided into the red and brown hematites, the ores of the oolitic formation, the white carbonates, and the magnetic oxides. The carbonates of the coal measures frequently contain silica as their predominating impurity; but these ores are classified with the argillaceous instead of with the siliceous ores of the oolitic and other formations, which do not contain any important quantity of carbonic acid.

ARGILLACEOUS ORES.

The argillaceous as well as the carbonaceous ores are obtained from the coal measures, in which they are found in seams of from a quarter of an inch to three feet in thickness, and in nodules varying from one inch to two feet in diameter. Lying parallel with and not unfrequently in close proximity to the coal seams, these ores are mined in a manner similar to that followed in the extraction of coal in the same locality. A large quantity is raised annually in Wales by open working, termed "patching," but the principal supply is derived from pits sunk in the coal measures to a depth varying from a few yards to a hundred and fifty fathoms.

All the great coal formations hitherto discovered contain argillaceous and carbonaceous iron ores in greater or less abundance. The Staffordshire, South Wales, North Wales, Derbyshire, Shropshire, and Scotch coal-fields, contain valuable seams of argillaceous iron ore. In the Durham, Lancashire, Somersetshire, and other minor coal-fields, the argillaceous ores exist in smaller quantities, and produce when smelted crude iron of an inferior quality.

The South Wales coal-field stands pre-eminent for the number and richness of its seams of argillaceous iron ores. The aggregate thickness of the seams measures twenty-one feet. The average per-centage of metal in the ores exceeds thirty-two per cent. We subjoin the analyses of the ores from a number of seams wrought by the Dowlais Iron Company, from which their blast furnaces at Dowlais are chiefly supplied. The Penydarran, Plymouth, and Rhymney furnaces are also worked with the produce of the same seams.

ANALYSES of the Principal Seams of Argillaceous Iron Ore in the South Wales Coal-Field.

	1	2	3	4	5	6	7
Carbonate of iron	74.5	86.	77.1	62.	42.7	50.5	68.2
Silica	14.5	8.3	15.9	27.5	42.7	36.9	21.6
Alumina	8.3	.2	3.8	7.3	7.5	1.9	5.4
Carbonaceous matter	—	4.2	1.8	2.1	2.6	—	3.8
Lime	.8	—	.4	—	.1	—	—
Moisture and Loss	.6	1.3	1.	.6	1.4	1.7	1.
Phosphoric acid	Trace	—	—	—	2.8	—	—
Manganese	1.3						
	100.	100.	100.	100.	100.	100.	100.
Per-centage of metallic iron	35.9	41.46	37.2	29.5	20.0	23.7	32.9

These analyses taken from the centre of the iron manufacture in this district may be considered as fairly representing the mean composition of the Welsh argillaceous ores, since the variation at other workings, eastward and westward, is inconsiderable.

The richness of the respective seams in this basin is influenced by the distance between them. Thus, where two or more seams of iron ore exist with only a thin parting, their mean per-centage will be found higher than that of seams having a greater thickness of ground interposed. The general character of the associated earths is influenced by the composition of the matrix, and also, but to a minor degree, by the adjacent seams of rock, shale, or clod. Seams of argillaceous ore, having either a roof or bedding of siliceous rock, invariably contain a large per-centage of silica. The lowest seams of ore, as they approach the mountain limestone, are found to contain a notable per-centage of lime, a substance almost entirely wanting in the richer seams of the upper series.

On analysing specimens from 68 seams, the produce of which is used in the Dowlais furnaces, including the whole of the argillaceous ores of the north outcrop, we found that 47, or more than two-thirds of the number, yielded 30 per cent. and upwards. Two seams exceeded 38 per cent., and 4 exceeded 37 per cent., while 5 reached to 36 per cent., 9 to 35 per cent.,

8 to 34 per cent., 3 to 33 per cent., 4 to 32 per cent., 3 to 31 per cent.; 9 averaged 30 per cent., and 3 seams only were under 20 per cent.

The South Wales basin contains, in addition to the workable seams of ironstone enumerated, several seams of ore yielding a low per-centage of inferior iron. They are known to the workmen by the local appellation of "jacks," or coarse ironstone. They are never used when the quality of the resulting metal is desired to be good. For the inferior irons, however, they are sparingly employed as a mixture with other ores. The general composition of these ores is represented by the accompanying analysis of a seam wrought by the Dowlais Company:

Carbonate of iron	27.8
,, lime	48.8
Silica	10.9
Alumina	10.5
Carbonaceous matter	1.0
Moisture and loss	1.0
	100.

Metallic iron 12.7 per cent.

The Staffordshire coal-field contains numerous seams of argillaceous iron ores, from which the blast furnaces of the district derive their principal supply. In richness they are slightly inferior to the average of the Welsh ores, but they are equal to them in the quality of the resulting iron. The analysis of a very rich specimen from this field, obtained near Dudley, gave:

Carbonate of iron	78.3
,, lime	5.2
,, magnesia	4.7
,, manganese	1.7
Alumina	1.8
Silica	5.6
Phosphoric acid	.2
Carbonaceous matter and loss	2.5
	100.

Metallic iron 37.7 per cent.

The analysis of another specimen, more nearly representing the average yield of the whole of the seams, gave:

Carbonate of iron	62.8
,, lime	4.6
,, magnesia	3.5
,, manganese	2.1
Alumina	5.6
Silica	16.8
Carbonaceous matter	2.3
Phosphoric acid	Trace
Moisture and loss	2.
	100.

Metallic iron 29.3 per cent.

The North Wales coal-field contains seams of argillaceous ore, but the average yield of metallic iron does not on the raw ore exceed 25 per cent.

The Derbyshire coal-field supplies a considerable quantity of these ores, but the product is generally inferior to that of the Welsh ores. According to M. Bunsen, the composition after calcination of those smelted in the Alfreton furnaces was as follows:

MANUFACTURE OF IRON.

Peroxide of iron	60.242
Silica	23.775
Alumina	6.553
Lime	3.510
Magnesia	3.188
Potash	.743
Manganese	Traces
	100.

Metallic iron 41.7 per cent.

The Yorkshire coal-field contains numerous valuable seams of argillaceous iron ores, and, when this district is supplied with greater facilities for the conveyance of the manufactured iron to market, it is probable that the make will be largely increased. Looking at the small per-centage of clay and the comparative freedom of these ores from sulphur and phosphoric acid, this district will no doubt eventually produce large quantities of very superior iron. We annex the composition of five of the seams under the manor of Healaugh Swaledale, according to analyses made by Dr. Odling:

COMPOSITION of Yorkshire Argillaceous Iron Ores.

	1	2	3	4	5	MEAN.
Carbonate of iron	80.50	70.80	75.80	79.00	65.59	74.3
,, lime	3.48	11.72	4.72	8.36	21.28	9.9
Silica and clay	8.72	10.72	10.00	10.30	6.16	9.3
Carbonate of magnesia	.25	.03	—	—	1.23	.43
,, manganese	Traces	Traces	Traces	—	—	—
Sulphur	—	—	—	—	—	.03
Carbonaceous matter } Moisture and loss }	7.05	6.13	8.88	2.33	5.74	5.44
	100.	100.	100.	100.	100.	100.
Yield of metallic iron	38.8	34.17	36.6	38.1	31.0	35.8

The Scotch mineral field contains large quantities of argillaceous iron ore. Before the discovery of the more fusible carbonaceous variety these ores formed the chief supply of the blast furnaces in this district, but of late years they have been comparatively neglected. Their great value, however, is very manifest from the following analyses by Dr. Colquhoun:

COMPOSITION of Scotch Argillaceous Iron Ores.

	1	2	3	4	5	6	7	8
Protoxide of iron	35.22	45.84	42.15	38.80	36.47	47.33	43.73	53.03
Peroxide of iron	1.16	—	.80	.33	.40	.33	.47	.23
Carbonic acid	32.53	33.63	31.86	30.76	26.35	33.10	32.24	35.17
Protoxide of manganese	—	.20	—	.07	.17	.13	—	—
Lime	8.62	1.00	4.03	5.30	1.97	2.00	2.10	3.33
Magnesia	5.10	5.90	4.80	6.70	2.70	2.20	2.77	1.77
Silica	9.56	7.83	0.73	10.87	19.20	6.63	9.70	1.40
Alumina	5.34	2.53	3.77	6.20	8.03	4.30	5.13	.63
Carbonaceous matter	2.13	1.86	2.33	1.87	2.10	1.70	1.50	3.03
Sulphur	.62	—	—	.16	—	.22	.02	—
Moisture	—	.99	—	—	—	—	—	—
	100.37	100.68	100.37	101.	98.00	97.94	97.66	98.59
Yield of metallic iron	28.4	35.3	33.	30.	28.4	36.7	34.	40.0

CARBONACEOUS IRON ORES.

The most valuable seams of carbonaceous iron ores hitherto discovered belong to the Scotch coal-field. The thickness of the seams in this field varies from a few inches to several feet. It is observed, however, that the thickest seams are not so rich in metal as the thinner, and as a rule the quality is also inferior.[*] The general composition of the richest of the Scotch carbonaceous iron ores will be seen from the following analyses, principally by Dr. Colquhoun:

Composition of Scotch Carbonaceous Iron Ores.

	1	2	3
Protoxide of iron	53.03	40.77	53.82
Peroxide of iron	.93	2.72	.93
Carbonic acid	35.17	26.41	34.39
Lime	3.33	.90	1.51
Magnesia	1.77	.72	.28
Silica	1.40	10.10	2.00
Alumina	.63	—	—
Carbonaceous matter	3.03	17.38	7.70
Moisture	1.41	1.00	
	100.	100.	100.
Yield of metallic iron	41.2	34.6	41.6

From the results of experiments we are led to believe, that the quantities of carbonaceous matter given in these analyses are below that actually existing in the mass of the Scotch ores of this kind. The variation in the composition of these ores is further exemplified by the following analyses:

	1	2
Carbonate of iron	85.44	29.03
„ lime	5.94	1.52
„ magnesia	3.71	3.59
Silica	1.40	24.76
Alumina	.63	20.10
Peroxide of iron	.23	—
Coaly carbonaceous matter	3.03	21.71
	100.38	100.71
Yield of metallic iron	41.3	14.

---

[*] By some writers these ores are termed "carboniferous," by others "blackband;" this last correctly designates particular seams in which the ore alternates with thin bands of coaly matter; but the majority of these ores, though abounding largely in carbonaceous matter, do not exhibit this stratification. We have adopted the term carbonaceous as being more comprehensive, embracing as it does all ores containing a considerable per-centage of carbon. We may also remark that from inattention to the appearance of the respective ores we frequently observe writers using "clayband" for "argillaceous" iron ore, thereby leading the uninformed reader to the erroneous conclusion that the clay exists in these ores in the form of thin bands similar to the coaly matter combined with particular seams of carbonaceous ore, instead of being equally disseminated through the entire mass.

In Scotland some of the beds of carbonaceous ironstone are known as Mushet's blackband, after the late Mr. Mushet, to whom the merit of discovering this iron ore is due. But it was not till about 1830 that it began to be extensively used in smelting.

Seams of this ore exist in the other coal-fields, but generally the produce of metal is not equal to that obtained from the Scotch varieties. In the Durham district carbonaceous ores are wrought to a limited extent. The North Wales field contains seams of this mineral, but the yield is inferior. In the North Staffordshire district this ore is worked to a considerable extent. A specimen analysed by Herapath gave:

Protoxide of iron	42.95
Bisulphide of iron	3.53
Protoxide of manganese	7.43
Silica	2.20
Alumina	.50
Lime	4.00
Magnesia	2.00
Bituminous matter } Carbonic acid } Water and loss }	37.35
	100.

Metallic iron 34.2 per cent.

In the South Wales field there are several valuable seams of carbonaceous ores, but they are wrought to a limited extent only in comparison with the seams of the other ore. A general dislike to them exists in the Welsh district because, from a want of sufficient attention to their peculiar composition, a crude iron is obtained, when they form the entire burden on the furnace, generally of an inferior description, and incapable of being converted into bars without great waste.

At the Beaufort works three seams of carbonaceous ore, measuring in the aggregate 3 feet 6 inches in thickness, and yielding 34 per cent. of metal, have been partially wrought for the furnaces. A seam at the Blaina workings averages 38 per cent. of metal, but at the Nantyglo workings in the same valley the yield is only 13 per cent.

In the western part of this coal-field the Cwm Afon carbonaceous ore yields 22 and the Oakwood 21 per cent. At the Yniscedwyn workings this ore yields 36 per cent. From these statements it will be seen that the variation in the yield of the carbonaceous iron ores of this basin is greater than in the Scotch, and we may remark that the development of the seams is more local and irregular.

The composition of a number of seams, principally those wrought by the Dowlais Company, may be seen in the annexed table of analyses:

Composition of Welsh Carbonaceous Iron Ores.

	1	2	3	4	5	6
Carbonate of iron	58.9	81.6	92.8	29.0	79.8	80.0
Carbonaceous matter	31.3	11.4	5.3	23.0	10.1	9.5
Carbonate of lime	.7	—	—	.2	.6	.2
Silica	3.5	2.9	.7	32.4	5.1	8.2
Alumina	3.9	1.7	1.1	14.6	2.4	1.0
Bisulphide of iron	1.0	—	—	—	.3	—
Moisture and loss	.7	2.4	.1	.8	1.2	1.1
	100.	100.	100.	100.	100.	100.
Yield of metallic iron	28.3	39.3	44.7	14.	38.4	38.5

CALCAREOUS IRON ORES.

The calcareous iron ores, or the sparry carbonate of iron, are principally obtained from workings in the carboniferous or mountain limestone. In the Forest of Dean large quantities of these ores have been mined and smelted in the local works; and more recently considerable quantities have been carried away and smelted along with the argillaceous iron ores in the iron works of Glamorganshire. These ores are also wrought from large deposits in Lancashire and Cumberland, whence they are principally transported to Wales, and to a minor extent to Staffordshire, Yorkshire, and Scotland. The carboniferous limestones of Derbyshire, Somersetshire, and South Wales contain deposits which are occasionally wrought to a limited extent; but it is from the Dean Forest, Lancashire, and Cumberland mines that the chief supply is at present obtained.

By analysis we find that the average composition of the calcareous ores of Dean Forest is nearly as follows:

Peroxide of iron	54.
Carbonate of lime	35.
Clay	7.
Moisture	4.
	100.

Metallic iron 37.5 per cent.

This result will probably seem a low yield to persons who use calcareous ores in mixture with others, but from numerous assays, as well as experimental trials in the blast furnace, we find that it represents the produce of the mass of these ores. When the specimens have been carefully selected we have found the produce higher, as in the following example from the same locality:

Peroxide of iron	67.0
Carbonate of lime	24.3
Clay	6.5
Moisture	2.2
	100.

Metallic iron 46.5 per cent.

In contrast with the preceding analysis we annex the produce of a calcareous ore offered by the vendors as containing a large per-centage of iron:

Peroxide of iron	10.1
Carbonate of lime	52.5
Clay	34.4
Moisture	3.0
	100.

Metallic iron 7 per cent.

SILICEOUS ORES.

The red hematites of Lancashire and Cumberland are probably the richest ores of iron that we possess in this country. Although their extensive use in the blast furnace with coke or raw coal dates but a few years back, they are now largely mined. And when the resulting crude iron is intended for conversion into malleable bars they are advantageously smelted along with the leaner argillaceous ores. Probably the time is not distant when these ores will be largely smelted without the admixture of the leaner varieties.

By analysis we find the average produce of the ore from Ulverstone, Lancashire, to be nearly as follows:

Peroxide of iron	70.6
Silica	27.9
Alumina	.5
Lime	.3
Sulphur	.4
Magnesia	.2
Phosphoric acid	.1
	100.

Metallic iron .49 per cent.

This we consider to be about the average yield of the red hematites. Some varieties of this ore will produce a greater yield of metal, but taking the average of a cargo as it comes from the mines the yield will not reach 50 per cent.

The analysis of a selected specimen from the same locality gave the following results:

Peroxide of iron	81.6
Silica	10.2
Alumina	5.0
Moisture	3.0
Lime	.2
	100.

Metallic iron 56.6 per cent.

But the analysis of a third sample taken promiscuously from various parts of a cargo gave a lower result than either of the foregoing, the quantities, viz.:

Peroxide of iron	60.4
Silica	17.2
Alumina	6.8
Carbonate of lime	7.9
Moisture	7.7
	100.

Metallic iron 41.8 per cent.

Limited quantities of hematite have been wrought in the Somersetshire carboniferous limestone. The following is an analysis of a very rich specimen from near Bristol:

Peroxide of iron	85.000
Alumina	6.250
Silica	3.304
Lime	1.087
Magnesia	1.458
Oxide of manganese	1.601
Sulphur	.210
Phosphoric acid	.457
Potash, soda, water, and loss	.633
	100.

Metallic iron 58.9 per cent.

Cornwall and Devonshire produce considerable quantities of hematite, but the average produce of metal of the ores from these counties is not equal to that from the Lancashire and Cumberland ores.

A piece of hematite ore from the Duchy mines, Cornwall, yielded by analysis:

Peroxide of iron	57.06
Silica	23.40
Alumina	7.32
Lime	7.99
Magnesia	4.22
Phosphoric acid	.35
Manganese	.36
	100.

Metallic iron 39.5 per cent.

This we consider superior to the average produce of the Cornish ores, which do not generally yield more than 36 per cent. for ordinarily clean ores.

Another specimen of Cornish ore, the richest in metal that we have operated on, when analysed gave the following results:

Peroxide of iron	86.62
Silica	1.35
Manganese	.86
Water and loss	12.17
	100.

Metallic iron 60 per cent.

The clay slate formation of North Wales yields a variety of iron ores of greater or less value for iron-making. The analysis of a specimen from Carnarvonshire gave the following results:

Peroxide of iron	79.5
Water	7.0
Clay	13.4
Lime	.1
	100.

Metallic iron 55 per cent.

The analysis of a selected specimen of iron ore from Merionethshire yielded:

Peroxide of iron	71.6
Clay	18.8
Water	6.6
Carbonaceous matter	3.0
	100.

Metallic iron 49.6 per cent.

The analysis of three other specimens of the Carnarvonshire ores, made by Dr. Haughton, will show the varied composition of the North Wales hematites:

	1	2	3
Protoxide of iron	32.90	33.24	49.92
Peroxide of iron	34.14	25.29	5.92
Silica	12.90	13.00	9.62
Alumina	3.66	7.09	3.12
Lime	5.00	1.85	8.57
Magnesia	1.00	—	—
Phosphoric acid	2.25	1.32	4.45
Sulphur	.25	—	—
Loss by calcination	7.90	18.21	28.10
	100.	100.00	99.93
Metallic iron	49.0	43.1	42.5

The use of siliceous ores in large quantities in the blast furnace, with coal or coke as fuel, has been much increased by the discovery of extensive deposits of these ores in Northamptonshire and Yorkshire. The comparatively low cost at which they are mined, taken with the large per-centage of iron which the best varieties yield when carefully selected, will probably operate as an inducement for their more extended use in the manufacture of particular qualities of crude iron. Hitherto a prejudice has existed against the use of these ores otherwise than as a mixture, from certain peculinrities displayed by the finished iron. But, doubtless, when their properties become better understood and they are reduced in suitably constructed furnaces with raw coal, they will yield crude iron which may be manufactured into bars little inferior to those now obtained from the argillaceous ores.

The general composition of the Northamptonshire ores is shown in the following analysis by Bernays, of Derby, of the ores mined by the Duston Company:

	1	2	3
Peroxide of iron	67.20	55.40	44.00
Sand and silica	11.00	21.60	34.00
Alumina	11.00	5.20	4.52
Water	10.40	12.00	14.08
Unestimated matter	.40	2.80	3.40
	100.	100.	100.
Yield of metallic iron	47.	40.3	30.8

On analysing portions of a sample obtained at different periods during the delivery of a large contract, we found the average composition of the ores from the Northamptonshire district to be nearly as follows:

Peroxide of iron	54.6
Carbonate of lime	19.3
,, magnesia	4.0
Protoxide of manganese	.5
Silica	10.3
Alumina	2.1
Water	9.2
	100.

Metallic iron 37.8 per cent.

SECTION I.
FUEL AND FLUX.

THE fossil fuel with which this country abounds is now exclusively used in all the various operations connected with the manufacture of iron. Charcoal, which was once considered as the only fuel with which good merchantable iron could be manufactured, is now from its high price and scarcity only used for the conversion of malleable iron into plates and bars for tinning, and other purposes where a very superior quality of metal is desired.

The South Wales basin is at present that from which the largest quantity of coal is being extracted and used in the iron manufacture, and its great area and the superiority of its products over those obtained from any other formation in this country will doubtless enable it to maintain this position for several centuries to come. It possesses coal of nearly every quality with which we are acquainted. On the eastern side the seams are generally of a bituminous character. Farther west following the northern out-crop we find them semi-bituminous, as at the Rhymney, Dowlais, and Penydarran works; and in the Neath Valley on the western out-crop, we find the different seams changed into anthracite. In the central portion of the basin, seams of a highly bituminous description are worked and used to a limited extent in smelting.

That characteristic of the Welsh coals which distinguishes them from all others, is the large amount of carbon they contain. In smelting as well as in the other operations of the manufacture of iron, the useful effect of coals of the bituminous and semi-bituminous classes is in direct proportion to their richness in carbon. The Welsh coals used in the blast furnace ordinarily yield from 80 to 92 per cent. of carbon.

On the north-eastern side of the basin near Pontypool, where the coal is of a bituminous kind and is coked for use in the blast furnace, an analysis gave the following results:

Carbon	80.4
Hydrogen	5.7
Oxygen	5.3
Nitrogen	1.2
Sulphur	.9
Earthy matters	6.5
	100.

Specific gravity 1.29. Yield of coke 66 per cent. The earthy matters show the proportion of ash.

At the Dowlais works raw coal is used both in smelting and refining. The composition of the upper four-feet seam—which is considered the best for smelting the various seams in the Dowlais mountain—is nearly as follows—the specific gravity being 1.30:

Carbon	87.3
Hydrogen	4.0
Oxygen	3.8
Nitrogen	1.7
Sulphur	.9
Earthy matter	2.1
	100.

Yield of coke 84 per cent.

Another seam wrought by the Dowlais Company, but which is not considered a good furnace coal, yielded:

Carbon	90.0
Hydrogen	3.8
Oxygen	3.2
Nitrogen	.3
Sulphur	1.3
Earthy matter	1.4
	100.

The thick coal wrought for the Hirwain furnaces, directly on the edge of the great anthracite formation, yielded by analysis:

Carbon	87.2
Hydrogen	4.0
Nitrogen	1.5
Sulphur	.7
Oxygen	2.0
Earthy matter	4.4
	99.8

The anthracite district on the western out-crop yields coal of a superior description for smelting. An analysis of a specimen from the Swansea Valley, intended as a sample of the quality of the coals used in the Yniscedewyn and Ystalyfera works (the two largest works in the anthracite district), afforded the following results:

Carbon	91.5
Hydrogen	3.5
Oxygen	2.6
Sulphur	.6
Nitrogen	.3
Earthy matter	1.5
	100.

The specific gravity of this coal is 1.38, and the produce of coke 93 per cent.

The Staffordshire coal-field, although inferior in extent to the South Wales, contains a number of seams with which iron of an excellent quality has been manufactured. Their compositions and qualifications for use in the blast furnace differ but slightly from those of the bituminous coals from the eastern side of the Welsh basin.

The bituminous coals used in the minor iron-making districts of Dean Forest, Shropshire, Derbyshire, North Wales, Yorkshire, and Northumberland, are of a weaker character than the Welsh, and contain considerably less carbon. The proportion which it bears in the composition of these coals being from 56 to 75 per cent., and the yield of coke from 55 to 75 per cent.

According to the analysis of Messrs. Bunsen and Playfair, the Alfreton Derbyshire furnace coal is composed of:

Carbon	74.98
Hydrogen	4.73
Oxygen	10.01
Nitrogen	.13
Water	7.49
Silica } Ash	2.61
Potash } Ash	.07
	100.7

The Newcastle blast furnace coal yielded by analysis:

Carbon	78.0
Hydrogen	7.3
Nitrogen	1.6
Oxygen	2.2
Sulphur	1.6
Earthy matter	8.3
	100.

The best furnace coals wrought in Yorkshire yielded by analysis:

Carbon	78.8
Hydrogen	5.5
Nitrogen	2.0
Oxygen	6.4
Sulphur	2.7
Ash	4.6
	100.

The coals obtained from the Scotch fields and employed for iron-making are also poor in carbon in comparison with the Welsh. They yield about 60 per cent. of weak coke. At the present time the Scotch coals are, with one or two exceptions, used in the raw state in the blast furnace. By analysis we find the composition of the coals used at the Gartsherry furnaces to be nearly as follows:

Carbon	77.5
Hydrogen	5.0
Oxygen	9.1
Sulphur	.5
Nitrogen	1.5
Earthy matter	6.4
	100.

Limestone is the flux almost universally used in the blast furnace. At some furnaces in the neighbourhood of Newcastle-upon-Tyne chalk is occasionally made use of, but that is, we believe, the only locality where it is so employed. The occurrence of limestone in conjunction with iron ore and coal, and the cheap rate at which it is generally to be obtained, are advantages which no other material hitherto discovered possesses.

The limestone used in the works in South Wales and Monmouthshire lies but a short distance below the seams of coal and ironstone, and in some parts of the out-crop it is of immense thickness. The blue mountain limestone from the upper part of the formation, as used at the Dowlais furnaces, yielded by analysis:

Carbonic acid and water	41.0
Clay	1.5
Silica	2.5
Lime	55.0
	100.

In Staffordshire, Dean Forest, and the other iron-producing districts of England, the limestone formation is much thinner, and the stone, judging from its yield of pure lime, which constitutes its value for iron-making, is inferior in quality to that from the quarries around Merthyr Tydvil. In some specimens from the Forest of Dean the quantity of lime is as low as 36 per cent., while the proportion of silica and clay rises as high as 30 per cent. of the whole. Such stone, however, is not used in the furnace when any other containing a larger per-centage of the alkaline earth can be obtained at a remunerative price.

The composition of the chalk used as a flux in the Newcastle furnaces is nearly as follows:

Carbonic acid and water	47.0
Silica	1.5
Lime	51.5
	100.

From containing so large a proportion of lime, chalk is well fitted to act as a flux in iron-smelting, but as it is only met with at considerable distances from the great iron-making districts, it becomes a costly material as compared with ordinary limestone.

The limestone used at the Alfreton furnaces yielded in the hands of M. Bunsen:

Lime	54.4
Carbonic acid	42.9
Magnesia	.6
Alumina	.8
Moisture and loss	1.3
	100.

The limestones used at the Scotch blast furnaces are extremely varied in their character and general composition. The purest specimen we have examined contained:

Lime	55.0
Carbonic acid	39.7
Alumina	.5
Silica	.7
Iron	1.0
Moisture	3.1
	100.

SECTION II.

CALCINATION OF ORES.

EXPERIENCE proves to us that the ores used in the manufacture of iron work better in the blast furnace if previously calcined. This preliminary operation is performed in various ways, but in Wales kilns are generally used for this purpose. These kilns vary greatly in their dimensions. The most satisfactory results are obtained with kilns of the description delineated in Plate I., Figs. 1—5. The floor of the kiln is formed of cast-iron plates, about 2 inches thick. The interior measures 20 feet long, 9 feet wide at top, and 18 feet high. It is built of masonry, and lined with fire bricks 14 inches long. In front are two arches with openings into the inside of the kiln, on a level with the floor, through which the calcined ore is drawn and filled into barrows or waggons for the furnace. Above these openings, but within the semicircle of the arch, it is usual to leave four or five apertures, 6 or 8 inches square, for regulating the draught. Around the upper edge of the kiln there is placed a cast-iron ring from 12 to 15 inches wide, with a flange about 6 inches high on the upper side to protect the brickwork from injury during the filling in of the raw ironstone.

At some works the kilns are of a circular form in the interior; at others they are built square and sharp in the angles, but preference is generally given to the form represented in the plates. Square kilns, or those having sharp angles in their interior, are objectionable on the ground that combustion is slower in the angles than in the centre. If the heat be regulated to properly calcine the centre of the mass, the stone lying in the angles will scarcely have altered from its raw state.

The operation of calcining in kilns may be described thus: Two or three small coal fires having been lit on the floor of the kiln, raw ironstone is placed on top and around them until the whole of the floor is covered with ironstone at a dull red heat. A fresh layer of ironstone, 8 or 9 inches thick, is then added, along with about 5 per cent. by weight of small coal, and, as soon as this layer has reached a red heat, another is added. This addition of fresh layers of raw ironstone and coal is repeated as fast as the previous layers have been heated to the necessary degree.

As a consequence of the small quantity of coal used in the process, by the time that the kiln is filled up with the successive layers of raw ironstone, the lower portions which were first ignited are comparatively cold and fit for drawing.

In Scotland and in Staffordshire the calcination of the ironstone is generally effected in the open air. A space is roughly levelled, on which a stratum of coal of a few inches in thickness is laid, upon this a layer of raw ironstone of 10 or 12 inches in thickness is placed, and then a quantity of small coal is thrown over the stone. Additional layers of ironstone and coal are added until the heap reaches to a height of 4 or 5 feet. The bottom stratum of coals is then fired, and in a few hours the whole mass will be ignited. The operation, from the time of firing till the heap has cooled down sufficiently for drawing, will occupy from eight to twelve days, depending on the nature of the stone, quantity and quality of fuel, and size of the heap.

Calcination in the open air is also carried on to a limited extent in some Welsh works, the operation being there known as burning in "clamp," in contradistinction to burning in kilns. The method of building and firing these clamps is nearly the same as that pursued in the Scotch works.

Upon the merits of these two systems of calcination there can be but one opinion. For if we admit that calcining is a necessary operation before ironstone enters the blast furnace—and there are few practical men indeed who question its utility—we must concede to the kiln the merit of performing it more effectually than can be done in the open air. Under the clamping system, even if the operation has been otherwise successfully performed, the outside stones are only partially burnt. But the great defect of the system is the difficulty experienced in maintaining an equable temperature throughout the heap. Being open, and exposed on all sides to the weather, air-draughts are created, and the adjacent stones are not unfrequently melted into a hard refractory mass. When such a result threatens any portion of the heap attempts are made to check the draught in that quarter; and if successfully, the changing direction of the wind will probably bring on the evil in other places. Again, should heavy rains occur during the burning, a considerable portion of the whole heap will be found but slightly affected by the operation, on account of the great surface exposed to the atmosphere, compared with the bulk of the heap. Indeed, when we consider the rapidity of atmospheric changes in this country, and the extent to which the calcination of ironstone, conducted on the open-air plan, is affected by them, it is a matter of surprise that such an inefficient process should be in use at so many old-established works.

We do not know of any advantage possessed by the open-air system over that of kilns, beyond the simple one that it saves the expense of erecting any kind of apparatus. But this saving in the first outlay of capital is very small in comparison with the benefits that would follow from the use of mineral kilns. The first cost of the kiln delineated in Plate I. will not, in most iron-making districts, exceed 160l. Its capacity is equal to 70 tons of argillaceous ironstone. With ordinary attention it will calcine 146 tons weekly, or 7592 tons annually. Dividing the interest at 5 per cent. on 160l., which equals 8l. by the number of tons calcined annually, we obtain one farthing as the cost entailed on each ton of ironstone calcined to cover the outlay of capital in the erection of kilns.

But if the open-air system saves this slight outlay to the manufacturer, it is by far the more expensive of the two systems in the matters of labour and fuel. And here we may remark that in this as in other cases the prices or items of cost given are such as have actually been paid at the Dowlais works, where the two methods have been tried on a larger scale than at any other place.

With kilns the expense of labour in tipping and filling-in the ironstone and small coal is barely one penny a ton. Small coal only is necessary for the operation, and the quantity used, if of an average quality, is 1 cwt. to the ton of ironstone. But, working on the open-air plan, the cost of the labour expended in stacking and arranging the heaps, and in subsequently watching them during the time they are under fire, amounts to fourpence per ton on the raw stone. The consumption of coal will average 2 cwt. of small and half a cwt. of large to each ton of ironstone. Estimating the small to be worth 2s. 6d., and the large 6s. per ton, the cost of calcining the common argillaceous ores in kilns will stand:

In Kilns.	d.	In Clamps.	d.
Labour in filling, &c.	1	Labour in stacking, &c.	4
Small coal, 1 cwt. at 2s. 6d. per ton	1½	Small coal, 2 cwts. at 2s. 6d. a ton	3
Interest on capital laid out on kilns	0¼	Large coal, ½ cwt. at 6s. a ton	1½
Total cost	2¾	Total cost	8¾

	d.
Cost of calcining in clamps	8¾
„ kilns	2¾
Difference in favour of kilns	6

A difference of sixpence per ton on the cost of preparing an ironstone yielding 32 per cent. of iron is equal to one-seventh nearly on the ton of pig-metal. Independently, however, of this saving, the effectual manner in which kilns perform the operation of calcination enables the ironstone to be worked in the blast furnace with less fuel, and the resulting metal is of a better quality.

The carbonaceous ironstone, or black band of Scotland, is calcined in large heaps by a process similar to that pursued with argillaceous ironstone. The operation is generally performed at the mouth of the pit. From the large per-centage of carbon contained in this stone, calcination is effected without using more fuel than is sufficient to ignite the mass at one or more places, and consequently is effected at a comparatively cheap rate for the open-air plan. All the disadvantages, however, belonging to this system which result from exposure to the ever-varying changes of the atmosphere, show themselves even more prominently when carbonaceous ironstone is being calcined. From the comparatively low temperature at which the metal in carbonaceous ironstone melts, it is a common occurrence to find thin plates of metallic iron wherever slight wind-draughts have existed. Other parts of the heap will probably be found cohering together with a tenacity requiring the use of steel wedges for their separation. In one instance which came under our notice the heap of ironstone had been raised to the height of 20 feet, with a breadth and length in proportion. It was fired, and allowed to burn for some weeks; when sufficiently cooled down, the operation of filling it for the blast furnace commenced. A small portion, about one-fourth, was got out without much difficulty, but the remainder of the heap was found adhering together in such immense masses that they had to be blasted with gunpowder by experienced quarrymen to reduce them to manageable dimensions. Even then the lumps sent to the blast furnace frequently weighed a ton each. The filling of the looser portions was done for about threepence per ton, but the labour employed in the separation of the large masses exceeded 2s. 6d. per ton of calcined ironstone.

We consider the employment of kilns, with careful men as burners, to be a matter of very great importance to the ironmasters of Scotland. Apart from the consideration of having the ironstone calcined with regularity and certainty, the use of kilns would enable the ironmaster to smelt these ores with a consumption of one-third or one-fourth of the fuel now used. In other words, a ton of pig-iron would be made with from 10 to 14 cwt. of coal, instead of 38, which is about the present average consumption.

By referring to the analyses of carbonaceous ironstone at page 5, the proportion which the carbon bears to the whole will be found to be about 30 per cent. In the same stone the metallic iron amounts to 28 per cent. Of such an ironstone we require 3.57 tons to produce one ton of pig-metal. The pure carbon being equal to 30 per cent. of the whole weight, the quantity contained in 3.57 tons of ironstone will be 2404 pounds. Under the open-air system of calcination in use at the Scotch works, this immense quantity of carbon is wasted in over-heating and partially fusing the stones into large refractory masses, and necessarily a large quantity of fuel is required in the blast furnace to convert the ironstone thus calcined into metallic iron. The general yield is 38 cwts. of coal containing 76 per cent. of carbon to each ton of pig-metal produced. This will give 3234 pounds of carbon in the 38 cwts. of coal, or an excess of 830 pounds only over the quantity combined with the ironstone previous to calcination. The difference of 830 pounds is equal to 25 per cent., and we thus discover that the carbon ordinarily contained in the raw carbonaceous ironstones of Scotland, which is now utterly wasted during their calcination, amounts in weight to three-quarters of the weight of carbon contained in the fuel subsequently added in order to effect their fusion and reduction in the blast furnace.

We are very far from supposing that the whole of the carbon combined with the ironstone can be retained and used for the operation of smelting, but we are of opinion that the addition of 8 to 12 cwts. of coal in the blast furnace will be amply sufficient to compensate for the loss during calcination in kilns.

That the carbon can be retained in the ironstone during the process of calcination, if that operation be carefully conducted in properly constructed kilns, there can be no doubt. If the workmen are attentive to their duties, the heat to which the ironstone is subjected can be regulated with a nicety and precision unknown with the open-air system. At no time need the heat be greater than is found in practice to suffice for coking the combined carbonaceous matter; and such being the case, the retention of the carbon for profitable use in the blast furnace may be as effectually accomplished as in coal undergoing the same process in an oven to fit it for a similar purpose.

The pecuniary profit which would accrue to the ironmasters of Scotland by using kilns in the way we have alluded to, will vary with the cost of coal in the district, but under existing circumstances the reduced cost of smelting will not be less than 10s. per ton of pig-iron.

The richer iron ores, such as the red hematite of Lancashire and the brown hydrated hematites of Cornwall and other places, seldom undergo any calcination before entering the blast furnace. The omission in the case of oxides of an operation universally performed on the leaner ores of the argillaceous and carbonaceous species, is owing to the small per-centage of volatile matters which they contain. Water appears to be the principal foreign substance which a well-regulated system of burning would remove from these ores. Under the most favourable circumstances, they contain about 6 per cent. of water, which it is advisable to expel before they are filled into the blast furnace. On numerous occasions, however, we have found these same ores mixed with as much as from 14 to 15 per cent. of water, a quantity which is injurious to the working of the furnace. A portion of this water may have been absorbed during the transit of the ores, but it also frequently happens that they are shipped in a very wet state from the mines in which they are raised. When in this wet state the ores, particularly if they are small and intermixed with a portion of their earthy matrix, have the consistency of concrete. Filled in by barrows, each load drops into the furnace a dense clotted mass, through which neither blast nor heat can penetrate until it has descended far down into the body.

The injurious effects on the working of the furnace and the deterioration in the quality of the resulting pig-iron will be treated of when we come to those sections relating to the working of the blast furnace. Meanwhile, we would here impress on all those who use these ores the necessity of adopting means for expelling the water they contain. Calcination in kilns would seem the most feasible way of accomplishing this desideratum. By itself, however, the red hematite lies too heavily to be properly roasted by the heat given out during the combustion of the small coal generally used in the kiln. Its great density also prevents the passage of the air necessary for combustion.

These difficulties in the way of calcining in kilns are probably the cause of hematite being so much used in the raw state. At the Dowlais works, however, the plan partially adopted some years since, was to calcine these ores in the same kiln along with the argillaceous ironstone. The proportions of hematite ore to one ton of argillaceous stone ranging from 2 to 6 cwt. With the last quantity the kilns worked well, but not so fast as with Welsh ironstone alone. The beneficial effects of this operation on the hematite were remarkable, while the additional expense at the kilns for labour and fuel was exceedingly trifling. Including the cost of the labour of filling into kilns, small coal as fuel, labour in wheeling to stocking places, and wear and tear of kilns, the cost amounted to about threepence per ton of raw ore.

Upon whatever system ironstone is to be calcined care should be taken that the fragments of ore intended to be treated at one time should be nearly uniform in size. This uniformity of dimensions is a matter of considerable importance, although it does not receive that attention which it deserves. We frequently see pieces of ironstone of 2 or 3 inches in the least diameter undergoing calcination along with lumps 12 to 18 inches in diameter. With such variations in the dimensions it is very evident that if the quantity of fuel be regulated to thoroughly roast the smaller pieces it will suffice to calcine the outside only of the larger lumps. On the other hand, if the proportion of fuel is sufficient to maintain a heat that will calcine the large lumps, the smaller pieces will have been overheated and fuel wasted. We have ascertained experimentally that the time necessary to heat argillaceous ironstones of different dimensions to the same temperature is nearly in proportion to their smallest diameters. Thus, if the time necessary for a piece of 12 inches in the smallest diameter is 24 hours, the time for a piece of 2 inches in diameter will be 4 hours only; whilst ironstone so divided that it will pass through a sieve containing 30 meshes to the lineal inch will only require 4 minutes for this operation.

At several works kilns have been erected with a tram-road sufficiently elevated to allow the waggons to discharge directly into the kiln. (Pl. II., Figs. 6—10.) This plan is attended with a saving of labour, amounting in value to about three-eighths of a penny per ton of ironstone; but otherwise we do not consider it to be a desirable practice. Each waggon probably holds 2 or 3 tons of ore, which fall in a single heap, measuring perhaps 2 or 3 feet in height. Over this we will suppose that a quantity of coal is thrown and then left to calcine. If an abundance of coal is used the whole will be properly burnt; but if the quantity of fuel is proportioned only to the requirements of a well-conducted kiln, the centre of the heap will be more or less imperfectly roasted. From careful observation we are inclined to believe that filling with the shovel is eventually the cheapest plan, and is attended with the most satisfactory results in the blast furnace.

Calcination, when performed with the requisite care and attention, effectually deprives the ironstone of water, sulphur, carbonic acid, and other bodies volatile at the temperature maintained in the kiln. It is necessary, however, that during the progress of the operation the heat should be gradually advanced to the point which experience has proved to be most advantageous. This is provided for in kilns by maintaining the greatest heat 2 or 3 feet below the surface of the incandescent mass; in the open-air system, by the slow rate at which the combustion proceeds from the original fire.

If the operation is too much prolonged, or if the temperature employed is too great, the ironstone will be more or less injured. When the water, carbonic acid, &c., are expelled, the operation is complete; but if it is continued after this, the stone again increases in weight by the absorption of oxygen, and when in the furnace is more difficult of fusion than properly roasted stone. In extreme cases this increase of weight by the fixation of oxygen may amount to 7 or 8 per cent. From the foregoing remarks it is obvious that great care bestowed on the preparation of the ores for the blast furnace is well repaid where the quality of the metal and cost of smelting are deemed objects worthy of attention.

When properly calcined the argillaceous ironstone is of a light-reddish colour throughout, friable and readily splitting into imperfect laminæ. In the partially calcined stone the depth inwards of the reddish colour shows the extent of the calcination, and there will be a portion of the stone towards the centre of a deep blue-black colour. If the operation has been so imperfect as to leave a considerable portion undone, the centre will retain its grey or indigo-blue colour unchanged. The breadth and presence of each band will show the extent of the calcination. Pounded ironstone calcined on a red-hot iron plate is observed gradually to turn black as it absorbs heat, but on allowing it to cool this colour finally changes into a light red.

Ironstone is found to lose considerably in weight by the expulsion of the water, carbonic acid, &c. This loss of weight by calcination varies with different ores, in some being as high as 50 per cent., while in others it is as low as 6 or 7 per cent. of the original weight. With the same class of ores the loss is generally in an inverse ratio to the yield of metal.

Argillaceous stones lose from 20 to 33 per cent.—the average of 18 assays was 27 per cent.

Carbonaceous ironstones lose more than any others. The actual loss on these ores varies with the different kinds, but it is seldom under 28 per cent. Stones containing a large per-centage of carbonaceous matter lose from 40 to 50 per cent. And in one specimen which we examined, and which is extensively used in Scotland, the loss reached 60 per cent. The lean carbonaceous ironstones of the Welsh basin lose from 28 to 37 per cent.

Calcareous ores lose weight in proportion as they contain more or less lime. The average loss of stones of this class may be taken at 33 per cent. Siliceous ironstones are amongst the leanest ores used in the blast furnace. They lose in calcination from 25 to 30 per cent.

The rich hematites of Lancashire and Cumberland lose about 6 per cent. in weight in passing through the calcining kiln. The hydrated hematites of North Wales, Cornwall, Devonshire, and other places, lose from 12 to 14 per cent. when clean. But if these ores are mixed with much extraneous matter, which unfortunately for iron-masters is now too often the case, they have been known to lose 26 per cent.

PREPARATION OF FUEL.

It is but a few years since raw coal was first adopted as a fuel in smelting. Previously, the preliminary process of coking was considered as indispensable to the success of smelting operations; and in the majority of the iron-making districts this erroneous impression prevails at the present day. The causes which have contributed to perpetuate this system of wasting a large portion of the calorific power of the coal in the coke-yard will be the subject of a separate section.

In the process of coking the coal is exposed to a slow combustion, by which the volatile gases are expelled, and the carbon retained for use in the furnace. If carefully conducted, the loss of carbon is not great, but in the ordinary way of coking, from one-fourth to one-half of the carbon is dissipated, and the calorific power of the coal in the furnace is reduced to this extent.

The operation is often conducted in the open air; large quantities, however, are prepared in brick ovens, variously constructed, according to the qualities of the coal, mode of working, and science displayed.

PREPARATION OF FLUX.

The limestone used as flux, is usually charged into the furnace in the state in which it comes from the quarry, the preliminary operations being limited to reducing the dimensions of the blocks, that calcination may be the more readily affected. In a few establishments, however, the stone is calcined in kilns, by which the water and carbonic acid is expelled, and lime obtained in the caustic state. This process is performed in kilns, of the construction employed for the calcination of ores, and is conducted throughout on nearly similar principles.

SECTION III.

BLAST FURNACES.

Erection.—In the erection of blast furnaces care should be taken to secure a firm unyielding foundation on which to build the superstructure. The weight of the masonry, brickwork, iron gearing, and plates is of itself great, and when to this is added that of the metal and materials within the furnace, it is evident that a sound foundation is indispensable. It is desirable to have the excavations in a dry soil, but where local considerations interfere, and water is met with, or a subsequent influx is to be apprehended, efficient drainage should always be provided. Also a sufficient distance must be maintained between the furnace and any combustible material, or such as would be liable to injury from heat.*

The thickness of the foundation will depend on the character of the soil and the description of furnace to be erected. Furnaces with a massive square stack tapering considerably in their height require a less depth than cupola furnaces, in which the entire weight of furnace and of the materials within its interior is borne by the cast-iron columns and the narrow space which they enclose. On the space enclosed by the base the square stack furnace presses with a force of 2 to $2\frac{1}{2}$ tons per square foot, and the cupola furnace with a force of $3\frac{1}{4}$ to $3\frac{3}{4}$ tons per square foot. In alluvial soils the former require a thickness of from 3 to 5 feet, the latter from 5 to 8 feet, with a proportionate breadth. The lower portion may be of common work, but in wet situations, as a precaution against the possible ascent of moisture, the centre of the upper portion should be carefully built in hydraulic lime. Having brought the foundation to the level of the existing or intended furnace yard, the next step is the erection of the furnace itself.

Form of Furnace.—The interior of the furnace is usually circular; the exterior is variously constructed. In South Wales the form generally preferred is that of a truncated pyramid; frequently, however, the lower half is built nearly vertical, whilst the upper is wrought to an irregular curve. On the eastern side of the district a considerable number of cupola furnaces exist. In the Staffordshire and Derbyshire districts the older furnaces have square stacks, the newer a circular stack on a square base. The majority of the Scottish furnaces have a square base, surmounted by a circular stack. On the continent of Europe a large number of the furnaces are built with square stacks; those in Russia, Norway, and Sweden often being a rude pile of stones, kept together by a few pieces of timber. Those in America, with the exception of a few of the more recently erected anthracite and coke

---

* The Blaenavon Valley furnace was erected (1853) on and in contact with a quantity of combustible débris, which subsequently ignited; for some time the insidious combustion was not perceived, but the gradual though unequal sinkings of the soil as the carbonaceous matter was consumed, caused fractures in the inferior erections; after a short period the engine-stack fell, the boiler seatings were broken up, the engine-house was destroyed, and the incline plane for raising the materials to the top fired, which necessitated a total abandonment of the furnace within a very few months after its erection.

furnaces, are scarcely superior to the Russian, as may be gathered from the many descriptions extant. The form of the exterior is not material; little attention, further than to secure the greatest economy, need, therefore, be given to this point.

The Material used in the erection of stacks, the lining excepted, may be either brick or stone. Economical considerations usually determine the most eligible substance. The principal qualities required are hardness, freedom from brittleness, and power to resist a moderate degree of heat.

The style of work varies according to the taste of the proprietor. In Wales the furnace stacks are generally built of plain unhewn rubble-work, in Staffordshire of brick, while the Scotch furnaces are not unfrequently composed of dressed stone blocks. A large outlay on the architectural features of a furnace, however, is not judicious, the points to be aimed at being a sufficient degree of strength and the retention of heat in the interior; the outlay should, therefore, be limited to securing these rather than spending large sums of money on ornamental work. The cost of erecting an iron-works, indeed, is so large that economy in the outlay on every part is indispensable to ensure the commercial success of the undertaking.

In building a blast furnace, as also in the numerous other erections belonging to ironworks, it should be borne in mind that they are required for *temporary* purposes, and that all outlay in securing unnecessary solidity and strength is so much direct waste. Improvements in the mode of manufacturing are daily being made, by which the cost of the finished product is largely reduced. It is desirable, then, that the ironmaster should be able to avail himself of the new methods with the smallest possible outlay of capital. This he cannot well do if the new mode involves the sacrifice of existing costly plant. And the reluctance and inability to sacrifice elaborately-constructed though antiquated apparatus eventually results in the possessor being left behind his compeers in commercial standing.

Building Blast Furnaces.—In erecting a large furnace with a square stack, the four pillars to carry the arches over the tuyere-houses are first marked out on the previously levelled floor. The distance between these pillars measures 8 to 10 feet, and they are usually built to a height of 8 or 10 feet before springing the arches. The inner portion of the pillars generally forms part of the internal diameter of the furnace (Pl. XIX., Fig. 103), but in certain cases the interior of the furnace below the boshes is of a square form; the inner portion is then of an angular figure. (Pl. XIV., Fig. 87.) Above the springings of the arches the stack is carried up with the requisite taper to the top, which may vary in height from 25 feet to 70 feet from the level of the foundation. The taper or batter of the stack is determined with reference to the material of which it is to be built, and the manner in which it is to be bound together. In cases where no expense is spared in the binding, the exterior walls have been carried up vertically; in others, where few or no binders have been employed, and the mason-work has been of a very common description, the batter has been from 2 or $2\frac{1}{4}$ inches to a foot. The interior is wrought to the required figure and diameter by a revolving trammel of framed wood. Those parts of the pillars which may at any time be in contact with the cinders or fire of the hearth are built with a facing of fire-brick. And in the wall of one side of the cinder-fall a cast-iron bracket is built, against which the wrought-iron crane used in working the furnace is subsequently hung.

The fire-brick lining is carried up simultaneously with the stack. It ordinarily consists of an inner course of the best fire-bricks, about 14 inches long, manufactured of the required segmental form, and laid endwise. It begins at the bottom of the pillars, and is carried up to the top of the furnace, or to the level of the charging plates. Over the arches that span the tuyere-houses and cinder-fall a second course of casing bricks commences, and is carried up along with the other.

To provide for the enlarged diameter arising from the expansion by heat of the brick lining, a space of from 2 to 3 inches is left between the inner and outer courses. In some instances this space is rammed with sand, fire-clay, or broken scoriæ, with numerous vertical channels, as outlets for any vapours that may arise. If the sand is rammed in solid, the steam generated during the drying of the furnace is very likely to cause a rupture of the casing and outer walling.

Also, in order to give vent to any aqueous vapours or gases that may be given off from the masonry during the drying and working of the furnace, air-holes are left all around; they are about 4 inches square, and proceed from the second course of bricks outwards. Their greatest distance apart, vertically or horizontally, should not exceed 8 feet. They are a precaution against fracture, which should never be omitted; and if the furnace is to be blown-in with very little previous drying, the distance between them should be reduced at least one-half. They afford, also, an escape into the atmosphere for any gas that may leak through the brick lining. In furnaces where they have been insufficient in number, the broken and dilapidated appearance of the masonry is an evidence of the force exerted by the gases during their liberation. It is usual to build in across each of the arches at the level of the springing a massive cast-iron mantle about 13 feet long, curved on the inner side concentric with the curvature of the interior of the furnace. These mantles are connected together by stout plates having lugs to fit into corresponding recesses in the mantle. The purpose of this circle of heavy castings is to bind together and strengthen the lower part of the furnace, where it has been so much weakened by the insertion of the arches. The space between the mantles and the crown of the arch, a distance of about 4¼ feet is walled up with fire-bricks. In some furnaces we have observed this space filled up with a large cast-iron plate, which had been better omitted. If convenience and facility for working the furnace are considerations, the permanent fixing of iron plates of any kind in the tuyere-house is objectionable. Cases may occur in the course of working when the presence of such plates may be highly detrimental to the success of the operations.

In the old blast furnaces, it was usual to leave in the bottom, underneath the hearthstone, numerous small channels or flues, but for what purpose is not very clear. They may have been intended to prevent the ascent of moisture, by draining the brickwork, but if the site has been judiciously selected, moisture cannot penetrate into the hearth. By some they are considered necessary for ventilating the lower portions of the furnace, but a layer of sand under the bottom answers every purpose. Certain it is, however, that this mode of constructing the bottom, though at one time universally practised and considered indispensable to its safety, is rarely adopted in modern furnaces.

Until within a comparatively recent period the bottom was invariably formed of large blocks of coarse sandstone, and wherever practicable, in a single course of from 2¼ to 3 feet high. The quarrying, dressing, and setting of these blocks was necessarily very expensive. Sandstone is still employed in the majority of instances, and, owing to the peculiar action of the hot blast in creating an intensely high temperature immediately contiguous to the tuyere, it will probably continue to be preferred. The bottom thus formed fills up the circular space between the pillars, and projects 2 or 3 feet into each of the tuyere-houses, and the same distance into the cinder-fall.

When finished, the surface of the bottom in the direction, from tuyere to tuyere, is perfectly level, but from the back tuyere to the front there is a fall of a quarter inch in a foot.

In numerous furnaces, recently erected or repaired, the bottom is formed of fire brick, and the experience of nearly twenty years enables us to state that such bottoms work well, and are less costly than stone. Bricks of the common size were tried in the first instance, but in practice they were found to be too small. After the furnace had worked a few days, they floated on the metal in the fluid cinder, from whence they were withdrawn by the workmen. It does not appear, however, that any permanent injury resulted from the displacement of these bricks, for the furnace has since remained in blast for a period of twelve years. But to prevent the possibility of their floating up, they are now made larger and of a peculiar form. (See Pl. XV., Fig. 90.) By contracting them in width in the middle and introducing corresponding half bricks, every brick is effectually locked into its place. The bottom is composed of two courses of these, laid on a course of flat bricks.

At Scotch works where brick bottoms are used, the means employed to retain the bricks in their position are equally successful. The bricks are made of a length equal to the height of the bottom, but are moulded to such sections that, when placed on the foundation level, they form an inverted arch. (See Pl. XX., Fig. 107.) This plan has the disadvantage of requiring several moulds, but it makes a sound bottom. The bricks being comparatively thin, a perfectly homogeneous quality can be insured.

When the surface of the bottom is completed and finished off, the hearth is marked out upon it. In practice hearths are of different forms and dimensions, and are variously constructed. (Pls. XIV., XVI., XVIII., XIX., XXI.)

In the old charcoal furnace the hearth was square, and in the present charcoal furnaces of the Continent of Europe and the United States of America, this form appears to be almost universal. As it is generally narrow—seldom exceeding 2 feet in width—we may reasonably infer that the first builders employed the square form as being the easiest of construction.

With the modern coke and raw coal furnaces of large dimensions, hearths of proportionate width have been adopted. Following the model presented by the charcoal furnace, square hearths are nearly universally used in Continental and American furnaces, and very generally in the furnaces of this country. In some cases the circular form is adopted, and there are a few instances of hearths having a pear-shaped section.

The material of which hearths are constructed may either be sandstone or brick. Ironmasters who use stone for bottoms employ the same material in building the hearths, while others who have adopted the less expensive material, brick, find that it answers equally well for the hearth. The suitability of this latter material, however, depends in a great measure on the particular mode of working the furnace, which may be contemplated. The quality of the fuel and density of the blast in cold blast furnaces exercise an important influence on the temperature in the several portions of the hearth. And the low specific gravity of heated blast also causes an inequality in the temperature at the sides of the hearth in comparison with that at the centre. Therefore in selecting a material, it is necessary to take into consideration the causes that will be brought into action to establish a high or low temperature contiguous to the tuyere.

If the furnace be a large one, and is intended to work up to its full power, there is left in the sandstone or brickwork on each side, and in the back of the hearth, a small arch about 2 feet in width, widening out or splaying to 5 feet on the outside, and reaching to the cast-iron mantles, the lower edge of which forms the outer face of the arch. In furnaces with brick hearths it is usual to start the openings of these arches from the bottom, the space between up to the tuyere being subsequently filled in with brickwork or other material. But where sandstone is adopted the tuyere arches are commenced at the required elevation, the solid sandstone block forming the lower side of the opening. The arch in front is of nearly the same width as the others, but the height decreases towards the outside, where it does not usually exceed $3\frac{1}{4}$ feet from the bottom.

The boshes commence at the top of the hearth; their interior diameter increasing with their height until they meet the inner lining of brickwork, built during the erection of the furnace. They are usually constructed of fire-bricks, about 15 inches long, carefully laid in fire-clay. Considerable diversity of opinion exists respecting the best angle at which they should incline outwards from the hearth. In our own practice we have generally adopted an angle of 70 deg. from a horizontal line, as being the most suitable, and the results warrant us in stating that this angle may be adopted in all furnaces for smelting argillaceous or carbonaceous ores. But when other ores are to be smelted, their character and that of the fuel will have an important bearing on the form of the boshes as well as that of the hearth and furnace generally. We purpose examining the relation which these should bear to each other in another section

The form of the furnace, from the boshes to the throat, is also a matter on which a difference of opinion exists amongst ironmasters. Formerly it was invariably that of a truncated cone, as is seen in the majority of the blast furnace sections (see Pls. VII., XII.), but of late years numerous furnaces have been built differently. In Scotland, the body of the furnace is frequently carried up cylindrically, or nearly so, for a considerable height, terminating with the usual truncated cone. We shall defer the consideration of the advantages which are supposed to attend the different forms to a more advanced portion of this work.

To complete the furnace, a chimney, or, as it is termed in South Wales, a "tunnel-head," is erected above the charging-plates. This tunnel-head is generally of a diameter larger than the mouth of the furnace, and is carried up to a height of 10 or 12 feet: and one or more openings are left in it, through which the furnace is charged. The number of filling places varies with the size of the throat. Where there is more than one, each opening is fitted with a metal door to protect the workmen from the draught. (Pl. XXX., Figs. 150, 153.) The tunnel-head is built of brick, strengthened by stout cast-iron rings at top and bottom, and cast-iron frames to the charging places. It is fitted also with four or five stout iron hoops, having tightening screws, which effectually secure the brickwork from being fractured by the great heat evolved from the ignited materials in the throat of the furnace.

In the erection of walled blast furnaces, the exterior line of which deviates from the vertical, we have found it advisable to work the stones with a square front, and set the courses with a dip from the level towards the centre of the furnace, corresponding to the batter in front. Besides the evident saving in labour and material, the work is considerably stronger and the face less liable to breakage from expansion. In the interior also we advise the setting of the bricks or stones forming the hearth, and the bricks forming the boshes, in a similar manner. By so doing the interior cavity, from top to bottom, may be worked without steps and with little waste of material. With the boshes this mode of setting should always be followed. We have observed furnaces in England and Scotland, in which the necessary angle has been given to the boshes by stepping back each course the required distance, and afterwards plastering over the interstices with fire-clay to produce the desired evenness. Were the other plan followed—the bed of the courses sloped downwards as they recede from the face of the work, the ends of the bricks form the correct angle of inclination without dressing or subsequent plastering. In the stone-work of the stack a strong mortar may be used in the face, but a weaker kind is better for the backing and filling-in, because it permits of slight movements without disturbing the outside.

The binders employed to prevent the work from opening require to be very strong and easy of renewal. For this purpose they should be on the outside, or otherwise so placed that they may be changed in a few hours. The furnace delineated in Pls. XV., XVII. is strongly bound, and has stood remarkably well. The lower portions are held together by cast-iron angle pieces and wrought-iron tension rods $2\frac{1}{4}$ inches square. The circular portion is bound throughout with wrought-iron hoops, $3\frac{1}{4}$ by $\frac{1}{4}$ inch, placed 6 inches apart, and retained at this distance by vertical bars of the same dimensions.

In Scotland the outlay on the materials for binding some furnaces has been very large. At the Muirkirk works a furnace is cased in malleable iron plates from top to bottom. At the Bilston new furnace also a similar expensive binding has been employed. Great strength is obtained by this method, but the expense is so considerable as to preclude its general adoption.

To expedite the operation of drying, two small arches are left in the base of each of the pillars of masonry of a size sufficient to contain a fire 3 feet by 1½ feet. From the crown a flue, about 10 inches square, is carried up through the masonry to the top of the furnace. (See Pls. XV., XVI., Figs. 88, 91, 92.) With this flue the whole, or nearly so, of the holes left in the masonry for ventilation should communicate. Where this is done, the masonry may be rapidly and perfectly dried without any of the usual unsightly fissures being produced.

The drying of the furnace previous to blowing in, requires time and fuel commensurate with its dimensions. If it is a large one, two months may be well spent in the operation, and a consumption of 70 tons of coal will not be too great. The interior brickwork will be best dried by a temporary furnace in the cinder-fall, communicating directly with the interior. While this furnace is in operation the tuyeres should be temporarily bricked up to prevent the ingress of cold air, and the mouth partially covered over to diminish the draught and retain the heat within the interior.

When the drying is completed, the temporary furnace in front is removed and the brick stopping in the tuyeres taken down.

Preparations may now be made for blowing in. These consist in building up the tuyere openings with brickwork or sandstone to a height of 2 feet on each side, and 2 feet 3 inches at the back. In some furnaces this height is made up with a hollow cast-iron block, through which water is allowed to circulate while the furnace is in blast. (See Pl. XXXIV., Figs. 194, 196.) Above this the cast or wrought-iron tuyeres are placed, with their points flush with the wall of the hearth, and the remainder of the space filled up with brickwork, 18 to 24 inches thick; or sometimes with a cast-iron breast containing a small pipe bent in a spiral form, through which water is made to circulate to keep it cool. (See Pls. XXXIII., XXXIV., Figs. 189, 193, 202.)

In front of the cinder-fall, a cast metal damplate (Pl. XXXIV., Figs. 205, 206) is bolted to two wrought-iron bolts built into the brickwork of the hearth. This plate measures about 6 feet long, 3 feet high, and 3 inches thick. Near the centre, an opening, 9 inches wide by 20 inches high, is left for tapping, the bottom being flush with the bottom of the hearth, and one side flush with the brickwork inside. In the upper edge a notch, 8 inches wide, is left for the cinders to flow through. The height from the brickwork of the bottom to the underside of this notch is an important measurement: in this instance it is 24 inches. To retard the wearing or burning away of the plate at the underside of the notch the thickness of metal is there doubled. On the outer side, close to the tapping-hole, a vertical flange is cast to sustain the end of a cast-iron plate set on edge, to keep the flowing cinders on one side of the fall.

At a distance of about 16 inches above the notch, and 26 inches inside the damplate, it is usual to fix a tymplate within a recess, provided for that purpose in the brickwork. The tymp is generally 3 feet high and 2 inches thick, with a short flange on the under side as a protection to the brickwork over the fall. Tymps having a small water-pipe laid in a serpentine form in the metal, are in use at several furnaces, where a high local heat prevails. (Pl. XXXIV., Figs. 197, 199.) At other works, however, we find the furnaces working with an unprotected breastwork of brick.

There are also fixed in the cinder-fall a wrought-iron crane; a cast-iron plate, having its upper edge serrated, to facilitate the removal of large masses of cinder; a cast-iron trough, about 6 feet long, to convey the fluid metal from the tapping-hole to the casting-bed or refinery; and two troughs on the cinder-bed for guiding the fluid cinder into the tubs. Immediately before filling, the portion of the damplate exposed to the fluid metal is protected by a stone or mass of brickwork, at a level with the cinder-notch. (See Pl. XXXVI.)

The conveyance of the blast to the furnace is accomplished in various ways—by leather bags, cast-iron pipes, wrought-iron fixed, and wrought-iron telescope pipes. Local circumstances and the temperature of the blast employed, principally determine the kind of apparatus to be used.

For cold-blast furnaces, the last-named is probably the most durable, and attended with the least waste of blast. It consists of a thin wrought-iron pipe, generally 10 inches in diameter and 6 feet long, having rivetted within one end a light cast-iron cylinder, bored and turned, and on the other a cast-iron flange. The large end of the sliding telescopic pipe is furnished with a metal ring, turned to fit the interior of the cylinder, and has a small groove to receive packing. The length of the sliding pipe should equal that of the fixed; the diameter at the small end being for the above size cylinder 5 inches, and at the large end 8 inches. To prevent its entire withdrawal, the interior of the cast-iron cylinder is provided at the outer end with a small hollow flange, against which the piston is ground air-tight to prevent leakage. The loose wrought-iron nozzles, placed on the small end of the sliding pipe, should be about 2 feet long, and of a diameter proportioned to the volume and density of blast to be delivered. (See Pl. XXXII., Figs. 169, 173.)

To the cast-iron flange on the rear of the wrought cylindrical pipe, there is attached a universal joint, consisting of a cup and ball, accurately ground to each other, and connected by two eye-bolts. This joint allows of any lateral or vertical movement in the pipes that may be rendered necessary, through changes in the position of the tuyere.

Connected with this joint, or to the elbow pipe leading to the main, is the valve for regulating the admission of the blast. Various descriptions of valves are employed for this purpose. One very commonly used in the old apparatus was formed of a stout disc of wood, faced with leather or sheepskin, and furnished with a spill and stalk, similar to the common spindle-valve of a steam-engine. (Pl. XXXI., Figs. 165, 166.) While in good order, it proves an effective stop-valve; but the return of cinders from the furnace through the pipes frequently destroys it, and causes delay and waste of material.

For a considerable period disc-valves turning on a pivot-spindle were very commonly used. In general they are neat in appearance and require little power to open or shut them

(Pl. XXXI., Figs. 158, 160.) Practically, however, valves of this description are about the worst that can be adopted. It is almost impossible, even with a large expenditure of labour and very careful fitting, to make them air-tight. The best allow considerable leakage of blast, and to this cause we attribute the general abandonment of valves of this description.

Slide-valves are now very generally used, and unquestionably are much superior to the others. The movement of the valve is effected by a rack and pinion in the box, with a spindle projecting through the side. (Pl. XXXI., Figs. 161, 164); or a rod working through a stuffing-box. (Pl. XXXI, Figs. 154, 157.) In either case, a simple iron slide planed and ground in tight on a planed face in the interior of the box is employed. The pressure of the blast being on the back of the slide, whether it is open or shut, causes sufficient adhesion to keep it in contact with the face, and to retain it in whatever position it may be left.

In several works the valve-boxes are so constructed that the movement of shutting off the blast from the furnace opens to the atmosphere an orifice nearly equal in size to the nozzle-pipe. (Pl. XXXI., Figs. 161, 163.) The object in view appears to be to equalise the resistance to the movement of the blowing-engine piston, where there is more than one furnace, by maintaining the previous area of discharge. The attainment of this object, however, by permitting a portion of the blast, compressed at great cost, to escape into the atmosphere, is not entitled to commendation. It should rather be sought by regulating the movements of the blowing-piston, which are perfectly controllable, and so adjusting the quantity of blast compressed to the reduced area of discharge.

Bolted to the stop-valve box is an elbow-pipe, 10 inches bore, with the curve upwards, joining other pipes of the blowing apparatus. In the majority of works it is usual to have this elbow turning down, and connected with larger pipes laid below the surface. However neat such an arrangement may appear, in practice it is attended with many disadvantages. For instance, when a sudden stoppage of the blowing apparatus occurs, the cinders not unfrequently flow back through the pipes into the subterraneous mains, and cause expense and delay; and in the event of leakage of blast from the joints, it is difficult to get at them to stop it.

In the back of the elbow an orifice, about one inch diameter, is drilled in a line with the centre of the tuyere, and fitted with a metal stopper. Through this orifice a small iron rod can be introduced to clean the tuyere when fouling; and when a heated blast is used it is also convenient for trying the temperature.

The pipes used for hot-blast furnaces differ from the preceding, the wrought-iron telescope apparatus being absent. Cast-metal pipes, diminishing in size as they recede from the cup and ball joint, with wrought-iron nozzles similar to those with a cold blast, are in general use. At some of the Welsh cupola furnaces, a lighter and more compact arrangement has been adopted on account of the limited room for the pipes, as may be seen in the plate of details. (See Pl. XXXII., Figs. 176, 177.)

At the majority of hot-blast furnaces the stop-valve for regulating or shutting off the supply of blast, is placed in the pipe leading to the heating-stove. But the employment of a single valve in this manner is objectionable, inasmuch as it necessitates the entire stoppage of the blast during repairs to the heating-stove, which, unfortunately, are of frequent occurrence. To avoid such interruptions to the working of the furnace, the heating-stove should be furnished with two valves, one in the inlet-pipe and another in a box between the stove and belly-pipes; to this box a range of pipes should be connected to admit cold blast when the stove is undergoing repairs. (Pl. XXIV., Fig. 123.)

Leather bags are employed at some works with a cold blast; and where the supply of blast is not dependent on a single engine or apparatus, and careful workmen are employed, the connexion lasts a considerable time. They form probably the simplest arrangement that can be devised, there being no fitting or other expensive workmanship required in their construction; while the flexibility of the leather permits of the nozzle being pointed to any part of the breast. (Pl. XXXIII., Fig. 182.) This mode of conveying the blast is in use at all the furnaces of the Plymouth and Duffryn works.

The top of the furnace round the tunnel-head is floored with cast-iron plates from three-quarters of an inch to an inch thick; and where the materials are stacked upon the level of the furnace top, a continuation of the plate flooring is carried out to the stocking place of the fuel, ore, and flux, forming a level barrow-road for the fillers to wheel the charges. In front of each stocking place it is desirable to have on a level with the floor a lock-up platform weighing-machine, weighted according to the burden on the furnace. The usual arrangement is to have two, sometimes three, beam weighing-machines at the bridge plates, where the quantities are adjusted, recourse being had to a small supplementary stock for supplying deficiencies. With platform machines, conveniently fixed at the stocking places, the barrow rests on the machine whilst being filled; the exact quantity is determined on the spot; greater accuracy is thus obtained and much labour economised.

Cupola Furnaces.—In the erection of cupola furnaces the masonry is limited to the foundation and the stone work of the bottom and hearth. This form of furnace possesses certain advantages over the massive square stack, but it has been ascertained through the experience derived from the working of several, that they also are subject to disadvantages of a very serious character.

The building of a cupola furnace commences with carefully bedding on the levelled masonry an iron ring of massive proportions, cast in four or more segments. Upon this ring cast-iron columns of from 12 to 14 feet high are bolted fast, one on each side of each of the tuyere openings. Upon the columns a second iron ring is bolted, of an internal diameter somewhat greater than that of the interior of the furnace, and ranging from 18 to 24 inches wide by about 3 inches thick, and strengthened by a deep flange on its outer edge. Four or more vertical binders are now set up, which support, at distances of from 8 to 12 inches from centre to centre, wrought-iron hoops about $3\frac{1}{2}$ inches wide by $\frac{3}{8}$ inch thick, made to fit the calculated exterior diameter of the furnace at their respective heights. (Pl. XVIII., Figs. 97, 100.)

The building of the furnace itself is performed, inside the network of binders, by starting from the upper cast-iron ring a course of walling of the required diameter, and at the usual distance of 2 or 3 inches a course of casing bricks; the space between them being rammed in the same manner as in blast-furnaces built with massive stonework stacks. The outer case of bricks abuts against the binders, which limit the thickness of the walls to the two courses of brickwork and the intervening space, amounting together to about 26 inches. At this thickness the walls are carried up to the top, upon which a tunnel head of the usual form is built.

Neither the construction of the bottom, hearth, or boshes, nor the materials used, differ from the more common form of furnace. Cupola furnaces are thoroughly dried in a very short time, on account of the small quantity of brickwork in their construction.

The advantages offered by the cupola furnace over the more common form are dependent in a great measure on local circumstances. Where the necessary massive iron framing can be obtained at a low price, and stonework is comparatively expensive, the cupola furnace can be erected at a cheaper rate, probably at half, or under half, the cost of the other plan. It is evident, however, that the question of expense turns on the cost of the ironwork of the one compared with that of the masonry walling of the other. For the height and internal capacity being alike, the foundations, bottom, hearth, boshes, and brickwork will be similar, and any difference must arise between the walling, in one case, and the iron framing in the other. Estimating the furnace to be 50 feet high and 275 cubic yards internal capacity, there will be in the stack, about 1250 cubic yards of masonry, against 30 tons of castings and 14 tons of wrought-iron jointed work in place, in the cupola. The difference in value between these two quantities, in any locality, will determine the comparative cheapness of the two modes of furnace building.

It must, however, be borne in mind that the ironwork of the cupola furnace possesses in proportion to its first cost a prospective value greater than that of the stonework of the walled stack furnace. The materials of the latter are valuable only as constituting a portion of the furnace, but the metal work of the former possesses an intrinsic value in whatever form it is employed.

The cupola furnace possesses a decided advantage in the period required for building and completion for blowing-in. The building and thoroughly drying of a walled stack blast-furnace of the largest dimensions will require from six to seven months; the cupola furnace may be built, dried, and blown-in in three months.

The disadvantages attending this form of furnace are an increased consumption of fuel in proportion to the quantity of iron smelted, and more serious irregularities in the operation of the furnace. The increase in the consumption of fuel is considerable, and in a few years the additional annual cost thus entailed is found in the aggregate to greatly exceed the original cost of the furnace.

The further consideration of this subject will be deferred to the section treating on the causes influencing the consumption of fuel.

APPARATUS FOR LIFTING MATERIALS.

The apparatus for raising the materials to the level of the charging-plates—where nature has not afforded facilities—is directly worked by a steam-engine, or by an hydraulic or pneumatic apparatus. In South Wales the ironmasters have taken advantage of the generally mountainous character of that country to build the blast-furnaces on hill-sides, having back-ground on a level with the furnace top, over which the materials are wheeled directly into the furnace, and, with the exception of a few instances, it has not been necessary to erect machinery for lifting the materials. But in the more level districts of England and Scotland machinery is very generally employed for this purpose.

One of the most common means of raising the loaded barrows is the inclined plane and stationary engine. An inclined plane is constructed to the furnace top at an angle of about 25 degrees, with two tracks of rails, each track being traversed by a platform carriage, which is drawn up and let down by a chain from the engine-drum passing over a pulley at top. When it is at the bottom of the plane the platform is on a level with the adjacent ground, the barrows are wheeled on to it, and it is drawn up to the top, where it is brought to a standstill, with the platform on a level with the staging around the furnace. The barrows having been discharged into the furnace, they are replaced on the platform, which is lowered, and the opposite carriage with its loaded barrows drawn up. By employing two carriages the one descending acts as a counterpoise to the one ascending, consequently the load to be raised at each time is simply the weight of the material in the barrows. To work an inclined plane which supplies four blast-furnaces requires an engine of ten-horse power. (Pl. XXIII., Fig. 118.)

The great wear and tear of the carriages, pulleys, and chains, together with their constant liability to derangement, and the space occupied by the plane, render this an expensive method of raising the materials. In the event of the chain breaking, which is not an unfrequent occurrence, considerable delay occurs in the supply to the furnace, occasioning a loss, independent of the cost of repairs and renewals. Hence, although in use at many old furnaces, the inclined plane is rarely adopted in new erections, and is likely to be eventually altogether superseded by simpler and more efficient machinery.

The water-balance lift employed at some furnaces is a cheap method of raising the materials. It consists of two cylindrical or rectangular sheet-iron buckets, or cisterns, suspended from a strong chain which works in a grooved brake-wheel, revolving in standards at a height of 10 or 11 feet above the level of the staging around the furnace top. Each bucket is provided with a platform to receive the barrow, and has a valve at the bottom for discharging the water; it is guided in its ascent and descent by guide-rods bolted to framing at top and bottom. An upright pipe, supplied with water (generally by a plunger-pump driven by the blowing-engine), and fitted on the upper part with a box containing two spindle valves, one for each bucket, completes the essentials of the apparatus. (Pl. XXIII., Figs. 114, 117.) The operation of lifting, premising that both buckets are empty, one at the top, the other at the bottom, is performed by letting into the upper bucket, upon which the empty barrow stands, a quantity of water rather more than sufficient to counterbalance the weight of the load in the barrow on the lower bucket. On lifting the friction-brake from off the wheel, the greater weight of the descending bucket draws up the opposite one with its load to the top, where the contents of the barrow are discharged into the furnace. To repeat the operation, the empty barrow is replaced on the upper bucket, and the valve in the lower bucket is opened, to allow the water to escape; a loaded barrow is wheeled on to it, and water is admitted into the upper bucket until it begins to descend. The velocity of the descent is regulated by the friction-brake, which should be sufficiently powerful to stop the buckets at any desired spot and to control their speed, so that on their arrival at top and bottom they may be brought to rest without that concussion so common with these machines. In order that this may be effected by means of the brake the buckets should exactly balance each other, and a chain should be hung to their bottoms, similar to the one employed in lifting. Unless a balance-chain be employed, the bucket will descend with an accelerated velocity and strike heavily upon the bottom framing.

Several modifications of the water-balance lift may be seen in English and Scotch works. One consists of a single bucket at one end of the chain with a platform at the other end. Water is admitted to the bucket at top until it overbalances the load on the platform, which is thus drawn up and wheeled off. The descent is caused by the excess of weight of the platform and empty barrow over that of the empty bucket, and is controlled by the brake. In another arrangement of this apparatus the descent of the water-bucket and the lift of the barrow platform are unequal; the bucket probably descends through a distance of not more than one-half that through which the materials have to be raised. Separate chain-drums on the same axle are employed, the diameters of which are proportioned to each other in the same ratio as the respective courses of the bucket and platform. The velocity in this case also is under the control of a brake.

The dimensions of a water-balance lift will depend on the size of the barrows and the number of furnaces it is to supply. At the Dowlais works four furnaces have each of them a water-balance lift. But one apparatus will generally suffice for three or four furnaces if the materials to be lifted do not exceed 400 tons daily. The greatest load to be sent up in the barrows will determine the size of the buckets. With barrows containing 15 cwt. the maximum size in use—wrought buckets 5 feet square and 2 feet deep—will not be too large, and if of any other form they should be of the same capacity. Inch chains are used for lifting and balancing, and the pipes for the conveyance and delivery of the water are 8 inches bore.

Though the water-balance apparatus is employed at several new furnaces, and is, on the whole, an inexpensive way of lifting the materials, especially where a sufficient fall of water can be obtained without having recourse to pumps, yet the liability to accident from the breaking of the chains must always prevent it from being extensively adopted. To diminish this risk two, and sometimes three chains have been combined together, each of sufficient strength to carry the load singly; but the use of these chains was attended with a serious objection. Where a single chain is employed it works tightly in a V-shaped groove in the brake-wheel, which thus has a controlling power; but flat chains, which have to be worked on a plain cylindrical sheive slip when the friction brake is applied to check the speed, and the brake has no controlling action whatever. At some furnaces steam power has been applied to the hoisting of the materials by a vertical lift. Two platforms are connected by chains to opposite sides of a drum keyed on the engine shaft. Guides for steadying the platforms and catches at the top to maintain them in the required position, similar to those employed in coal-pits, worked by steam power, are also necessary. But the risk from accident is equally great, if not greater, than in either of the foregoing machines, and doubtless this is the reason why vertical lifts, worked by steam power, are comparatively rare.

The pneumatic lifts are of recent date, but already they are in use at several Scotch, English, and Welsh works. They supply a desideratum of long standing in numerous iron-works, being superior to either of the machines already described in freedom from accident, quietness of motion, and facility of management.

The pneumatic lift consists of a well in the rear of the furnaces, about 7 feet diameter, and 8 to 10 feet deeper than the height of lift, made watertight by a brick or metal casing. A wrought-iron cylindrical tube, open at the lower end, and closed at the top, works up and down in this well. On the top of the tube a suitable platform is fixed to carry the loaded barrows. Four chains are attached to the platform and passed over pulleys on the top of the frame-work, weights nearly sufficient to balance the tube and platform being hung to their extremities.

Perpendicular timbers act as guides to the platform, which is furnished with four angular pulleys as guide rollers. A pipe, fitted with a stop valve, is brought from the blast main, carried down one side of the well to the bottom, turned up in the centre, and brought to within 4 or 5 feet of the surface. The well is filled with water to within 5 or 6 feet of the top. The wrought-iron tube, open at the lower end, stands in it, surrounding the central upright pipe. (Pl. XXIV., Figs. 119, 122.)

Loaded barrows having been wheeled on to the platform, the stop valve in the blast pipe is opened, the blast presses against the top of the tube with a force proportionate to its density, and to the superficial area of the end of the tube. This force raises the platform, carrying the loaded barrows to the top. On arriving there the blast valve is partially closed, and the tube is sustained by the elasticity of the blast within. The loaded barrows having been wheeled off, and their contents discharged into the furnace, they are replaced on the platform for a descent. The inlet blast valve at the bottom is closed by means of a vertical rod carried up alongside the framing, and the escape valve in the top of the tube is opened to allow the confined air gradually to escape into the atmosphere, the pressure being removed from beneath, the platform descends with a greater or less velocity, dependant on the area of the escape valve. The density of the blast being fixed, the requisite lifting power will be obtained by proportioning the diameter of the tube to the load.

The great recommendation possessed by the pneumatic lift over all others consists in the perfect control which the workmen have over its movements, and in its freedom from concussion in stopping. In ascending, the speed is easily regulated, the quantity of blast admitted being adjusted to the requirements of the load and velocity; and though the motion may be rapid, yet, by partially shutting the inlet valve before arriving at the top, the whole weight in motion, amounting probably to 20 or 25 tons, may be brought to rest without any perceptible concussion. While this valve is wholly or partially open, the pressure of the blast will maintain the platform against the stop plates at top, unsupported by catches. The control over the motion in descending is equally perfect. When all is ready for the descent the inlet valve is entirely shut, and the escape or discharge valve in the closed end of the tube opened. If this valve were of very large dimensions on opening it, the apparatus would descend with great rapidity, but with the small valves employed the removal of the pressure is so gradual that the machine cannot descend so rapidly as to produce injury. By partially closing this valve the velocity may be reduced; by shutting it, and thus preventing the further escape of the confined air, the apparatus may easily be brought to a standstill at any desired point without any concussion. These are advantages which no other kind of lift possesses in the same degree.

The employment of additional levers to the valves at top and bottom, acted on by projecting arms, renders the apparatus to some extent self-acting. On approaching the top or bottom the levers partially shut the valve, so as gradually to destroy the motion by the time the platform arrives at the stop plates.

At the Corbyn's Hall new furnaces, one pneumatic lift, with a tube about $5\frac{1}{4}$ feet in diameter, lifts the materials for four blast furnaces. The inlet pipe is equal to 7-inch bore, and a pressure of blast $2\frac{1}{4}$ lbs. to the square inch is used. The area of the cylindrical tube in square inches, multiplied by the pressure, 342 in. $\times$ $2\frac{1}{4}$ lbs., gives a lifting power of 7981 lbs. The load of materials lifted each time, including barrows and workmen, averages 5040 lbs., leaving a surplus power of 2941 lbs. to cover the unbalanced weight of tube and all contingencies. With a denser blast, such as is used at some Welsh works, the same load could be raised by a tube of one-half that area; but in practice it is preferable to use a large tube and increase the number or weight of the barrows in proportion to the increased power.

The working cost of lifting the materials with a pneumatic apparatus is equally as great as with an inclined plane or water-balance lift, but the cost of repairs and renewals is undoubtedly less. With an apparatus of the foregoing dimensions, lifting vertically 50 feet, the consumption of blast is about 1200 cubic feet for every $1\frac{1}{4}$ tons lifted. Allowing that it requires 8 tons of material to each ton of pig-iron made, an expenditure of 6400 cubic feet of blast, at a pressure of $2\frac{1}{4}$ lbs. to the square inch, will be required to raise this weight. The cost of compressing atmospheric air will be affected by local circumstances, but at several Welsh works the cost of compressing 100,000 cubic feet to that density, including all expenses incidental thereto, will not exceed 3d. This is equal to $\frac{7}{8}$ths of a penny per ton, and if to this be added another $\frac{7}{8}$ of a penny for the cost of erecting and maintaining the apparatus, we have a charge of ⅜ths of a penny per ton on the pig-iron made as the cost of lifting the materials 50 feet high.

HEATING APPARATUS.

The use of heated air for the furnaces having been extensively adopted in the manufacture of iron, a description of the apparatus employed will be necessary. We may mention here that the great saving of fuel and increased make of iron, which the advocates of the hot-air system so strenuously maintain as invariably following its application, is almost entirely due to other causes. But we shall enter more fully into this common mistake regarding the hot blast in our description of blast furnace operations.

In furnaces recently erected, sufficient space is generally left on each side and at the back to erect a separate stove to each tuyere; but in many old-established works using the hot blast, owing to the limited room between the furnaces, a single stove placed at the back, or at a distance from the furnace, is used to heat the blast for all the tuyeres. The plan of single stoves possesses many advantages over the other, and is adopted wherever it is practicable to do so. The size of the stove should bear some relation to the quantity of blast to be heated, but in practice we do not find any general rule observed. At some works, a single stove employed to heat for one tuyere will be as large as one at other works heating for an entire furnace.

The plan of stoves generally used, and which we have found capable of maintaining a great heat, is delineated in Pls. XXV., XXVI., Figs. 127, 131. It consists of two horizontal pipes, 14-inch bore and 2 inches in thickness of metal, having cast on their upper sides a number of sockets to receive the same number of small pipes, of a horseshoe figure, which stand in a vertical position, one leg in each horizontal pipe, and form a communication between them. Below and between the horizontal pipes a suitable fire-grate is constructed, furnished with a close-fitting door. The exterior of the whole structure of pipes is surrounded with walling arched at the top concentrically with the curve of the vertical pipes, and lined throughout with fire-brick. At one end a flue is constructed for conveying the smoke, &c., to a chimney about 8 or 9 feet higher than the roof, having a damper to regulate the draught. To prevent the heated products of combustion from escaping too rapidly by this flue, the communication to it is through a number of small apertures distributed over the further end of the interior; and as a protection to the horizontal pipes from the great heat of the fire, with which they would otherwise be in close contact, they are cased with brickwork the whole length of the fireplace. Vertical binders, resting in cast-iron sockets built into the walling at the bottom, and connected at top by wrought-iron bolts, are necessary to enable the walls to withstand the great heat and the thrust outwards of the arched roof.

The blast is admitted to one of the horizontal pipes at the end furthest from the fire, from whence it passes up through the vertical pipes and down into the opposite horizontal pipe, one or both ends of which are closed. During its passage through the vertical pipes, the blast will have absorbed sufficient heat from them to raise its temperature to 600 deg. or 620 deg. We have here supposed that the cold blast is admitted at the end of one of the larger pipes, and the hot air, after passing once over the vertical pipes, is delivered at the furthest end of the opposite horizontal main—the plan adopted at several works. But another, and perhaps a superior arrangement, consists in coursing the air through a portion only of the vertical pipes at one time; this is accomplished by fixing stop plates in the horizontal pipes at any required distance, and so causing the blast to take a circuitous course. If the stove consists of twenty-six vertical pipes, and the first stop is between the fifth and sixth pipes, the blast will first pass through five pipes to the opposite side; then if the next stop is between the eleventh and twelfth, it will return through six pipes; and the next stop again between the eighteenth and nineteenth, it will pass through seven; finally returning to the same pipe through eight vertical pipes, after having coursed a distance of between 90 and 100 feet.

The increase in the number of pipes for each course as the blast approaches the end, compensates for the greater volume of the hot air in the latter courses. The blast enters probably at a temperature of 50 deg., but leaves at a temperature of about 600 deg. If its volume be equal to 1000 at entering the stove, it will have expanded to 2050, or just twice its original volume, on leaving; hence the area of the pipes must be increased in a similar ratio, or the velocity of the blast will be very great. And since an increase in the velocity is attended by a great increase of friction, and consequently by a diminution of useful effect, the utility of the increased area given to the finishing courses is generally admitted.

Although the usual mode of connecting these pipes is by having sockets cast on the body of the horizontal pipe to receive the feet of the vertical pipes, a much superior plan is to cast spigots on this pipe about 6 inches long, of a size and bore similar to the vertical pipes; around this spigot, a loose socket-piece, 12 inches long, is clayed and cemented, and the foot of the vertical pipe is fixed into the part projecting above the spigot. (Pl. XXV., Figs. 128, 129.) This plan of joining the pipes is attended with additional expense at first, but when a defective or burnt-out pipe needs to be changed—a matter of very frequent occurrence in all hot-blast apparatus—the time required for the operation is very much less than if fast sockets were used. The pipes standing so close together, it requires considerable time to cut out a defective one; indeed, the labour of getting out the old pipe is two or three times greater than that of putting in the new one; but with socket rings, if any difficulty occurs, the ring may be broken off and its place supplied by another.

At the Dowlais works, each of four blast furnaces (Nos. 15, 16, 17, and 18) is fitted with three hot-blast stoves, one to each tuyere. The horizontal pipes are 14 inches internal, and 18 inches external diameter. Each pipe has on its upper side 26 sockets, 6 inches deep and 8¾ inches between centres. These sockets receive the ends of the vertical pipes, which measure over the foot and crown 8 feet 3½ inches, and over the legs 5 feet ½ inch; the sectional area of the interior, which is of a V-shape, is 18 inches. The fireplaces, two to each stove, measure 2 feet 3 inches wide by 6 feet 11 inches long.

The superficial area of the pipe surface exposed to the action of the fire in each stove is 1001 square feet. This quantity of surface is heated by two grates of an aggregate area of 31 square feet. The quantity of blast passing through the inlet pipe of each stove, at an average pressure of three pounds to the square inch, is 2020 cubic feet per minute. Therefore in these stoves there are 500 square feet of heating and 15¼ square feet of grate surface for each 1000 feet of blast heated to a temperature of 600 deg.

At three other furnaces at the Dowlais works (Nos. 12, 13, and 14), the stoves are considerably smaller than the foregoing. The horizontal pipes are 14 inches bore and 14 feet long, with 16 sockets for the vertical pipes. These measure 7 feet 9 inches over foot and crown, by 4 feet 8¼ inches over the legs, which are of a plain cylindrical section, 4 inches bore and 6¼ inches in diameter outside. A single grate, 6 feet 11 inch by 2 feet 3 inches, heats the apparatus. The total surface exposed by the vertical pipes above the sockets was 503 superficial feet. The grate surface is 15 feet 8 inches, and the quantity of cold air entering the inlet pipe, at a pressure of 2¾ lbs. to the square inch, was 1860 cubic feet per minute. So that in these stoves, for each 1000 cubic feet of blast entering the stove per minute, there is 270 square feet of heating surface, and 8¼ square feet of grate surface, or a little more than one-half of the proportional areas in the other stove.

In the small stoves it was difficult to maintain a constant temperature sufficient to melt lead, but in the large ones this temperature was maintained with great regularity; we may therefore conclude that these stoves present the maximum and minimum proportions which the heating surface and grate surface should bear to a given quantity of blast to be heated to about 600 deg. in a given time.

The vertical pipes we have described have their sides parallel with each other, but they are occasionally constructed with a greater span at foot than crown as represented in Pls. XXV., XXVIII. The sectional construction is also occasionally varied from that given. Circular, V-shape, flat, oblong, and eliptical forms are employed with the view of obtaining the greatest area of heating surface in the least space.

SECTION IV.

BLAST FURNACE OPERATIONS.

The blowing-in of blast furnaces is an operation demanding great care and an intimate acquaintance with their management. If it is hastily done, the injury to the furnace may be such as to require its being blown out to be repaired; and if due attention is not paid to the mixture of materials with which the working is commenced, the results will be unsatisfactory, much difficulty being experienced, and time lost in bringing the furnace into a healthy working condition.

The arrangements for blowing-in having been completed, as described in a previous section, a quantity of rough dry timber is placed in the hearth, filling it to a height of five or six feet. On this a quantity of coke is deposited from the top, filling the remainder of the hearth and also the boshes. Fire is applied to the timber, which quickly communicates it to the coke above. Regular charges of calcined ironstone, limestone, and coke are now filled in till the materials reach the throat of the furnace. The proportions of ironstone and limestone to the coke vary with the locality, but at the works around Merthyr Tydvil, the proportions are generally $5\frac{1}{2}$ cwt. of calcined ironstone and $1\frac{3}{4}$ cwt. of limestone to 4 cwt. of coke, containing a large per-centage of carbon. Where the rich hematites are to be smelted, the filling above the coke is conducted in a different manner.

These ores cannot be successfully introduced in quantity before the furnace is brought into working order. And if leaner ores are not to be obtained, the mixture of materials at the commencement may be good grey cinders, with a very small burden of calcined ore and limestone. On these materials it will be well to let the furnace run for some days, until a regular flow of good cinder is obtained at the fall, when the proportion of ore may be increased and the cinders diminished.

Everything having been arranged for its admission, blast is let on to the tuyeres, and the furnace is "blown in." At first the tuyere pipes are of small diameter, but in this as in too many other matters connected with iron-works no fixed rule exists, and a great difference in the sizes employed in blowing-in furnaces at the same works may be observed. And yet with similar ores and fuels, smelted in furnaces of the same interior dimensions, the diameter of the nozzle-pipes first used should bear some proportion to those eventually adopted with a full blast. We have endeavoured to arrive at some fixed ratio, and from the dimensions of those employed in blowing-in eleven blast furnaces under our own immediate observation, we find that the average area of the pipes through which blast is first used, is one-fifth of the area of the pipes ultimately employed. By using nozzles upon this proportion, all risk of failure in the blowing-in and subsequent injury to the furnace will be avoided.

For a furnace of an interior capacity of 275 cubic yards, and intended to be blown with 4-inch nozzles, the first set will be $1\frac{3}{4}$-inch bore. After blowing about thirty hours, these may be replaced by a set of $2\frac{1}{4}$-inch bore, and at the expiration of three days by a set $2\frac{3}{4}$ inches. In ten days from the time of blowing-in, the pipes may be increased to $3\frac{1}{4}$ inches, and in three weeks to $3\frac{3}{4}$ inches. Full size pipes may be used in four or five weeks after blowing-in.

The burden of materials above described should be kept on unaltered for ten days, in which time the furnace will go to from four hundred to four hundred and fifty charges. It may then be increased to 6 cwt. of calcined mine and $2\frac{1}{4}$ cwt. of limestone to the 4 cwt. of coke; with this burden it will go about four hundred charges the first week after altering, increasing, however, to six hundred and fifty or seven hundred in the third or fourth week. If the furnace is intended for forge-iron, the alteration in the burden should not be made until it has worked successfully three or four weeks on grey iron.

After the application of the blast, the founders will commence cleaning the hearth below the tuyere for the reception of cinders. These will make their appearance about twelve hours after blowing. In twenty-four hours they will have filled the bottom of the hearth to a level with the notch in the damplate, and in three days may be directed through the troughs to the tubs.

The metal will appear in about ten hours after the cinders, and will collect in the hearth to the amount of 3 or $3\frac{1}{2}$ tons in sixty hours after blowing-in. In about eighteen hours afterwards, another casting of about 2 tons may be made, and from this time the operation of casting may be performed at the usual stated periods. The quantity of metal at each casting will increase from 2 tons at the second cast to about 5 tons each cast in the fourth week. From the first week's blowing the make of metal will be about 21 tons; from the second, about 36 tons; from the third, 50 tons; and the fourth week's work will not fall far short of 75 tons. With the burden stated and full blast, the make will reach 95 or 100 tons at the expiration of ten or twelve weeks; but a greater make than this cannot, under existing circumstances, be obtained from a furnace of this size working on lean ores for foundry purposes.

Forcing the furnace so that a greater make of iron may sooner be obtained from it is attended with the most injurious effects on its subsequent working. In the present day the majority of furnaces blown-in are permanently injured by this practice. The desire for making large and immediate returns outweighs all considerations respecting the destruction of the boshes and hearth. The blowing-in is performed with large pipes, and the furnace filled and worked with rich ores, or with calcined ironstone and forge or finery cinders. White pig-iron and a dark scouring cinder are the natural results of such a proceeding. The make is considerable for a few weeks, but after that time it diminishes, and great difficulty is experienced in maintaining the furnace at all in working order. Alterations are then made in the burden, the quantity of blast is diminished, and the forcing system suspended for a period, in order to remedy the evils which it inevitably occasions. If the altered mode of working is persevered in for some weeks the condition of the furnace usually improves, and although irreparably injured, it may continue in work for a considerable period. But too often, however, the system is carried on till the boshes are entirely destroyed, the hearth nearly so, and the brickwork around the tuyeres and over the fall so thinned, that the outside remains at a red heat. The breast is generally a mass of red-hot bricks, and through this and the tuyere stoppings the pent-up flame will frequently burst, showing that the interior work has been destroyed. The bricks, indeed, are distinguishable in the cinders, and it is from the quantity raked out that we are enabled to judge of the state of the hearth and boshes. The bottom of the hearth is repaired with fire-clay: from the front, but there is no access to other portions of the hearth, or to the boshes while the furnace is in blast. This circumstance should be well considered when it is proposed to force a furnace to produce a great make of metal. Eventually the make is greatly diminished, the metal produced is of the worst quality, and the amount of fuel to the ton of metal increases in an inverse ratio to the quantity made. The amount of ironstone is also increased, and a dense black cinder flows slowly from the hearth. In a few weeks the increase of cost consequent on the increased yield of materials, and the diminution in make, becomes so great, that the furnace is blown out, and the interior refitted as the only practicable remedy.

A notable instance of this forcing system occurred a few years since at the British Iron Company's works, Abersychan. No. 6 furnace was blown-in with such volumes of blast and rich burden of materials, that a cast of several tons was obtained within 14 hours after applying blast. And the first week's blowing resulted in a make of nearly 200 tons, at which rate it continued for two or three weeks, when it rapidly diminished, falling as low for one week as 19 tons. From this deplorable state it was got to produce 26 tons a week, and after some time the make reached 100 tons, but with a considerably increased expenditure of materials as compared with the other furnaces.

The introduction of blast of great density and in large volumes during the "blowing-in" of furnaces, must produce a very prejudicial effect on the duration of the brickwork of the interior. If the volume is so great as in the Abersychan furnace, where the melting temperature of pig-iron was created and pervaded the hearth and the materials within the boshes, in a few minutes, the destruction of the boshes and hearth is inevitable. Brickwork cannot stand a sudden accession of temperature like this. Stonework will also fail to continue sound under such an ordeal. Even if the bricks are well manufactured and carefully set the great heat of the ascending gases will loosen them from their beds, and the descending materials striking on them, they are displaced, and descend along with the current of materials into the hearth. This destruction of the boshes is accelerated if the materials smelted are of a rich quality, and there is a deficiency of flux. It is well known that the cinders ordinarily produced in a furnace will, on flowing over brickwork, give it a glaze which materially protects it from the influence of the metal. This effect is successfully produced where a small blast and suitable burden of materials is used at first. But with a large blast and rich burden the cinders produced are of a hot scouring nature containing a large per centage of iron, and the temperature of the brickwork being kept too high it does not receive the glaze, and it therefore suffers more readily from the action of the metal. The corroding effect (if we may be allowed the term) of the fluid metal on the unprotected brickwork is forcibly shown by the rapidity with which certain portions of the hearth in well-regulated furnaces are destroyed. The front work at and below the level at which the metal stands before tapping, has to be renewed every six or eight days by lumps of fire-clay tightly rammed into the hollows. This fire-clay during the few hours which elapse before it is covered with metal, has not time to receive a glaze from the cinder, and is therefore speedily destroyed by the metal, to be again and again renewed.

THEORY OF THE BLAST FURNACE.

The blast furnace employed for the reduction of iron ores into metallic iron may be considered as an immense laboratory, wherein the most varied chemical processes are conducted with a regularity and rapidity equalled only by the magnitude of the operations performed. In the largest furnaces the weekly consumption of atmospheric air amounts to 2318 tons by weight, and of solid materials, ore, fuel, and flux, 883 tons—total 3201 tons, or more than 20 tons per hour. By the chemical processes of decomposition and recomposition in operation within the furnace, this weight of gaseous and solid materials is resolved into 485 tons of liquid and 2716 tons of gaseous matter. The solids are introduced into the furnace at the tunnel head, the gases—atmospheric air—through the tuyeres at the hearth. The liquid products of the furnace are obtained from the hearth in the form of cinder, slag, or scoria, from a high level, and crude iron from the lowest level. The gaseous products escape at the tunnel head, and comprise nitrogen, oxygen combined in determinate proportions with carbon forming carbonic acid; and carbonic oxide, hydrogen, hydrogen in combination with carbon, as light carburetted hydrogen, and other gases in lesser quantities.

Hence it will be seen that in the smelting furnace, we have a descending column of solid materials which enters at the throat, and is resolved into gaseous and liquid products, the latter escaping at the bottom, and the former at the throat, and an ascending gaseous column which enters at the bottom and escapes at the throat of the furnace.

The transformations which the ore, fuel, and flux undergo during the smelting process, will be best considered if we examine first the changes produced on the descending mass of materials; secondly, those effected in the ascending body of atmospheric air; thirdly, the chemical action produced by the contact of the descending materials with the ascending column of gases; and, finally, the composition of the gaseous products resulting from the operations of the furnace.

The changes which take place in the descending iron ores when uncalcined ores are used, commence in the mouth of the furnace. They there begin to lose their moisture, sulphur, and other volatile ingredients before they reach the level of the boshes. Below this the ore is gradually converted from peroxide into magnetic oxide, or, as sometimes occurs, into metallic iron, having in combination with it a portion of carbon from the fuel to form a fusible carbide of iron. In the space from the bottom of the boshes to the level of the tuyeres, the reduction of the ore and flux to a fluid state is completed. Complete fusion takes place at a height of 6 or 8 inches above the tuyere, and from thence the resulting fluids descend into the hearth, where the metal from its greater specific gravity falls to the bottom more or less freed from the cinder which floats on its surface and protects it from the oxydizing influence of the blast.

Little change takes place in the fuel if coke be employed, until it arrives within the boshes. But when raw coal is used its distillation commences immediately on its entering the furnace mouth, and during its descent to the boshes it parts with its volatile constituents and becomes converted into coke. During the further descent of the fuel a portion of its carbon is absorbed by the ore, and between the top of the hearth and the tuyere it is completely consumed—the most active combustion taking place a few inches above the centre of the tuyere.

The flux commences to undergo a change from the time of its reception amongst the ignited materials. Raw limestone being employed, the carbonic acid is expelled by the heat evolved, and the stone is converted into caustic lime. In this state it descends until it reaches a level immediately above the tuyere, where it is fused, and combining with the earthy constituents of the ore, it falls into the hearth, and floats upon the surface of the metal in the form of cinder.

The ascending column of air entering the furnace through the tuyeres at bottom is decomposed on coming in contact with burning fuel, oxygen is absorbed to form carbonic acid, and nitrogen is liberated. When it reaches the line of fusion the carbonic acid parts with a portion of its oxygen to the descending fuel, and carbonic oxide is produced, and as the gaseous column proceeds upwards, the proportion of carbonic oxide increases until it arrives at the boshes, from which point up to about half the height of the furnace the carbonic oxide diminishes, and carbonic acid again increases in quantity. Above this point the relative proportions of nitrogen, carbonic oxide, and carbonic acid remain nearly the same; but the volume of hydrogen increases, and steam begins to make its appearance, increasing in quantity up to the throat, when the ascending gases as they escape from the furnace mouth consist of carbonic acid, carbonic oxide, hydrogen, nitrogen, and aqueous vapour. These form the principal constituents of the escaping gases of the blast-furnace, but the composition of the ore, fuel, and flux used in particular instances will modify their composition, and in some cases add to their number.

The whole of the chemical operations taking place in the interior of the furnace are not well understood, but from the data at our disposal, however, and from our own observations, we believe that comparatively little chemical action takes place in the upper portion of the body. The ore, flux, and fuel, part with their volatile constituents, principally hydrogen and aqueous vapour, which are thus evolved in great abundance in the vicinity of the throat. Lower down the carbonic oxide of the ascending column reacts on the oxygen of the ore, producing carbonic acid, and converting the ore into a magnetic oxide. This reaction appears to be continued further down, but the rapid descent of the materials when once they have reached the boshes leaves the deoxydation and carbonization to be performed principally in the centre and lower regions of the boshes. Down to the top of the hearth the fuel contains nearly its original proportion of carbon, but below this level its consumption is astonishingly rapid. In the hearth the chemical effects of the blast result in the ore losing its remaining oxygen, which goes to form carbonic acid and carbonic oxide. The metal thus completely deoxydised, combines with a small portion of carbon, and still descending arrives with the flux within the region of the intense heat generated by the action of the blast upon the fuel just above the tuyeres. They here enter into a state of complete fusion, and form a compound of silica, lime, oxide of iron, and alumina, &c., which with the fused metal drops below the tuyeres and beyond the disturbing influences of the blast into the lower part of the hearth. This compound eventually resolves itself into two distinct layers. In the lowest stratum metallic iron will preponderate; carbon, silica, alumina, and lime, phosphorus, sulphur, manganese, &c., being present in small quantities. The upper stratum consists of various fused earthy silicates. But when the furnace is improperly burdened and the working deranged, the stratum of cinder will contain an undue proportion of oxide of iron.

CHEMICAL COMPOSITION OF THE PRODUCTS OF THE FURNACE.

The attention of chemists has been frequently directed to ascertain definitely the composition of the various products of the blast-furnace, both solid and gaseous, with a view to learn the nature of the operations going on within, and to obtain data upon which to base efforts both to improve the quality of the crude iron and also to render more certain the action of the furnace, as well as to utilize to the greatest possible extent the materials employed in the process of smelting.

Beginning with the gases escaping from the throat, we give the results of the experiments made at one of the Alfreton furnaces, Derbyshire, by Messrs. Bunsen and Playfair, and of those made by MM. Ebelman, Scheerer and Langberg, and others upon furnace gases at Clerval, Baerum, and other places on the Continent.

The composition of gases withdrawn from various depths in the interior of the Alfreton furnace is given in the following table. The apparatus used for collecting the gases consisted of a vertical tube suspended over the top of the furnace, and freely descending at the same rate as the materials charged. Connexions were attached at the upper end for collecting the gases, and also an apparatus for ascertaining the pressure exerted within the tube at different depths.

The materials charged into the Alfreton furnace during twenty-four hours consisted of 80 charges of 420 lbs. of calcined ironstone, 390 lbs. of coal, and 170 lbs. of limestone, producing 140 lbs. of crude iron.* We have previously shown that this furnace received 1020 cubic feet of atmospheric air per minute. Calculated by weight and reduced to the consumpt per minute, we have:

Atmospheric air	58.91 lbs.
Calcined ore	23.33 „
Coal	21.65 „
Limestone	9.44 „

And by referring to the analyses of the ore, coal, and limestone, the weight of the gaseous matters in pounds per minute introduced into the furnaces, or evolved from the respective materials, will be nearly as follows:

Nitrogen, by the blast (atmospheric air)	58.91 lbs.
„ „ coal	.03 „
	58.94 „
Oxygen, by the blast	17.80 „
„ ore	4.30 „
„ coal	2.17 „
„ ditto	1.43 „
„ limestone	2.05 „
	25.74 „
Carbon, by the coal	16.23 „
„ limestone	1.10 „
	17.33 „
Hydrogen, by the coal	1.21 „

From the amount of carbon we must deduct the quantity which combines with the crude iron, equal to 3 per cent. on 777 lbs. of iron, or 23 lbs., leaving 17.10 lbs. of carbon available.

The carbon combines with the oxygen, forming carbonic acid and carbonic oxide. The 17.10 lbs. of carbon combining with 28.74 lbs. of oxygen produces 29.2 lbs. of carbonic oxide and 16.6 lbs. of carbonic acid. Hence the weight of the issuing gases is 105.95 lbs., composed as follows:

Nitrogen	58.94 lbs.	=	55.6 per cent.
Carbonic oxide	29.20 „	=	27.6 „
„ acid	16.60 „	=	15.6 „
Hydrogen	1.21 „	=	1.2 „
	105.95 „	=	100. „

This is the composition by weight of the ascending column of gases at the level of escape, calculated from the analyses furnished by Messrs. Bunsen and Playfair. By comparing these results with the analyses of the gases from the same furnace, collected at a depth of 5 feet from the surface of the materials, the consumption of carbon even at this shallow depth, as represented by the richness of the gases in carbon, is very evident.

* We have adopted Messrs. Bunsen and Playfair's quantities, but comparing the produce of crude iron (140 lbs. per charge) with the consumption and richness of the ore, there is a marked discrepancy. For every 100 lbs. of crude metal obtained, there was consumed 300 lbs. of calcined ore, containing 60.242 of the peroxide of iron, yielding 122.3 lbs. Now, as crude metal does not average 95 per cent. of iron, it follows that for 95 lbs. obtained, 122.3 lbs. were smelted, showing a loss of 24 per cent. on the metal contained in the ore.

	Five feet deep.	Surface.
Carbonic oxide	25.97	27.6
,, acid	7.77	15.6

At a depth of 5 feet every 100 lbs. of the ascending column contained 13.46 lbs. of carbon, which is augmented at the level of escape to 17.1 lbs. by the combustion of carbon. The high temperature has consequently caused the combustion and escape of 20 per cent. of the carbon in this short depth. Calculated on the number of charges introduced, the time occupied was only 1 hour and 48 minutes. Now, as the latter weight represents the maximum quantity of gaseous carbon, the deficiency at the lower level clearly proves the combustion of not less than 20 per cent. of the carbon charged in this short distance. With one-fifth of the carbon consumed in the first hour and three quarters after charging, we should naturally infer that the quantity ultimately available for combustion before the tuyere, is but a small portion of that charged into the furnace.

The composition of the gases escaping from the Baerum charcoal furnace is remarkably confirmatory of the position we have taken: That from an imperfect mode of construction a considerable consumption of coal takes place in the upper part of the coal and coke-fed furnaces of this country, but which is not seen in the best regulated charcoal furnaces abroad.

In the Alfreton coal-fed furnace we have seen that the quantity of carbon is diminished one-fifth by combustion in the first 5 feet of descent, and that at the top it forms 17.1 per cent. by weight of the escaping gases. The analyses by Messrs. Scheerer and Langberg of the gases from the Baerum furnace are valuable as showing an important difference from those of Alfreton. The composition of the gases escaping at top from the respective furnaces is nearly as follows:

	Baerum.	Alfreton.
Nitrogen	58.98	55.6
Carbonic acid	31.68	15.6
,, oxide	7.23	27.6
Carburetted hydrogen	2.00	—
Hydrogen	.09	1.2
	100.	100.
Carbon in carbonic acid and carbonic oxide	11.76	17.1

The excess of carbon in the Alfreton gases is very remarkable, and sufficiently explains the greater yield of fuel.

But the contrast is still greater if we descend to a lower level. At half the depth of the furnace the composition of the Baerum and Alfreton gases is shown by the following comparative analyses:

	Baerum.	Alfreton.
Nitrogen	63.70	60.46
Carbonic acid	6.64	10.83
,, oxide	28.90	19.48
Carburetted hydrogen	6.69	4.40
Hydrogen	.07	4.83
	100.	100.
Carbon in carbonic acid and carbonic oxide	44.19	11.29

By these analyses the immense difference in the richness in carbon of the ascending column of gases in the respective furnaces, and the consumption at different heights, is readily seen. In the charcoal furnace the 14.19 per cent. of carbon in the gas at half the depth is diminished to 11.76 per cent. at the surface of the materials. The carbonic acid expelled from the limestone, entering into combination with the gases, augments their volume and increases the per-centage of carbon as they approach the surface level. In the coal-fed furnace, however, notwithstanding the carbonic acid evolved from the limestone and the gases escaping from the coal, the per-centage of carbon in the ascending column is rapidly augmented from 11.29 per cent. at half the depth to 17.1 at the surface.

The presence of carbonic oxide in the gases from the charcoal furnace shows that the arrangements of blast and fuel in that furnace are not such as attain the greatest possible economy of fuel. Carbon should escape at the top only as carbonic acid. So long, then, as carbonic oxide forms a portion of the escaping column, the carbon is in excess of the oxygen for combustion. With more perfect arrangements the 11.76 of carbon escaping from the charcoal furnace may be reduced to 10.2; and the 17.1 from the Alfreton furnace to 10.0 without causing any disturbance to the smelting process, or impairing the quality of the resulting metal.

The richness of the blast-furnace gases in carbonic oxide has caused an undue importance to be attached to them for heating purposes. While carbonic oxide enters so largely into their composition, there can be no doubt but that burnt with air to carbonic acid, a considerable quantity of heat is evolved, though the disturbance to the smelting operation caused by the withdrawal of the gases more than compensates for their heating value. But the formation of carbonic oxide in such considerable quantities occurs only with arrangements deficient in protection against the combustion of carbon in the upper part of the furnace, or incapable of supplying the air requisite for more perfect combustion at the tuyere. With other arrangements such as we have described carbonic oxide will disappear from the escaping gases, and with it also their value for heating purposes, except as regards the hydrogen; and its calorific value is insufficient to warrant the expense necessary for its utilization.

Since the proportion of carbonic oxide determines the value of these gases for heating purposes, and this gas is not produced unless from defective arrangements, a large yield of it, and consequently a successful example of its utilization, can only be taken as evidence that the smelting arrangements are more than ordinarily defective. With a very small supply of air in proportion to the carbon, which is the rule throughout Scotland, the greater value of the gases for heating, and the greater success which has attended their application, compared with other districts, is readily explained. It must be borne in mind, however, that whatever means are adopted for the combustion and application of the caloric evolved, the value of the gas is not equal to that of the carbon unnecessarily consumed in its formation. If we examine the consumption of gaseous materials at the Gartsherry works, we shall find that the consumption of oxygen is rarely sufficient to oxidise the carbon which escapes at the top in the form of carbonic oxide, carbonic acid being entirely wanting. The proportion by weight which the respective gases form in the ascending column is nearly as follows: Nitrogen, 55.6; carbonic oxide, 43; hydrogen, 1.4; total, 100—the carbon forming 18.4 per cent. of the whole.

However desirable it may be that carbonic oxide should not appear amongst the issuing gases, it is impossible, with the form of furnace generally in use, to prevent its existence to the extent of from 20, to 42 per cent. of the entire quantity of gases escaping. In the existing furnaces the carbonic acid formed by the union of the oxygen of the ore with carbon, and the carbonic acid expelled from the limestone, ascend to the throat, and absorb from the ignited fuel a second volume of carbon, thereby converting the carbonic acid into carbonic oxide.

The composition of the gases withdrawn from various depths in the interior of the Alfreton furnace, Derbyshire, is given in the following table:

Depth in feet from top.	Nitrogen.	Carbonic Acid.	Carbonic Oxide.	Light Carb. Hydrogen.	Hydrogen.	Olefiant Gas.	Cyanogen.
5	55.35	7.77	25.97	3.75	6.73	.43	—
8	54.77	0.42	20.24	6.23	6.40	.85	—
11	52.57	9.41	23.16	4.57	9.33	.95	—
14	50.95	9.10	19.38	6.64	12.42	1.37	—
17	53.49	12.43	18.77	4.31	7.62	1.38	—
20	60.46	10.83	19.43	4.40	4.82	—	—
23	58.28	8.10	29.97	1.64	4.92	—	Trace
24	56.73	10.08	23.19	2.33	5.65	—	Trace
34	58.05	—	37.43	—	3.19	—	1.34

In reference to this table it may be remarked that the furnace was driven with a hot blast, the temperature being 626. Fahr., and pressure, 3.375 lbs. to the square inch. The coal was used in the raw state. The ore consisted of calcined argillaceous ironstone, The last line of the table shows the composition of the gaseous column at 33 inches above the tuyere, and 6 feet above the hearth-stone.

The relative proportions of oxygen to nitrogen, in the ascending gases, as deduced from the table of analyses, appear to have been as follows:

Depth.	Nitrogen.	Oxygen.
5	79.2	24.9
8	79.2	23.6
11	79.2	24.6
14	79.2	19.5
17	79.2	25.7
20	79.2	23.7
23	79.2	28.2
24	79.2	27.7
34	79.2	27.8

The pressure within the tube, as measured by the apparatus above described, appears to have been equal to that of a column of water of the following heights, the depths being in feet from the top:

Depth.	Pressure.
5	.12 inches
8	.40 ,,
11	1.10 ,,
14	1.60 ,,
20	1.80 ,,
23	4.70 ,,
24	5.10 ,,

Analyses have also been made of the gases produced by the charcoal furnace of Vickerhagen, Westphalia, the results of which differ materially from those obtained from the Alfreton furnace. The composition, by volume, of the Vickerhagen furnace gases appears to have been as follows; the heights are in feet above the tuyere:

Height above tuyere	17.75 ft.	16.25 ft.	14.75 ft.	13.25 ft.	11.75 ft.	8.75 ft.	5.75 ft.
Nitrogen	62.34	62.25	66.29	62.47	63.89	61.45	64.58
Carbonic acid	8.77	11.14	3.32	3.44	3.60	7.57	5.97
Carbonic oxide	24.20	22.24	25.77	30.08	29.27	26.99	26.51
Light carburetted hydrogen	3.36	3.10	4.04	2.24	1.07	3.84	1.83
Hydrogen	1.33	1.27	.58	1.77	2.17	.15	1.06

The results obtained at the charcoal furnace of Baerum, Norway, again, differ very considerably from those obtained at either the English or the German blast furnace. The composition, by volume, of the gases from this furnace, taken at various heights above the tuyere, is represented by the following table:

Height above tuyere	23.00 ft.	20.50 ft.	18.00 ft.	15.50 ft.	13.00 ft.	10.00 ft.
Nitrogen	64.43	62.65	63.20	64.28	66.12	64.97
Carbonic acid	22.20	15.21	12.45	4.27	8.50	5.09
Carbonic oxide	8.04	15.33	18.57	29.17	20.28	26.38
Light carburetted hydrogen	3.87	1.28	1.27	1.23	1.18	—
Hydrogen	1.46	2.53	4.51	1.05	3.92	2.96

The composition of the gases issuing from the top of this furnace, estimated by weight, will be as follows: Nitrogen, 58.95; carbonic acid, 31.68; carbonic oxide, 7.28; light carburetted hydrogen, 2.00; and hydrogen, .09.

The composition, by volume, of the gases produced in the working of the Clerval furnace, using charcoal as fuel, is stated to have been:

Height above tuyere	25.50 ft.	22.50 ft.	17.50 ft.	13.30 ft.	9.50 ft.	8.00 ft.
Nitrogen	57.70	57.80	58.15	59.14	60.54	63.07
Carbonic acid	12.88	13.06	13.76	5.86	2.23	—
Carbonic oxide	23.51	22.24	22.65	28.18	33.04	35.01
Hydrogen	5.82	6.00	5.44	3.82	3.50	1.92

At the top of the Clerval furnace the ascending column consisted of the following gases, by volume:

Aqueous vapour	11.7
Carbonic acid	12.5
Carburetted hydrogen	3.6
Carbonic oxide	15.6
Nitrogen	56.6
	100.

A second series of experiments on the Clerval furnace gave the composition of the issuing column as consisting of:

Carbonic acid	12.88
Carbonic oxide	23.51
Hydrogen	5.82
Nitrogen	57.79
	100.

At the Audincourt furnace, consuming a mixture of charcoal and wood as fuel, the composition of the gases at the furnace mouth was:

Carbonic acid	12.59
Carbonic oxide	25.24
Hydrogen	6.55
Nitrogen	55.62
	100.

The composition of the gases from the coke furnaces of Vienne and Pont l'Evêque, as discharged at the throat, appears to have been:

	Vienne.	Pont l'Evêque.
Carbonic acid	11.58	7.15
Carbonic oxide	25.24	28.37
Hydrogen	2.48	2.01
Nitrogen	60.70	62.47
	100.	100.

At the coke furnaces of Ougrée, Belgium, experiments were made on the composition of the gases at 6 feet below the top, and the following results obtained:

Hydrogen	0.45
Carburetted hydrogen	0.31
Carbonic oxide	28.68
Carbonic acid	8.64
Nitrogen	61.92
	100.

The foregoing analyses show the grounds upon which the various attempts at the utilization of the blast furnace gases have been based; and from the very various results recorded, an idea may be formed of the difficulties attending the application of any one general plan of collection and utilization. We shall give this subject further consideration in a section specially devoted thereto.

In addition to the gases, a considerable discharge of particles of solid matter takes place in the majority of blast furnaces. The chemical composition of this discharge is not known; it probably contains a quantity of carbonaceous matter, along with other substances. Some of the dust which collects in the interior of the tunnel-head was taken from one of the Dowlais furnaces and analysed. The results were as under:

Silica	30.33
Peroxide of iron	47.06
" manganese	1.77
Sulphate of lime	4.42
Lime	2.30
Phosphate of lime	.75
Potash	1.80
Soda	.36
Copper	

The composition of the waste material escaping at the bottom of the furnace, the cinder which issues over the damstone or damplate, has also engaged much attention. This cinder is of very variable composition, and alters, in fact, with every change in the working of the furnace; and seldom remains constant in its character for any lengthened period. On it, however, the practical metallurgist relies for information as to the working of his apparatus; the appearances which it presents are carefully noted, and any important change in its colour, rate of flow, or general properties, is immediately taken as indicating a corresponding change in the interior action of the furnace. A full consideration of this subject will be found in another section; at present we shall only consider the chemical composition of the cinder.

The twelve following analyses are of cinders from the Dowlais works, where raw coal is used as fuel in the furnaces.

Blast-furnace cinders are commonly classified by their colour and external aspect. A grey, semi-transparent cinder gave the following composition:

Silica	38.40
Alumina	14.60
Protoxide of iron	.54
" manganese	1.02
Lime	35.66
Magnesia	4.45
Sulphide of calcium	3.26
Potash	1.40
Soda	.29

A grey, opaque cinder, breaking with a rough stony fracture, yielded:

Silica	46.94
Alumina	15.47
Protoxide of iron	3.92
" manganese	1.33
Lime	24.65
Magnesia	5.55
Sulphide of calcium	.79
Potash	2.33

A brown-coloured cinder, transparent on the surface, opaque underneath, yielded:

Silica	40.92
Alumina	14.85
Protoxide of iron	1.57
" manganese	.07
Lime	32.29
Magnesia	4.85
Sulphide of calcium	1.61
Potash	1.83

A cinder of a black colour, stony opaque fracture, semi-transparent at the edges, gave:

Silica	34.96
Alumina	16.66
Protoxide of iron	6.83
" manganese	.99
Lime	29.48
Magnesia	5.36
Sulphide of calcium	1.45
Phosphoric acid	2.63
Potash	1.83

A cinder of a dark green colour on the exterior, and a greenish black in the centre of the masses, smooth glossy fracture, yielded by analysis:

Silica	40.04
Alumina	12.69
Protoxide of iron	7.81
,, manganese	1.12
Lime	32.36
Magnesia	1.65
Sulphide of calcium	1.32
Potash	1.23
Phosphoric acid	1.08

A cinder of a deep olive-green on the exterior, nearly black in the centre of the cinder pig, gave:

Silica	45.60
Alumina	15.70
Protoxide manganese	1.40
Lime	21.65
Magnesia	4.85
Sulphide of calcium	.65
Potash and soda	2.03
Protoxide of iron	8.03

A blast-furnace cinder, of a heavy, dark colour, approaching to black, and of a dull stony fracture in the interior, yielded:

Silica	39.99
Alumina	15.50
Protoxide of iron	4.80
,, manganese	.79
Lime	30.64
Magnesia	3.30
Potash	2.07
Sulphate of lime	.51
Sulphide of calcium	1.96
Phosphoric acid	.23

A cinder, somewhat similar to the preceding in colour and fracture, but of a glassy smoothness on the exterior, yielded:

Silica	40.75
Alumina	17.30
Protoxide of iron	1.20
,, manganese	.54
Lime	31.59
Magnesia	4.68
Potash	1.41
Sulphide of calcium	2.41

A cinder, of a greenish colour on the exterior, approaching to the description known as "half-scouring," gave:

Silica	40.10
Alumina	16.41
Protoxide of iron	.76
,, manganese	1.18
Lime	31.49
Magnesia	5.08
Potash	1.96
Sulphide of calcium	2.51

A cinder similar in appearance to the last, but rather deeper in colour, and likewise known as "half scouring," gave:

Silica	38.29
Alumina	17.17
Protoxide of iron	1.31
,, manganese	.68
Lime	35.20
Magnesia	2.34
Potash	1.89
Sulphide of calcium	2.18

A grey, stony cinder, of a bluish colour on the exterior, rough stony fracture in the interior, yielded:

Silica	39.51
Alumina	16.87
Protoxide of iron	.54
,, manganese	.95
Lime	36.23
Magnesia	2.71
Potash	1.60
Sulphide of calcium	2.98

A grey cinder, of smooth fracture in the interior, transparent on the edges, in thin pieces, and of a glassy smoothness on the exterior, gave on analysis:

Silica	41.03
Alumina	19.47
Protoxide of iron	.32
,, manganese	.47
Lime	27.18
Magnesia	5.43
Potash	2.40
Sulphide of calcium	3.53

The following analysis is of a cinder of a dull leaden fracture, from one of the furnaces in the Aberdare valley; and the mass from which the sample was taken contained numerous cavities of from 2 to 6 inches in diameter, filled, more or less, with cinder in a peculiar state of crystallisation. The crystals consisted of straight needles of black cinder, crossing and interlaced with each other, but of so fine a texture as not to bear handling without breaking:

Silica	44.99
Protoxide of iron	9.86
Alumina	10.91
Protoxide of manganese	1.10
Lime	28.43
Magnesia	3.61
Sulphuric acid	1.66
Phosphoric acid	Traces

A sample of these needles was submitted to analysis with the following results:

Silica	39.90
Protoxide of iron	7.26
,, manganese	1.53
Alumina	13.50
Lime	31.16
Magnesia	4.09
Sulphur	0.48
Phosphoric acid	0.61

The examination of a number of crystalline cinders, produced by blast-furnaces near Dudley, gave results not dissimilar to the foregoing. Four samples of hot blast, coke-smelted cinders, yielded by analysis:

	1	2	3	4
Silica	38.05	38.76	37.63	37.91
Alumina	14.11	14.48	12.78	13.01
Lime	35.70	35.68	33.46	31.48
Magnesia	7.61	6.84	6.64	7.94
Protoxide of iron	1.27	1.18	3.91	0.93
,, manganese	0.40	0.23	2.64	2.79
Potash	1.85	1.11	1.02	2.60
Sulphide of calcium	0.32	0.98	0.68	3.05

A fifth sample of Staffordshire cinder, cold blast, yielded:

Silica	39.53
Alumina	15.11
Lime	33.53
Magnesia	3.49
Protoxide manganese	3.89
" iron	2.03
Potash	1.06
Sulphide of calcium	2.15

A sample of cinder, taken from the Oldbury furnaces, is chiefly remarkable for the large per-centage of lime and sulphide of calcium:

Silica	28.32
Alumina	24.24
Lime	40.12
Magnesia	2.79
Protoxide manganese	0.07
" iron	0.27
Potash	0.54
Sulphide of calcium	3.39

Two samples of cinders from Belgian coke-furnaces gave:

Silica	42.06	55.77
Alumina	12.93	13.90
Lime	32.53	22.22
Magnesia	1.06	2.10
Protoxide manganese	2.26	2.52
" iron	4.94	2.12
Potash	2.59	1.73
Phosphate of alumina	0.31	—

The analyses of two cinders from the blast-furnaces of Olsberger, on the Rhine, yielded results less complicated than the foregoing:

Silica	53.37	53.76
Alumina	5.12	4.76
Lime	30.71	29.48
Magnesia	9.50	9.82
Protoxide of manganese	1.41	1.30
" iron	0.95	1.48

The analyses of cinders thus far given are the results of researches made with the object of determining the chemical composition of these products of the blast-furnace. The following were undertaken with a view of ascertaining their chemical constitution, and the relation which exists between the composition of the cinder and that of the crude iron, obtained at the same time.

A hot-blast slag, of a grey colour, and presenting the qualities of a good cinder as it came from the foundry iron furnace at Dowlais, gave by analysis:

Silica	39.64
Protoxide of iron	Traces
Alumina	24.05
Protoxide of manganese	1.16
Lime	32.49
Magnesia	2.61
Sulphur	0.19

The foregoing cinder was accompanied by the production of No. 1 pig-iron, of the following composition:

Iron	94.57
Silicon	1.30
Carbon	2.06
Sulphur	00.9
Phosphorus	Traces
Manganese	1.36
Calcium	0.60
Magnesium	0.11

A blast-furnace cinder of a grey colour, but not quite so good in quality, discharged by the same furnace as the preceding, yielded:

Silica	39.40
Protoxide of iron	1.08
" manganese	Trace
Alumina	23.20
Lime	32.70
Magnesia	1.60
Sulphur	0.80
Phosphoric acid	0.40

This cinder was accompanied by the production of pig-iron of No. 2 quality, which yielded as its composition:

Iron	93.46
Silicon	1.42
Carbon	2.36
Sulphur	0.08
Phosphorus	0.31
Manganese	1.57
Calcium	0.67
Magnesium	0.13

A cinder, produced by one of the Dowlais furnaces, working with a cold blast, and heavy mixed burden of materials, gave the following composition:

Silica	40.60
Protoxide iron	1.66
" manganese	0.55
Alumina	17.87
Lime	37.15
Magnesia	2.38
Sulphur	0.76
Phosphoric acid	0.28

The blast-furnace discharging the preceding cinder yielded a white pig-iron of the following composition:

Iron	95.16
Silicon	0.43
Carbon	2.49
Sulphur	0.75
Phosphorus	0.53
Manganese	0.55
Calcium	0.95
Magnesium	0.22

A cinder similar to the last, and also from one of the Dowlais furnaces, working with a heavy mixed burden, but blown with a hot blast, gave the following result:

Silica	43.13
Protoxide of iron	1.50
Alumina	17.50
Protoxide manganese	Trace
Lime	31.24
Magnesia	5.55
Sulphur	1.14

This cinder was accompanied by a white pig-iron of the following composition:

Iron	93.96
Silicon	1.19
Carbon	2.10
Sulphur	0.50
Phosphorus	0.62
Manganese	0.33
Calcium	0.45
Magnesium	0.20

A white pig-iron smelted at one of the Dowlais furnaces, from a mixed burden of calcined argillaceous ore, hematite ore, and forge and finery cinders mixed, with a limestone flux, raw coal, and a hot blast—the furnace being in that condition known to the smelter as "scouring badly," that is, throwing a dense black cinder, containing a large per-centage of protoxide of iron—gave by analysis the following composition:

Iron	93.44
Silicon	0.92
Carbon	2.23
Sulphur	1.18
Phosphorus	1.04
Manganese	2.02
Calcium	0.25
Magnesium	Traces

The "scouring cinder" yielded by this furnace gave by analysis the following results:

Silica	44.60
Protoxide of manganese	2.62
" iron	2.63
Alumina	18.10
Lime	29.19
Phosphoric acid	0.10
Sulphur	1.06
Magnesia	1.70

A cinder from one of the Abernant furnaces in the Neath Valley, working with anthracite as fuel, yielded a composition as follows:

Silica	30.85
Protoxide of iron	0.90
" manganese	0.13
Alumina	16.06
Lime	41.80
Magnesia	0.83
Sulphur	0.92
Phosphoric acid	0.54

This cinder was accompanied by the production of a grey anthracite pig-iron of the following composition:

Iron	95.81
Silicon	1.34
Carbon	1.56
Sulphur	0.17
Phosphorus	0.31
Manganese	1.56
Calcium	0.25
Magnesium	0.12

The blast on this furnace was hot, the throat large and open, and the entire circumstances favourable to the production of a comparatively pure iron. From these figures some idea may be formed as to the derivation of those qualities for which anthracite pig-iron is so well known.

A blast-furnace cinder of a green colour, discharged by one of the Ebbw Vale furnaces, working with a mixed burden, of which the spathose ores of the western district formed part, a hot blast, and the throat of the furnace closed for collecting the combustible gases, gave by analyses:

Silica	43.55
Protoxide of iron	3.74
,, manganese	0.25
Alumina	20.40
Lime	28.85
Magnesia	1.10
Sulphur	0.65
Phosphoric acid	0.35

This cinder was accompanied by the production of a white pig-iron for the forge, of the following composition:

Iron	89.75
Silicon	2.02
Carbon	1.88
Sulphur	1.23
Phosphorus	1.52
Manganese	4.13
Calcium	0.21
Magnesium	0.05

At Cwm Celyn the furnaces are worked with closed tops, hot blast, and a mixture of coal and coke as fuel; the cinder produced by one of these furnaces, under a mixed mineral burden, yielded:

Silica	50.50
Protoxide of iron	10.10
Alumina	17.20
Protoxide of manganese	2.24
Lime	13.07
Magnesia	5.04
Sulphuric acid	0.27
Phosphoric acid	0.15

The cinder was accompanied by the production of a white pig-iron, for forge purposes, which presented the following composition:

Iron	95.618
Silicon	1.012
Calcium	0.320
Carbon	1.590
Sulphur	0.640
Phosphorus	0.820

At the Rhymney works some of the furnaces are worked with a mixed burden, hot blast, and the top closed for utilisation of the gases. A partial analysis of a cinder from one of these furnaces gave:

Silica	42.50
Protoxide of iron	9.75
,, manganese } Phosphoric acid } Alumina	16.90
Lime	28.56
Magnesia	1.13
Sulphur	0.54

This cinder was accompanied by white pig-iron, for forge purposes, which gave as follows:

Iron	93.11
Silicon	0.46
Carbon	1.35
Sulphur	1.82
Phosphorus	1.10
Manganese	0.93
Calcium	0.37
Magnesium	0.21

The Rhymney Company have other furnaces working on a mixed burden, and blown with a hot blast, but having the throat open and uncontrolled. The white pig-iron produced by these furnaces is for forge purposes, and a sample taken from one gave the following results:

Iron	91.25
Silicon	0.33
Carbon	2.22
Sulphur	1.49
Phosphorus	1.37
Manganese	2.62
Calcium	0.50
Magnesium	0.17

Experiments were made on the Continent, at the charcoal blast-furnace of Hamm, where the ore is smelted without the addition of any material as flux. The burden of ore was successively largely augmented, and cinders of the following composition appear to have been discharged under three different proportions of burden:

Silica	40.57	45.30	37.50
Alumina	0.00	5.66	2.10
Protoxide of iron	0.04	0.06	21.50
" manganese	25.54	33.96	20.20
Magnesia	15.15	10.22	8.60
Sulphur	00.S	00.S	0.02

The crude irons produced with these cinders were of very different qualities. The first was accompanied by a grey pig-iron; the second by a white, lammelar, pig-iron; the third by a granular pig-iron, white, and containing small cavities. With this last the augmentation of burden had been carried so far as to endanger the furnace:

Iron	85.73	89.74	95.21
Manganese	7.42	4.50	1.79
Silicon	1.31	0.56	—
Graphite	2.35	—	—
Carbon	2.08	5.14	2.91
Sulphur	Traces	Traces	0.01
Phosphorus	0.08	0.08	0.05
Magnesium	Trace	Trace	Trace

A blast-furnace cinder from Torgelow, in Pomerania, smelted with charcoal fuel, from bog ores containing much phosphorus, yielded by analysis:

Silica	53.60
Alumina	3.80
Lime	24.00
Protoxide of iron	1.70
" manganese	3.90
Magnesia	1.20

The above cinder was of a bluish-white colour, and was from a furnace which produces grey pig-iron of the following composition:

Iron	91.10
Manganese	2.80
Carbon	2.00
Silicon	0.40
Phosphorus	3.10

This crude iron is chiefly remarkable for containing a large quantity of phosphorus; from another furnace, however, similarly worked, pig-iron was obtained containing a still larger amount of this body. The composition of some from Pertz was:

Iron	91.40
Manganese	0.90
Carbon	1.00
Silicon	0.20
Phosphorus	5.00

We will now give examples of the composition of various English and foreign pig-irons, produced under circumstances differing either as to character or proportion of fuel, flux, ore and blast. These analyses have more especial reference to the elucidation of the sources from which pig-irons derive their peculiar and characteristic properties, as developed in the cast and manufactured state.

A white pig-iron, smelted at the Dowlais works with a cold blast, from refinery cinders, and argillaceous shale and limestone as flux, raw coal as fuel. This iron is known in commerce as "kentledge," and gave the following compositon:

Iron	91.25
Silicon	0.33
Carbon	1.63
Sulphur	1.40
Phosphorus	2.43
Manganese	1.04
Calcium	0.52
Magnesium	0.15

No. 1, grey pig-iron, smelted at the Dowlais works, from the cleanest varieties of calcined argillaceous ores, the best furnace coal, and a cold blast, in a furnace of smaller dimensions than those now in use at that establishment, gave by analysis:

Iron	95.05
Carbon	3.24
Silicon	.73
Aluminium	.36
Sulphur	Traces
Phosphorus	Traces

A white pig-iron, smelted at the same works, from a lean argillaceous ore, yielded by analysis:

Iron	90.50
Carbon	1.27
Silicon	0.96
Aluminium	0.33
Sulphur	0.32
Phosphorus	Traces

The iron made at the same works, with a mineral burden composed of two parts of the local carbonaceous ore and one part of forge cinders, gave a composition of:

Iron	89.84
Carbon	1.22
Silicon	6.92
Aluminium	0.30
Sulphur	0.43
Phosphorus	0.85
Manganese	Traces

The composition of two specimens of pig-iron, from the Level furnaces, Dudley, smelted from the local ores, with a cold blast, is stated to have been:

Iron	94.10	96.57
Combined carbon	1.87	0.95
Free carbon	1.92	1.67
Silicon	1.30	0.51
Manganese	1.12	1.16
Calcium	0.05	Trace
Sodium	0.19	Trace
Potassium	Trace	0.62
Sulphur	Trace	0.11
Phosphorus	0.21	0.36

The composition of two specimens of pig-iron, from the same furnaces, smelted under similar circumstances as regards the minerals and fuel, but with a hot blast, is stated to have been:

Iron	95.23	95.80
Combined carbon	1.77	2.72
Free carbon	0.49	0.36
Silicon	0.31	0.11
Manganese	0.34	0.54
Calcium	0.10	0.06
Sodium	0.19	0.14
Sulphur	Trace	Trace
Phosphorus	0.12	0.37

In making the preceding and other analyses of irons from the Level furnaces, the analyst (Wrightson) was led to infer that the temperature of the blast affected the quantity of phosphorus in the pig-iron. The proportion found in eight samples of each description of iron is represented in the following table:

	Cold blast.	Hot blast.
No. 1	0.47	0.51 per cent.
2	0.41	0.55
3	0.31	0.50
4	0.20	0.71
5	0.21	0.54
6	0.36	—
7	0.03	0.07
8	0.36	0.40

The analysis of a specimen of Staffordshire pig-iron, the furnace not known, gave a composition of:

Iron	95.73
Combined carbon	2.22
Free carbon	0.58
Silicon	0.95
Sulphur	0.15
Phosphoric acid	Traces

The difference in the composition of pig-irons smelted by a cold blast and those smelted with a heated blast, is attempted to be given in the following analyses (by Thomson); but the absence of phosphorus and the single reference to sulphur, an ingredient which unquestionably exists in nearly all irons smelted with coal or coke, must cause much distrust as to their general correctness:

Analysis of Cold-blast Pig-irons Smelted in Scotland.

	Muirkirk.	Muirkirk.	Muirkirk.	Carron.	Clyde.
Iron	90.98	90.29	91.38	94.010	90.824
Manganese	—	7.14	2.00	.626	2.458
Sulphur	—	—	—	—	.045
Carbon	7.40	1.706	4.83	3.086	2.458
Silicon	.46	.830	1.10	1.006	.450
Aluminium	.48	.016	—	1.022	4.602
Calcium	—	.018	.20	—	—
Magnesium	—	—	—	—	.340

Analysis of Hot-blast Pig-irons Smelted in Scotland.

	Clyde.	Carron.	Carron.	Clyde.	Clyde.
Iron	97.096	95.422	96.09	94.966	94.345
Manganese	.332	.336	.41	.100	3.120
Carbon	2.400	2.400	2.48	1.560	1.416
Silicon	.280	1.820	1.49	1.322	.520
Aluminium	.385	.488	.26	1.374	.599
Magnesium	—	—	—	.702	—

The following analysis of a grey pig-iron from the Clyde furnaces presents results different from those exhibited by the preceding analyses of Scotch irons. The composition of a white pig-iron from these furnaces is likewise given:

```
                    Grey iron.   White iron.
Iron . . . . . . .    92.30   . .  92.24
Free carbon . . . .    1.60   . .   1.52
Combined carbon . .    0.40   . .   0.30
Sulphur . . . . . .    1.40   . .   0.60
Phosphorus . . . .     1.30   . .   0.95
Silicon . . . . . .    2.50   . .   1.79
Manganese . . . . .     —     . .   2.00
```

A grey pig-iron from the Calder works gave the following as its composition:

```
Iron . . . . . . . . . . .  94.63
Free carbon . . . . . . .    1.40
Combined carbon . . . . .    1.20
Sulphur . . . . . . . . .    0.55
Phosphorus . . . . . . .     0.39
Silicon . . . . . . . . .    1.53
Manganese . . . . . . . .    0.50
```

The quantities of silicon and sulphur in some of the pig-irons smelted from carbonaceous ores, with raw coal as fuel, may be seen by the following table:

```
              Silicon.     Sulphur.
Monkland . .   1.53  . .   0.300 per cent.
Coltness . .   2.69  . .     —
Eglinton . .   3.12  . .   0.336
Dalmellington  4.42  . .   0.956
```

The composition of two samples of coke-smelted grey pig-iron, is stated, by Brande, to have been as follows:

Iron	95.15	94.85
Carbon	2.45	1.66
Silicon	1.62	3.00
Phosphorus	.78	.49
Manganese	Trace	Trace

The composition of two samples of white pig-iron is stated to have been:

Iron	96.12	94.08
Carbon	2.33	2.64
Silicon	.84	.26
Phosphorus	.71	.29
Manganese	Trace	2.14

Experiments were made at Königshütte, in the Hartz, for the purpose of determining the effect of temperature on the chemical composition of the pig-iron produced. The first analysis is that of a pig-iron, mottled, with a cold blast; the second, of iron from the same furnace with the blast heated to 470°. The specific gravity of both samples was 7.166:

Iron	93.20	91.42
Combined carbon	2.78	1.44
Free carbon	1.90	2.71
Silicon	0.71	3.21
Phosphorus	1.23	1.22

Similar experiments, made on the Leerbach furnace, in the same district, resulted in the production of pig-irons of the following composition—the first with a cold blast, the second with the blast at 230°. Specific gravity, cold blast iron, 7.081; hot blast, 7.077:

Iron	93.66	91.98
Combined carbon	0.43	0.05
Free carbon	3.85	3.48
Silicon	0.79	1.91
Phosphorus	1.22	1.68

The pig-iron smelted at Danville, Pennsylvania, from the fossiliferous red oxide, with anthracite and a hot blast, is stated to yield by analysis:

Iron	90.10
Carbon	6.48
Silicon	1.96
Phosphorus	1.50
Sulphur	Traces

The Lehigh iron of the same district, with similar fuel and blast, but different ores, yielded:

Iron	94.30
Carbon	4.40
Silicon	1.03
Phosphorus	Traces
Sulphur	0.05
Copper	0.02
Calcium	0.02
Aluminium	0.04

During the working of the blast-furnace belonging to the Anglo-Asturian Company, in Spain, pig-irons, presenting some unusual properties, were occasionally met with. On one occasion the iron produced was of a tin white colour, smooth on the upper side of the pig, and remained unaffected by some years' exposure in the open air to rain and sun; it was brittle, and capable of being pulverised in a mortar. Its analysis gave the following composition :

Iron	81.99
Silicon	12.98
Sulphur	0.31
Manganese	2.60
Carbon	1.70

The furnace at these works also produced, from another class of ores, a pig-iron of great strength, and remarkably tough under the cutting tool. An analysis is stated to have furnished the following results :

Iron	87.50
Silicon	5.77
Manganese	0.94
Phosphorus and arsenic	1.37
Sulphur	.37
Carbon	3.60

SMELTING.

The smelting process, or that by which the iron ore is converted into metallic iron, is the most important operation of an iron-works. The working of the blast-furnace, therefore, requires great attention from the ironmaster and his workmen. Any irregularity in its action, if allowed to go on unchecked, may endanger its safety; and apparently very trifling circumstances will often produce the most extraordinary changes in the operations within the furnace. After carefully arranging the proportions of the materials for the production of grey pig-iron, we shall probably obtain an inferior description several times in a week, and sometimes, without any apparent cause, the furnace will produce white iron of a coarse quality for a week together. Irregularities equally great also occasionally occur in the make, or quantity of metal produced in a definite time. Indeed, the operations connected with the blast-furnace are more uncertain in their results than any other of those carried on in iron-works. Moreover, when we consider that the quality of bar-iron is dependant on that of the pig-metal from which it is manufactured, and that every irregularity in the working, and every stoppage of the furnace, arising from whatever cause, is attended with loss, we can easily understand why the healthy working of the furnace, is an object of paramount importance to the ironmaster.

Having already described the various materials used in iron-making, and the manner of construction of the furnace, we will now proceed to examine the various processes employed in smelting iron on the large scale.

Where pig-iron of very superior quality for foundry or other purposes, is desired, the materials used are confined to selected varieties of argillaceous ironstone; coal, either raw or coked, and limestone. The ironstone, having been previously roasted, is filled into the furnace by barrows, or, as is still the practice at some few works, by iron baskets. Between each barrowful of calcined ore the proper quantities of fuel and flux are filled in. The weight of calcined ironstone which is charged into the furnace for a definite measure of the fuel used is termed the "burden." This burden varies in different works, and frequently at different furnaces in the same works, but it is governed by the qualities of the ironstone and fuel, by the blast and the state of the furnace, as well as by the kind of pig-iron to be produced. The burden commonly carried by the South Wales furnace coals may be set down at 10 cwt. of calcined mine to 9 cwt. of coals. The weight of limestone used for flux depends on the nature of the earths combined with the iron in the ore, but may be taken at $3\frac{1}{4}$ cwt.

We have mentioned in another place the loss of metal consequent on the heavy burden carried by the coal in numerous works, and will here draw attention to the great pecuniary loss which occurs from so overburdening the coal. A dark or black cinder is produced at the majority of the forge-iron furnaces in this country; but by using a larger quantity of coal grey or yellowish cinders are obtained. It is a question, therefore, for the consideration of ironmasters whether the quantity of metal lost in the cinders produced with a heavy burden is not of more value than the coal saved. The dark and black cinders will average 12 per cent. of metal, and will weigh about two tons per ton of pig-iron obtained. The grey cinder will average about 6 per cent. of metal, and will weigh per ton of pig-iron rather less than the dark. So that if the furnace is making 120 tons of iron weekly, the cinders will weigh 240 tons, and will contain 28.8 tons of metal in one case, and 14.4 in the other. Estimating the excess of 14.4 tons in the dark cinder at the price of forge pigs, 3*l*., we have a weekly loss of 43*l*. in metal sent to the tip. Yet, on the plea of economy, we see nearly one-fourth of the metallic iron of the ironstone carted away in the cinders; while, with a more rational proportion of fuel, a great part of it might be retained in the shape of good pig-iron. The quantity of fuel required to be used to produce grey cinders exceeds that required when black or dark ones are made by about 8 cwts. per ton of pig-iron, or 48 tons weekly, which, valued at 6s. per ton, does not amount to 15*l*.

A definite quantity of ore with its assigned proportion of fuel and flux is termed a "charge," such, for instance, as the quantities just named. And every time this weight of minerals is filled into the furnace it is said to have "gone one charge." By the number of charges which the furnace goes in a given time—say twelve hours, the period usually taken—the probable make of iron is estimated.

SECTION V.

OBSERVATIONS ON THE WORKING OF BLAST FURNACES.

The plan usually adopted for charging is to fill with barrows, containing according to the materials to be filled and local custom, from 4 to 16 cwts. each. This mode of filling is attended with the least labour, but we question whether it is the most advantageous as regards either the yield or quality of the pig-iron. Where the respective materials are thrown into the furnace in quantities of from 15 to 16 cwt. at once, we cannot expect that complete commingling which takes place when they are filled in quantities of a few pounds only. On the Continent it is usual to mix the limestone and ores before filling, but the higher price of labour in this country is generally given as a reason for not adopting a similar plan. It is probable, however, that some such method might be adopted with considerable advantage. The Continental ironmaster, smelting with charcoal, produces a ton of iron with about one-half the quantity of carbon consumed in this country; and as this superiority is doubtless in some degree owing to the more thorough commixture of the materials, the additional labour employed would be more than compensated by the small consumption of coal and the superior production.

The mode of filling at present adopted here is the occasion of much irregularity in the working of the furnace. We have observed fillers, either to avoid a little trouble, or perhaps from ignorance of the serious nature of the consequences, charge several rounds of ironstone through one side of the tunnel-head without the usual complement of coal, which has been charged at the opposite side. In such cases the ironstone in its descent arrives at the tuyeres with an insufficient quantity of fuel, and the temperature attained is consequently too low for the perfect reduction and separation of the metal. The nearest tuyere becomes clogged, and probably entirely closed, by the adhesion of the partially fused mass. These ill consequences are most apparent with a cold blast. The effect of the immense volume of cold air on a mass of materials not possessing sufficient carbon to maintain combustion is to produce rapid cooling, which not unfrequently results in the loss of the tuyere.

The proper proportion of ironstone, flux, and fuel having been determined by analysis or experiment, it is most important that the workmen engaged in filling should maintain it regularly in the consecutive charges. For their guidance one or more weighing machines are placed in the barrow-road to the tunnel-head, having suitable weights placed beyond their control. We are of opinion, however, that this arrangement fails to guarantee the requisite accuracy, from leaving too much at the discretion of the workmen. Supposing each charge to be correctly weighed by the filler, the existing arrangements would answer very well; but as the operation of weighing both occupies time and is attended with labour, it is too generally omitted when the superior agents are not by, and even in their presence it is at best but a rough approximation to the actual weight. It is easy to see that while so much is left to the judgment and care of a class of workmen but little superior to common labourers, the operations of the blast-furnace must be subject to numerous irregularities in yield and quality, besides those which may justly be attributed to atmospheric and other known causes.

The desirableness of having the materials accurately weighed is generally admitted, but the labour and supervision required for it with existing appliances are considered to make this advantage too expensive. It is necessary, therefore, that the machines intended for this purpose should not add to the labour or render necessary any expensive supervision. With these views we some years since pressed upon the proprietors of the Dowlais works the value of a self-acting machine which required no exertion on the part of the workman; and as the necessity for exercising a rigid economy in materials will eventually compel the adoption of a machine of this kind at the majority of works, we will briefly describe the principle on which it was constructed.

In the frame-work and general arrangement it was similar to the ordinary weighing-machine, the platform being level with the surface of the ground, and so placed that the materials from any given spot were obliged to pass over it. To the end of the lever on which the scale-pan is usually hung a small hollow iron plunger is attached, guided in a vertical direction by a slender parallel motion. The plunger worked in a small cylindrical cistern, partially filled with mercury, and the levers were so proportioned that a resistance of one pound to the descent of the plunger in the mercury equipoised a weight of 1 cwt. on the platform. The plunger was also so proportioned in diameter to the load, that it made a stroke of 3 inches in the mercury for every 12 cwt. on the scale (or about $\frac{1}{4}$ inch per cwt.), while the platform descended only $\frac{1}{74}$th part of an inch. So that on a load being placed upon the platform, the plunger descended until the resistance, multiplied by the leverage, equalled the weight, the amount of which was indicated by an index and pointer.

To render the machine altogether independent of the filler, a registering apparatus was attached to it, so constructed that the weight of every barrow-load that had passed over the platform during a given time could be ascertained at intervals of a few days. The circumference of a light metal cylinder was covered with paper sufficiently large for a week's working: a pencil was attached to the end of the plunger-rod, and was caused to press against the paper by a spiral spring in a case. The surface of the cylinder was turned through a distance of $\frac{1}{16}$th of an inch each time the plunger ascended, and whenever it descended the pencil drew a line equal to the distance through which it travelled. By this means every movement of the plunger was accurately registered, and by referring to the measurements of the lines representing the movements, the agreement of the quantities charged with those ordered could be easily ascertained. A weighing-machine of this kind would be of great value to ironmasters, as showing the exact consumption of materials, and would also be an effectual check on the present careless system of weighing.

SCAFFOLDS.

Obstructions to the descent of the materials are called "scaffolds," and may be usually traced to the adhesion of masses of material above and around the boshes. The primary cause of these we believe to be the increase of bulk which the fuel undergoes in its descent. Hence coal-fed furnaces are more subject to scaffolding than those fed with coke; and in furnaces fed with coal this liability is increased by the sectional form of the furnace. If the throat is small, and the enlargement immediately below inconsiderable, the liability to scaffold will be very great.

Irregularities in filling will occasion partial obstruction in the deeper parts of the furnace, and variations in the quantity and quality of the blast at a tuyere may produce similar effects. When it is known that a partial obstruction exists in the hearth or in the bottom of the boshes, the furnace is turned on hot fluid grey iron. The proportion of ore and flux to coal is largely diminished, and a greater temperature being thus obtained, the refractory mass gradually melts and a clearance is effected. The operation may be expedited by turning on a greater volume of blast of undiminished density, proportionate to the more rapid consumption of fuel. Similar measures are adopted when, from accident or other cause, the hearth becomes partially filled with cold material.

A different course is sometimes pursued in the removal of obstructions which may have accumulated around the tuyere. Fresh tuyeres are formed above the accumulated matter, and the proportion of ore to fuel is largely increased. This alteration of burden is followed by the production of a sharp irony cinder, that seldom fails to penetrate and carry away the obstruction. Great caution must, however, be used in the employment of this remedy, or it will entail effects upon the furnace quite as injurious as those which it is intended to remove. The diminished consumption of fuel consequent on the production of scouring cinder reduces the temperature of the hearth below the point necessary for the separation of the metal and the flowing of the cinders; hence, if the production of scouring cinder is of long continuance, there is always a danger of the lower half of the hearth being filled with solid matter, in order to the removal of which the original proportion of coal to ore or iron-stone is restored, if not exceeded, that a hot fluid metal may be produced. The high temperature now maintained in the hearth, with the fluid character of the iron, gradually fuses the solid mass and cleans the hearth.

TUYERES.

The height of the tuyere above the bottom, though usually dependent upon the position of the cinder-notch, is partly regulated by the quality of the coal and local custom. In some furnaces we have observed the centre of the tuyere placed only 20 inches from the bottom, while in others it is as high as 48 inches.

The distance to which the blast penetrates in the hearth is the principal distinction between dark and bright tuyeres. The quality of the fuel being similar, a soft voluminous blast causes a bright tuyere, while a dense concentrated blast produces a dark one. The oxygen of the weak blast being absorbed by the fuel close to the tuyere, an intense local heat is created, and on looking through the blast-pipe a spot of dazzling brightness is presented to the eye. But with a dense blast the velocity of escape is so much greater that the principal part of the air is carried further into the interior of the hearth, consequently, the fuel next the tuyere is but scantily supplied with oxygen; the dark tube is thus caused, the great heat being produced in the centre of the hearth.

The bright tuyere is more common with weak, spongy coke than with that of a harder kind.

Formerly, the blast entered the furnace through a cast-iron dry tuyere. The metal at the point was protected by a nose of fire-clay, which was renewed at casting-time, and on other occasions when, from the stoppage of the blast or other cause, it broke off into the hearth. If it was not immediately replaced, the metal, being unprotected, began to burn, and the point of the tuyere became contracted. The blast being thus partially intercepted, the heat increased, and the burning proceeded so rapidly that it was not an unusual thing to be obliged to change the cast-iron shell at every casting.

The bright tuyere is universal with charcoal furnaces. This is doubtless owing to the soft blasts generally used, and to the large surface which the fuel presents to the action of the air. An intensely high local heat is consequently produced, displaying in these furnaces the most perfect examples of the bright tuyere.

Bright tuyeres are also occasionally seen with a dense blast; but, if the circumstances be examined, a sufficient cause is usually discernible. The most common one is removing the nose of the blast-pipe to a great distance from the point of the tuyere. This causes the blast to diverge on escaping from the tuyere, and an effect, similar to that of a soft voluminous blast, is produced on the fuel.

It is not an unusual circumstance with the bright tuyere to find accumulations of metal adhering to the point, which obstruct the passage of the blast. These adhesions, from being more commonly met with in certain localities, are supposed to arise from some peculiar property of the iron-stone; but our own observation has been that they occur most frequently when the burden is temporarily so rich in metal that the usual proportion of cinder to iron is not maintained. Their removal is usually effected by damming up the cinder to a level above the tuyere, so that being immersed in a fluid bath they are eventually melted, and a free passage allowed for the blast. In adopting this method of clearing the tuyere, particular attention must be paid to the blowing-engine, so that no stoppage of the blast may occur while the cinders are at this high level. Should the blast cease even for a few minutes the fluid cinder runs back into the pipes, and causes material injury thereto, as well as delay in refitting.

The dark tuyere is produced, as we have already stated, by the dense concentrated blast causing the most active combustion at a considerable distance in the hearth. The intermediate materials being deprived of the air necessary for combustion are kept in a comparatively cool state, and form a kind of vitreous tube for the passage of the blast to the central portions of the hearth. This is broken off by the pressure of the superincumbent materials in their descent after each casting; but its formation commences anew on the re-admission of the blast. Between the castings it will extend inwards from the iron tuyere from 12 to 20 inches. But should it extend farther, and fail to be broken off by the descending materials, measures are adopted for its removal. This is usually accomplished by the use of iron bars; but if it cannot be dislodged by this means, and the elongation continues and threatens to extend across the hearth, the tuyere is temporarily abandoned, and a fresh one cut out higher up in the hearth. The new tuyere by fusing the materials at a higher elevation, eventually removes the refractory tube beneath.

By some writers the formation of the dark tuyere is attributed to the use of a coke less instantaneously combustible, which, at the tuyere orifice, has its temperature lowered by an incessant discharge of blast. Our own experience leads us to a different conclusion. That the nature of the coke has an influence on its formation we freely admit; but the density of the blast is no doubt the primary cause. We do not hear of any such effect being produced in charcoal furnaces blown with a soft blast. Here the air diverges at once, and is completely decomposed within a few inches of its emission; but the dense blast of modern furnaces it penetrates deeply amongst the materials, and the quantity which diverges in the immediate vicinity of the tuyere is very trifling. Now, as the quantity of air brought into contact with the carbon of the fuel in a given time regulates the degree of heat attainable, it follows that when a dense concentrated blast is used, the fuel next the tuyere being sparingly supplied with this element, the temperature maintained there will be proportionately low.

We question the correctness of the late Mr. Mushet's opinion, "That the coke has its temperature lowered by the blast." Whatever heat the coke attains is the effect of the blast, and the supply of fuel being kept up the degree of heat evolved will be in exact proportion to the quantity of air brought into contact with the carbon of the fuel. The theory of a reduction of the temperature by the blast is contrary to all known laws of combustion. A less degree of heat may be maintained at a particular spot, but this is the result of a *diminished supply* of air to the carbon at that place, and not of an *excessive* quantity, as this author states.

A soft blast and porous coke invariably produce a bright tuyere, and the cause is sufficiently evident. The blast diverges on its emission from the tuyere, and a large proportion of air is thus brought into contact with the fuel, which by its porosity exposes a large surface of carbon; hence the rapid combustion of the fuel and the high temperature maintained close to the tuyere. With a dense blast the effect would be different—the volume of blast would be carried further into the hearth, and the material next the tuyere being partially deprived of air would exist in a comparatively cool state.

Blowing into the cinder is largely practised in some districts, and, to some extent, in several Welsh works. The centre of the tuyere is usually placed 4 or 5 inches above the bottom of the cinder-notch in the damplate; but, in some cases, not more than 1 or 2 inches. But where blowing into the cinder is practised, we find the centre as much as 5 or 6 inches below the notch. When thus situated, a dense blast is required to keep back the cinder, and great care is demanded at the blowing-engine so that no stoppage of the blast may occur except at casting time. And care must also be taken that the depth of the tuyere in the cinder is not greater than the descent of the level of the cinder after the metal has been tapped.

It was formerly supposed that blowing into the cinder would deteriorate the quality of the iron, in consequence of the thinner stratum of cinder which protected it, especially when, towards casting time, the metal rose in the hearth; and, were the thickness reduced below a certain point, this effect would undoubtedly occur. But under ordinary circumstances the thickness of cinder is from 18 to 30 inches, or from three to five times that of the substratum of metal, and it may be diminished to twice without injury to the quality of the iron; consequently, the tuyere may be safely brought so much lower.

Blowing into the cinder is more applicable to narrow than to wide hearths. When the breadth is small the mean temperature within the zone of fusion is proportionably high, and the fuel within so contracted a space, is consumed too rapidly to yield a maximum effect. This is partly obviated by blowing into the cinder. The ascending column of heated air, on reaching the zone of fusion, is equally distributed throughout the whole mass of material, maintaining a less intense but more lasting combustion.

Bright tuyeres are usual with the hot blast. They have been accounted for on the supposition that the heat carried into the furnace increased the temperature around the tuyere, instead of lowering it, as with cold air. But we are of opinion that the occurrence of bright tuyeres with hot blast is due to the same causes to which we have attributed them when produced in furnaces where a soft blast and porous fuel are used. The oxygen in the hot blast combines more readily with the carbon, and does not penetrate so far into the interior of the hearth before acting on the fuel, as a cold blast of the same pressure. Besides which, the elevation of its temperature to the melting point of lead, more than doubles its volume, and as heat is not considered ponderable, this expansion of the air is followed by a corresponding reduction of its specific gravity. Now the distance to which the blast penetrates is of course due to the momentum acquired by it at its exit under pressure from the pipe, and if its specific gravity be diminished by heating, as in the case of the hot blast, the momentum acquired will also be diminished, and, consequently, its ability to penetrate among the materials.

The experiment of blowing into the furnace through a tuyere, situated above the boshes, has been tried more than once at the Dowlais works. By some practical men it is held that blowing at this elevation would increase the temperature of the descending materials, lighten the work at the lower tuyeres, and, consequently, increase the make of the furnace. But the results with the elevated tuyere were very unsatisfactory, though such as might have been anticipated on attentive consideration. The blast poured in on the materials caused a high local heat, which threatened to destroy the surrounding portion of the furnace. A portion of the fuel was consumed, partially fusing the adjacent pieces of ironstone, and rendering them less permeable to the ascending gases and less fusible in the hearth. Hence the consumption of coal was increased.

PRODUCTION OF PIG-IRON.

The relative proportions of ore, fuel, and flux employed vary considerably in the same locality, while the difference in the practice obtaining in different districts using the same class of ores is very great. At some of the large Welsh works an assayer is maintained for the purpose of assisting the furnace manager in determining the proportions best adapted for the metal to be manufactured; but at the majority of the works the proportions adopted are the result of experimental trials made in the furnace, often with a great waste of materials, injury to the furnace, and loss through a deficiency of make, amounting, on the whole, to a large item in the cost of production. Too much stress cannot be laid on the importance of having all the materials that are used in the furnace properly analysed. Unless this be done the pig-iron will be uncertain in quality, the consumption of fuel and flux being likely to be as often below as above the requirements of the case. This has become the more necessary now that the consumption of hematites and siliceous ores is on the increase. The yield of metal from such ores varies exceedingly, being in some cases less than one-eighth of that in others. And although the ore containing the greater per-centage of metal is always more or less easily distinguishable by its heaviness, no test short of actual assay should be relied on. The chief consideration with an iron-master in forming an opinion of an ore is richness in metal, but an ore may be metallurgically poor, and yet more valuable than a richer one. If it contains lime in considerable quantities, it may be both used as an ore and the excess of lime made to act as a flux for other ores. Or, if it contains a large per-centage of carbonaceous matter, though poor in metal, the cost of smelting it may be so low, through the reduction in the quantity of fuel and flux consumed, that metal is manufactured from it at a cheaper rate than from richer ores. Indeed, with our present knowledge of the blast-furnace, an ore that has in combination a large proportion of silica, cannot successfully compete in low cost of manufacture with those having clay or lime as their gangue. The real value, however, of any ore at a given spot can be determined only by an accurate analysis, and comparing the results with those obtained from other ores.

To produce pig-metal of the best quality a single variety of ore is used. The production of good metal with a mixed burden is difficult and uncertain. Numerous circumstances concur to render it so. The shape of the furnace may be well adapted for one description of ore, but not for another. The proportions of fuel, flux, and blast may also suit one and be altogether unsuitable for the other. Consequently, the best pig-metal is smelted from a single variety of ore, to which has been added proper proportions of fuel and flux.

The qualities of the metal which the respective classes of ironstone and iron ores yield differ greatly, and these differences may be traced in the manufactured bars.

The superiority of the metal produced from one stone or ore over another partially arises from the greater or less fusibility of the combined earths. The melting temperature in all cases considerably influences the quality of the metal produced, but its strength and other valuable properties are also materially affected by the presence of minute quantities of various earthy and other impurities. When the foreign matter present consists of several different minerals, the quality of the pig-iron is not so low as it would be, if the same amount of impurity being present, its composition were less varied; while a similar quantity of a single earth would often so deteriorate the metal as to render it comparatively valueless for all purposes requiring strength and ductility.

We have stated that the quality of pure iron is the same in all ores. This is obviously the case, since otherwise iron, instead of being a simple metal, must be a compound body, which we have no reason at present to suppose. The iron of commerce, however, is a compound. Pig-iron consists of iron combined with carbon, calcium, silicon, and aluminium, in varying proportions, besides other substances in more minute quantities. Bar-iron and the various productions manufactured therefrom also contains carbon, silicon, and other substances. Absolutely pure iron is a chemical curiosity, and cannot be manufactured in large quantities in the present state of metallurgical science.

After what has been already advanced we need hardly observe that the terms good or bad iron apply only to the metal in its manufactured state, as variously affected by the impurities combined with it, and in this sense alone we employ them, always intending, unless it be otherwise specified, the pig and bar-iron of commerce.

The metal smelted from ironstones of the argillaceous class is the best this country produces. The earthy part of these ores being composed chiefly of alumina and lime, with an inferior proportion of silica, the stone is of an open porous nature after calcination, and offers an extended surface for the action of the carbon of the fuel both in a gaseous and solid state. The earthy matrix, combining with the flux, forms a fluid cinder, from which the metallic iron readily separates in a comparatively pure state. From this metal malleable iron, possessing great strength and ductility, may be manufactured, containing a minimum per-centage of earthy matters.

The carbonaceous ironstone of the coal formation has, in combination with the metal, carbon, alumina, silica, lime, and occasionally small quantities of magnesia, sulphur, and manganese. By calcination the sulphur is expelled and the carbonaceous matter partially consumed. The remaining earths combine with the limestone flux and form a cinder, which is fluid at a lower temperature than that from argillaceous ironstone. From this cinder the metallic iron separates by its superior gravity, but from the smaller quantity of cinder produced, and the lower temperature at which it melts, the separation of the metal is not so perfect as with the generality of argillaceous ironstones. In consequence of the carbonaceous matter contained in the stone, and the excessive quantity of fuel used in proportion to the fluid products obtained, the metal is combined with a large per-centage of carbon and minor quantities of aluminium, silicon, and manganese. It is inferior in point of strength and hardness, but melts at a lower temperature, and is preferred to iron smelted from argillaceous stone where fusibility and softness are desired. From the comparatively low temperature at which this metal melts, its conversion into malleable iron is attended with greater waste, and the finished bar is altogether inferior to that from argillaceous ore.

Ironstones of the calcareous class contain lime as their chief earthy mixture, alumina and silica in smaller proportions. Lime is sometimes present in sufficient quantity to smelt the ore without the addition of flux, and in some cases is in excess. When this occurs the complement of clay is made up by the addition of burnt argillaceous shale. In consequence of the large quantity of lime, in comparison with the other earthy matters, carried by these ores, the cinders produced are thin and exceedingly fluid. The metal readily separates from this thin cinder, falling to the bottom, but retains in combination a small per-centage of cinder. This being composed chiefly of lime, the pig-metal produced consists of iron with calcium and minute portions of carbon, aluminium, and silicon. This metal is inferior in strength and hardness to that from argillaceous ironstone. If manufactured into malleable iron bars it possesses great strength and ductility when cold, but is brittle at a red heat. This red-short property is eminently characteristic of metal smelted from calcareous ironstone, and constitutes a defect for which no remedy has hitherto been discovered.

The class of ironstones termed siliceous, from their containing a very large per-centage of silica, with less quantities of alumina and lime, are not extensively used in the manufacture of iron. From the large proportion of silica in combination they require a greater quantity of lime for fluxing; and the excess of silica also renders the cinder infusible at the temperature at which other ores are ordinarily smelted. A higher temperature has, therefore, to be maintained, rendering necessary an increased consumption of fuel. In this case the quantity of cinder is great, but of too thick a consistence for a perfect separation of the metal, which consequently retains a considerable portion of slag. The pig-iron will be composed of iron, combined chiefly with silicon, aluminium, calcium, &c., being present in minute quantities. It is inferior in strength, and melts at a higher temperature than either of the foregoing descriptions of metal. On account of this last quality its conversion into malleable iron is attended with greater expense in fuel and labour, and the finished bar is hard and brittle. All iron manufactured from siliceous ores is cold-short, and not unfrequently red-short also. In fine, the general quality of the metal from siliceous ores is greatly inferior to that from any other class, and no improvement in its quality has yet been effected in the course of its manufacture into bars.

From the great variation in the qualities of the metal produced from the different classes of ironstones, we may safely conclude that the quality of pig-iron is affected chiefly by the nature of the earthy components of the stone. Where a particular matrix predominates in the ore the quality of the iron will be more or less affected thereby. Thus we observe in Scotch iron, smelted from the carbonaceous ironstone, that an excess of carbon is followed by the production of a very grey metal, greatly deficient in strength and hardness. The siliceous ores are the most difficult to manage. The silicon, combined with the metal, is infusible at ordinary temperatures, and during the process of manufacture in the forge and mill, it is incorporated in the bar, to the manifest injury and deterioration of the metal for commercial purposes.

Iron ores having alumina, lime, and carbon in nearly equal portions, but a smaller quantity of silica, would smelt with the greatest facility, and produce metal of good quality. In the manufacture also of malleable iron this equality of the earthy constituents would be attended with the best results; for since the red and cold-short characteristics in bar-iron are mainly owing to an excess of one or other of these earths, their presence in nearly equal proportions would conduce to the production of metal free from either defect.

This property of the calcareous and siliceous ironstones of producing iron deteriorated by the presence of an excess of calcium in one case and silicon in the other, is an effectual barrier to their being worked alone when the resulting metal is intended for conversion into malleable iron; and even for castings (except for such as are intended either for ornament or dead weight) these metals do not possess the requisite strength, and are unsuitable for machinery subject to vibration and working under great strain. The defects in metals produced from these ores are now well understood, and the smelter, whenever he has recourse to them, combines them with an equal or superior weight of argillaceous ores in order to produce metal suitable for the forge. But the defects incident to each variety of ore will invariably appear more or less strongly in the finished bar. If a siliceous ore has been used the metal will be hard and cold-short in proportion to the quantity of such ore used. If calcareous ores are employed, the hot-short tendency will prevail in a similar ratio. By mixing all these—argillaceous, calcareous, and siliceous—the resulting metal will exhibit in the manufactured bar the defects incidental to an excess of the predominating matrix in the mixture.

The addition of either of these ores to the argillaceous ironstones results in the production of a metal inferior to that from the clay ironstone. Mixing an inferior with a superior metal cannot result in the production of a metal superior to either. Yet we frequently observe these ores used for improving the argillaceous ores of the coal formation. That the use of rich ores of these classes results in an increased make of iron from the same sized furnace we readily admit, but as to the improvement in quality we are sceptical, never having witnessed such a result in practice.

In South Wales the argillaceous ironstones are invariably selected for the production of superior iron. But great difference exists in the quality of these ironstones, even when extracted from the same mine, while some produce, when smelted alone, iron of the finest quality, equal, indeed, to any manufactured in this country, the metal from others is of a coarse, inferior description. Having ascertained from observation and experiment the great superiority of certain seams, the Welsh ironmaster selects these for the production of pigs for foundry purposes, and for the manufacture of cable bolts and other wrought bars requiring metal of the first quality.

BURDEN OF FURNACE.

The proportion of materials for the production of No. 1 foundry iron in Wales will range from 45 to 55 cwts. of calcined argillaceous ironstone, 40 to 50 cwts. of coal as fuel, and 15 to 20 cwts. of limestone for flux. The average yield may be taken at 48 cwts. calcined ironstone, 45 cwts. of coal, and 17 cwts. of limestone to the ton of pig-metal produced. Estimated upon the raw stone, the consumption of ironstone will be about 65 cwts. With these proportions dark grey metal should be obtained at each casting, and if a lower quality is produced it indicates a deranged condition of the furnace.

In the anthracite district of South Wales dark grey pig-iron is manufactured with a yield of materials averaging 50 cwts. of calcined ironstone, 40 cwts. of anthracite coal, and 18 cwts. of limestone to the ton of pig-metal. If estimated upon the raw stone the consumption of ironstone will be 70 cwts.

The yield of materials at the Staffordshire furnaces is probably greater than at the Welsh works. The average will probably be near 48 cwts. of calcined mine, 50 cwts. of coal, and 18 cwts. of limestone to the ton of pig-iron produced.

At the Scotch blast furnaces, working entirely on carbonaceous ironstone, the consumption of materials is lower than in any other district in this country. The yield of calcined ironstone will range from 32 to 45 cwts., coal 35 to 45 cwts., and limestone 4 to 6 cwts. to the ton of pig-iron. The average yield may be taken at 35 cwts. of calcined ironstone, 38 cwts. of coal, and 5 cwts. of limestone. Estimated on the raw stone the consumption of ironstone will be about 70 cwts.

The make of the Dowlais furnace, on the yield of 48 cwts., will average 90 tons weekly; consumption of blast at a pressure of 3 lbs. to the square inch, 6540 cubic feet per minute; cubic capacity of furnace, 275 yards. Materials consumed per week: coal, 202 tons 10 cwts.; calcined ironstone, 216 tons; limestone, 76 tons 10 cwts.; atmospheric air, 65,914,800 cubic feet, or, at the ordinary temperature, 2215 tons.

The make of a Staffordshire furnace of 162 cubic yards capacity on the abovementioned yield of materials will average about 65 tons weekly. Consumption of blast at a pressure of 2¼ lbs. to the square inch, 4100 cubic feet per minute. Materials consumed per week: Calcined ironstone, 156 tons; coal, 162 tons (in the form of coke); limestone, 58 tons 10 cwts.; atmospheric air, at an ordinary density and temperature, 41,328,000 cubic feet, weighing 1388 tons.

The average weekly make of an anthracite furnace, equal in capacity to 112 cubic yards, is 50 tons. Consumption of blast at a pressure of 4 lbs. to the square inch, 4000 cubic feet per minute. Materials consumed per week: Calcined ironstone, 125 tons; anthracite coal, 100 tons; limestone, 45 tons; atmospheric air, at its ordinary density and temperature, 40,320,000 cubic feet, weighing 1,355 tons.

The capacity of the Scotch furnace represented in Pl. X., Fig. 64, is 167 cubic yards. Average weekly make with carbonaceous ironstone, 140 tons. Consumption of blast, 3120 cubic feet per minute, under a pressure of 2½ lbs. to the square inch. Materials consumed per week: Calcined carbonaceous ironstone, 245 tons; coal, 266 tons; limestone, 35 tons; atmospheric air at common density and temperature, 31,169,600 cubic feet, weighing 1047 tons.

From the foregoing figures we ascertain that the Dowlais furnace on foundry iron consumes of solid materials weekly, 485 tons; the Staffordshire furnace, 322 tons; the anthracite furnace, 270 tons; and the Scotch furnace, 546 tons. The space occupied by these materials will be nearly as follows: Dowlais, 731 cubic yards; Staffordshire, 603; anthracite, 400 yards; Scotch, 802 yards.

PROPORTION OF MATERIALS TO BLAST, ETC.

With the foregoing data for our guidance, the accuracy of which may be relied on, we will examine the more prominent features of the operations of the blast furnace in these districts. The anthracite and Scotch furnaces employ heated air, but this circumstance will not materially affect our inquiries, which will relate to the ratio which the size of the furnace bears—1stly, to the quantity of materials smelted; 2ndly, to the quantity of pig-metal produced; 3rdly, to the production of cinder and metal; 4thly, to the volume of blast; 5thly, to the ratio which the volume of blast bears to the metal and cinder produced; 6thly, to the ratio which the carbon of the fuel bears to the weight of metal produced; 7thly, to the relation the carbon bears to the metal and cinder produced; 8thly, to the velocity and time occupied by the descending column of materials.

1. The Dowlais furnace has a capacity of 275 cubic yards, and smelts 485 tons, or 1¾ tons for each cubic yard; the Staffordshire furnace, of 162 cubic yards, smelts 322 tons, or 2 tons nearly to the cubic yard; the anthracite furnace, of 112 cubic yards, 270 tons, or 2¼ tons to the cubic yard; the Scotch furnace, of 167 cubic yards, smelts 546 tons, or 3¼ tons to each cubic yard. Hence the smelting powers of the respective furnaces per yard capacity range from 1¾ to 3¼ tons of ore, fuel, and flux per week.

2. The Dowlais furnace makes 90 tons, or 6½ cwts. of metal per cubic yard of capacity; the Staffordshire 65 tons of metal, or 8 cwts. nearly per cubic yard; the anthracite furnace makes 50 tons, or 9 cwts. to each cubic yard; and the Scotch furnace 140 tons, or 17 cwts. nearly to each yard capacity: the highest being 17 cwts., and the lowest 6½ cwts. for each cubic yard of capacity. This shows that with rich carbonaceous ironstone nearly three times the quantity of grey metal can be produced from a given capacity of furnace as can be done with lean argillaceous ironstones.

3. The weight of the iron and cinder produced will be nearly equal to the weight of the calcined ironstone, the flux minus its carbonic acid, and the earthy matter or ashes of the fuel. This mode of estimating the weight of metal and cinder produced, we have ascertained experimentally, gives within 3 or 4 per cent. of the actual weight; we shall therefore adopt it in estimating the weight of the products from the other furnaces. The produce of cinder and metal at the Dowlais furnace amounts to 268 tons per week, equal to 1 ton nearly for

each yard capacity of furnace; of the Staffordshire furnace, 198 tons per week, equal to 1 ton 4 cwts. per yard capacity; of the Anthracite furnace, 154 tons, equal to 1 ton 7 cwts. per yard capacity; of the Scotch furnace, 283 tons, or 1 ton 14 cwts. for each yard capacity The variation in the produce of cinder and iron per cubic yard capacity, 1 ton to 1 ton 14 cwts., is not so great as in the consumption of materials and make of pig-iron.

4. Into the Dowlais furnace is blown 6540 cubic feet of atmospheric air per minute, or 24 feet for each yard capacity; into the Staffordshire furnace, 4100 feet per minute, or 25 cubic feet per yard; into the Anthracite furnace, 4000 cubic feet, equal to 36 cubic feet nearly for each cubic yard; into the Scotch furnace, 3120 cubic feet per minute, equal to 19 cubic feet per cubic yard of capacity.

5. For each ton of metal and cinders flowing from the Dowlais furnace, 245,940 cubic feet of atmospheric air is blown into it; at the Staffordshire furnace the consumption is 208,630 cubic feet to the ton of iron and cinder; at the Anthracite furnace it is 248,800 cubic feet; and at the Scotch furnace, 110,140 cubic feet for each ton of cinder and iron obtained.

Estimated on the pig iron produced, the consumption of blast per ton will be as follows: Dowlais furnace, 732,386 cubic feet, weighing 25 tons; Staffordshire furnace, 635,800 cubic feet, weighing 22 tons nearly; Anthracite furnace, 806,400 cubic feet, weighing 27 tons; and Scotch furnace, 222,600, cubic feet, weighing 8 tons.

6. By the analyses given in a preceding chapter, we ascertain that the carbon contained in the Dowlais coal is equal to 87 per cent. of its weight. At this rate 2 tons 5 cwts. of coal, the quantity consumed per ton of pig-iron made, will contain 4384 lbs. of carbon, or 2 lbs. nearly for each pound of metal produced. Calculating on the reduced quantity of carbon in the Staffordshire coals, the consumption of carbon in that furnace is equal to 4480 lbs., or 2 lbs. to each pound of metal obtained; in the Anthracite furnace the yield of carbon is 4076 lbs., or 1¾ lbs. to the pound of metal; in the Scotch furnace the yield of carbon will be 3234 lbs., or 1¼ lbs. to each pound of metal obtained.

7. If the quantity of carbon is estimated on the cinder and metal, the total quantity of solid rendered fluid, the yield will appear more uniform at the several furnaces. At the Dowlais furnace for each ton of fluid material obtained 1472 lbs. of carbon will have been consumed; at the Staffordshire furnace, 1454 lbs.; at the Anthracite furnace, 1309 lbs.; and at the Scotch furnace, 1600 lbs.

8. Employing the bulk of materials and capacity of furnace as previously given, we find that the solid materials are in the Dowlais furnace 63 hours from the time of their being filled to their reduction at the tuyere; in the Staffordshire furnace, 45 hours; in the Anthracite furnace, 47 hours; and in the Scotch furnace, 35 hours.

In the Dowlais furnace the velocity of the descending materials is nearly as follows: Through the throat 18 inches per hour, above the boshes 5¼ inches, and in the hearth 28 inches per hour. In the Staffordshire furnaces these velocities are respectively 36 inches, 7¼ inches, and 48 inches per hour; in the Anthracite furnace they are 15 inches, 5 inches, and 31 inches per hour; and in the Scotch furnace they are 31 inches, 10 inches, and 41 inches per hour.

In the production of white pig-iron for forge purposes, a mixture of calcareous or siliceous ores and forge, or forge and finery cinder together, is often employed. By using these ores and cinders the make of the furnace is increased, and the yield of fuel and flux diminished. The proportion in which they are used at the Dowlais works is varied according to the quality of bar metal desired; but under ordinary circumstances the yield of the furnace in common forge iron may be stated as follows :—Calcined argillaceous ironstone 28 cwts., calcareous and siliceous ore 10 cwts., cinder (forge generally, but sometimes forge and finery mixed) 10 cwts., coal 38 cwts., limestone 14 cwts. With these materials the furnaces generally average 110 tons of pig-iron weekly.

For the production of a more inferior forge iron, used only where the quality is not an object, the furnaces have been burdened with calcareous and siliceous ores and refinery cinders only. The yield under such burden is usually 16 cwts. of ores, 25 cwts. of cinders, 16 cwts. of limestone, and 36 cwts. of coal. The make, when thus burdened, will average 120 tons a week.*

For the production of cinder-iron, to be used for ballast or other similar purposes, the furnace is burdened with finery cinders and burnt argillaceous shale. The yield is nearly 36 cwts. of cinders, 14 cwts. of shale, 14 cwts. of limestone, and 38 cwts. of coal to the ton of iron produced. On ballast, or "kentledge" metal, the make of the furnace will probably average 110 tons a week.

The capacity of the furnace used for cinder-iron is the same as that for grey iron, and the quantity of blast is also nearly the same in the three cinder-iron furnaces. These, for facility of reference, we will call Nos. 1, 2, and 3, cinder-iron furnaces, and will proceed to reduce the quantities of materials and the ratio which they bear to the metal made, &c., as in the case of the grey-iron furnace.

At the same yield and make as in the No. 1 cinder-iron furnace, the weekly consumption of calcined ironstone will be 154 tons, calcareous and siliceous ores 55 tons, cinders 55 tons, coal 209 tons, limestone 77 tons. At the No. 2 cinder-iron furnace the consumption will be 96 tons of ores, 150 tons of cinders, 96 tons of limestone, and 216 tons of coal. At the No. 3 cinder-iron furnace the consumption of cinders will be 198 tons, coal 209 tons, shale 77 tons, and limestone 77 tons.

These quantities give a weekly consumption of solid materials weighing at No. 1 furnace 550 tons, at No 2 furnace 558 tons, and No. 3 furnace 561 tons. If measured their bulk will be equal to 745 cubic yards for No. 1 furnace, 686 cubic yards for No. 2 furnace, and 699 cubic yards for No. 3 furnace.

On comparing these quantities with those of the foundry iron furnace of the same works, previously described, we arrive at some important facts, viz.—

---

* For the week ending June 11, 1843, No. 3 and 11 furnaces produced 319 tons 10½ cwts. of cinder iron. The yield of materials being, refinery cinders 2½ cwts. 3 qrs. 4 lbs.; red ore, Lancashire and Denn Forest, 16 cwts. 0 qrs. 15 lbs.; limestone, 16 cwts. 3 qrs. 29 lbs.; coal, 36 cwts. 0 qrs. 4 lbs. Each of these furnaces is of 275 yards' capacity; but during this experiment the volume of blast was not more than sufficient for a furnace of 140 yards'. With this burden and a volume of blast proportioned to their capacity, these furnaces would have made over 300 tons each in the week.

MANUFACTURE OF IRON.

The grey-iron furnace smelts 1¼ tons of materials weekly for each cubic yard of capacity, the No. 1 cinder-iron furnace 2 tons, the No. 2 cinder-iron furnace 2 tons, and the No. 3 cinder-iron furnace 2 tons.

The grey-iron furnace makes 6½ cwts. of metal weekly for each cubic yard capacity, the No. 1 cinder-iron furnace 8 cwts., the No. 2 ditto 8⅜ cwts., and the No. 3 ditto 8 cwts.

The grey-iron furnace makes 268 tons of cinder and iron weekly, equal to 1 ton nearly for each cubic yard capacity, the No. 1 furnace makes 310 tons, or 1 ton 3 cwts. per yard, the No. 2 furnace 314 tons, equal to 1 ton 3 cwts., and the No. 3 furnace 333 tons, equal to 1 ton 4 cwts. per yard capacity.

For each ton of metal and cinder from the grey-iron furnace 245,940 cubic feet of air is consumed. In No. 1 furnace the consumption is 212,900, in No. 2 furnace 210,000, and in No. 3 furnace it is 199,000 cubic feet nearly.

The weight of the blast consumed for each ton of iron made from the grey-iron furnace is 25 tons, No. 1 furnace 20 tons, No. 2 furnace 18 tons, and No. 3 furnace 20 tons nearly.

The consumption of carbon in the grey-iron furnace amounts to 4384 lbs. per ton, or nearly 2 lbs. for each pound of metal. With the No. 1 cinder-iron furnace it is 3659 lbs., or 1¼ lbs. per pound of metal; in No. 2 cinder-iron furnace 3466 lbs., equal to 1½ lbs. per pound of metal, and in No. 3 furnace 3659 lbs., or full 1½ lbs. per pound of metal.

On the total quantity of cinder and iron produced the yield of carbon is 1472 lbs. per ton at grey pig-iron furnace, 1313 lbs. at No. 1 cinder-iron furnace, 1374 lbs. at No. 2 furnace, and 1230 lbs. at No. 3 furnace.

The iron-making materials are changed in the grey-iron furnace every 63 hours; in the No. 1 cinder-iron furnace, every 62 hours; in the No. 2 cinder-iron furnace, every 67 hours; and in the No. 3 cinder-iron furnace, every 65 hours.

From the diversity of opinion which exists respecting the most proper dimensions and form for the interior of blast furnaces, it is not surprising that the yield of fluid materials from some furnaces, should be greater for a given capacity than that from others working under similar conditions of ore, fuel, &c. There is an opinion current amongst ironmasters that the power of the furnace to smelt is in proportion to its capacity, and that large furnaces are more economical in fuel and other materials than small ones. The economy of fuel and materials we shall consider subsequently; but we may here state that the yield of metal from furnaces similarly burdened does not depend only upon their capacity.

We have stated that the Dowlais grey-iron furnace has a capacity of 275 yards, and that the average weekly make is 90 tons, or 6½ cwts. for each cubic yard capacity. With similar ironstones the Staffordshire and Anthracite furnaces, of 162 and 112 yards capacity, smelt 8 and 9 cwts. to each yard, being an increase of 23 and 38 per cent. over that obtained at Dowlais. Whence is this inferiority of the Dowlais furnace? Looking at the facts we have produced relative to each furnace, it is not difficult to account for this disparity.

The conversion of the iron-making materials into grey pig-iron is an operation involving a certain time. In the laboratory, it is true, such iron is produced in two hours;

but this is accomplished by crushing the stone to an impalpable powder, and by the employment of an excessive quantity of carbon for the results obtained. The materials remain in the Dowlais furnace, 63; in the Staffordshire, 45; and in the Anthracite furnace, 47 hours. Now, there is no necessity for the materials to be in the Dowlais furnace 63 hours before smelting: for if 45 and 47 hours are respectively sufficient for completing the deoxydation and cementation in small furnaces, a similar period will be amply sufficient for larger furnaces. If the materials were to pass through the Dowlais furnace in 47 hours, the make in pig-metal would be 120 tons weekly, or $8\frac{3}{4}$ cwts. per cubic yard capacity. But the materials can descend no faster than they are consumed in the hearth. The rate at which the fuel is consumed and the iron-making materials melted, will depend on the volume and pressure of blast employed. Without the aid of the blast no reduction could take place. With a small soft blast the materials will descend slowly, and the make of metal will be small. Increase the quantity and pressure of the blast, and the materials descend faster, and the make is increased. But there is a limit to this increase of volume, and, we believe, that as yet blast of a greater pressure than 8 lbs. to the square inch has not been applied to smelting. The maximum volume and pressure should be regulated by the size of the furnace qualities of the ore, fuel, and flux, and finally, by the degree of carburization desired in the resulting metal. Where the other conditions are similar, the volume of blast should be in proportion to the cubic capacity of the furnace.

The Dowlais grey-iron furnace consumes 2330 tons, or estimated on a make of 90 tons of pig-iron weekly, 25 tons of atmospheric air per ton of metal made; the Staffordshire furnace, 22 tons; and the Anthracite furnace 27 tons—the average of the three furnaces being a fraction under 25 tons. Hence the consumption of atmospheric air at the Dowlais furnace is merely the quantity due to the make of pig-iron. To produce, then, 120 tons of pig-iron weekly, instead of 90 tons, as at present, this furnace should have a corresponding increase in the volume of blast. Instead of 6540 cubic feet per minute, there should be 8720. That it is at present working under a column of blast too small and weak we may infer from the fact that a furnace at the same works averages, when on grey iron, 70 tons weekly, though of no more than 160 cubic yards capacity. This is at the rate of $8\frac{3}{4}$ cwts. nearly per cubic yard. In its consumption of blast this small furnace averages from 26 to 28 tons to the ton of metal obtained; of materials the yield is nearly the same as in the large furnace.

We have thus far considered furnaces working under a burden of clean argillaceous ironstone, producing grey pig-iron; but a similar deficiency of blast exists at the large furnaces smelting ores and cinder for the production of forge iron, and as the number of furnaces on this description of iron is five or six times the number on grey iron, the loss of smelting power at some works from this cause must be great indeed.

The average make of the large furnaces on a mixture composed of calcined ironstone, ore, cinders, fuel, and flux, as previously described, is 110 tons a week, or 8 cwts. per yard capacity, with a blast of 6540 cubic feet per minute. At the Dowlais works there are two furnaces with a capacity of 139 yards each, or just one-half of the large ones, but having a blast of nearly the same volume and density. They are generally kept on common forge iron, and, when the burden is similar, these small furnaces produce nearly the same quantity of metal as the large furnaces of double their capacity; the production being as high as 15¼ cwts. for each yard capacity.* This high produce is obtained solely by the increased blast, which amounts to 47 cubic feet per minute per yard capacity of furnace, against 24 feet per yard in the large furnace. Were the large furnaces blown with an equal volume of air, at the requisite density, for each yard of their capacity, their produce of pig-metal would be augmented in a similar ratio; and instead of 110 or 115 tons of forge pigs weekly, the make would be from 220 to 230 tons of metal of equal quality.

This deficiency of blast is a very common feature with the majority of large furnaces. It has very probably resulted from ironmasters not sufficiently considering that the cubic capacity of furnaces of the same height is nearly as the square of their largest diameter. Were the dimensions of the hearth and throat determined by any established rule, the exact capacity of a furnace might easily be ascertained, if the diameter were known: but since these dimensions vary in practice, we may state that a furnace, 13 feet 3 inches diameter at the boshes, and 44 feet high in the interior, will contain about 140 cubic yards; and a furnace 18 feet diameter, and of the same height, 280 cubic yards. Hence an increase from 13 feet 3 inches to 18 feet in the diameter doubles the capacity of the interior. Furnaces built prior to the last 25 years were 13 to 14 feet diameter; since then they have been built as large as 18 feet and 18 feet 6 inches. With this increase of size there should have been an increase in the volume of blast, if an augmentation of the make, in ratio with the capacity, was contemplated; but if a greater volume was employed, it is certain that it was not in proportion to the increased capacity.

The Plymouth new furnaces are of nearly the same capacity as the Dowlais, and work under very similar conditions. The volume of blast thrown in is nearly the same, and when smelting argillaceous ironstone for foundry or other purposes, the make of pig-iron is as low in proportion to their capacity as at the Dowlais furnaces. We could mention other furnaces in the South Wales and other districts, which, from a similar deficiency of blast, are not producing metal in proportion to their capacity; but it is needless to multiply instances.

The advantage which would be obtained by working blast-furnaces to their maximum power of smelting, in some establishments, would be very considerable. With a full blast the make of many grey-iron furnaces might be increased one-third, and the make of cinder iron furnaces doubled, without deteriorating the quality of the pig-metal. This increase would be equivalent to so much additional smelting power; but when greater power is not desired the employment of a full blast will cause a smaller number of furnaces to be sufficient, and will be attended with a corresponding economy in the working charges of the furnaces.

* The make of these two furnaces, No. 6 and 7, for the four weeks ending July 3, 1852, amounted in the aggregate to 875 tons 10 cwts. of cold-blast forge iron, equal to a weekly produce of 109 tons nearly from each furnace. During the same period six other furnaces—mostly new ones or recently repaired—averaging 275 cubic yards capacity each, produced 2700 tons of hot and cold blast forge iron, equal to a weekly make of 112½ tons per furnace. On going over a period of twenty-one years, we find that the yield of the small furnaces approaches within 4 or 5 tons of the larger.

SECTION VI.

PRODUCE AND QUALITY OF METAL.

The blast-furnaces employed for the reduction of iron ores vary considerably in their dimensions, and in the quantity of metal they are capable of producing. With furnaces working under similar conditions of ore, fuel, flux, and blast, the produce of metal will vary in nearly the same ratio as their cubic capacities. With furnaces of similar capacity and working on similar materials, but differing in the volumes of blast they receive, the produce will be in nearly the same ratio as the volume of blast. However, in the production of grey iron the power of the furnace is limited as regards quantity. Thus with similar solid materials the capacity of furnace and volume of blast principally determine the produce of metal of a given quality. It is essential to the economical manufacture of iron that the furnace should be worked to its maximum power. As this subject is one of considerable importance to the smelter, we will give particulars of the quantities of metal produced from different furnaces under varying circumstances of blast, ore, and fuel, and of the various proportions which the different materials bear to each other, to the resulting metal, and to the capacity of the apparatus.

The foundry iron furnace at the Dowlais works is of 275 cubic yards capacity, and is blown with a blast of 5390 cubic feet of air per minute. The materials charged at the top in addition to fuel, consist of calcined argillaceous ore, coal, and limestone. The yield, or consumption averages 48 cwts. of calcined ore, 50 cwts. of coal, and 17 cwts. of broken limestone for every 20 cwts. of crude iron obtained. The weekly make of iron is occasionally over 130 tons, but we may assume this as sufficiently high for our calculations. The produce of cinder weekly amounts to nearly 250 tons.

The weekly consumption of solid material at top will be as follows: Calcined ore 312 tons, coal 325 tons, limestone 110 tons 10 cwts.—Total, 747 tons 10 cwts. By measurement, these materials in a mass would occupy 1066 cubic yards.

The air delivered by the tuyeres weekly weighs 1695 tons and measures 50,550,400 cubic feet, or 1,872,223 cubic yards.

From these quantities we deduce the following ratios which are the extreme proportions when the iron is of a grey quality, and smelted from argillaceous ores:

The weekly consumption of solid materials at top is at the rate of 54 cwts. per cubic yard capacity.

The weekly produce of liquid matter from the hearth is nearly 28 cwts. per cubic yard capacity.

The produce of metal from the hearth is at the rate of 9.5 cwts. weekly for each yard capacity.

Each ton of coal charged into the furnace suffices for the production of 23.4 cwts. of liquid matter in the hearth.

Estimated on the carbon in the coal, the ton of iron is produced with a consumption of 43.5 cwts. of carbon, and the ton of liquid matter—iron and cinder—deposited in the hearth with a consumption of 17.1 cwts. of carbon.

The solid materials introduced into the furnace weekly measure, in their original form, 1166 cubic yards, the liquid matter obtained measures 172 cubic yards.

The solid materials charged at the top are in the furnace 40 hours before they are reduced to a liquid state.

The solid materials descend through the throat at the rate of 28 inches per hour, at the top of the boshes the descent is reduced to 7 inches per hour, but is accelerated at the hearth to 35 inches per hour.

The consumption of blast per minute is at the rate of 20 cubic feet of air to each yard capacity of furnace.

The ton of iron is produced with a consumption of 3,888,490 cubic feet of air.

The air decomposed in smelting one ton of iron weighs 13 tons.

The weight of the air introduced through the tuyere is to the weight of the solid materials introduced at the top as 16 to 7.

The materials, solid and gaseous, charged into the furnace for each ton of iron smelted, weigh 18.8 tons.

The weekly consumption of solid and gaseous materials weigh altogether 2442 tons, of which 380 tons are obtained in a liquid form from the hearth, the remaining 2062 tons escape in the gaseous form at the top. Hence for each ton of liquid matter obtained 129 cwts. of gases are evolved from the furnace.

The atmospheric air introduced weekly measures 1,872,223 cubic yards; the gases evolved from the tunnel-head measure 7,488,000 cubic yards.

The ascending gases traverse the furnace at its largest diameter at the rate of 415 feet per minute, increased at the throat to 1660 feet.

The time which elapses from the admission of the atmospheric air at the tuyere until its escape at the tunnel-head in combination with the gaseous products of combustion is nearly 7 seconds.

For the production of white-iron for the forge, in furnaces of the same capacity as the foregoing, a larger volume of blast is employed with a different burden of materials. The blast averages 7370 cubic feet per minute. The consumption of materials to a ton of crude iron averages 28 cwts. of calcined argillaceous ore, 10 cwts. hematite, 10 cwts. of forge and finery cinders, 42 cwts. of coal, and 14 cwts. of limestone. With these materials the weekly produce of liquid matter amounts to 170 tons of crude iron and 310 tons of cinders.

Consumption of solid materials 884 tons, measuring 1103 cubic yards; and of air 2318 tons, measuring 68,983,200 cubic feet. Hence the total weekly consumption amounts to 3202 tons, which is resolved during the process into 480 tons of liquid and 2722 tons of gaseous matter.

Under these circumstances the consumption of solid materials is increased to 64 cwts. per yard capacity; but the volume is not sensibly greater, consequently they are in the furnace nearly the same time as in the case of grey iron.

The liquid and gaseous products bear nearly the same relation to each other as in the production of grey-iron.

But the ton of crude iron is produced with 36.5 cwts. of carbon, and the ton of liquid matter with 13 cwts. of carbon.

In consequence of the larger volume of blast and comparatively dense manner in which the materials lie in the furnace, the gaseous column escapes with the increased velocity of 2900 feet per minute; hence the time occupied by the ascending gases in traversing the height of the furnace is reduced to 4 seconds.

For the production of an inferior iron for the forge, the burden is composed of the following materials: Hematite 16 cwts., refinery cinders 25 cwts., coal 36 cwts., and limestone 16 cwts. to the ton of crude iron. The capacity of furnace and volume of blast are the same as in the last instance. From this furnace a weekly produce of 190 tons has been attained accompanied by the production of 295 tons of cinder. The weekly consumption of solid materials amounts to 883 tons, measuring 934 yards; of air 2318 tons.—Total, 3201 tons, which is resolved into 485 tons of liquid and 2716 of gaseous matter.

On the production of this cinder-iron then, the consumption of solid material is at the rate of 64 cwts. per yard capacity, but from their greater density the time during which they are passing through the furnace is increased to 46 hours.

The ton of iron is produced with a consumption of 31.3 cwts. of carbon, and the ton of liquid matter with a consumption of 12 cwts.

The materials used being so much more dense, the ascending column of gases traverses the height of the furnace in 3.5 seconds.

The Hirwain foundry iron furnace measures 200 cubic yards in capacity nearly, and is blown with 2541 cubic feet of air per minute. Yield of materials: Calcined ore 46 cwts., coke 34 cwts., limestone 16 cwts., to a ton of crude iron. Produce weekly, 90 tons of crude iron and 150 tons of cinder.

The solid materials introduced weekly weigh 432 tons, and measure 732 cubic yards, and the air weighs 800 tons and measures 23,783,000 cubic feet.

Consumption of solid material per yard capacity 43 cwts.

Produce of crude iron per yard capacity 9 cwts., of liquid matter 24 cwts.

The ton of iron is produced with a consumption of 32 cwts. of carbon, and the ton of liquid matter with 12 cwts.

The solid materials composing the descending column are in the furnace 43 hours nearly.

In consequence of the comparatively small volume of air used and the porosity of the coke, the ascending column is 12 seconds passing through the furnace.

The employment of a greater volume of blast would enable the quantity of iron yielded by the Dowlais and Hirwain foundry furnaces to be largely increased; but unless a larger proportion of carbon were at the same time used, the quality of the iron would change from grey to white. The grey quality along with the increased production may be maintained by the employment of a greater quantity of carbon, and conversely if the volume of blast be diminished, grey iron may be produced with a lower proportion of carbon, but in less quantity.

Furnaces smelting carbonaceous ores are not subject to the same limits in point of production as others. From the large quantity of carbon in combination with the metal, a greater make of iron may be obtained from the same capacity of furnace. The volume of blast moreover is much smaller, and the quantity of cinder scarcely exceeds in weight that of the crude iron.

The furnaces at the Dandyvan works average 167 cubic yards capacity. Blast 3040 cubic feet per minute. Yield of materials: Calcined carbonaceous ore 33 cwts., coal 40 cwts., and limestone 5 cwts. to the ton of crude iron. On these materials the furnaces average 150 tons of iron and 140 tons of cinders weekly. The consumption of solid materials is 584 tons 10 cwts., and measures 785 cubic yards. The blast weighs 950 tons, and measures 28,454,000 cubic feet. Hence, the consumption of materials amounts to 1434 tons, which is resolved into 290 tons liquid, and 1144 tons of gaseous matter. A ton of fluid products is thus accompanied with 78 cwts. of the aëriform against 129 cwts. with the argillaceous ore.

The weekly consumption of solid materials is at the rate of 70 cwts. per yard capacity of furnace.

The weekly produce of liquid matter from the hearth is 34 cwts., and the crude iron 18 cwts. per yard.

Each ton of coal charged into the furnace suffices for the production of 21 cwts. of liquid matter.

Estimated on the carbon, the ton of iron is produced with 30.4 cwts. of carbon, and the ton of liquid matter with 15.6 cwts.

The solid materials charged into the furnace at the top are in the furnace 33 hours.

The consumption of blast per minute is at the rate of 18 cubic feet per yard capacity.

The air consumed in smelting one ton of crude iron weighs 6.3 tons.

The gases escape through the throat with a velocity of 1500 feet per minute.

The gaseous column is 7.5 seconds in ascending from the tuyeres to the throat.

Iron smelted from carbonaceous ores with the fuel and blast described, contains a larger per-centage of carbon than is found in Welsh irons, as will be seen by referring to the analyses of crude irons. This constitutes the principal defect of the Scotch pig-iron, the excess of carbon rendering it excessively fluid, and incapable of being readily converted into malleable iron. On reviewing the proportion, the liquid matter obtained from the hearth bears to the weight of carbon consumed, we find that the Scotch furnace occupies a most anomalous position. Smelting the most fusible ore in use 15.6 cwts. of carbon are consumed for each ton of liquid matter produced. At the Hirwain foundry iron furnace smelting a less fusible ore the consumption is only 12 cwts. It is this excessive consumption of carbon, coupled with the comparatively slow ascent of the gaseous column, which lowers the quality and strength of the crude iron.

For the production of crude iron from carbonaceous ores, suitable for conversion into malleable iron of a superior quality, the proportion of carbon to liquid matter should be reduced above one half, and the velocity of the ascending gaseous column doubled. The metal would then contain less carbon, and might be the more readily converted into malleable iron.

The larger consumption of carbon necessary to produce grey iron with a volume of blast exceeding 20 feet per cubic yard capacity of furnace, is partly due to the more rapid descent of the materials not permitting a greater quantity of carbon to combine with the metal, but chiefly, however, we believe to the accelerated velocity with which the ascending column of gases pass through the furnace. In the Dowlais furnace the ascent occupies 7 seconds, in the Hirwain 13 seconds. In the latter the reducing gas in the ascending column is in contact with the materials nearly twice the length of time that it is in the former, and doubtless the lower yield of carbon per ton of liquid matter in the case of this furnace is mainly due to this circumstance; the degree of carburization being dependent much more on the velocity of ascent of the gases than in the quantity of solid carbon charged at top; otherwise we find it difficult to account for the superior reducing power of a given weight of carbon in the Hirwain furnace.

The proportions of carbon per ton of crude iron and per ton of liquid matter are almost identical in the Dowlais crude iron and the Hirwain foundry iron furnaces; but in the former, notwithstanding that the materials are in the furnace 3 hours longer, the quality of the iron is an inferior white, while in the latter it is fair ordinary grey. In the velocities with which the gases pass through the furnace there is a wide difference. They escape from the Dowlais furnace with a velocity of 2900 feet per minute, and traverse its height in 3.5 seconds; in the Hirwain furnace the escape is at the reduced rate of 788 feet, and the time of traversing the height of the furnace is increased to 12 seconds.

If the degree of carburization were entirely dependent on the quantity of vapour of carbon brought in contact with the metal, the Hirwain furnace should enjoy no superiority over the Dowlais, excepting that arising from the quality of the materials employed. The like quantites of gaseous carbon being evolved for each ton of crude iron produced. But if it be allowed that the velocity of the gaseous column affects the degree of carburization, the difference in the quality of the product of the two furnaces is immediately explained. When the important part the gaseous matter plays in the reduction of the ore is considered, the opinion that the velocity of ascent exercises a great influence on the quality of the metal is greatly strengthened. In the Dowlais furnace, the aëriform matters ascend at the rate of nearly 50 feet per second, and it is while in this rapid motion that the gases have to effect the deoxydation of the ore and carburization of the metal. The perfect combination of the oxygen of the ore with the gaseous carbon is certainly to some extent the work of time, and the great velocity of the ascending column in the Dowlais furnace cannot be so favourable as the reduced speed of that of the Hirwain furnace; and no doubt the difference in quality arises, to a great extent, from this cause.

When superior quality is not an object to the ironmaster, the make may be largely increased by augmenting the volume of blast. The weekly produce of inferior white-iron may be doubled, and a make of 300 tons be readily attained. These large makes, however, are not so economical in manufacture as more moderate quantities.

The quantity of ironstone or other material consumed in the manufacture of one ton of iron is spoken of amongst smelters as the yield of that material. When the consumption is small for the quantity of metal produced, the yield is considered good, but if large a contrary judgment is pronounced. This term, although not, strictly speaking, a correct one, is used in connexion with nearly all the operations of iron-works. In well-regulated establishments the expenditure of materials, labour, stores, &c., in every department per ton of metal made is recorded, and by inspecting the books the yield of each item may be ascertained for any given period. It may be necessary, however, to remark here, that in all other cases throughout this work the term yield is also used in its proper sense—namely, for the net produce of metal or other substance from a given quantity of material.

The consumption of argillaceous ironstone in the manufacture of dark grey-iron will generally be in an inverse ratio to the quantity of metal in the ore. If it contains 29 per cent. the consumption will be 4 tons to each ton of metal produced; if 38 per cent., 3 tons of stone will be required; but if it contains 46 per cent., the consumption will be reduced to 48 cwts. of ironstone per ton of iron. A few of the argillaceous ironstones yield 50 per cent.; when calcined with such, the consumption will average 44 cwts. per ton.

The whole of the metal contained in the stone is never obtained: a portion remains in the cinder even when the smelting has been conducted under the most favourable circumstances. The quantity of metal lost in this way will vary with the richness of the ore. With the leaner ironstones the loss will range from 12 to 14 per cent. of the quantity of iron in the ore; with richer stones it will range from 8 to 12 per cent.

The grey cinder from blast furnaces using mineral fuel usually contain from 4 to 7 per cent. of iron. Occasionally instances occur of a lower per-centage, but much more frequently the higher number is exceeded; so that if the furnace be producing a large proportion of cinder to iron, it is evident that the loss from this cause must be very considerable.

In smelting one ton of pig-iron from an ironstone containing 29 per cent. of metal, 4 tons of stone are consumed. This quantity contains 23.2 cwts. of metal, 20 cwts. of which are obtained as pig, and 3.2 cwts. remain in the cinder. With such an ironstone a large quantity of limestone will be required for fluxing, and the product of cinder will range from 60 to 70 cwts. per ton of pig-iron. Then if we estimate that the cinder contains no more than 5 per cent. of metal, the 3.2 cwts. will be fully accounted for. A loss of 3.2 cwts. on 23.2 cwts. is equal to 14 per cent. nearly.

With richer ironstones the loss of metal in the cinder becomes less; in smelting an ore containing 50 per cent. of iron the production of 1 ton of pig-metal requires the consumption of 44 cwts. of stone. This will contain 22 cwts. of metallic iron, showing 2 cwts. left in the cinder for every 20 cwts. produced.

The quantity of limestone required will not be so great as in the former case, in consequence of the smaller proportion of earthy matter present, and the cinder will not necessarily exceed 40 cwts. per ton of pig-iron.

But this proportion of cinder, at the same low estimate which we previously adopted, will contain 2 cwts. of metal, representing a loss of 9 per cent. in this instance against 14 per cent. in the last.

An ironstone may be so lean that the metal remaining in the cinder may equal in quantity that obtained in pigs. Such ironstones are not used when others containing a greater per-centage of metal can be obtained. But the obvious disadvantage attending on the use of lean ores, on account of the large proportion of metal carried away in the cinder, should induce smelters to consider well how far by a want of attention to this point the cost of manufacture is increased. In smelting a stone containing only 20 per cent. of metal, more than 6¼ tons must be used for each ton of pig-iron obtained, showing metal left in the cinder to the extent of 25 per cent.; whilst with one so low as 15 per cent. the consumption of ore will exceed 9 tons, and the loss of metal 35 per cent., or more than one-third of that existing in the ore will remain in the cinder.

The carbonaceous kind of ore probably produces a ton of pig-iron from a smaller quantity of stone than any other species. The average per-centage of metal in calcined Scotch carbonaceous ironstone is nearly 60 per cent.; the quantity consumed per ton of iron averages 35 cwts. The metal in this quantity of stone weighs 21 cwts., 1 cwt. only remaining in the cinder. This comparatively small loss, consequent upon the smallness of the quantity of cinder produced, places this ore in most favourable contrast with lean argillaceous ironstone. Instead of a loss of 10 to 14 per cent., as with this latter variety, the carbonaceous ironstone is smelted with a loss of only 5 per cent. of its metal. This great produce of metal from a given weight of stone is an important advantage to ironmasters who use carbonaceous ores, and has doubtless contributed in no small measure to the greatly extended use of this class of ironstones in the blast furnace of late years.

Calcareous ironstones also yield better than the argillaceous kinds, in consequence of the small quantity of cinder produced. Lime being already present in them in nearly sufficient proportion for fluxing the other earths, the quantity of cinder is necessarily limited. Besides which weight for weight the cinder usually contains rather less metal than the average of that from argillaceous ironstones.

The yield from siliceous ironstones, in proportion to the iron they contain, is inferior to that from either of the other varieties. On account of the infusible nature of the earthy constituents of the ore, a larger quantity of limestone is required for fluxing. This forms, with the siliceous earths, a cold sluggish cinder, from which the metal does not freely separate. The quantity of cinders is consequently large, and they contain from 6 to 7 per cent. of metal. In practice a siliceous ironstone yielding 45 per cent. of metal will not produce more than 40 per cent. of pig-iron, the cinder retaining the remainder.

The produce of pig-iron from the primary iron ores—the red and hydrated hematites—is lower in proportion to their richness than from argillaceous or calcareous ironstones. These ores contain generally about 50 per cent. of metal, but they require the addition of considerable quantities of burnt argillaceous shale and limestone for flux when grey pig-iron is desired. In consequence of this addition the flow of cinder is comparatively large—from 45 to 50 cwts. per ton of pig-iron. These cinders retain a portion of the metal originally in the ore, therefore the quantity required for smelting 1 ton of pig-iron is raised from 40 cwts.—the theoretical yield—to 45 cwts. A loss of 5 cwts. on every 45 cwts. is equal to 11 per cent. The loss thus exceeds by 2 per cent. that with argillaceous ironstones containing an equal quantity of metal.

The burnt shale generally used to supply the deficiency of fusible earths in the primary ores contains a small per-centage of iron. This unites with the metal in the ore, and so raises the yield of pig-iron slightly above that due to the ore alone.

Hitherto we have supposed that the furnace is working well on grey pig-iron, and that the cinders produced are of a grey stony fracture, but alterations in the quantity or quality of any of the materials may result in the production of a white metal and dense cinder of a black glassy exterior and of a dull lead colour within. Whenever from accident or any other cause such an alteration takes place, the produce of pig-iron in proportion to the ironstone rapidly diminishes, and the per-centage of metal in the cinder is augmented in a similar degree. Under ordinary circumstances, a ton of pig-iron will require, as stated already, 44 cwts. of a stone yielding 50 per cent., and the grey stony cinder produced will contain metal to the amount of about 5 per cent. of their weight; but when the operations of the furnace are deranged, the consumption of ironstone will sometimes rise as high as 60 cwts. per ton of pig-iron, and the cinder will contain metal to the extent, in extreme cases, of 20 per cent. of its weight. The consumption of 3 tons of such an ironstone to produce 1 ton of pig-iron, involves a loss of 10 cwts., or 33 per cent. of the metal contained in it. This quantity of metal is left in the cinder and lost. A large quantity of ironstone being consumed, the quantity of cinder corresponds, and, through the imperfect separation of the metal from it, it will weigh 3 tons per ton of pig-iron. These 3 tons of cinder contain 10 cwts. of metal, or $16\frac{1}{2}$ per cent. of their weight, instead of 5 per cent. as before.

A furnace may work several months without producing a cinder containing so much metal as 16 per cent.; but in large establishments it is not difficult to find cinder containing this and larger quantities of metal, even up to 20 per cent. The average yield of metal in the furnace-cinder made throughout South Wales will not fall far short of 10 per cent. It is supposed by some smelters that the grey cinder contains no metal, but on reference to the analyses of cinders produced under different states of the furnace, it will be seen that even the grey varieties contain from 4 to 7 per cent. of iron.

The greater consumption of materials for a given quantity of iron which occurs when the furnace is working badly, is shown in the most striking manner by the weekly statement of materials consumed. For the week ending April 25th, 1846, the make of the foundry iron furnace was 115 tons 10 cwts.; consumption of calcined ironstone 257 tons, or 45 cwts. per ton of pig-iron obtained. This was considered a good yield; but from this point the make declined, the quality deteriorated, the cinder changed to a dull black colour, and the yields were in an inverse ratio to the diminished make. In the succeeding month the week's make was 86 tons 11 cwts.; calcined ironstone consumed 278 tons, or 65 cwts. per ton of pig-iron obtained. Calculating that the per-centage of metal in the ironstone was the same on both occasions, and with argillaceous ironstone, the variation from week to week is very trifling, the 278 tons of calcined ironstone should have produced 123 tons 10 cwts. of pig-iron instead of 86 tons 11 cwts. Thus in the May week the loss of metal from the deranged condition of the furnace amounted to 37 tons, or 30 per cent. of the quantity obtainable under more favourable circumstances. From this ruinous condition the furnace recovered in a few weeks, and in July made, in one week, 121 tons, with a consumption of 48 cwts. of calcined ironstone per ton; but this was evidently forcing it beyond its powers, for in the succeeding weeks the make fell to 82 tons 14 cwts., and the consumption of ironstone rose to 60 cwts. Where the furnace is forced to the production of a quantity of metal greater than its dimensions warrant, irregularities, such as we have mentioned, will occur, attended with an increased consumption of ironstone, fuel, and flux, and the cost of the resulting pig-iron, though inferior in quality, will be greatly above that of the best grey iron made in less quantities.

The production of pig-iron for forge purposes from a mixed burden is usually accompanied by a great loss of metal. The quantity of fuel allowed for smelting a given weight of materials is in nearly every establishment too little for the perfect reduction of the metal with existing appliances. From a mistaken idea of economy the burden carried by the fuel is fixed so high that the yield and quality of the pig-iron are reduced below the proper level. The cinders are dark brown, black, or lead colour, according to the per-centage of iron they contain, and a great quantity of metal is lost in the cinder. Were smelters to consider for an instant the very different values of pig-iron and coal, it is probable that the quantity thus wasted would be considerably reduced.

We have stated elsewhere that a common burden for forge iron of ordinary quality consists of 28 cwts. of calcined ironstone, 10 cwts. of calcareous or siliceous iron ores, and 10 cwts. of forge, or forge and finery cinders for each ton of pig-iron produced. The ironstone will yield on an average 48 per cent. of metal, the ores 50 per cent., and the cinders 55 per cent. The quantity of metal in the respective ironmaking materials will be as follows: Calcined ironstone, 13.44 cwts.; ores, 5. cwts.; cinders, 5.5 cwts.; total, 23.94 cwts., or 3.94 cwts. beyond the quantity of pig-iron obtained. The cinders flowing from a furnace thus burdened weigh nearly 2 tons for each ton of pig-iron made, and contain by analysis from 10 to 12 per cent. of metal. If this quantity of cinder contains 3.94 cwts. of metal, the difference between the supply and the yield, the proportion will be within a fraction of 10 per cent. The loss of 3.94 on 23.94 cwts. is equal to 17 per cent.

But the majority of the forge iron furnaces in South Wales work with a greater loss than 17 per cent. The cinder produced contains on an average more than 10 per cent. of metal. It is not an unfrequent circumstance to see furnaces burdened so high, that for a period of some months 15 to 18 per cent. of the weight of the cinder is oxide of iron.

The loss of iron under such circumstances is very great indeed. At a moderate computation the amount of pig-iron annually thrown away in cinders—the greater portion from an utter disregard of the simplest principles that govern the action of blast furnaces—cannot be less than 250,000 tons in the South Wales district alone. In other districts smelting pig-iron for manufacture into bars, the waste in proportion to the quantity smelted, is scarcely inferior to that in Wales.

This great waste of metal is of comparatively recent origin. It is not more than 30 or 35 years since manufacturers commenced using a mixture of cinder and the richer ores for the production of an inferior description of pig-iron for refining and conversion into bars. Prior to the year 1820 the forge-iron was smelted from the argillaceous ironstone of the coal formation without any foreign mixture. The cinders produced were usually grey, and contained a minimum per-centage of metal. This was in a great measure owing to the large consumption of coal—4 to 6 tons—prevalent at that time. Since that period, while the consumption of fuel has diminished, the burden has been composed in part of cinder and primary ores—at first in small quantities—3 cwts. of Lancashire ore to the ton of pig-iron being considered a large proportion; latterly, however, the consumption has increased to so great an extent that these ores frequently form the largest portion of the burden. Wherever this is the case, unless accompanied by an increase in the quantity of fuel, and the adaptation of the furnace to the altered burden, the resulting cinders are black in colour, and contain large quantities of metal. The smelting power of the fuel having previously been taxed to its utmost, it is unable to carry the furnace through any alteration of burden.

That the general quality of forge pig-iron has been lowered, in consequence of the increased use of cinder and rich ores, there can be no question; but we may remark that for many purposes to which bar iron is now applied quality is a secondary consideration, and the use of cinder and rich ores in moderation is attended with numerous advantages to the manufacturer.

The quantity of coal consumed to smelt one ton of pig-iron evidently varies with its richness in carbon and general quality, but is also affected by the nature of the ironstone, flux, and blast. Considering them by their richness in carbon, and estimating that a given quantity of anthracite coal is capable of producing 1000 lbs. of iron, an equal quantity of the best Dowlais coal would reduce 954 lbs.; Pontypool bituminous coal, 878; and Scotch coal, 835 lbs.

In no operation connected with an iron-works has there been a greater reduction made in the consumption of materials than in the coal for smelting. The rigid economy of fuel practised in several Welsh works has resulted in a saving of nearly two-thirds of the quantity formerly considered necessary. In 1791 the consumption of coal to each ton of pig-iron averaged 6 tons; in 1821 it had diminished to 4 tons; and in 1831 to 2 tons 5 cwts., which is nearly the quantity required at the present day.

The maximum quantity of coal for smelting an ironstone will depend on the quality and fusibility of the combined earths and the yield of metal. The siliceous varieties, on account of their infusible matrix, require the largest quantity of fuel in smelting; the red and hydrated hematites the next largest quantity; the calcareous ores require less; the argillaceous ironstones are smelted with comparative facility, but the least consumption of fuel takes place with the carbonaceous ironstones.

The presence of carbon greatly increases the fusibility of ironstones, and diminishes the consumption of fuel. Siliceous ores which contain a portion of carbon, although abounding largely in silica, are smelted with greater facility, and produce a superior metal to those where this constituent is wanting. In several of the carbonates of the coal formation silica is the predominating impurity; but owing to the presence of carbon they are smelted with a low yield of coal. If the quantity of carbon be large, as in the carbonaceous ironstones, the consumption is reduced nearly one-half, and the fusibility of the ore is so great, that with this reduced proportion of fuel the production is augmented to nearly twice the quantity which it is possible to obtain from the same furnace, working on other descriptions of ironstone.

The demand for fuel is affected by the richness of the ironstone. It is greatest with the poorest stones; but when an ironstone contains more than 50 per cent. of metal (carbonaceous ironstones excepted) the consumption of fuel is not diminished below the proportion due to a stone of that per-centage. To produce iron of good quality from the richest ironstones a quantity of shale is, as before stated, used to compensate for the deficiency of earths in the stone, and to form a fluid-cinder for the protection of the iron in the hearth. The quantity of shale used increases in proportion to the per-centage of metal in the ore, sufficient being added to reduce the mean yield of metal to 50 per cent. or under: consequently, the consumption of fuel will equal that for an ironstone of the richness of the aggregate.

In smelting argillaceous ironstone, 45 cwts. of a coal containing 87 per cent. of carbon is consumed for each ton of grey pig-iron produced. This is nearly 2 lbs. of carbon to each pound of iron, and this proportion holds good with coals containing less carbon, the quantity of a coal used being generally in an inverse ratio to its yield of carbon. But numerous other circumstances, also, more or less affect the reducing power of the fuel.

Among raw coals, ton for ton, anthracite reduces the largest amount of metal; and the semi-bituminous coal, mined to the east of Merthyr Tydfil, comes next in order. Scotch coal is that most extensively used in the raw state; but its power is lower than that of either of the above-mentioned kinds.

It is with coke as with coal—the harder and denser the coke and the more concentrated the carbon, the greater the reducing power. A light, hollow, spongy-looking coke, exposes too great a surface to the action of the blast; it consumes quickly, without producing a very intense heat; and to maintain the requisite temperature the quantity requires to be largely increased, and the consumption of carbon—estimated on the amount in the raw coal—is sometimes double or treble what it would be with coal of a superior description.

The consumption of coal or coke will also depend on its hardness, and its capability to resist fracture in the furnace.

Breakage or crumbling in the furnace may occur from several causes—either from the natural weakness of the coke, the great height of the apparatus, the dense character of the ore, or, if the coke be soft, from its grinding to dust against the ore and flux. Such pieces only as reach the zone of fusion in a comparatively whole state contribute to the maintenance of the temperature. The small fragments and dust are injurious, and do not assist in the reduction of the metal; so that as much carbon as they contain is consumed in addition to the quantity that would be required of unbroken coke. The presence of dust and small coke is proved by their constant discharge at the tunnel-head and under the tymp immediately after casting.

The consumption of coke is increased when it contains much water. The actual quantity of carbon charged is diminished, and a portion of the heating power of the fuel is expended in evaporating the water. If this water amounts to 12 per cent. by weight of the coke—not an unusual circumstance—the smelting powers of the fuel are diminished 12 per cent. by the weight of the water, and then further by the weight of the fuel consumed in vapourising this water and restoring the temperature of the materials. This diminution of heating power has to be met by an increased consumption. If 36 cwts. of dry coke suffice to produce good pig-iron, the consumption of wet coke, to produce iron of an equal quality, will be not less than 45.5 cwts. But the consumption of wet coke is usually greater than this, which is attributable to the partial disintegration of the pieces by the escaping vapour.

The admission into the furnace of water in any shape is attended with an increased consumption of fuel. If it enter with the ironstone the increase in the quantity of fuel will be in proportion to the degree of saturation, but it will at all times be in excess of the quantity necessary to evaporate the water.

Where water enters the furnace through the tuyere in the form of moisture in the blast, the consumption of fuel is increased in proportion to the increase of moisture over that usually existing in the atmosphere. Water exists in comparatively dry air to the extent of 1.42 per cent., and the quantity contained in the 25 tons of blast thrown in for each ton of pig-iron weighs 71 cwts. A portion of the $2\frac{1}{4}$ lbs. of carbon consumed for each pound of iron is evidently wasted in evaporating this water. In a damp state of the atmosphere the quantity of water in the blast is 6 or 7 cwts. in excess of this weight, and necessarily a correspondingly increased weight of carbon is consumed.

In the summer-time, on account of the greater quantity of moisture in the atmosphere, the consumption of fuel is greater than in winter. By reference to the records of the monthly yields of materials at the Dowlais furnaces, we find that the difference is very considerable, probably more than is generally believed. Taking the average of five years, selected promiscuously from twenty-two years' working, we find that at the foundry iron furnace the yield of coal per ton of pig-iron was, in the winter months, 49.7 cwts.; spring, 52.2 cwts.; summer, 53.1 cwts.; and autumn, 55.4 cwts. The excess of the autumn over the winter months, 5.7 cwts., is equal to an increase of 11 per cent. At the forge iron furnace the yields in the winter months are 43.6 cwts.; spring, 44.2; summer, 44.6; and autumn, 45.8 cwts. The excess of autumn over winter, 2.2 cwts., is equal to 5 per cent. The variation of yield with the season is still more marked with the ballast iron furnace, the yields being in winter 43.2 cwts.; spring, 44.1; summer, 50.1; and autumn, 49.5, or 6.3 cwts. more in autumn than in winter, equal to 13 per cent. nearly. The greater uniformity in the forge iron furnace yields we attribute to the variation in the composition of the burden. The average consumption of ores during five years was, in winter, 6.6 cwts.; autumn, 8.4 cwts.; and of cinder, in winter, 8.3 cwts.; and autumn, 11.8 cwts. With this increase of ores and cinders in autumn, the yield of local ironstone was reduced from 47 cwts. in winter to 41.2 cwts. in the autumn. An increased use of rich Lancashire ore and forge cinder, without the addition of clay or other material to improve the quality of the iron, would result in a diminished yield of fuel.

Throughout the Welsh works the consumption of primary ores is largest in summer and autumn. In these seasons the trade in sea-borne ores is prosecuted with the greatest activity, and the manufacturers are, in consequence, well supplied; but in winter and spring the falling off in the shipments causes a larger consumption of the local ironstones.

The yield of fuel in the furnace is diminished when caustic lime is substituted for limestone. This diminution in the weight of carbon is nearly equal to one-third of the difference between the weight of the caustic lime and limestone. If the burden of 17 cwts. of limestone be replaced by an equivalent quantity of caustic lime, say 10.2 cwts., the reduction in weight will be 6.8 cwts., and one-third of this, 2.26 cwts., will give nearly the reduction in the weight of carbon, arising from the substitution. If the coal yields 87 per cent. of carbon, the saving will equal 2.57 cwts. of coal.

But against the diminished consumption in the blast furnace there must be placed the quantity of coal consumed in calcining the limestone. This will amount to 1.5 cwt. per ton of limestone, or 1.7 cwt. per ton of iron, leaving an apparent saving of .87 cwt. only; but the value of the large coal saved from the blast furnace is greatly above that of the fuel used in the kiln. For calcining, slack or other small coal may be employed which cannot be used in the furnace, and which would otherwise be comparatively valueless.

Raw coal will reduce and smelt a greater weight of ironstone than the coke from such coal. At one period of the manufacture the use of coke was universal, but within the last twenty-five years numerous furnaces have been worked on raw coal. The number of kinds of coal which may be advantageously used in the existing furnace in the raw state is not large; but wherever the change from coke to raw coal has been made, the results are greatly in favour of raw coal. The advantage is most apparent with coals, which lose considerably in weight when coked, and least with those approaching to the character of anthracite. The best of the furnace coals raised at the Dowlais colliery contain 87.3 per cent. of carbon and 2.1 of ash. These coals lost in coking 25 per cent., thus reducing the weight of the coke below the contents of carbon. A portion of the carbon was consumed in the process of coking, and was consequently unavailable for smelting. The quantity thus consumed is represented by the difference between the weight of the carbon and ash in the coal and that of the coke obtained. The carbon and ash in the Dowlais coal amounts to 89.4 per cent.; the coke weighed 75 per cent., leaving a loss of 14.4, or 16 per cent. nearly of carbon. With such a loss of carbon attendant on the use of coke, the raw coal which retains its carbon undiminished may be expected to afford a greater weight of iron, and in practice it is found to do so. Prior to the use of raw coal in the furnace the coal used for coking averaged 50 cwts. to the ton of pig-iron, but since the abandonment of coking this weight of iron is smelted with a mean consumption of 45 cwts.

In Scotland the use of raw coal is attended with a still greater economy. The furnace coals of that country average 76.4 per cent. of carbon and 6 per cent. of ash; total of carbon and ash, 82.4. They lose 55 per cent. by weight in coking, or 37.4 below the amount of carbon and ash. This loss of 37.4 parts out of 76.4 is equal to a diminution of 50 per cent. on the smelting power of the coal. Assuming that the quantity of carbon in 38 cwts. of raw coal is required to reduce 1 ton of pig-iron, it will take 76 cwts. of such coal converted into coke to yield the same quantity of carbon. Indeed in the earlier period of the manufacture a much larger quantity than this was consumed in producing a ton of pig-iron.

The consumption of fuel is increased whenever the working of the furnace is deranged from causes connected with the ironstone flux or blast, in a similar manner and to the same, if not to a greater extent than the increased consumption of ironstone. To restore the furnace to a healthy state the relative quantity of fuel to ironstone must be largely increased, in order that a greater temperature may be attained for the fusion of the refractory masses adhering to the sides of the hearth and around the tuyeres. The amount of this increase varies according to the nature of the case, from 45 cwts.—the usual yield per ton of iron—to 60 or 70 cwts.

We have stated that the consumption of fuel per ton of pig-iron is smallest with the carbonaceous ironstones, but if their richness in metal and carbon, and great fusibility be fully considered, the consumption of fuel still appears excessive. The yield averages 38 cwts. of a coal containing 76 per cent. of carbon, or 3234 lbs. of carbon for each ton of iron obtained. To this must be added the carbon mechanically combined with the ironstone in the proportion of 30 parts of coal to 28 parts of ironstone, equal to 2404 lbs., or a total of 5638 lbs. of carbon consumed for each ton of pig-iron. The average consumption with the argillaceous ore is 4480 lbs., or 1158 lbs. less than with the carbonaceous. Judging from the greater consumption of carbon in smelting this ore, it might be inferred that the metal was extracted with difficulty, but such is not the case. It is now well known as the most fusible of ironstones. Yet for its reduction one-fourth more carbon is expended than is found necessary with other stones melting at a much higher temperature. But if the consumption be estimated on the quantity of materials rendered fluid—the iron and cinders—the excessive quantity of carbon used in smelting the carbonaceous ironstone becomes still more apparent. For each ton of fluid materials, with argillaceous ironstone, 1463 lbs. of carbon are consumed; with the more fusible carbonaceous ironstone, 2785 lbs., or nearly twice as much. It is difficult to account for the larger consumption of carbon in smelting a more fusible stone, except upon the supposition that corresponding waste is incurred through imperfection in the mode of working. In corroboration of this view, it may be stated that the consumption of atmospheric air is less in proportion to the consumption of carbon than with other furnaces. For each pound of carbon consumed in smelting the argillaceous ironstone 168 cubic feet of atmospheric air are blown into the furnace, but for each pound of carbon consumed in smelting the carbonaceous ironstone of Scotland, scarcely 40 cubic feet of atmospheric air enters the furnace—a quantity greatly below that required for the complete combustion of the fuel.

The carbon, mechanically combined with the ironstone, is partially consumed in the operation of calcination. This loss, however, may be avoided by using kilns instead of conducting the operation in the open air. With properly constructed kilns and a moderate degree of attention, the carbon, combined with the ironstone, may be made to suffice for the requirements of the blast furnace.

The consumption of fuel is reduced when a hot blast is substituted for a cold one. This diminution is with some kinds of coal considerable, but with others it is trifling, and scarcely compensates for the greater outlay of capital. In Scotland the reduction in the consumption of coal in the blast furnace when smelting carbonaceous ironstone amounts to from 8 to 10 cwts. of coal per ton of iron. In consequence of the low temperature at which the carbonaceous ironstone melts—a simple wind-draught frequently being sufficient—the increase of temperature from 50° to 610° approaches to the melting point of the materials, and the carbon previously consumed in the stove in elevating the blast to this temperature may be withheld, but with the more refractory ironstones the reduction is not so great. The elevation of the temperature of the blast to 610° bears a comparatively small proportion to the intensity required in the blast furnace, therefore the saving obtained by heating the blast is proportionally less. The economy arising from the use of heated air in the furnaces of Wales amounts to from 4 to 5 cwts. of coal per ton of pig-iron.

Against the saving in furnace coal, however, there must be placed the coal used in the stoves in heating the blast. The quantity usually required for this purpose averages in weight one-half of the amount saved in the furnace, but the coal consumed in the stoves is usually of a very inferior quality, incapable of being used in the blast-furnace for smelting. The saving in fuel, therefore—the relative values of the furnace and stove coal being considered—may be fairly estimated at 3 cwts. in Wales, and 6 to 7 cwts. in Scotland.

In 1844 and 1845 seven of the Dowlais furnaces were blown with heated air, and the other eleven with cold. The average yield of coal at the cold-blast furnace was 47.8 cwts., and at the hot-blast furnaces 44.4 cwts. The coal used in the heating stoves of the hot-blast furnace averaged $2\frac{1}{4}$ cwts. per ton of iron.

The consumption of limestone is dependent on its richness in lime, and on the quality and quantity of the earths combined with the ironstone. Other things being equal, the consumption of limestone will vary with its richness in lime. If the per-centage be about that of an average good limestone, yielding 54 to 55 per cent. of lime, the quantity for argillaceous ironstones yielding 48 per cent. of metal will be from 15 to 20 cwts. per ton of iron. If the limestone yields less lime or contains much silica, the consumption may be roughly estimated by adding the silica in the flux to that combined with the ironstone, and charging a sufficiency of limestone to produce the lime necessary for the fusion of both.

As the varieties of ironstone smelted in this country are not numerous, we may state in reference to them that the consumption of lime will generally be directly as the quantity of silica and inversely as the quantity of lime in their composition. One of the seams of argillaceous ironstone, extensively mined at the Dowlais works, yields 33.5 per cent. of metallic iron, and contains 13.6 of silica. The consumption of raw ironstone of this richness is 65 cwts. per ton, and of limestone 17 cwts. The quantity of silica in the ironstone and limestone by calculation amounts to 9.2 cwts., and the lime in the limestone to 9.4 cwts. In this instance the lime is slightly in excess of the silica. We purpose showing by the quantities consumed with different ironstones and limestones that the proportion of silica in the ore and flux may be safely taken as a correct measure of the quantity of lime necessary to be added.

The argillaceous ironstones of Scotland contain on the average 30 per cent. of metal in the raw stone, and 11.3 per cent. of silica. When smelted by themselves the consumption of raw ironstone to the ton of pig-iron averages 78 cwts., yielding 8.82 cwts. of silica and 3.1 cwts. of lime. The consumption of limestone is 12 cwts. to the ton, yielding 6.48 cwts. of lime and .25 cwts. of silica. Here the weight of the silica amounts to 9.1 and the lime to 9.6—a difference of about 5 per cent. only.

The Scotch carbonaceous ironstone yields on an average 28 per cent. of metal. The consumption of raw stone averages 77 cwts. per ton, yielding 2.5 per cent. of silica and 1.5 per cent. of lime. The consumption of limestone with this ironstone averages 5 cwts., yielding 54 per cent. of lime and 3 per cent. of silica. With these quantities we ascertain that the silica weighs 2.0 cwts. and the lime 3.85 cwts. Apparently there is a large excess of lime over the silica, but the excess is accounted for by the ash of the coal. These weigh 2.3 cwts. per ton, and are principally composed of silica.

The calcined ironstone used at the Alfreton furnace, Derbyshire, yields, according to the analyses made by M. Bunsen, 42 per cent. of metal. The consumption per ton of pig-iron is 60 cwts. of calcined ironstone, containing 25.7 per cent. of silica and 3.5 of lime. The limestone yields 54.4 per cent. of lime, and the consumption is 24.3 cwts. per ton. On these quantities we find that the silica amounts to 15.4 cwts., and the lime in the limestone and ironstone amounts to 15.3 cwts.

At the Abersychan furnace, for the production of a forge iron with grey cinder, the following burden is used: Calcined ironstone 4 cwts., containing 16 per cent. of silica; forge cinder 5 cwts., containing 28 per cent. of ditto; Northamptonshire ore 5 cwts., averaging 12 per cent. of silica; caustic lime 3 cwts. Hence the quantity of silica in the iron-making materials is 2.64 cwts. against 3 cwts. of lime.

As far, then, as iron-smelting in Great Britain is concerned, the foregoing examples, together with the constant result of our own observations, enable us to state with confidence that if the quantity of silica entering the furnace be known, an approximation may be made, sufficiently accurate for all practical purposes, to the quantity of limestone necessary for fluxing. We have applied similar calculations to furnaces working on mixed ores at the Dowlais works, and have invariably found that where a cinder comparatively free from iron was produced, the quantity of lime was slightly greater than the silica, but in no instance have we known a furnace to work well when the consumption of lime was less.

The exception will be when the silica bears a very small proportion to the quantity of alumina. The consumption of limestone will then be greater than we have stated; but we may remark that in the ironstones and ores smelted in this country, the proportion of silica to alumina on the average is fully as high as three to one. It is on the quantity of silica, therefore, that we have to calculate the flux.

If the limestone yields a low per-centage of lime, the consumption is rapidly augmented. It is not unusual for limestone to contain 5 to 10 per cent. of silica, and in some instances as much as 25 per cent. of this substance is present. The purest stones contain from 1 to 2 per cent. With the knowledge, then, that for the fusion of the silica in the limestone, a corresponding weight of lime is needed, we see the importance of employing a limestone as free as possible from this mineral. If silica were present in the flux to the extent of 8 per cent. instead of 2.5, the yield of lime would be reduced to 48, out of which 8 parts must be deducted for fluxing the combined silica, leaving 40 parts only available for the reduction of the ironstone, instead of the 52.5 as at present. Under such circumstances an increase of 5.5 per cent. of silica is followed by a diminution of the fluxing powers of the limestone of 18 per cent.; and instead of 17 cwts. being consumed as at present, the excess of silica would require nearly 21 cwts.

An excess of limestone over the quantity required for fluxing the combined earths is injurious, inasmuch as its fusion absorbs a portion of the heat evolved by the fuel, and to this extent weakens its reducing power. The temperature in the hearth is lowered, and the separation of the metal rendered less perfect. If the lime be greatly in excess, and the consumption of coal is augmented in proportion, the resulting pig-iron will bear all the characteristics of having been smelted from calcareous ores. The red-short peculiarity will be strongly developed, and the strength and general quality sensibly deteriorated.

The consumption of blast is immediately dependent on the quantity of fuel used. For the combustion of one pound of carbon 31.5 cubic feet of oxygen gas is chemically required. To afford this gas 155 feet of atmospheric air must be consumed. It remains, then, to ascertain how far the quantities of blast actually blown into the furnace agree with the theoretical amounts.

The Dowlais foundry iron furnace consumes 732,386 cubic feet of air for the combustion of the 4384 lbs. of carbon supplied by the fuel, or 167 cubic feet of air to each pound of carbon—an excess of 12 feet over the theoretical quantity. This is probably as near to the actual requirement as can be obtained in practice, taking into account that with the best constructed blowing apparatus, leakage and loss of a portion of the blast must occur.

The Staffordshire foundry iron furnace consumes 635,800 cubic feet of atmospheric air to 4480 lbs. of carbon, equal to 144 feet per pound of carbon, showing a deficiency of atmospheric air of 11 feet as compared with the theoretical requirement.

The anthracite furnaces in the Swansea Valley consume 806,400 cubic feet of air to 4076 lbs. of carbon ; or 195 cubic feet to each pound of carbon—an excess of 44 feet over the theoretical quantity. The great difference here between the actual and theoretical quantities is probably owing in some measure to the leakage from a large number of small tuyeres, coupled with the circumstance that the pressure is considerably higher than at other furnaces.

The average of these three furnaces is 168 cubic feet for each pound of carbon—a result sufficiently near the theoretical quantity ; and it is not probable that perfect combustion of the carbon of the fuel is attained with a smaller consumption.

Applying similar calculations to other cases, we find the No. 1 cinder iron furnace at the Dowlais works consumes 599,200 cubic feet to 3659 lbs. of carbon, or 163 cubic feet to each pound.

At the No. 2 cinder iron furnace the consumption of air is 540,900 cubic feet to 3466 lbs. of carbon, or 156 feet to the pound.

At the No. 3 cinder iron furnace (ballast-iron) the consumption of air is 599,200 cubic feet to 3659 lbs. of carbon, equal to 163 cubic feet to the pound. The average of the three cinder iron furnaces is 161 cubic feet to the pound of carbon, or 6 feet above the theoretical quantity required.

The Scotch blast furnace smelting carbonaceous ironstone consumes 222,600 cubic feet of atmospheric air to 3234 lbs. of carbon in the coal, equal to 67 cubic feet per pound, or 88 cubic feet under the quantity theoretically required for the complete combustion of the carbon. But this disproportion between the carbon and the amount of blast in the Scotch furnace becomes still more apparent if we add to the carbon contained in the coal the quantity mechanically combined with the ironstone—viz. 2404 lbs., making a total of 5638 lbs. This gives only 40 feet of air per pound of carbon, instead of 153 feet—the least quantity with which, theoretically, perfect combustion can be effected.

Assuming the consumption of blast at the Scotch furnaces to be sufficient for fusing the ironstone and reducing the metal, the quantity of carbon which can combine with the oxygen of the air is limited to 1436 lbs., or a little more than half of that existing in the ironstone. This quantity of carbon, with proper arrangements, would maintain an equal, if not greater heat, for the reduction of the metal than the present consumption. By using four times the quantity of carbon that the volume of blast thrown in can possibly consume, the heat maintained in the hearth is kept very low, compared with furnaces having a full blast, and shows in the most decisive manner, the fusible nature of carbonaceous ironstone. With such a disproportion between the carbon and the blast no other ironstone could be smelted. In the Welsh furnaces using argillaceous ironstone, the use of so low a proportion of air as 40, or even 60, feet to the pound of carbon, would inevitably result in such an immediate reduction of temperature as to occasion a setting together of the materials and an entire suspension of operations. The Scotch ironmaster is saved from such a catastrophe solely by the low temperature at which his carbonaceous ironstone melts.*

The effects upon a furnace of a diminished volume of blast are, waste of fuel, lowering of the temperature, and the production of a metal more or less debased by the presence of impurities. In the smelting—and, indeed, in all other operations connected with the manufacture of iron where heat is essential—a high temperature and active combustion conduce to economy both of time and material. In the more advanced stages of the manufacture, where the effects of variation are more readily observable, a dull, heavy draught results in loss of time, a rapid waste of the metal, a large consumption of coal, and the production of an inferior bar. Similar effects cannot fail to be produced in the operations of the blast furnace whenever the supply of atmospheric air is inadequate to maintain active combustion. In the case of carbonaceous ironstone it has been shown that the quantity of air supplied is scarcely more than one-fourth of that chemically required, and, if compared with the actual supply at other furnaces, the deficiency appears greater rather than otherwise.

There is an opinion current amongst furnace managers that any excess of coal over the quantity absolutely required for smelting is so much waste, but nothing more. There is ground, however, for the opinion that when an increased quantity of coal is used, without a corresponding increase in the amount of blast, the additional fuel is decidedly injurious to the working of the furnace, both as regards the quantity and quality of the metal.

For the complete combustion of the carbon a definite quantity of oxygen is required, which must be supplied from a sufficient volume of air. The temperature attained will depend entirely on the quantity of air supplied in a given time. If the necessary quantity be

---

* It must be remembered that in addition to the oxygen supplied by the blast, a certain amount of fuel is consumed by the oxygen in the ores themselves.

admitted slowly, the rate of combustion will be slow in proportion, and a minimum temperature attained. But if the air be supplied rapidly, the combustion becomes active, and although the same quantity of heat is evolved from similar quantities of carbon and oxygen, as with a slower combustion, yet in consequence of its evolution occupying a shorter period, the temperature attained is proportionately higher. Every increase in the quantity of atmospheric air admitted to the ignited fuel elevates the temperature of the products of combustion. So that by the employment of suitable mechanical means for the introduction of sufficient quantities of atmospheric air, almost any desired heat may be maintained in the interior of a furnace.

The reverse occurs if the quantity of fuel is increased. The addition of carbon lowers the temperature.[*] The volume of air admitted is insufficient to maintain the same active combustion throughout the larger quantity of carbon. An increase in the quantity of fuel is equivalent to a reduction in the volume of blast: in either case the quantity of oxygen, in proportion to carbon, being reduced, the combustion is slower, and the heat maintained less intense. Of course, just so much as the additional fuel lowers the temperature of the furnace, it is positively injurious.

Furnace managers generally, however, entertain a different opinion respecting the effect of an increased quantity of fuel in the furnace. Additional fuel is supposed to maintain a greater heat and produce a superior pig-iron. With this impression, whenever the quality is low, or the furnace working badly, the weight of fuel is considerably increased—frequently so much so that the evil which it is intended to remedy is augmented. In corroboration of what we have already advanced respecting the necessity of proportioning the quantity of blast to the carbon in the coal, we may remark that in derangements of the blast-furnace, followed by a maximum yield of fuel, a minimum make occurs, and the weekly consumption of carbon, and, consequently, its relation to the volume of blast, is but slightly altered. In a case where the weekly make declined from 98 to 74 tons, the yield of fuel was increased from 39 to 54 cwts.; but the week's consumption of coal increased from 193 to 202 tons only. In another month the weekly make declined from 80 to 56 tons; the yield of coal rose from 39.5 to 55 cwts.; but the week's consumption of coal diminished with the higher yield from 158 to 154 tons. And in the following month the make declined to 48 tons; the yield of fuel increased to 65 cwts.; but the weekly consumption of coal—156 tons—remained nearly the same. We have selected these as extreme cases of variation in the yield of fuel without sensible alterations in the weekly consumption; but lesser departures from the usual yield with similar results are of daily occurrence.

Through these reduced makes and augmented yields of fuel the volume of blast remained unaltered. Carbon was freely supplied; but as the other element necessary to generate a high temperature was not furnished in the same proportion, the benefits which might have been produced were lost, and results the opposite of those sought were obtained.

The supply of blast is fixed; no increase in the volume can be effected without altera-

[*] Owing to the production of carbonic oxide.

tions of the engine or boilers. Since an increase of blast from the blowing-machine is not readily attainable, if even it were considered desirable, attempts are made to remove the derangements occurring in the furnace by the simple addition of fuel. When derangements occur, and additional blast is not obtainable, no alterations should be made in the quantity of fuel; but the weight of ironstone, or other ironmaking material, should immediately be reduced. If this be done, the greater heat maintained in the hearth and boshes, through the absence of absorbing materials, speedily restores the furnace to a healthy condition.

The power of the blowing-engine at ironworks is almost without exception much below what the dimensions of the present blast furnaces require. A large surplus ought to be available for cases of emergency; but, as a rule, the engines are not sufficiently powerful to maintain in a thoroughly efficient manner their ordinary duty—that is to say, they are incapable of discharging air in such quantities and of such a density as would conduce to the greatest economy of materials and a maximum make.

The blowing machinery at the Scotch ironworks is manifestly incapable of supplying the air necessary for the perfect combustion of the fuel in the limited time permitted by the descent of the materials. A low temperature consequently prevails in the hearth, a considerable quantity of the carbon of the fuel is wasted, and, as a necessary result of the immense consumption of fuel, the pig-iron produced is surcharged with carbon, both mechanically mixed and chemically combined, by which its strength is diminished, its manufacture into bar-iron rendered more difficult, and the finished bar, when tested, rendered of an inferior quality.

Although we advocate the employment of ample engine-power and a sufficient blast for the combustion of the fuel, we are very far from agreeing with the opinion entertained by some ironmasters that with a blast increased in volume and density a diminution in the yield of coal may be effected. What we desire to impress is the importance of proportioning the volume of blast to the consumption of fuel, wherever economy in materials and regularity in the working of the furnace are desired.

A volume of blast, greatly beyond that required for supplying the requisite oxygen to the fuel, can only be attended by the reverse of beneficial results. What air is not decomposed to supply oxygen ascends with the gaseous products of combustion, and, by absorbing heat, reduces the general temperature of the surrounding materials. An excessive supply, therefore, may produce effects scarcely less injurious than those occasioned by a deficiency.

The quality of the pig-iron from a furnace working upon the same kind of ironstone may be affected by various causes, but the most common are the variable qualities of fuel and flux, variations in the pressure and volume of blast, and in the state of the atmosphere. The quality is probably more dependent on the fuel than on the other materials. If the coal or coke be deficient in carbon, and contains a large proportion of earthy matters, it is unfit to be used for smelting. The best grey pig-metal cannot profitably be manufactured with such coal; and experience has demonstrated that if the fuel contain a notable per-centage of sulphur it is unfit for smelting the finer qualities of metal. If such coal be coked the sulphur is partially expelled during the process, but its complete volatilization requires a higher temperature. A portion is consequently present in the fuel when it reaches the hearth, and there combines with and contaminates the metal, diminishing its strength and other valuable properties.

A weak coal, if used in the blast furnace in its raw state, is very liable to be splintered by the heat of the ascending gases immediately it has entered the throat. The cohesion of its particles is weakened, and ultimately destroyed by the rapid expansion and escape of its volatile constituents. Fragments descend with the materials, filling up the interstices and obstructing the passage of the ascending column of gases and their free action on the ironstone, until, on arriving at the hearth, they drop through the melting zone and below the direct action of the blast, and are finally discharged with the escaping gas under the tymp, or more commonly cleaned from off the fluid cinder. Under these circumstances, the metal being deprived of the beneficial effects of a considerable portion of the fuel, is of a quality below that due to the quantity or composition of the fuel, and from the comparatively low heat maintained at the tuyeres with such fuel, the metal does not freely separate from the cinder, and consequently is charged with impurity.

If a weak coal is coked before entering the furnace, its injurious effects on the quality of the metal are equally apparent. The coke produced being of a light spongy hollow nature, offers an extended surface for the action of the blast, an intense local heat is generated, and the fuel is consumed too rapidly for its due action on the ores treated. A furnace working with such coke will, as a general rule, produce metal of a low quality.

If the coke has been overdone by allowing the coking process to proceed too far, a portion of the carbon will have been consumed; and as the proportion of fuel is generally estimated by barrows of a known capacity, the same charge of overdone coke will contain more ash and less carbon than if properly prepared. Its power of producing metal will, therefore, be diminished, and since a slight reduction in the quantity of carbon is perceptible in the quality of the metal, the employment of such coke invariably results in an immediate deterioration in the metal produced.

Under the old system of coking in the open air, the coke produced was seldom overdone. The conversion of the coal into coke was the operation of several days—generally eight or ten—and, being open to inspection, the combustion of every portion of the heap was under the control of the workmen. Lately, however, at several works the process has chiefly been conducted in brick ovens. A greater yield of coke is supposed to follow the use of this method, but from our own observation we do not find that this increase of yield is at all commensurate with the defects of the coke so prepared. The operation is conducted with great rapidity, 3 or 4 tons of coal being charged into an oven, coked and withdrawn every 24 hours. We have yet to learn that this high-pressure system of coking produces a fuel capable of carrying a higher or even as high a burden as that prepared upon the older and slower plan. It is certain that coke prepared in ovens is commonly either burnt or underdone, and wherever it is used the quality of the metal and working of the furnace are most variable.*

The use of coal partially coked deranges the working of the furnace, and has an injurious effect on the quality of the metal. This deterioration in quality will be greater or less according to the character of the coal. If it be of a highly bituminous description, swelling considerably in coking, the deterioration will be considerable; but if of a semi-bituminous character, increasing but slightly in bulk, the bad effect will not be so great. The cause of this mischievous effect from the use of partially-coked coal is probably that the hydrogen and other volatile substances are not completely expelled from the centre of the individual masses. On being suddenly thrown into the hot furnace the coking process recommences; the uncoked coal expands, bursting the external crust of coke into fragments, and the rapid expulsion of its volatile constituents so weakens the cohesion of its particles that it is crushed by the weight of superincumbent materials. In the hearth the dust and broken pieces of coke are incapable of maintaining a sufficiently high temperature for the production of grey metal, the usual quality under such circumstances being white or mottled.

A large quantity of inferior coke is also prepared from the small of highly bituminous coal. This practice is of very recent date. If, however, the coal, before it has had time to lose its good qualities by exposure to atmospheric influences, is carefully coked in properly-arranged ovens, very excellent fuel may be produced. But if, on the other hand, it be allowed to remain for a long period stored in large heaps, as we have frequently observed it, the coke produced is of a very inferior quality. This is readily accounted for. While lying in heaps the coal heats, and slow spontaneous combustion commences, setting free the volatile parts. If the heap be examined afterwards, or while this is going forward, the coals in the centre will be found bearing evident signs of partial charring, having lost their bituminous property, and presenting appearances similar to those of underdone coke. This heated small coal, when charged into the oven, is converted into a hollow spongy coke, of so weak and friable a character as to be quite unfit for the blast furnace. If, however, it be used in the furnace, it is crushed and partially ground to dust by the descending materials, like all very weak coke under a considerable burden, and, as already stated, the metal suffers both in the quality and quantity produced.

Coke containing a large quantity of water is at all times injurious to the quality of the metal. Most kinds of coke will absorb water to the extent of 10 to 12 per cent. of their weight. Under the old system of burning in the open air it was not general to use water for cooling the coke, and a considerable quantity, therefore, could be obtained for the furnace comparatively dry. The coke, however, was often saturated from exposure to the weather. Where the operation is performed in ovens, the common practice is to cool the coke with water before or immediately after drawing; a quantity of water consequently becomes fixed in the coke. The employment of water doubly impairs the power of the coke. In the first

* The best coke at the present time remains 92 hours in the oven.—Eds.

place, the stream thrown on the red-hot mass causes it to cool irregularly, breaking into fragments from the sudden contraction, and a number of the pieces become too small to carry a proper burden of ore. The larger pieces, through the operation of the same causes, become brittle and break up when heated under pressure in the furnace, and can only carry a small burden. In the second place, the water absorbed by the coke is vaporised by the heat of the furnace. This is attended by a direct consumption of fuel, further reducing the carrying power of the coke. But the presence of water in the furnace in any shape is injurious, and when introduced along with the materials at top, it lowers the temperature in the throat and body of the furnace. A reduction of temperature in these regions is equivalent in effect to a reduction in the height of the furnace, and causes a corresponding diminution in its smelting power. From the inferior temperature prevailing, the upper portions of the furnace are rendered comparatively ineffective in the reduction. The production of cast-iron from ironstones of the argillaceous class requires that the materials should be in the furnace about 40 hours, exposed to the heat and gases generated by the ascending blast. If, then, the effective working height of the furnace is from any cause diminished, the descending materials will be in the effective portions of the furnace a shorter period. The deoxidation and cementation commences at a lower level than usual, and is only imperfectly accomplished when the materials are fused in the hearth. The metal produced will be of an inferior quality, and usually, under such circumstances, the cinders contain a considerable per-centage of metal.

Coal of this kind expands rapidly under the action of the heat, and presses with the other materials against the sides of the furnace with such force that the whole mass, cemented together by the partly-melted coal, remains immovable sometimes for several hours. During the time this obstruction lasts the operation of filling is discontinued. In the mean time the descent of the materials below the obstruction continues, leaving a vacancy of greater or less depth, according to the time and rate of driving. The suspended materials remain fixed in this position until their cohesion is destroyed by the gradual progress of combustion, and the whole mass suddenly descends several feet to the surface of the other charges.

With the smelter this suspension of the materials is termed "scaffolding," and the subsequent sudden descent "jumping." The time which the materials remain fixed is measured by the number of charges which the furnace would have gone during the period that the filling has been suspended. When the obstruction is removed, the furnace is said to jump so many charges. Scaffolding may occur from other causes, but we have found it most common in furnaces using bituminous and other raw coals.

The injurious effect of "scaffolding" upon the metal is very apparent. It changes in a few hours from a warm free-running grey to a cold thick white metal of the worst quality. This may be readily accounted for. A considerable portion of the carbon is consumed during the retention of the materials, and the value of the fuel is to that extent diminished. When the mass falls the partially consumed coke is broken up into small pieces, so that its power is again diminished. This diminution of the power of the coal is of itself sufficient to alter the quality of the metal from grey to white, but this is not the only mischievous cause at work. To produce superior metal the materials must be in the furnace the whole time requisite for their complete deoxidation and cementation before reduction. When the furnace is scaffolding, the materials are there the usual period, it is true, but the time during which they are suspended below the throat, out of the influence of proper reducing agents is so much time lost. If they remain for 10 or 12 hours—a very common occurrence—the time for deoxidation and cementation will be reduced to this extent. Therefore, instead of remaining under the regular action of the furnace, the time necessary for the production of good grey iron—say about 46 hours—the time occupied in their descent is 34 or 36 hours only—a period much too short for the production of grey metal from any but the richest carbonaceous ironstones.

Such obstructions occasionally occur with coal containing but little bituminous matter. But as nearly every kind of fossil fuel expands when heated, there is no difficulty in accounting for scaffolds and their injurious effects on the metal, upon the same grounds. If a high temperature is maintained at the throat, the expansion of the fuel is very rapid, but if the throat be cool the full expansion is not attained till the materials have descended 17 or 18 feet, where, from the increased diameter of the furnace, the liability to form scaffolds is greatly diminished.

The total increase in bulk is much less in the semi-bituminous coals; and as the rate and amount of increase determines the risk from obstructions, coals which expand but slightly in coking may generally be used in the raw state with satisfactory results.

One prominent disadvantage attending the use of raw coal containing a large per-centage of volatile substances, is the comparatively low temperature prevailing in the upper portions of the furnace. The volumes of gas and aqueous vapour distilled from the fuel combine with the ascending column of heated gases, reducing their temperature and that of the adjacent materials to a degree incompatible with the perfect deoxydation and cementation of the ore before reduction in the hearth.

The use of small coal is attended with an immediate deterioration of the quality of the metal. It is rarely, however, that such coal is intentionally introduced into the furnace; all the fuel, whether coal, coke, or charcoal, is filled into the barrows by "pikes," formed of iron bars (Pl. XXXV., Fig. 213), having sufficient space between each of the bars for the small to fall through. But if finely broken coal or coke from any cause gains admittance in considerable quantity as part of the fuel, the injury to the furnace and metal may be very great. We have ascertained that a proportion so low as 7 per cent. of the weight of the fuel will change the metal from dark grey to mottled and white, and if this proportion be exceeded the deterioration becomes still greater. That this change should result from the presence of so low a per-centage of small coal, may appear surprising; but it must be remembered that for the production of every pound of dark grey iron two pounds of carbon are consumed, and that no portion of this is supplied by the small coal; consequently, whatever proportion the small bears to the large coal, by so much will the effective power of the fuel be diminished. This subject has already been fully discussed.

Injurious effects, similar to those which result from using coal of a weak fusible nature, are sometimes caused by employing coal that has been exposed to the atmosphere, though for a few weeks only. Several of the most valuable Welsh coals deteriorate in quality if stocked in heaps. They lose a great portion of their heating power, become brittle, and finally, if suffered to remain for a few months, disintegration commences, and the whole heap crumbles into small pieces. The effective power remaining in these coals will depend on the length of time they have been exposed and the season of the year. Under ordinary circumstances three months exposure will reduce their carrying power one-third; six months, more than one-half. Coals which have been exposed more than six months cannot be used in the blast furnace with safety, since under the action of heat they crumble to pieces.

The reduced power of small coal, broken coke, or other fuel in small pieces, when compared with that of larger coal, although already treated of at some length, may require additional explanation. It is known that a given quantity of large fuel, yielding a certain portion of carbon, will smelt a definite quantity of metal, but with the same fuel broken into small pieces good metal cannot be produced; and if broken very small the effect is the total stoppage of smelting operations. The quantities of carbon charged into the furnace are the same in each case; but the results are widely different. We are of opinion that this arises from two causes.—Firstly. On account of the small dimensions of each piece the coal is partially consumed in the upper regions of the furnace, and that which does descend burns too rapidly under the immediate action of the blast for the requisite quantity of carbon to combine with the metal.—Secondly. On account of the blast acting on a number of fragmentary pieces of fuel, mingled with iron ore and lime, the temperature maintained is too low for perfect deoxydation and the complete separation of the iron from the cinder; the result is the production of an inferior white metal. To illustrate the subject more fully, let the fuel, originally in lumps of 32 lbs. each (the average weight of lumps of raw coal for the furnace) be broken into eight pieces, averaging 4 lbs. each, the cross dimensions of each piece will be one-half of those of the original; but the aggregate surface for the blast to act on will be doubled. Now we have ascertained by experiment that the duration of the fuel under blast of a known intensity is nearly as the thickness, and inversely, as the surface exposed; therefore the duration of the small fuel will be one-fourth only of the larger. The fuel being consumed so rapidly, the metal fails to absorb the same quantity of carbon which it would take up under a slower combustion. Again, the coal being thus split up, the pieces occupy, including the ironmaking materials in their interstices, a space nearly four times the area of the original piece. Over this extended surface the blast plays on the divided lumps of coal; but the heat generated under these circumstances is too low for the complete reduction and separation of the metal.

The quality of the metal is affected both by the nature of the limestone used as flux, and by the way it is filled into the furnace. Uncalcined limestone is generally used for fluxing. If it be broken small before it enters the furnace—say into pieces of not more than one pound each—it works well, and the cinder produced along with good grey metal will be of an even quality. But if large pieces are used—and furnaces may be found where the lumps range from 5 to 20 lbs. each—the effects will be discernible in the inferiority of the metal and in the altered appearance of the cinder, which, in contrast to its former smooth flow and even surface, will now contain pieces of partially fused stone. The larger the pieces of stone charged, the more apparent will be the alteration in the general quality of the metal and cinders. On the other hand, the smaller the stones the more easily are they fused, and the more readily will they unite with the earthy matrix of the ore, and thus form a fluid cinder from which the metal separates without difficulty. When large stones are used the heated blast fuses the exterior only, leaving an unmelted core. The fused part unites with the other earths to form cinder, but while this is going on the mass is descending, and ultimately the unfused portions float on the melted materials below the action of the blast. The cinders being deprived of the beneficial effects of so much limestone will be thick, and as the metal will separate but imperfectly, they will contain a larger portion of iron. And if they be examined when cold, they will be found of a dark colour, and spotted with lumps of partially fused limestone.

Apart from the impossibility of reducing large lumps of limestone in the limited time, during which they remain exposed to the intense heat in the region of the tuyeres in their rapid descent in the hearth, they considerably lower the temperature of the furnace.

At some works the limestone before being used in the furnace is calcined in kilns similar to those used for roasting the ore. It loses about 40 per cent. of its weight of carbonic acid and water. By so much, of course, the weight of calcined stone for fluxing may be reduced below that of raw limestone. The beneficial effects of burnt limestone are considerable One of much importance being, that the temperature at top is not so diminished as with raw stone; to this circumstance no doubt it is owing that a given weight of fuel will produce a greater weight of iron with burnt than with raw limestone. Yet with this marked advantage burnt lime is not extensively used as a flux. The reason probably being, the readiness with which it absorbs moisture from the atmosphere. If care is not taken to have it conveyed promptly from the kiln to the furnace the quantity of water absorbed will be greater than that contained in the raw stone, and all the benefit of calcination be thus lost.

In selecting a stone for flux, its comparative freedom from clay, silica, and other earths, should guide the judgment. The presence of small quantities of clay and silica is not injurious to the quality of the metal, but as these earths generally exist in sufficient abundance in the ironstone, it is desirable to have a flux as free from them as possible.

The effects produced on the quality of the metal by changes in the atmosphere, are both serious and constantly recurring. It is known that the metal produced in winter and spring is, on the whole, superior to that produced in summer and autumn, and that the difference of quality is due to the condition of the atmosphere in these seasons; the immediate cause, however, is not so well understood.

We have already stated that the introduction of water into blast furnaces is attended with the most prejudicial effects. At certain seasons of the year the atmosphere contains a considerable quantity of water, which is forced into the furnace through the tuyeres along with the blast; at other periods the materials collected for smelting are saturated with rain falling on them, and water is thus also conveyed into the furnace, but through the throat, so that at certain times water is discharged into the furnace at top with the materials, and at bottom with the blast.

The quantity of water conveyed into the furnace along with the materials at top, will depend on the fuel, burden, and other circumstances. If the furnace is working on argillaceous ironstone, coke, and limestone, and working 120 tons per week, the weekly consumption of materials will be about 288 tons of calcined ironstone, 204 tons of coke, and 102 tons of limestone. If the coke is made in ovens and quenched with water, it will contain on an average 12 per cent. of water, amounting on 204 tons of coke to $24\frac{1}{2}$ tons. The quantity absorbed by the calcined ironstone will vary with the state of the atmosphere and method of calcining, the stone calcined in the open air absorbing more than the stone calcined in kilns, but it may be estimated at 8 per cent., or on 288 tons of ironstone 23 tons of water. The limestone will contain about 20 per cent. of water, or in 102 tons of stone $20\frac{1}{4}$ tons of water. Hence the quantity of water discharged weekly into a furnace with the materials at top, may, and often does, exceed 68 tons, or 11 cwts. of water for each ton of pig-metal produced. The atmosphere has little influence upon the water absorbed by coke in being cooled, and that in limestone used raw, but the water in the calcined ironstone is altogether due to absorption from the atmosphere, and in numerous instances the water carried by the coke has been obtained from the same source. The quantity of water introduced with the materials at top may be diminished or increased by alterations in the ore, fuel, and flux. Raw coal absorbs and conveys into the furnace less water than coke. From burnt lime the water has been expelled, and if used immediately the quantity of moisture absorbed will be inconsiderable; but if it be exposed to the air for a short time, it will absorb more water than the original stone. Quantities of iron ores are smelted containing even more water than that which we have stated.

The quantity of water discharged into the furnace through the tuyere, will depend on the consumption of blast and quantity of moisture in the atmosphere. For dark grey pig-iron the consumption is 25 tons of air per ton of metal made. Estimating, then, that the make is 120 tons weekly, the consumption of blast will be 3000 tons. Now, according to the most trustworthy authorities on the composition of atmospheric air, it appears that in ordinarily dry weather it contains 1.42 per cent of moisture. At this rate, then, the water in 3000 tons of air will amount to nearly 43 tons. This, however, refers to comparatively dry air. The generally moist atmosphere of this country contains at periods full twice this per centage of water; on such occasion, the volume of water discharged into the furnace along with the blast will not fall far short of 100 tons weekly, or from 50 to 60 tons above the quantity discharged into it in favourable seasons.

If to the quantity discharged into the furnace along with the blast there be added the quantity entering with the materials at top, it will be seen that there are periods when, from a superabundance of moisture in the atmosphere, the enormous quantity of 160 tons of water is discharged weekly into a blast furnace, making 120 tons of metal, and that under ordinary circumstances the quantity entering is equal in weight to the make of iron. The deteriorating effects which such volumes of water produce in the quality of the metal are very apparent. With a dry easterly wind, the quality and make will be greatly superior to that obtained when the wind is from any other point of the compass. A sudden shift from east to south-west occasions a deterioration in quality from dark to bright grey, and if the alteration continues, from grey to mottled and white. Thus the importance of a dry atmosphere for blast furnace operations can scarcely be overrated.

Some years ago hydrostatic regulators for equalising the pressure of the blast were common at the ironworks of this country. Their construction evinced much ingenuity, and was necessarily attended with great expense. The effect produced by them on the metal was remarkable. By closely observing the blast from a water regulator in comparison with that from an engine blowing directly into the furnace, the fact became known that a quantity of water was absorbed by the blast and carried into the furnace whenever the water regulator was used. The effects produced by this water was a diminished make, an inferior yield of materials, and the production of a thick, sluggish, white pig-iron. We have no means of ascertaining the quantity of water absorbed by the blast in its passage, but looking at the fact that the sectional area of the air-chamber in the hydrostatic regulator was about twice the area of that of the blowing cylinder, the velocity of the air current would be about $1\frac{1}{4}$ feet per second, and as only a very small portion of the air was in actual contact with the water, the quantity absorbed must have been small. And yet, inconsiderable as it may have been in itself when added to that already present in the atmosphere, it would be sufficient to produce the most prejudicial effects on the quality of the metal and the working of the furnace.

RATE OF PRODUCTION.

The yield of cast-iron from blast-furnaces of a given capacity, and blown with a fixed volume of blast, will be affected chiefly by the richness of the ore and the quality of the fuel, and, to a minor extent, by that of the flux. The smelting powers of the furnace are limited to the production of a definite quantity of materials in a stated time. With ironstones of the argillaceous class the extreme production of fluid cinder and iron at the bottom is at the rate of 25 cwts. per week for each yard capacity. This rate cannot be exceeded without deteriorating the quality of the metal. But with a richer stone the production of *metal* may be augmented, the produce of *cinder* remaining nearly constant. If a calcined ironstone, yielding 38 per cent. of metal be employed, 3 tons will be required to produce 1 ton of metal; but if one containing 46 per cent. be employed, 48 cwts. will be sufficient.

The time required for deoxydation and cementation is about 46 hours, and if the furnace smelts the lean ores at the rate of 25 cwts. of iron and cinders per yard capacity, it will also smelt this quantity with the richer ores. But the proportion of metal to cinders, which with the lean ores would be as 7 to 18, becomes as 8 to 17 with the richer stones. The make of metal is consequently augmented in this ratio.

There is, however, a limit to this increase of production by the use of rich ores. The materials must be in the furnace the stated time, and the gross weight of the liquid products not exceed 25 cwts. If very rich ores are employed, additional clay and lime becomes necessary as flux, and, consequently, an increased consumption of fuel; so that the proportion of metal to cinder is not sensibly affected, and the rate of production is not increased. Also if the stones are very lean, the large quantity of lime necessary to flux the earths, combined with the metal, causes the proportion of iron to cinder to be diminished. If the yield of the calcined stone is only 27 per cent., 4 tons will be required for 1 ton of metal, and the proportion which this metal will bear to the cinder will be nearly as 6 to 19. The make consequently will be reduced in this ratio.

If the capacity of the furnace be equal to 160 cubic yards, with the stone yielding 46 per cent., it will produce on an average 64 tons; with the stone yielding 38 per cent., 56 tons; and with that yielding 27 per cent., the average will be 48 tons per week.

An exception must be made in the case of the carbonaceous ironstone so much used in Scotland. This stone yields, after calcination, from 44 to 64 per cent. of metal; the average is nearly 60 per cent. The matter, in combination with the metal—about 40 per cent. of the whole weight—consists of carbon, alumina, silica, and lime. This last is generally about 5 per cent. of the weight. In consequence of the presence of this lime and the small per-centage of earths, the additional quantity of lime required for flux is usually less than 6 cwts. The carbon is consumed before the blast, and the earthy matrix of the stone, combining with the lime, forms cinder, but in comparatively small quantities. With argillaceous iron-stones the weight of the cinder will never be less than twice that of the metal; but with carbonaceous ore, from the peculiar manner in which the carbon is combined with the metal, grey-iron is produced with not more than an equal weight of cinder. And instead of a gross fluid product, 25 cwts. per cubic yard of furnace capacity, 34 cwts. is obtained. The greater facility with which pig-iron can be produced from the carbonaceous ironstone is made still more apparent on comparing the quantities of blast consumed per ton of pig-iron. This, with argillaceous ironstone, averages 25 tons, but with carbonaceous ironstone 8 tons suffice. If we carry the comparison to the total fluid products, we find that on an average 1 ton of metal and cinder is produced with carbonaceous ironstone with 4 tons of air for each ton; with argillaceous ironstones 8 tons are required.

The rate of production is affected by the qualities of the fuel. A hard dense semi-bituminous coal, containing a large per-centage of carbon, and yielding little ashes, will reduce the greatest quantity of metal. Coke prepared from a coal too bituminous for use in the raw state will reduce metal in proportion to its density and the carbon it contains.

With a weak friable coal, or the coke prepared from such coal, the production is lowest. Since the height of the blast furnace has been increased to 40 and 45 feet, a blast of $2\frac{1}{4}$ to 3 lbs. to the square inch has become general. But with weak coals this pressure of blast is attended with an increased consumption of fuel, if the make and quality of the metal are to be at all maintained.

The make will be less with coke prepared from a given coal than with the raw coal itself—with such coals as expand in coking. The coke, consisting chiefly of carbon combined with the earthy matters of the coal, is qualified for the immediate action of the blast, and undergoes little alteration in its descent to the hearth; but, bulk for bulk, the coke does not contain so much carbon as coal. Consequently, as it occupies a greater space, the quantity of other materials in the furnace at the same time is diminished. And since the time of descent cannot be reduced without deteriorating the quality, the quantity of stone smelted and the produce of metal are diminished.

With anthracite coal the greatest make is effected, the relative dimensions of the furnaces being considered. And since this coal contains the largest per-centage of carbon of any hitherto discovered, and alters but slightly in descending through the furnace, it appears eminently adapted, in conjunction with a powerful blast, for smelting the finer qualities of metal.

The quality of the limestone used as a flux will affect the make of the furnace. If it contains a notable per-centage of alumina and silica its practical value is diminished by nearly twice the amount of these earths. Their presence in quantity involves disadvantages equivalent to those attendant on the use of a lean ore. The alumina and silica combined with the limestone requiring fuel and lime for their fusion just as though they were combined with the ore. These additional materials occupy space in the furnace without contributing to the produce of metal, and of course exclude a proportionate quantity of iron-stone. The quantity of cinders, in proportion to that of the metal, will be increased by the quantity of earths in the limestone and the lime necessary for their fusion. The make, therefore, will be diminished by the lower yield of iron from the liquid materials at the hearth.

The smaller space occupied by caustic lime, together with its comparative lightness and freedom from moisture, favour a large production from the furnace. Where it is used an increase of 3 to 4 per cent. is observable in the make. This is accounted for by the reduced consumption of fuel in smelting, and the smaller space occupied by the flux, enabling the furnace to drive more charges in a given time.

The make of the blast furnace varies with the season of the year, as the reader will doubtless be led to conclude, from our remarks upon the effect of the hygrometic state of the atmosphere upon the quality of metal and yield of fuel. It is well known to smelters that with materials of similar quality, and volume of blast unaltered, the make of the furnace is greater in the winter months than at any other season. Until within the last few years this was attributed to the coldness of the air; and on the introduction of the invention of the hot blast to the manufacturers of iron this superiority of cold winter air over warm summer air was adduced as a reason against the use of the heated blast. The greater efficiency of the colder air was considered by some writers to arise from its increased density, which augments in proportion to the decrease of temperature, a given volume of air containing more oxygen in winter than in summer. The cause of this superior make in winter is now, however, generally ascribed to what is doubtless its real cause—the greater dryness of the atmosphere in winter as compared with summer.

Taking for our data the make of the 18 blast furnaces at the Dowlais works during a period of seven years, we find that the actual increase of make in winter over that of summer —premising that the furnace is working on a similar burden—is between 4 and 5 per cent.; and with this increase there is also a marked improvement in the quality of the iron obtained. If we consider the state of the atmosphere of this country in summer we shall arrive at the conclusion that its dryness or dampness is amply sufficient to cause these alterations in the operation of the blast furnace.

SECTION VII.

DENSITY OF BLAST.

THE pressure or density of the blast is a matter of considerable importance in smelting. The considerations that determine it are the height of the furnace, size of the hearth, and quality of the fuel.

In the infancy of the iron manufacture, through the then low state of the mechanical arts, the blowing machines employed were very deficient in the power necessary for compressing the air. The volume of the blast was small and the pressure low, and the furnaces, being of correspondingly small capacity, the produce of metal was on the same limited scale. But with the progress of improvement in the manufacture of machinery blowing machines were constructed of greater power and capacity, so that larger volumes of blast at a higher pressure were obtainable, and, with additional blowing power, the capacity and height of the furnace was increased and the produce of metal augmented proportionately.

The degree of compression of the blast depends upon the height of the furnace, because the weight of the column of materials affects the density of the stratum of fuel under combustion. However, the blast furnaces of the present day are nearly uniform in height, a deviation of more than 5 feet from the average being rare. The variation, therefore, in the pressure of the superincumbent materials on the fuel, arising from the greater or less height of the column in different furnaces, is not great. So that in proportioning the density and volume of blast, we need only consider the internal dimensions of the furnace and quality of the fuel.

In the present state of the manufacture 2 lbs. to the square inch is a minimum degree of compression. A few years since a blast of a lower pressure was tried at the Wingerworth furnaces, but after great expense was incurred and waste of materials caused, it was abandoned, and a blast of $2\frac{1}{4}$ to $2\frac{1}{2}$ lbs. to the square inch substituted. More recently we have ourselves witnessed the injurious effects of a weak scattered blast upon the make and quality of pig-iron.

The maximum density of blast is dependent to a certain extent on the fuel; if the coal is of a hard compact quality, containing a large per-centage of carbon, a pressure of 4 to 5 lbs. to the square inch may be advantageously adopted. With a weak friable coal, containing less carbon, from 2 to 3 lbs. is very commonly used. The compact coke of a highly bituminous coal supports a blast of $2\frac{1}{4}$ to $3\frac{1}{4}$ lbs. to the square inch.

As a general rule, and one to which we have seen no exceptions, the density of blast applicable to any given coal—other things being equal—is proportionate to the density of the coke produced from such coal. Hence the hardest and heaviest coke will carry the strongest blast, and *vice versâ*.

Generally speaking, the increase in the density of the blast has not kept pace with the enlarged dimensions of the furnace, and yet they are intimately related to each other. The density must be sufficiently great that the requisite quantity of air shall penetrate through the materials to the opposite side of the hearth, so as to maintain active combustion in the descending fuel situated farthest off from the tuyere. The broader the hearth of the furnace the more numerous will be the obstructions to the passage of air across it. Any increase, then, in breadth should be met by a corresponding increase in the density of the blast. The degree of compression is undoubtedly higher now than formerly; but it is not yet sufficient for the large hearths at present constructed.

In the old blast furnaces the breadth of the hearth seldom exceeded 3 feet, and the blast had only to penetrate through a mass of that thickness. The density was usually $1\frac{1}{4}$ to 2 lbs. to the square inch. If the obstructions offered by this thickness of material required a blast of such a density for the effectual reduction of the metal it is very evident that a greater width of hearth requires an increased density in nearly the same proportion. If to penetrate 3 feet requires a mean pressure of $1\frac{4}{5}$ lbs. to the square inch, to penetrate twice this distance would require a proportionately greater pressure. Assuming that a pressure of $1\frac{4}{5}$ lbs. was suitable for 3 feet hearths, an approximation may be made to the pressure required for any other width. The proportion may be taken equal to 6-10ths of a pound for each foot in width. Hearths are now constructed up to 8 feet in breadth, and upon this proportion the pressure of blast for such should be $4\frac{4}{5}$ lbs. to the square inch; for the more common breadth of 6 feet the pressure would be $3\frac{1}{2}$ lbs. But in practice a lower density is used, partly because the relation which the density of the blast should bear to the breadth of the hearth is not fairly considered, and partly because the blowing engines having been constructed to produce blast of a given density, an increase, though it may be desired, is not often obtainable. Furnaces with the widest hearths are blown with engines which maintain a pressure of $2\frac{1}{2}$ to 3 lbs. to the square inch; but the diameter of the discharging pipes is such that at their termination a greater pressure than 2 lbs. to the square inch is seldom realised.

Perfect combustion of the fuel with so low a pressure of blast is not to be expected; the portions farthest from the tuyere do not receive the requisite quantity of oxygen for creating a rapid combustion and intense heat; and consequently the carbon of such fuel does not become fully effective in the reduction of the materials. The full powers of the coal are not brought to bear on the metal, and the quality consequently suffers.

The distinction between volume and density is not sufficiently attended to by ironmasters. Accompanying the enlarged capacity of the furnace the volume of blast has been increased, but augmentation in volume *alone* is not sufficient to obtain the entire benefits which ought to accrue from the employment of large furnaces. To suppose that the same density of blast is equally suitable to a large as to a small furnace, is to assume that a blast of given density can penetrate across any hearth in sufficient quantities for combustion, whatever may be its breadth. This is obviously erroneous. From inattention to this point the capacity of the furnace has been increased from about 80 yards to 260 and 280 yards; and in consequence, an equally great, if not greater, increase in the volume of blast has taken place, but the density remains nearly the same. Had the density of the blast been augmented in the same ratio as the increased dimensions of the furnace, the produce of large blast furnaces would be more in unison with their capacity.

While, however, we advocate the employment of a blast of adequate volume and density, we freely admit that no form of tuyere yet invented can produce a perfect combustion of the carbon. The blast of low density supplies the nearest fuel with oxygen, but fails to penetrate the materials farthest off, while a high density affords ample air to the most distant fuel, and scarcely any to that in contact with the sides. A tuyere which shall afford to all parts of the hearth the requisite quantity of air for maintaining a uniformly perfect combustion is much wanted, and until it is brought into use a high economy of fuel cannot be attained.

We believe that a compound tuyere, consisting of a central discharge of very dense blast, and an exterior annular discharge of a less dense blast, will eventually supersede the single tuyere.

The necessity for maintaining a certain pressure of blast is generally admitted by ironmasters. By no other known means can sufficient air be brought into contact with the fuel; however, the patent records of this country contain many ingenious substitutes for the common plan of forcing a draught. A furnace was built not long since in the neighbourhood of Caerphilly, and an attempt was made to obtain the requisite supply of air by exhaustion, but without success, and the operation was discontinued. A different result could scarcely have been anticipated after a moment's careful consideration. For the rate of combustion necessary to the maintenance of a high temperature is so rapid that the impossibility of supplying the necessary quantity of atmospheric air by an indraught becomes manifest. On the furnace-grates of ordinary stationary engine-boilers the rate of consumption is not often above 15 lbs. of coal per square foot of grate per hour. This rate can be easily maintained by having a chimney-stack from 110 to 120 feet high, when the grate surface is 180 to 200 square feet. In locomotive engines, by employing a portion of the available power of the steam, the rate of combustion is increased to 60 lbs. per foot per hour; but this is greatly under the requirements of the blast furnace. The furnace delineated in Pl. XV., consumes, when working in full blast, 270 tons of coal weekly. The combustion of this coal is effected in the hearth, which for the time being we may consider as a species of grate; but in estimating the surface for combustion we must deduct the space occupied by the ironstone and flux, leaving as available surface an area not exceeding 20 square feet. Dividing the consumption of coal by the hours in a week and by the surface for combustion, we obtain 180 lbs. as the rate of combustion per foot per hour, or three times the quantity consumed in the locomotive engine-grate with the violent indraught created by the escaping steam. But the free consumption of the fuel in the blast furnace at the above rapid rate is impeded by the weight of the superincumbent materials—say from 150 to 200 tons. So that if it were possible to create a sufficient draught by exhaustion to burn 180 lbs. per foot of grate per hour, the obstruction which this column of materials would offer to the passage of the ascending gas would destroy it. No contrivance short of forcing the air into the furnace by compression can possibly produce such a rapid combination of the fuel and such a supply of oxygen as is demanded by the high temperature necessary to be maintained in the interior of a blast furnace.*

But the waste of steam-power in the locomotive engine, in order to create a draught for the combustion of 60 lbs. of fuel per square foot per hour, is immense. Of the power generated by each 60 lbs. of fuel consumed fully two-fifths is expended in maintaining the draught. The 24 lbs. of coal thus consumed is capable of generating sufficient steam to produce four-horse power; this expenditure, then, is required to maintain the combustion of 60 lbs. of coal per hour by this mode of creating a draught. But by the method of compressing the air in cylinders 50 lbs. of coal are consumed in one-third of the above time for each horse-power expended. Measuring, then, the comparative efficiency of the two systems in this manner, the power expended in compressing the blast to the requisite density is scarcely a fraction of that expended in creating an indraught of inferior velocity.

Considerable diversity of opinion exists as to the best mode of applying the blast. The most usual method is by three tuyeres, one on each side and the third at the back; but other modes are to be seen at several works. It is seldom that fewer than three are employed in modern furnaces, but a greater number is considered by some ironmasters as more advantageous, and furnaces may be seen receiving blast through 10 and even 12 nozzles.

The volume of blast is fixed; therefore, when the number of pipes is increased, if the density of the blast is to be maintained at the tuyeres, their diameter is reduced so that the total sectional area of orifice remains unaltered. The same quantity of blast then being discharged through a greater number of pipes the quantity passing through each will, of course, be less in proportion to its reduced sectional area.

The advantages supposed to attend the use of a large number of small pipes are a more perfect combustion of the fuel, and, consequently, economy of blast and smelting materials, and an increased make of iron. By some ironmasters it is maintained that these advantages have been actually realized wherever the number of tuyeres has been increased, and on more than one occasion letters patent have been obtained for the supposed discovery of this improved mode of bringing the blast in contact with the fuel, and the employment of 4 or more tuyeres is now common in several districts. Our own experience, however, does not permit us to subscribe to the general approval of numerous tuyeres. After a lengthy trial at several furnaces we were unable to discover any superiority possessed by the greater over the

* The consumption of fuel in locomotive fireboxes is occasionally at the rate of 150lbs. per foot, per hour, a rate not far short of that maintained in many blast furnaces; and there is little reason to doubt that the temperature of the burning fuel is often quite equal. The real reason that the attempts to provide draught for iron furnaces by exhaustion have failed, no doubt, is that the volumes of gaseous material to be dealt with are so prodigious, and their temperature so high, that it is impracticable rather than impossible to provide suitable apparatus.—EDS.

fewer number, but rather the contrary. If due consideration be paid to the circumstances by which the volume and density of the blast should be determined no other result could be expected. The admission of the blast at several points in the circumference of the hearth is doubtless productive of a more perfect combustion of so much of the fuel as may be within its influence, but it is detrimental to the combustion of the remoter portions. For the profitable combustion of the fuel, every portion of it lying within the zone of fusion should be supplied with the requisite quantity of atmospheric air. This can only be accomplished by using a blast properly proportioned in volume and density to the size of the hearth and quantity of fuel consumed in a given time. This last, supposing the degree of fusibility of the ore and capacity of the furnace be known, may be easily ascertained. If then the volume be apportioned to the breadth of hearth and quantity of carbon, and the density of the air be fixed, the comparative efficiency of a greater or less number of tuyeres may be measured by the relative quantities of blast decomposed by the fuel at or a little above their level.

If the blast is cut up into a number of small jets their intensity and ability to penetrate the materials is inferior to that of larger jets. The pieces of fuel in the immediate vicinity of the issuing blast are liberally supplied with oxygen, but the quantity of atmospheric air intended for the remoter positions, unable to force a passage through the materials, ascends undecomposed into the higher regions of the furnace, absorbing heat in the ascent, and so far reducing the available temperature. A portion of the fuel failing of its full supply of oxygen, the ironstone is deprived of the reducing power of so much carbon, and, consequently, the consumption of coal is increased.

The deficient intensity of the small jets to penetrate to the remotest parts of the hearth is partially understood by the advocates of the numerous small tuyeres, and to remedy the defect a high density of blast, up to four pounds per square inch, is employed. At the ironworks in the Swansea Valley, and at the Aberdare, Abernant, and other works, a high pillar of blast is used with furnaces which are under the average height. But although an increased density of blast may produce combustion of the remoter fuel, it necessarily increases the evils occasioned by the presence of undecomposed air in the furnace. The quantity of blast is considerably above the actual requirements of the fuel, and the excess only absorbs caloric in its passage, which is so much loss. At the above-named works the blast delivered into the furnace exceeds the quantity required for combustion by nearly one-third.

Apart from the detrimental effects on the furnace, this waste of blast is itself attended with great expense, and coupled with the high density required, tells very much against the small tuyere system. The increase in the density of the blast has usually exceeded one-third, and a similar increase has been made in the volume, or, for 3 cubic feet of atmospheric air at 3 lbs. per inch, there is now employed 4 cubic feet at 4 lbs. If then a given power sufficed to generate blast for a furnace with the minimum number of tuyeres, with the larger number the power required is augmented in the proportion of 9 to 16. The cost of compressing the blast varies at different works, but (with the exception of those where iron is smelted from carbonaceous ironstone) it will, with very superior engines and the fewer number of tuyeres, not exceed two shillings per ton of pig-iron. The additional expense then to the manufacturer using small tuyeres is very considerable for engine-power alone.

The effects of the change at the Dowlais works were not so apparent, but this, however, was probably owing to the smaller number of tuyeres employed. In the Swansea Valley the furnaces are generally blown with 10 tuyeres, three each side and back, and one in the breast; but at the Dowlais furnaces six tuyeres were substituted for three, two on each side and back instead of one, and no alteration was made in the volume or density of the blast. Whatever alterations then occurred in the working of the furnace were the result of the increased number of tuyeres. In 1847-48, during a period of 15 months blowing with the double set of tuyeres at each furnace, the average yield of coal for smelting was 50.1 cwts. The average yield with single tuyeres during the two years preceding the experiment was 45.3 cwts. With the single tuyere in each house the average weekly make of each furnace was 93 tons 15 cwts., but with the double tuyere it was 92 tons. A loss consequently occurred from the small tuyeres of 4.8 cwts. of coal on each ton of iron, and a diminution of two tons nearly in the weekly make. Estimated on the make of pig-iron at that establishment during the above period the additional consumption of coal in the furnace consequent on the alteration amounted to 25,750 tons. If to this coal be added the expense of the alteration, the increased consumption of the iron-making, materials, and the deficiency in make, it will be apparent that the policy of using, under any circumstance, a number of small tuyeres, is, to say the least, very questionable.

The working expense of the small tuyere system is also greatly in excess of the large tuyeres. Twice or three times the number of pipes, tuyeres, and joints have to be kept in repair. The leakage of blast is increased in a similar ratio, and, owing to the quantity of air, supplied to the fuel near the tuyeres, the heat generated at each group is so intense that recourse is had to water breasts around and hollow water blocks below the tuyeres. The water circulating through these keeps the tuyeres cool at the expense of the heat destined for the reduction of the ironstone. (Pls. XXXIII., XXXIV., Figs. 189, 190, 202.)

In Scotland it is a rare circumstance for a furnace to be blown with so few as three tuyeres. At the Langloan works they are blown with four tuyeres, 2 on each side; at the Dandyvan works 5 tuyeres are used; at the Gartsherrie, 4, 5 and 6 are used; at the Monkland works, 5; and at the Govan furnaces 8 tuyeres, 3 on each side and 2 in the back. All these furnaces have large hearths. The consumption of fuel to the quantity of blast is excessive, as we have already shown. May not a portion of this excess be accounted for by the use of numerous small tuyeres. We have seen that the employment of 6 small instead of 3 large nozzles at the Dowlais works caused an increased consumption of fuel of nearly 5 cwts. per ton of iron. We do not know of any circumstance connected with the Scotch furnaces which should exempt them from using a greater quantity of coal under like circumstances.

The small tuyere system is in use at some English works. Several of the Yorkshire furnaces are blown with six tuyeres, but we are not aware of a single instance where the adoption of the plan has been followed by a saving of fuel, blast, or other material, or, indeed, by any other advantage commensurate with its greater cost both in construction and maintenance.

TUYERE AND NOSE-PIPE—ADMISSION OF BLAST.

The beneficial effects which result from a blast of the requisite volume and density may be, and often are, destroyed by the use of improper pipes for its delivery into the furnace. The longitudinal section of the nose-pipe and tuyere has a most important bearing on the efficiency of the blast. Unless these are properly proportioned at first and carefully maintained to their original section it is hopeless to expect that the blast delivered will produce a maximum effect.

The most common error committed in the construction of nose-pipes is making their horizontal section to converge too rapidly—the difference between the diameters of the ends is too great for their length. With pipes having much taper, the distance to which the blast is projected is materially diminished; and at a very short distance from the outlet the density of the blast is very little superior to that of the atmosphere. The tapering form of the pipe favours the divergence of the blast, while, in smelting, a dense concentrated blast is required at a distance of several feet from the pipe, for under no other conditions can the blast penetrate through a mass of materials to supply the air necessary for the combustion of the fuel.

The effects produced on the furnace from using pipes of too much taper usually show themselves in an increased yield of coal, and the burning of the work around the tuyere. The increase in the coal is often very considerable. In consequence of the density of the blast being reduced so quickly after its emission from the pipe it is unable to penetrate far into the mass of materials; the quantity of air to the fuel in the vicinity of the tuyere is consequently so great that an unnecessarily high temperature is created, to the injury of the brickwork of the hearth.

The diameter of the pipe, its length and thickness, should be determined after mature consideration by a responsible person, instead of being left, as is generally done at present, to one of the workmen, and a careful supervision should be exercised in the smithy while it is being made. In numerous instances that have come under our own immediate knowledge the diameter of the bore has been given, but the length and the diameter at the large end have been left to the discretion of the workmen. The pipe conveying the blast into the nose-pipe is usually placed at a fixed distance from the furnace, and if the position of the tuyere be altered, a different length of nose-pipe is required. If the distance is shortened—the two diameters of the pipe remaining unaltered—the taper is increased, but if it is lengthened the same quantity of taper is retained, but being distributed over a greater length the angle is less, and the tendency of the blast to diverge on escaping is reduced. Short pieces of pipe of different lengths are sometimes employed to connect the large end of the nose-pipe to the blast-pipe. They maintain the taper of the nose-pipe, but as their employment increases the number of joints for leakage, and causes obstructions to the free delivery of the blast, they should be, if possible, avoided. A better mode of adjusting the distance between the tuyere and fixed blast-pipe is by a telescope pipe properly fitted with a ring piston working airtight in a cylinder, as delineated in Pl. XV., Fig. 88, Pl. XXXII., Fig. 169. Pipes of this description have now been in use for several years at the Dowlais works, and for facility of working and economy of blast are probably unequalled. Their first cost is greater than the usual fixed pipe, but the numerous advantages which they possess amply compensate for the outlay.

The breadth of the hearth should be considered in determining the taper of the nose-pipe, a wide hearth requiring less taper than a narrow one. With the old hearths the shape of the pipes was of less importance, as they were usually not more than 3 feet across. A pipe which would answer well for a hearth 3 feet wide, and supply sufficient air to all the fuel it held, would be totally unsuitable to one of 6 feet in width. The diameter of the nose is usually determined by the quantity of atmospheric air intended to be delivered, and with regard to the taper, from numerous observations, we are of opinion that for modern-sized hearths the large end should be one-fourth greater than the small for each foot in length. By this rule the outer end of a 4-inch nose-pipe, 18 inches long, would be $5\frac{1}{4}$ inches in diameter. If the metal in the end of the connecting pipe is very thick a socket should be made on the nose-pipe to go over it, so that the interior of the connexion may offer as little irregularity as possible to obstruct the passage of the blast.

The condition of the nose-pipe should be occasionally examined, that any upsetting of the metal or burning away may be remedied. For want of such examination and repair the point often becomes battered up and the intensity of the escaping blast reduced. At some furnaces thin pipes are used, and from the weakness of the metal when heated they soon lose their original form. Pipes made from $\frac{3}{8}$ or $\frac{1}{4}$-inch boiler-plate are preferable in every respect, and no thinner metal should be used. Their interior should be quite circular, the ends piled up true and square, leaving the angles sharp, and the nose filed out or bored to a gauge of the exact dimensions desired, taking care, however, that the thickness is not materially reduced by the fitting.

In many iron-works, from a mistaken notion of economy, the pipes are roughly made, presenting in their transverse section some resemblance to a circle, but differing in figure at different parts of the pipe. As the use of such pipes is attended with a certain waste of blast, it is not difficult to see that any saving effected in their manufacture is more than counterbalanced by the imperfect manner in which the blast is delivered. From our own experience we can safely say that the additional expense incurred in making a well-finished pipe is amply compensated by the greater efficiency of the blast.

The interior of the water tuyere is usually made as represented in Pl. XXXIII., Figs. 180, 181. About two-fifths of its length inside, measuring from its inner end, is made parallel; from this point to the outer end the bore is enlarged to about $1\frac{1}{4}$ times the diameter of the inner end. The diameter of the smallest part of the tuyere is made nearly the same as that of the nose-pipe. The space around the nose-pipe, inside the large end of the tuyere, is generally rammed tight with fire-clay or other filling, to prevent the escape of air.

The diameter or bore of the water-pipe varies from $\frac{1}{4}$ to 1 inch, according to circumstance. The thickness of the cast metal around the bore of the tuyere at the inner end is just sufficient to encircle the water-pipe and to protect it from the direct action of the heat, diminishing at the outer end to about 1 inch. In turning the water-pipe to the spiral form great care should be taken to avoid flattening it or opening it at the weld. For want of care in bending the tube many tuyeres are rendered useless, and leakage has occasioned much injury to the furnace.

The connexion of the inlet-pipe to the fixed water-pipe should be such as will admit of a ready separation and re-connexion when changing tuyeres. This is best accomplished by having one or two universal joints by which the direction of the pipe may be suited to the position of the tuyere, and a pair of small flanges united by screw-pins for disconnecting.

To keep the tuyere sufficiently cool at the point the water should circulate at the rate of 10 to 12 gallons per minute for each square inch of sectional area of orifice. The height of the reservoir above the tuyere should, wherever practicable, be little inferior to that of the furnace.

SECTION VIII.

INTERIOR OF FURNACES.

The form of the interior of the blast furnace has an important bearing on its duration, economy of materials, and smelting power. The nature of the fuel and ores to be smelted, and the quantity of metal desired weekly, should regulate the principal demensions; but in many districts they are determined by local usages, without reference to propriety or suitability.

Of late years some attention has been given to the form of furnace best calculated to yield a maximum quantity of metal with a minimum consumption of materials, and considerable departures have been made from the old shape. Considering, however, the great improvements which have been effected in the manufacture of iron generally, we are of opinion that in the construction of the blast furnace itself the improvement has not kept pace with that in the other departments. This is doubtless owing in a great degree to the little attention paid to the subject by smelters; but much is also due to the serious consequences which would be entailed in the event of the failure of any experiment. In most of the other departments the cost of making the necessary alterations for testing the value of any supposed improvement is small compared with the expense which must be incurred in experiments on the construction of blast furnaces. And if the trial prove unsuccessful the change back to the former arrangements may generally in other departments be made in a few days; but in the case of the blast furnace any alteration of the interior construction involves blowing out, and is attended with stoppage of works for weeks or even months. Since any deviation from established forms is attended with the risk of heavy loss, it is not a matter of surprise that ironmasters continue to build their furnaces of the present form. And until some enterprising ironmaster with ample means at command steps out of the well-beaten path, and constructs his furnaces in accordance with correct scientific principles, no considerable improvement can be expected in this direction.

Great as has been the improvement in the manufacture of iron in the present century, any very marked step in advance has generally been the work of years of perseverance. The difference between the present blast furnace and blast furnace of sixty years since, though confined principally to increase of dimensions only, is the result of numerous cautious experiments. On comparing the lines of furnaces recently built with those of furnaces erected half a century back, we find the difference to consist chiefly in the enlargement of the diameter at the boshes. The great increase in size has been arrived at by successive enlargements; the individual steps have been small through uncertainty as to the result of a great and sudden departure from the established proportions. Except in size, the majority of the furnaces of the present day are very little superior to those of a former period, and it is evident from their design that the laws that regulate combustion and the ascent of heated air are little understood amongst the great body of practical smelters.

The opinions of ironmasters are divided as to what form of hearth is the most advantageous. Leaving the size for future consideration, we may endeavour to ascertain which form appears to produce the best results. Square hearths are common in Staffordshire, and are frequently used in South Wales, and a few are to be met with in Scotland. At the Plymouth (Pl. XIV., Fig. 87) and Aberamman (Pl. XIX., Fig. 104) works near Merthyr Tydfil, and in the Anthracite furnaces of the Swansea Valley, and in some of the furnaces on the eastern side of the coal basin, square hearths are in use. The angles of the square hearth are sometimes rounded off, as in the Langloan furnace, or their sharpness diminished, as in the Aberamman furnace. In Scotland hearths of a circular form in plan are general, and they are also used in some modern Staffordshire furnaces. At the Rhymney, Tredegar, Sirhowy, Ebbw Vale, Cyfarthfa (Pl. XIV., Fig. 86 ; Pl. XVIII., Fig. 100 ; Pl. XIX., Fig. 105) ; and other works, this form is generally adopted, and probably this form of hearth will be found in one-half the Welsh blast furnaces. In some of the Scotch works the plan partakes of a pear-shape ; the back circular, and diminishing in breadth from the side tuyeres to the damplate either by a straight or curved wall.

Each kind of hearth has its advantages. The square form is especially applicable when more than one tuyere is blown at the side, as in Anthracite furnaces, but the combustion of the fuel is not generally so well accomplished. That portion which lies in the angles is out of the direct influence of the blast, and consequently gives out an inferior heat. In facility for working also this form is inferior to others. The angle between the cinder-fall and tuyeres is beyond the direct action of the blast, and cannot be reached by any instrument from the fall. Collections of cinder and partially fused matter consequently lodge in these corners, and reduce the available area of the hearth. Indeed after being in blast for a short period all the angular spaces in the square hearth become filled up by the adhesion of vitrified matter to the brickwork, and the plan of the working portion thus approximates to a circle.

The circular hearth approaches more nearly to the form produced by the fusion and flow of the materials, but it is defective in the sharp angles at each side of the cinder-fall. The portion of the hearth covered by these angles is inaccessible to the workmen from the front, and the removal of any substance which may lodge there is attended with great difficulty. A variety of the circular hearth, having a portion of the circumference opposite to each tuyere flattened for a space of 18 to 30 inches, is adopted at some works. It places the tuyeres a few inches nearer to each other than the diameter of the circle, but we are not aware of any advantage arising from this modification which would not be better obtained by a perfectly circular hearth of a diameter equal to the diminished distance.

The plan used at some Scotch works, and exclusively at the Dowlais works, fulfils the conditions required in a hearth better than any other form. (Pl. XVI., Fig. 92.) By having no sharp angles anywhere in the plan, the entire bottom is accessible to the workman, and the opportunity for semi-vitrified matter to lodge in or adhere to any part of the hearth much diminished. We have observed in furnaces which have been blown out, after having been in blast three or four years only, that the working part of the hearth has more or less approximated to this form, whatever might have been its original shape. This would indicate the propriety of adopting it at first, instead of leaving the metal and cinder to round the angles and fill up the hollows. Certain it is that where the circular or square form is adopted, the fluid metal acting on the material of the hearth widens the fall at its junction, and repairs are frequently required. It has a similar effect on the sides of the pear-shaped hearths, but from the absence of angles the necessary repairs can be made with great facility.

The breadth of the hearth from tuyere to tuyere is regulated partly by the fuel employed. In the old charcoal furnaces, smelting rich ores, successful results were obtained with narrow hearths. But in the present furnace, where coal and coke are used, the hearth is made wider in proportion to the diameter at the boshes; and when raw coal is used the hearths are generally wider than with coke. The size of the pieces of fuel to be used must be taken into consideration in proportioning the size of the hearth. A few of the lumps of raw coal charged into some of the present furnaces would be enough to choke the descent of the materials in the old narrow hearth.

In Scotland the breadth varies from 6 to 8 feet; the furnaces at Langloan and Kinneil are 6 feet; those at Dandyvan, 7 feet; while the breadth of the hearths at the Muirkirk new furnaces is 8 feet. The Staffordshire hearths are usually small; the alteration being but slight from the old dimensions. In the Welsh works the breadth varies from 5 to 8 feet; the Abernamman and Ystalyfera are 5 feet; the Sirhowy, 5¼ feet; Tredegar, 6 feet; Plymouth, 7 feet; and Dowlais, 8 feet in the large furnaces, and from 6 to 7 feet in the smallest.

Where coke is used as the fuel we are of opinion that 6 feet is wide enough for all purposes, but in full size furnaces, 16 to 18 feet in diameter across the boshes, and if using coal, 7 feet or 7½ feet is more advantageous. With a full volume of blast at the requisite density a maximum produce of metal will be obtained with hearths of these dimensions.

In the charcoal furnaces the hearths are usually about 2 feet square, but the largest diameter of these furnaces rarely exceeds 9 feet. The charcoal furnaces of Sweden and Russia have narrow hearths, but their mechanical arrangements for supplying blast are defective, and for this reason the produce of metal is very small.

The height of the hearth up to the commencement of the boshes is, similarly with the breadth, subject to variation. In the Welsh furnaces the height varies from 6 feet to 8 feet 6 inches; at the Tredegar and Aberamman furnaces it is 6 feet; at the Plymouth furnace 6 feet 6 inches; at the Anthracite furnaces 7 feet; and at the Dowlais furnace the hearths are from 7 to 8 feet 6 inches high. In Staffordshire they vary from 5 to 6 feet; and in the Scotch furnaces 5 feet appears to be the most common measurement.

We are disposed to consider 5 to 6 feet as the best dimension. A greater height can be attended with no advantage in point of economy, but may considerably reduce the smelting power of the furnace. If the hearth be carried high up the capacity of the furnace is proportionately diminished, and its powers of production reduced accordingly. In some of the furnaces of 18 feet diameter at boshes the hearths are built 8 feet 6 inches high, the interior capacity being 275 yards. Were they 6 feet high only the capacity gained (supposing all the other dimensions remained unaltered) would equal 20 cubic yards, nearly; that is to say, the contents of a cylinder 18 feet in diameter by 2 feet 6 inches deep, minus the amount by which the hearth would be diminished. By thus reducing the height of the hearth to the most profitable dimension the capacity of the furnace is increased one-fourteenth, or from 275 to 295 yards. The smelting power of the furnace is equal to 9 cwts. of metal for each yard of capacity, consequently an increase of 20 yards would augment the weekly make 9 tons.

The breadth of the hearth at top is in some instances the same as at the bottom, the walls being carried up plumb; but in other instances they widen considerably as they ascend. The necessity for any considerable enlargement upwards is not very apparent. It tends rather to retard the descent of the materials. Where the hearth is very wide it probably may be advantageous, inasmuch as it tends to lighten the pressure on the bottom. With the usual width, however, the boshes support the weight of the materials, and the perpendicular pressure on the bottom of the hearth is not so great. On the whole, a batter of about 1 in 12 would seem to be a desirable proportion. In the Tredegar and some other furnaces it is $1\frac{1}{4}$ in 12, but this appears to be a maximum amount.

A slight widening of the hearth upwards also favours the ascent of the gaseous column. This increases rapidly in bulk in the first two feet of its ascent, and should therefore be allowed ample space for expansion.

The boshes commence from the hearth, and form the frustrum of a cone, the smallest end down, and the base forming the largest diameter of the furnace. The angle at which the boshes are inclined is a matter of considerable importance to the successful working of a furnace, for while it should not be so steep as to throw too great a pressure on the hearth, it should have a sufficient rise to allow of the uninterrupted descent of the materials as fast as the lower strata are melted in the hearth below. In determining the most advantageous angle for a special case the nature of the ironstone and the fuel require to be considered. If the ores are of a dense character and the fuel light the slope is usually very steep.

From the measurement of numerous furnaces which have come under our notice it would appear that the flattest boshes are at an angle of about 60 deg., with a horizontal line, while the steepest rarely exceed 80 deg. At the Dowlais works there are boshes at 68, 73, 74, 76, 78, and 81 deg.; the steepest are in the smallest furnaces. And it is worthy of remark that these furnaces produce a larger quantity of iron in proportion to their capacity than the others. At the Plymouth furnace the angle is 68 deg.; Tredegar furnace, 69 deg.; and Sirhowy, 71 deg. The Scotch do not differ greatly from each other: the angle at Dandyvan is 69 deg.; Kinneil, 71 deg.; and Muirkirk, 72 deg. In the Alfreton furnaces, Derbyshire, the angle is about 62 deg. The charcoal furnace hearths are constructed with boshes at 76 to 78 deg.

Formerly the boshes were constructed at a much lower angle—54 deg. was not uncommon—but in modern furnaces the increase in rise has been most beneficial. A less angle than 70 deg. should not be adopted where the full reducing power of the furnace is desired. On a slope of 38 deg. the tendency of the materials to slide down is nil. As the angle increases the action of gravity is correspondingly brought into play. With so flat an angle, then, as 38 deg. the regular and equable descent of the whole of the materials in the furnace would not take place. The centre column resting on the hearth would move most rapidly, the surrounding cylinder of materials at a slower rate, while the materials immediately resting upon the boshes would descend into the hearth with the least velocity. On the other hand, a greater angle than 70 deg. is not desirable, as the boshes then rise so high in the furnace that its capacity for reduction is decreased without producing any corresponding advantage.

Of late years much discussion has arisen respecting the form of the section of the hearth and boshes. Some writers maintain that the walls of the hearth should rise perpendicularly, or nearly so, and that the boshes should start off from the top of them at the desired angle. Others state that the interior of the vertical section of the hearth and boshes should be formed by a line nearly, or even quite, straight, starting from the desired breadth at bottom and continued to the side of the furnace at the determined angle. The walls of the hearth falling back with the same inclination as the boshes, the distinct angular junction of the two consequently disappears.

The advocates of this form of hearth assign as their reason for its adoption that it approaches most nearly to the form observed in furnaces which have been blown out after working several years. Upon this ground some ironmasters have altered the construction of the hearths and boshes of their furnaces to these lines, and, it is stated, with considerable advantage in respect both of yield and make. Among other works where this form of furnace is in use, we may mention the Sirhowy (Pl. VII., Fig. 43), Ebbw Vale, and Abersychan, in Wales, and the Corbyns Hall, in Staffordshire, to the proprietor of which the merit of introducing this description of hearth to the trade is due.

At first sight the form which is produced by the continued action of the furnace may seem the most correct, but on further examination this argument, we believe, will appear fallacious. If this form were really the best, a furnace should work better after being in blast some years than when new, for the improved form would then be attained; but the reverse of this is found in practice. Furnaces constructed with properly proportioned hearths, and boshes at a moderately steep angle, will, if properly blown in, produce as much metal, and be in as good working condition at the end of three months as at any future period. We believe it may be different with the very narrow hearths common in Staffordshire; but that would be on account of the form of construction. Let the size of the hearths be increased to not less than two-fifths of the diameter of the furnace, and the produce of metal and yield of materials will reach the maximum a few weeks after first blowing.

During every year in which the furnace is in blast, a portion of the hearth and boshes is removed by the attrition of the descending materials, so that in a few years the boshes are worn down very flat, the hearth is enlarged, and the working of the furnace becomes more difficult, the yield of materials increasing while the make diminishes. Effects of a similar kind are produced when the blowing in has been hastily done, and the power of the furnace prematurely forced to the production of a large quantity of metal before the surrounding brickwork has been thoroughly glazed and heated. In either case, when the boshes are much worn, the consumption of materials and the diminution of make progressively advance, until the expense of manufacturing becomes so great as to render it necessary to blow out and repair the furnace. If, then, the hearth and boshes are rightly proportioned at first the furnaces will work best while they retain their original form; but if they are improperly shaped, the wear caused by the descending materials may effect an improvement. If, however, it be deemed advisable to leave the hearth and boshes to be worn into a proper form by the friction of the materials, the evils of an extravagant yield and low make must be naturally expected.

We freely admit that for a limited period of time this form of hearth makes a large quantity of metal, and works to a good yield; and since the peculiar shape increases the capacity of the furnace about one-tenth part, such a result could reasonably be expected. But we must call to mind that the wear of the brickwork of the hearth and boshes proceeds as rapidly in furnaces of this construction as in those of the more usual form; and consequently every year that the furnace is in blast the boshes are flattening, the hearth enlarging, and the yield and produce deteriorating. No matter at what angle with the horizon the boshes are set so that it be less than 90 deg. the wear of the brickwork—supposing the furnace has not been improperly managed—goes on regularly year by year; hence if the hearth is unnecessarily large at first, the period which will elapse before it has arrived at such a size as to render blowing out necessary will be so much the shorter.

If this form of hearth and boshes is to maintain its efficiency unimpaired by the action of the materials, the laws of friction and abrasion must be suspended in its favour; and its advocates would almost seem to imagine that something of this kind really occurs. Amongst the objections urged against the old form, the inventor of the improved hearth states as a general fact that one-third of the substance of the hearth and boshes is commonly carried away in the first six months working, leaving it to be inferred that with the improved hearth the brickwork does not so suffer. If the hearth is excessively narrow, the heat maintained may be so intense as to soften the work, and render it less able to resist abrasion; but this evil cannot occur with a wide hearth, though it be built with vertical walls. Unless, then, we grant that the new hearth is exempt from the destruction elsewhere occasioned by the pressure and descent of the materials (and we are not aware of any circumstance which can warrant such an assumption), we are unable to perceive any ground for the alleged superiority of this description of hearth over that commonly in use in Wales and Scotland.

The statement that one-third of the substance of the hearth and boshes is carried away in the first six months, is very far from being verified by our experience. That instances may have occurred in which this quantity has been removed, even in a much shorter time, we are fully prepared to allow; but to maintain that such is the rule rather than the exception is manifestly incorrect. It takes on an average from ten to twelve years to carry away so large a quantity of the brickwork. From the dimensions of furnaces built under our own immediate superintendence, we have ascertained that the quantity of brickwork destroyed after having been under blast four years and three months, is not more than one-sixth of the original quantity in the hearth and boshes: and as a proof that this was not carried away in the first blowing, we may mention the case of a furnace which was blown out, after having been in blast seventeen months, where the loss was, if anything, still less in proportion to the time it had been at work. The work at the junction of the hearth and boshes was rounded off, but in all other respects it was so little the worse for the eighteen months' blowing that the furnace was put in blast again without any repairs, and has so continued since.

It is maintained by some theoretical writers on iron-making that the boshes do not wear; but as they disappear after a long blowing, it is very evident that they must either wear or melt away. If we admit that the material of which they are composed melts, we must account for the presence within their compass of a temperature greatly above that required for fusing the ironstone; and as this cannot satisfactorily be done, we must seek another explanation in the friction produced by the passage of the materials along the walls. When the immense quantity of materials which annually slides over the boshes is taken into consideration, we are only surprised that they last as long as they do. At a moderate calculation, each foot of surface of the boshes is abraded by the contact of nearly 1000 tons of materials sliding over it, under a pressure of 2 to 3 tons per square foot, every year of their duration.

No material yet discovered, available for the construction of the interior work of blast furnaces, can remain unaffected under such circumstances.

It is very rarely that opportunities occur for ascertaining the amount of wear of the boshes, for except under some peculiar circumstances a furnace is not blown out until they are nearly, if not altogether, destroyed. Circumstances, however, occurred at the Dowlais works in 1848 which resulted in the blowing out of furnaces which had not long been in blast, and an opportunity was thus afforded for measuring the direct loss which had taken place during the period they were under blast. In one furnace which had been in blast four years and three months, and had averaged 108 tons weekly during that period, the deficiency was 11 inches, measured at right angles to the slope. This is at the rate of $2\frac{1}{4}$ inches nearly per year. At another furnace which had been in blast a little more than sixteen months, the deficiency, as nearly as could be measured, did not exceed 3 inches. In both instances the wear was very regular, the original inclination of 70 deg. was maintained, and there was a corresponding enlargement in the upper part of the hearth.

The duration of the boshes varies with the quality of the material of which they are built, and the mode of working the furnace. From twenty-four blowings out by the Dowlais company, we find that the average duration of their furnaces was twelve years; the longest period during which any one furnace was in blast was seventeen years, and the shortest eight years; the blowing out being in each case for repairs only.

The diameter of the furnace at the boshes has been largely increased in some localities, while in others the size is not greatly varied from that prevailing in the last century. The furnaces of Staffordshire are usually 10 to 14 feet diameter; those of Scotland, 12 to 16 feet; the Welsh anthracite furnaces are from 10 to 14 feet; while those in other parts of the South Wales district range from 13 to 18 feet 6 inches in diameter. The new furnaces at the Dowlais, Rhymney, Hirwain, and Plymouth ironworks are 18 feet diameter, and are certainly the largest hitherto constructed. But the size of the furnace is a mere matter of choice. If they are large, the consumption of materials, blast, &c., is in proportion to the increased capacity and make; and the cost of erecting is also greater, though not to quite the same extent. The most advantageous dimension will be regulated by local circumstances.

Furnaces of 12 to 14 feet in diameter are preferred by some ironmasters as being more manageable than larger ones. But since the controlling influence is exerted through mechanical agents we do not see how this holds good. Other things being equal, quality or make depend on the descent of the materials, and this being the same, the time required will be the same also, whether the furnace be large or small. The interior of the hearth may be more accessible to the workmen; but, after all, the difference in linear dimension is not great. In one respect, however, small furnaces are advantageous, especially in small establishments, for the manager has a greater command over the production of small quantities of metal of any particular quality.

The form of the interior of the furnace from the boshes to the throat is subject to no fixed rule. The usual form is that of a frustrum of a cone. (Pls. VII.—XXII.) In some furnaces the interior is carried up cylindrically for a short distance above the boshes; but more commonly the base of the cone rests upon the top of them. If greater capacity be desired, a curved line is substituted for the straight one; the centre for striking this curve is generally on a level with the top of the boshes, and the radius is so adjusted that an arc of a circle may pass through the extreme diameters of the boshes and throat. (Pl. XV., Fig. 88.)

An enlargement of the furnace above the boshes is considered by some ironmasters as an improvement, and some furnaces are accordingly so constructed (see Pls. VII., IX., XII.), with the view of increasing their capacity. This, however, is merely continuing the boshes into the lining of the furnace, and, while we admit the utility of greater capacity, we doubt the expediency of so exposing any part of the lining to the destructive action of the materials. Wherever it is done the same wearing process will go forward as that which destroys the boshes, and consequently the linings will be worn out nearly as soon as they now are. And the renewal of the lining of a furnace is not only a very expensive operation, but is also dangerous. When the lining is built vertically, or with an inclination inwards, the wear is inconsiderable; we have not found the bricks shortened more than 3 or 4 inches in furnaces that have been under blast twenty years. If greater capacity is desired than the conical or conoidal form will give, the object will be best attained by building the furnace of an enlarged diameter.

A large number of the Scotch blast furnaces are constructed with a considerable part of the interior cylindrical, or only slightly coned. The height of the cylindrical part is sometimes, but not generally, more than twice the largest diameter. The body is rapidly drawn in at the top to the diameter of the throat, diminishing commonly at the rate of 6 inches in diameter per foot of height, until it is reduced to 7 or 8 feet. (Pl. X., Figs. 63—65.)

The cylindrical form, though general in Scotland, does not in our opinion possess any superiority in point of make or yield over others, beyond what is due to the greater capacity it affords. For the same consumption of building material it probably gives the largest capacity, and in this respect must be considered economical, besides which we are inclined to believe that the sudden enlargement under the throat is advantageous when raw coal of a weak character is used.

There is an opinion current in Scotland that the large weekly makes obtained there are connected with this form of furnace, but it would probably be more correct to ascribe them to the fusible nature and richness of the carbonaceous ironstone operated upon.

The diameter of the throat or filling place is a matter of the greatest importance to the working of the furnace. It influences the make and yield more than any other dimension; and yet it receives little attention in designing the furnace. Local custom is generally considered the safest guide, and yet it is a matter which above all others is likely to cause loss and create difficulty in the working of the furnace.

In the old blast-furnaces the top was generally narrow, the breadth scarcely averaging one-fourth of the diameter of the furnace; and in Staffordshire, Derbyshire, and other districts, furnaces are still in operation with throats bearing this proportion. In other furnaces in these districts a width of one-third of the diameter at the boshes is considered sufficient. The breadth most common in Scotch furnaces erected or altered within the last twenty-five years is one-half the diameter of the furnace—extended, however, in some instances to as much as two-thirds. In the Welsh district the breadth ranges from one to two-thirds of the diameter; but the proportion which prevails in the majority of the Welsh furnaces is one-half, or nearly so.

Although it is now generally admitted by smelters that with a narrow throat a furnace will not carry as much burden or work as well as with a wider one, the largest throats hitherto constructed have not exceeded 10 feet. This appears to be considered as a maximum width. But if the enlargement of the throat from one-fourth or one-third of the diameter of furnace has been productive of advantage, what is to prevent further enlargement still leading to improved results.

With the narrow-throated furnace formerly employed in smelting, the average yield of coal to each ton of pig-iron was 6 tons. By increasing the diameter of the throat to one-third of that of the furnace, and using a more powerful blast, 4 tons were made sufficient; increasing it again to one-half, the yield diminished to $2\frac{1}{4}$ tons. We believe that after making every allowance for the operation of other causes, three-fourths of this saving in fuel must be attributed to the enlargement of the throat, and that by continuing the enlargement a further saving might be effected.

In support of this opinion we may adduce the effects produced by a narrow throat at one of the Dowlais furnaces. The diameter of this furnace at the boshes was 18 feet, and it formerly worked with a throat 9 feet in diameter. Repair being necessary, the furnace was blown out, new hearth and boshes put in, and a new lining carried up beyond the boshes, but on approaching the top the curve of the section of the body was quickened, so that the width of the throat was reduced to 6 feet, or one-third of the diameter of the furnace. Prior to the alteration this furnace had been in blast fifteen years; the average make was 90 tons of pig-iron weekly, and consumption 45 cwts. of coal to the ton. After the alteration the make became irregular, varying from 50 to 70 tons; the consumption of coal rose to 70, 80, and even 90 cwts. per ton of pig-iron. The quality of the iron also was excessively bad, and the loss of metal in the dense black scouring cinder produced was very great. The average yield of coal with this narrow throat was near 4 tons, but if the deterioration in the quality of the metal be also taken into account, the consumption may be fairly considered as just twice the quantity which would have sufficed with a wider throat. Yet this proportion of throat is not less than may be seen in numerous furnaces in England.

As more satisfactory results could not be obtained, the materials in the furnace were let down nearly to the boshes, and the upper portion of the lining taken out and placed farther back, and a throat of the original width—9 feet—obtained. With this enlarged throat the make of the furnace has several weeks exceeded 170 tons, and for a period of six months has averaged more than 160 tons, the yield of materials being good.

There was one other circumstance connected with the working of this experiment worth recording. Whenever the furnace was let down and maintained at a depth of 7 or 8 feet, so that the throat was practically enlarged, partaking of the diameter of the furnace at the level of the materials, the yield and make greatly improved. The former would be as low as 50 cwts., while the latter rose to 80 and 85 tons. This circumstance clearly points to the confined throat as the cause of unsatisfactory results. Other narrow throated furnaces have yielded similar results under our observation, working better when the surface of the materials has been kept a few feet below the charging plates.

Where narrow throats are in use we need only to refer to the velocity of the upward current to find a sufficient cause for the diminished reducing power of the fuel in the lower regions of the furnace. The volume of gas produced there being the same, the velocity of escape through the throat will be in an inverse ratio to its area, and may be calculated with sufficient accuracy to show the beneficial effects which must arise from larger throats.

We have already stated that a furnace 18 feet diameter at the boshes, working up to its full power, should receive 8720 cubic feet of air per minute. A portion escapes by leakage, but for our present purpose we may assume that this volume of air actually enters the furnace, and, combining with the carbon of the fuel, ascends to the throat. To this there must be added the carbonic acid gas expelled from the limestone, and the volatile matter escaping from the coal during its coking in the upper regions. The amount of these cannot be determined with accuracy, as they vary with the constituents of the fuel, but the total volume of the ascending column will not, at any rate, be less than 10,000 cubic feet per minute. This would be the volume at the mean temperature of the atmosphere, but the temperature of the throat cannot average less than 1000°. This increase of temperature increases the volume, according to the law of Mariotte, at the rate of .00208 for each degree of temperature. At the temperature of 1000°, then, the 10,000 feet of gas will be expanded into, say 30,000 cubic feet nearly.

If the 18-feet furnace is provided with a 9-feet throat, the area for the passage of the volume of heated gases will be 63.6 feet, and the velocity of the current will be 472 feet per minute. Diminish the diameter of the throat to one-third of the diameter of the furnace—6 feet—and the area will be 28.3 feet, and the velocity of the issuing gases 1060 feet per minute. Reduce the diameter to one-fourth, or 4½ feet, the area will be 15.9 feet, and the velocity will be increased to 1868 feet per minute.

But the entire area of the throat is not available for the escape of the gases. The space occupied by the materials must be deducted. Considering the comparatively dense manner in which the materials lie in the furnace—the ore and broken limestone filling up the interstices between the pieces of fuel—five-sixths of the area may be assumed to be obstructed by the descending materials, and but one-sixth left for the ascending gases. The area being diminished to this extent, the velocity is increased in an inverse ratio, and thus the velocity of escape with the 9-feet throat becomes 2830 feet per minute; with the 6-feet, 6360 feet per minute; and with the 4½-feet, 11,208 feet per minute.

Now 1800 feet per minute is a high velocity for the air entering the fire-place of steam-engine boilers burning 15 lbs of coal per hour for each square foot of grate. Yet in the case of a blast furnace we have the fuel exposed to a much more rapid current the instant it is precipitated into the furnace. With the large-size throat the draught is one-third greater, while with the small size it is five times greater than that under engine-boilers. Exposed to such a rapid draught, then, can it be a matter of surprise that a considerable portion of the fuel is consumed in the throat? or that the temperature at the mouth of the narrow-throated furnace is higher than at one having a wide throat?

The consumption of fuel in the throat by the rapid draught explains the superior produce and yield when the materials are let down a few feet. The expansion of the furnace at the lower level affords a larger area for the ascending column of gases; they consequently pass through the upper stratum of materials at a reduced velocity, and escape through the narrow throat unimpeded by the materials.

But a reduction of the velocity of the current of escaping gases below the minimum above stated—2830 feet per minute—would doubtless be attended with beneficial results. A portion of the fuel now consumed in the throat would remain available for smelting, and the yield of carbon to iron might eventually be reduced considerably below 2 lbs. of carbon to 1 lb. of iron. We observe, from a drawing of the Baerum charcoal furnace in Norway, that the throat is two-thirds of the largest diameter. The yield of charcoal is a little more than 1 lb. per lb. of iron. May not the superior reducing power of this furnace be partly attributed to the large throat? for in many other respects the mechanical arrangements are inferior to those in use in this country.

There is another circumstance well known to smelters that may be adduced as a reason for enlarging the throat. Furnaces are observed to work remarkably well during the blowing out. This has been seized on by some writers as an argument against building furnaces so high as is usually done; but whatever be the height or diameter, several species of ironstone require to be in the furnace 46 to 48 hours to yield metal of pure quality, and any reduction of capacity arising from a diminution in the height will be followed by a similar reduction in the make. But we believe that the superior action of the furnace during the blowing out results from the diminished temperature of the upper layer of materials; for the area for the passage of the ascending gases, constantly enlarging as the level descends, their velocity is reduced, a lower temperature prevails, and, consequently, a much larger proportion of the fuel is available for reduction before the blast.

The utility of at all reducing the diameter of the furnace at top may be fairly questioned. The throat appears to have originated in an impression that the furnace could be filled better through a contracted orifice. It was supposed that the commingling of the different materials so essential to the production of superior iron would be accomplished by charging through a narrow throat, but that wide throats did not afford an equal advantage. However, the success that has attended the use of the throats recently introduced has proved that this is a groundless prejudice.

By some writers on iron-making the contraction is asserted to be beneficial, inasmuch as it retains the heat, and thus prevents a waste of fuel. Others advocate a considerable arching of the top on the score of its reflecting the heat back on the materials. This principle was carried to its full extent at the Wingermouth furnaces, but was abandoned, and the furnaces altered to the usual form, giving us good ground for presuming that the economy of fuel and other advantages anticipated from it were not realised. With respect to the concentration of the heat at top or its reflection on the materials, it should be remembered that the maintenance of a high temperature at the top involves the consumption of a portion of the fuel in a region where it can be of no service, and only impairs its efficiency in the lower regions.

The important effect of a cool top on the produce and yield of the furnace is understood by some ironmasters, but the means by which they accomplish this desideratum are original. Instead of widening the throat—the true remedy—they use wetted coke when the top is working hot. In the vaporisation of the water thus introduced into the furnace a portion of the fuel is consumed, but not so much as would be lost by the higher temperature.

The injurious effects which result from a narrow throat are not produced to an equal extent in all furnaces. The temperature of the top will depend in a great measure on the inflammability of the fuel. Coke or charcoal will remain comparatively unimpaired by a draught which would partially consume coal. The evils engendered by a narrow throat are consequently most apparent in coal-fed furnaces.

As far as regards *convenience* of filling the narrow throat is certainly superior, but when economy of materials, quality of metal, and weekly produce are at stake, mere considerations of convenience to the fillers must give way. Let the width be largely increased, and no real difficulty will be met with in properly filling the materials.

We are of opinion that the time is not distant when the contracted top will be altogether abandoned, and the interior wall of the furnace be built vertically from the boshes upwards. (Pl. XIII., Fig. 84.) By such a construction a minimum temperature would be maintained at the surface and throughout the upper stratum of the materials. The velocity of the issuing gases would be reduced to about 600 feet per minute—a draught too slow for the combustion of any portion of the fuel in the upper regions; consequently the yield of coal would improve. The diameter remaining constant, the capacity also would be largely increased, and the make, with a corresponding increase of blast, would be augmented in the same ratio. Furnaces of 275 cubic yards capacity would be enlarged to 340, and those of a smaller capacity in a similar proportion.

No difficulty need be felt in filling such a furnace. The top should be surmounted with a tunnel-head of the usual height, but provided with a greater number of filling places, and instead of wheeling in the materials as at present, the filling should be done with the shovel and pike. The largest furnaces in use measure about 18 feet in diameter; the tunnel-head of this class would be 20 feet in its exterior diameter; so that the greatest distance to which the materials would have to be thrown would not exceed 10 feet, the average distance being under 4 feet.

The height of the furnace from the bottom of the hearth to the level of the charging-plates varies considerably in the different districts. The anthracite furnaces on the western side of the Welsh district are the lowest. The average height of these furnaces is under 40 feet; 36 feet is a general dimension, but there are several under 30 feet. In the central and eastern portion of the same district the height ranges from 42 to 48 feet. The Staffordshire furnaces probably are more irregular in height than any other; they range from 40 to 60 feet, this last being the greatest height of any furnace at work in this country. In Derbyshire the furnaces are from 40 to 45 feet; and in Scotland from 42 to 46 feet high.

Other things being equal, the height of the furnace should be regulated by the fusibility of the ore and also by the carbon it contains. Ironstones devoid of carbon, chemically and mechanically, will be smelted more economically and be converted into a superior description of pig-iron in lofty furnaces; but with low furnaces the quality will be inferior. A lengthened exposure to the carburizing influence of the ascending gaseous products of combustion partially supplies the ironstone with carbon, by which its reduction in the hearth is greatly facilitated. Siliceous, calcareous, and other ironstones containing a very small per-centage of carbonic acid, should invariably be smelted in furnaces above the average height.

The argillaceous class of ironstones, on account of their more fusible nature and the large per-centage of carbon mechanically combined with them, can be reduced in furnaces of an average height. The associated carbon possessed by all the carbonates of the coal formations very much facilitates the reduction of these ores, and unquestionably improves the quality of the metal. Wherever it is absent, the generally refractory character of the ore is well known.

The argillaceous ironstone is smelted in the anthracite district in low furnaces, but no sufficient reason has been assigned for their use. The limited scale on which the operations were at one time carried on in this district may account in part for the small dimensions of the furnaces. And when the method of smelting with anthracite coal was not so well understood as at present, it was considered that, from the dense character of the coal, the blast would be unable to penetrate through a column of materials as high as usual. There is no doubt, however, that furnaces of the height of those used in other districts would be more advantageous. This is becoming partially understood by the proprietors, and the elevation in some cases has been increased, as for instance at the Ystalyfera works, 10 or 12 feet. (Pls. X., XI., Figs. 67, 68.)

The very fusible nature of the carbonaceous ironstone and the excess of carbon chemically and mechanically combined with it, render the production of metal of good quality easy under almost any circumstances. With the present furnaces it is produced in about two-thirds of the time required for argillaceous ironstone, and in about one-half of that necessary for siliceous ironstones. Yet we observe that the Scotch furnaces using this ironstone are uniformly of a maximum height; quite as high, indeed, as those used in Wales for an ironstone melting at a much higher temperature, yielding a less per-centage of metal, and only producing grey iron under careful management. Judging from the character of the ore, and from the results obtained in Wales, the Scotch furnaces appear unnecessarily high.

No doubt one cause for this apparently unnecessary height is that a considerable number of the existing furnaces were originally constructed for smelting the argillaceous stone prior to the general introduction of the carbonaceous variety, and these have served as models for the construction of others in more recent years. That elevation which a long experience had proved to be the most suitable for the argillaceous was retained for smelting the more fusible carbonaceous ironstone. Alterations have been made in the breadth of the

T

hearth and diameter at boshes and throat to meet the change from coke to raw coal, and an alteration in form might also have been made on the change of ironstone with considerable advantage.

The use of such high furnaces for the reduction of the most fusible ironstone known is chargeable to some extent with the comparatively high consumption of coal. The fuel being of a highly inflammable nature, a large portion of its heating power is unprofitably expended in the upper parts; the remainder suffices for the requirements of the ironstone already surcharged with carbon; and thus the true magnitude of the waste of carbon going on in these furnaces escapes observation.

SECTION IX.

QUALITY OF CRUDE IRON AS AFFECTED BY THE STRUCTURE AND COMPOSITION OF THE ORES.

The very different behaviour of the various ores of iron in the same furnace under similar conditions of fuel and flux as shown by their greater or less fusibility, and the quality of the resulting metal, is a subject of paramount importance to the iron-smelter. Having witnessed the reduction of large quantities of ore of nearly every description, and noted the peculiarities bearing on its fusibility, and on the quality and fusibility of the resulting crude iron, presented by each in the blast furnace, we conclude that the quality of the iron, as estimated by the quantity of carbon in combination, is directly dependent on the structural arrangement of the ore; and that the fusibility is dependent on the same causes, also varying with the per-centage of associated carbon.

It is known to intelligent smelters that in its descent the ore is deoxydised, the oxygen of the oxide of iron combining with carbon forms carbonic acid; in its further descent the deoxydised metal combines with a greater or less quantity of carbon from the ascending gaseous column and is fused, uniting with a certain proportion of carbon, and finally falls into the hearth. This quantity of carbon is absorbed prior to the descent of the metal into the lower hearth. The volume absorbed at the instant of fusion is inconsiderable, therefore in our explanations it may safely be omitted, and the degree of carburization calculated on the supposition that the entire quantity is absorbed from the gaseous column by the metal while yet in the ore.

The velocity of descent of the solid column and the period of exposure to the carbon of the gaseous column being alike, the volume combining will vary with the surface of metal presented to its action. If the pieces of ore are large and of a dense structure and consequently impermeable to the gases, crude iron containing a minimum per-centage of carbon will be produced. The proportion of fuel to ore may be largely augmented, but under no circumstances will the quality of the resulting iron be superior to the lowest white.

With ores of similar structure, but of smaller dimensions, the quantity of carbon will be augmented in the same ratio as the increased surface of metal presented to its action.

Ores of a high specific gravity and yielding a large per-centage of metal when in pieces of large dimensions, produce crude iron of the lowest quality; whilst with smaller pieces the degree of carburization is augmented, but cannot be carried above an inferior white.

On the other hand, ores of a low specific gravity, but yielding a high per-centage of metal when in pieces of a medium size, produce crude iron containing the largest amount of carbon.

The richest hematites and ores of a similar dense structure produce iron having a minimum degree of carburization, for in consequence of their high specific gravity and the absence of volatile matters in their composition a comparatively small surface of metal is presented to the action of the gases of the ascending column. The quality is improved when the surface is augmented by diminishing the size of the ores to the lowest practicable limits compatible with its complete reduction and the free action of the furnace. It may be further improved by reducing the velocities of the descending solid, and ascending gaseous columns. The volume of carbon combining may be taken as inversely as the velocities; hence with diminished velocities the degree of carburization is higher, but the weekly produce from the same furnace is reduced. On the Continent the production in charcoal furnaces of superior irons from rich ores of a dense structure is accomplished by reducing their dimensions and proportioning the velocities of the respective columns to the requirements of the case.

The superior quality of the crude iron smelted from the densest ores of certain continental districts, as compared with the iron obtained from similar ores smelted in this country, is generally considered as due to the different qualities of the fuels employed. While it must be conceded that the quality of the fuel has an important bearing on that of the resulting iron, and there is every reason to believe that the difference arises more from the mode of working the furnaces. Certain it is that when filled with ores of varying dimensions and driven at the rate common in this country, the quality of the metal produced from the foreign charcoal furnaces is very little superior to that produced from coke and coal furnaces.

From the carbonates of the coal formations iron of a superior quality may be smelted. The degree of carburization varies with the composition of the ores. With those of the argillaceous class it is at a medium, but will be greater or less according to the per-centage of metal and size of the pieces of ore.

In the absence of other sources of information the loss by calcination correctly indicates the fusibility of the ore, the volume of carbon taken up under similar conditions, and the fusibility of the resulting crude iron.

The production of a superior iron from the argillaceous ores is favoured by their comparatively low per-centage of metal and the large volume of gaseous matters given off during calcination. The extended area presented by the exterior surfaces of the ore facilitates the deoxydation, but when to this there is added the surface created by the distillation of its gaseous constituents, the facilities afforded for the absorption of carbon are immensely increased. During calcination these ores lose from 20 to 33 per cent. by weight of gaseous matters, principally in the form of carbonic acid, which renders the ore of an open, porous structure, permeable to the carbon of the ascending column, and at a moderate computation renders four times the surface available for deoxydation. Hence the comparatively large absorption of carbon and the fusible character of the ore and resulting metal.

The degree of carburization is carried furthest with ores of the carbonaceous class.

Containing large quantities of carbonaceous matter, in addition to the carbonic acid common to all carbonates, these ores present after calcination a maximum surface for deoxydation and absorption of carbon. The loss in this preparatory operation ranges from 28 to 60 per cent. The evolution of the latter quantity of gaseous matter has the effect of multiplying the surface from ten to twenty-fold. It is entirely owing to the volatile character of a moiety of its constituents and the consequent porosity of the calcined ore that the rapid deoxydation and large absorption of carbon is effected, as shown in the high velocity of the descending column and the amount of carbon combined with the metal.

The per-centage taken up by ores of this description is further augmented by the larger space left open for the gaseous column, causing it to ascend with a reduced velocity, and to this extent facilitating the deoxydation. The carbonates of the coal formations exclusively possess the property of thus augmenting the space, for although the other ores may be reduced in their linear dimensions so as to offer an equally large surface to the action of the gaseous column, they retain their original dense structure, and by filling up the interstices between the fuel and flux, contract the area, thereby augmenting the velocity of ascent and diminishing the amount of carburization.

The fusibility of the respective ores is influenced in the same manner as the volume of carbon by the surface of metal exposed to the action of the heat and gases, but is modified to a certain extent by the quantity and character of the associated earths. With ores similarly composed the degree of fusibility will be directly as the per-centage of gaseous constituents, and inversely as the quantity of solid earthy matter.

The per-centage of gaseous substances in the ore, by determining the amount of carbon, regulates the fusibility of the resulting crude iron; other substances impart fluidity, but in this country carbon is the principal modifying ingredient. Irons containing a minimum quantity are less fusible, and exhibit a marked deficiency of fluidity compared with those more abundantly supplied with this body.

In extreme cases the quantity of carbon amounts to nearly 8 per cent. by weight of the crude iron.* When re-melted the larger portion is volatilised, and the fusibility and fluidity is proportionately diminished. If again re-melted, the deficiency of these properties is still further manifested; eventually the most fusible iron by having its carbon oxydised becomes difficult of fusion and devoid of its former fluidity.

* At first sight it may seem surprising that this per-centage can be the cause of the great fluidity and low melting temperature of certain crude irons, especially those smelted from the carbonaceous ores; but if the proportion be estimated by volume, it is seen that, owing to the low specific gravity of carbon, it forms nearly 30 per cent. of the bulk; and since the fusibility is directly dependent on and proportionate with the volumes and melting temperatures of the respective ingredients forming the crude metal, the sufficiency of this large volume of carbon to produce these characteristic results must be apparent. In crude irons sparingly supplied, say to the extent of 2¼ to 3 per cent., the carbon forms, by volume, from 9 to 12 per cent. of the entire bulk.

SECTION X.

THE HOT BLAST.

THE effects of the hot blast on the manufacture of iron in this country have been exaggerated by writers. According to the statement of many, the great reductions which have taken place within the last twenty-five years in the quantity of fuel and flux required to smelt a given weight of iron, and the large increase of make from the furnaces, are mainly owing to the use of this invention. Without intending in the least degree to detract from the real value of the hot blast, which is unquestionably very great, we must maintain that powers have been ascribed to it which it does not possess. It is undeniable that, under certain circumstances, the hot blast has effected a saving in the consumption of fuel, and also augmented the weekly make. But the saving in fuel and increase of make due to it is not in general one-fourth of that which has been asserted to have been effected. Some have even gone so far as to state that by the mere substitution of heated air for the cold air formerly used two-thirds of the coal requisite for smelting a ton of pig-iron were saved at the Scotch ironworks—among others, the late Mr. Mushet. Before the introduction of the hot blast the consumption of coal at the Clyde works in smelting is stated by that gentleman to average 7 tons 3 cwts.

This appears to have been the quantity used in the year 1797, for in another part of his work we find the following: "Abstract of the quantity of materials required to manufacture one ton of pig-iron at the Clyde blast furnace No. 2, in 1797:

	Tons.	Cwts.	Qrs.	Lbs.
Coals for coking	7	5	0	4
Ironstone (raw)	3	1	2	0
Iron ore	0	2	0	0
Limestone	0	17	1	4
Engine coals, including coals for calcining	3	16	0	0

And then, to show the saving effected by the use of the hot blast, a statement of the consumption of materials to produce one ton of iron in 1839 is given as follows:

	Tons.	Cwts.	Qrs.
Coals used to the ton of iron	2	3	2
Mine (calcined)	2	6	2
Limestone	0	11	2

The lapse of a period of forty-two years showing us a reduction of 5 tons on the quantity of fuel required for 1 ton of pig-iron. This saving is carried "at once" to the credit of the hot blast. With all deference to the acknowledged authority on matters connected with iron-making of the late Mr. Mushet, we must confess that in our own opinion the saving of fuel due to the use of heated air would be more nearly represented by 5 cwts. than 5 tons.

For if we are to attribute the whole of this saving to the hot blast, we must also maintain that in the forty-two years between 1797 and 1831, with the exception of this single improvement, the iron manufacture remained stationary. But we know that this was not the case, for during that period very great improvements were made in the preparation of the fuel and ironstone, as also in the furnaces and blowing engines.

Were the hot blast universally applied to furnaces in Great Britain, instead of to about one-half of them only, it would be more difficult to distribute the credit of the saving effected between the hot blast and the other improvements which have assisted in accomplishing it; but since there are numerous furnaces to which it has never been applied, the progress made with these within the period above mentioned will enable us to approximate nearly to a correct judgment. At the Dowlais furnaces in 1791 the ton of pig-iron was made with the following materials:

	Tons.	Cwts.	Qrs.
Coal for coking	6	6	0
Ironstone (calcined)	2	19	0
Limestone	1	8	0
Engine coal	1	15	0

Forty years afterwards, namely, in 1831, the hot blast having been some months in operation at the Clyde works in Scotland, the Dowlais furnaces were making one ton of foundry iron by the consumption of the following materials:

	Tons.	Cwts.	Qrs.
Coal	2	10	0
Ironstone (calcined)	2	16	0
Limestone	0	18	0
Engine coal	0	10	2
Coal for calcining	0	6	2

From these data we perceive that the improvements in smelting have been such that, while still using cold blast, a reduction of three-fifths of the quantity of coal required to smelt a ton of iron has been effected. These results having been commonly obtained before the introduction of hot blast, in one of the largest works in Wales, with furnaces which have been blown with cold air without intermission since their erection, we must conclude that other causes besides the use of a heated blast have shared in producing this remarkable saving of fuel.

The use of carbonaceous ironstone, which melts at a low temperature, and, from its comparative freedom from earthy matters, requires but a minimum quantity of limestone for fluxing, and the enlargement of the throat of the furnace permitting the substitution of raw coal for coke, have both materially contributed to reduce the consumption of coal. But in almost every place where it is noticed—including Mr. Blackwell's lecture, delivered before the Society of Arts, in connexion with the Great Exhibition of 1851—the hot blast is credited as the cause of the diminished consumption of fuel. The enlargement of the throat from one-third to one-half of the diameter of the furnace, in the case of one of the Dowlais cold-blast furnaces, as we have already stated, was followed by a reduction in the consumption of coal from 80 to 45 cwts., without referring to the waste of carbon in the coking process.

Again, in the Welsh district, cold-blast furnaces, when working entirely on carbonaceous ironstone, smelt with a consumption of fuel no greater than that used in the Scotch furnaces. Yet we frequently see it stated that it is by the use of the hot blast that the Scotch ironmasters are enabled to smelt their carbonaceous ores. If so, how then are we to account for the success of the Welsh ironmaster with a cold blast?

The hot blast has also been credited as enabling anthracite coal to be successfully used as a fuel for smelting. The statement has been repeated by nearly every writer, as if the hot blast were more necessary to this kind of coal than to others. But it is now well known that this coal may be advantageously used in smelting with a cold blast of proper density; and that the iron so made is decidedly superior to that smelted with a heated blast.

The merit of augmenting the make in a surprising degree has also been attributed to the hot blast, but not correctly. We allow that the hot blast does increase the make, but not more than 10 per cent.

In 1791 the average weekly make of each of the Clyde furnaces appears to have been 17 tons. In 1839, with the advantage of a hot blast, but using argillaceous ironstone, the make was 52 tons weekly.

At the Dowlais furnaces the average make in 1791 was 20 tons weekly; in 1831 it had risen to 80 tons; and in 1839 to 91 tons, when working foundry iron. Cold blast being used through the whole period.

It is through the general use of carbonaceous iron ores that the comparatively large make has been obtained, and were a cold blast substituted, the reduction of make consequent upon the change would not exceed one-tenth.

The Scotch furnaces, using hot blast and carbonaceous iron ore, yielding on an average 60 per cent. of metal, average 146 tons a week. Welsh cold-blast furnaces, smelting a much leaner and more refractory ore, have averaged quite as much. Several of the cold-blast furnaces at the Dowlais works make 170 tons, and have exceeded 190 tons. The furnaces at the Plymouth works are all cold blast, yet they often exceed 130 tons a week. With these facts before him we feel that the candid reader must acknowledge that our statements respecting the exaggeration of the importance of the hot blast are fully justified.

HEATING HOT AIR STOVES.

With the view of economising the fuel ordinarily used in heating the blast, stoves have been constructed in some places in which a portion of the heat generated in the blast furnace has been applied to this purpose. This plan was extensively adopted at the Ystalyfera works (Pl. XXIV., Fig. 127), and has lately been applied at the Gartsherrie works. At Ystalyfera the stoves were placed at a suitable height between the furnaces, and flues were made from the furnaces to them. A tall chimney furnished with a damper was built to each stove to draw from the furnace a sufficient quantity of the hot gases to impart the requisite degree of heat to the blast.

By thus arranging the stoves so as to heat them without the usual coal fire, a large saving was stated to have been effected. "Neither coal nor labour was required," and "the working of the furnace was not at all interfered with." This is the statement of the proprietors, after they had had some experience of the working of the new method.

In reference to this plan, and our remarks are equally applicable to other inventions of this kind, we would ask: "If the blast was heated without the intervention of coal, from what source did it obtain its heat?" There can be no question but that it was derived from the coal in the furnace. But then the difficulty arises: How was it that such quantities of heat could be spared? Simply by filling in a larger quantity of coal than was otherwise necessary.

There is an error committed by many patentees of improvements in iron-making which cannot be too widely known. We frequently hear of the "waste heat" of blast and other descriptions of furnaces, and if an explanation is requested, it will be found that from $\frac{8}{10}$ths to $\frac{7}{10}$ths of the whole heat generated by the combustion of the fuel is included in the term. In each of the different operations of the manufacture a certain quantity of fuel is used to generate the necessary high temperature. Of this heat the largest portion goes up the chimney, or otherwise escapes into the atmosphere; this is considered as so much "waste heat." But can the requisite heat, with our present knowledge of combustion, be produced with a less quantity? Unless it can, the caloric escaping into the atmosphere can no more be considered as "waste," than the caloric from the chimneys of an engine boiler, or any other apparatus consuming coal as a fuel.

It is frequently observed by those who have not thoroughly studied the subject, and put the matter to the test of experiment, "But this lost heat may be seized in its passage to the atmosphere, and turned to profitable account." It is here that a great mistake is committed. For if the consumption of fuel is duly proportioned to the work to be done, no contrivance yet invented has ever enabled an ironmaster to turn this heat, or any part of it, to profitable account in serving a secondary purpose, without impairing in a corresponding degree the efficiency of the fuel in the primary operation.

This mistake was committed in erecting the hot-blast stoves at the Ystalyfera works. The heat for raising the temperature of the blast was abstracted from the furnace, and the quantity which would have been consumed in the stove grate was now added to the necessary consumption of the furnace. If the yield of coal had previously been unnecessarily large, sufficient caloric could be spared for this purpose, without greatly affecting the furnace operations, but if not the consumption must have been largely increased.

In the case now under our notice, the gases were drawn off at a depth of about 5 feet from the top of the furnace, or one-fifth of its height at that time. The tall stove-chimney, together with the pressure of the ascending column, caused so strong an indraught that besides depriving the coal of a portion of its reducing power, the materials in the part above the flues were robbed of the effect of the ascending gases, and the smelting power of the furnace was in consequence largely diminished. After a time the height of the furnace was increased nearly one-half, but the disadvantages of this mode of heating the blast were still apparent. We are justified in assuming that no saving of fuel was really obtained in practice, from the circumstance that after a lengthened trial the plan of abstracting heat from the materials was abandoned, and other means were adopted for heating the stoves. Very probably the consumption of coal in the blast furnace was augmented to even a greater degree than the saving of fuel usually consumed in the stoves.

In the sections on bar-iron we purpose drawing the attention of the ironmaster to a somewhat analogous instance of supposed saving of fuel in the mill and forge operations, but which in reality is equally founded in error.

WATER BLOCKS.

Mention has been made in this work of water blocks, breasts, and other contrivances (Pls. XXXIII., XXXIV.) for keeping the brickwork around the tuyeres and cinder-fall cool. The necessity for these contrivances has arisen with the wide hearth and numerous tuyeres blowing into it. With the old narrow hearth the blast penetrated to the opposite side, but in the modern enlarged hearth, where the density of the blast has not been correspondingly increased, the result has been that a greater temperature is produced in the immediate vicinity of the tuyeres at the expense of the other portions. And this evil has been further aggravated by the substitution of two or three pipes in each tuyere-house, instead of the single one formerly used. Thus a scattered blast is produced, creating an intense heat in the immediate vicinity of the tuyere, and rapidly destroying the brickwork.

The water blocks and breasts were designed as a remedy for this burning of the brickwork, and wherever they have been applied appear to have been successful. But it is a question whether the saving in brickwork by their use is not more than counterbalanced by the extra consumption of coal.

We have ascertained experimentally that the quantity of water passing through the various tuyeres, blocks, &c., of a furnace, averages about 17 gallons per minute. The temperature on entering is 45 degs., and on escaping 155 degs. Now to raise the temperature of this quantity of water 110 degs. requires the expenditure of rather more than $1\frac{1}{4}$ lbs. of coal. The weekly expenditure at the same rate will be nearly 7 tons.

This consumption of coal is not readily perceived, but it is undoubtedly going on. The coolness of the breasts and tuyeres is preserved by the water rapidly abstracting a portion of the heat evolved by the coal, which is thus lost to the operations of the furnace.

The weekly cost of these cooling contrivances in coal being ascertained, a comparison may be made with the expenses usually incurred with brickwork; the result, we anticipate, will be in favour of the latter.

The application of water breasts certainly evinces much ingenuity, but the evils of an intense heat around the tuyeres remain undiminished, and are to be removed only by proportioning the density and volume of the blast to the size of the hearth and power of the furnace. By due attention to these points the breast may be kept comparatively cool, and a minimum consumption of fuel ensured with a full weekly make.

SECTION XI.

EMPLOYMENT OF FURNACE GASES.

THE economical application of the combustible gases emitted from blast furnaces has been attempted at several works in this country with varied degrees of success. They have been collected and burnt under the boilers belonging to the blowing engines; but in only one instance have we observed the engine working from the heat given out by the gases alone. A quantity of coal—in some instances quite sufficient of itself to keep the engines going, if properly applied—is consumed in addition to the gases.

They have also been applied to heating hot-blast stoves, and with a measure of success. For this purpose they may be used more advantageously than under the boilers. The heat maintained is sufficient for this purpose; but is not usually high enough for the rapid generation of steam.

From M. Bunsen's analysis of the gases escaping from the Alfreton furnace it would appear that they are capable of yielding 81.54 per cent. of the heat yielded by the fuel consumed. The consumption of coal in the furnace was at the rate of 13 tons 17 cwts. per 24 hours. At this rate the gases are capable of yielding as much heat as would be produced by the combustion of 11 tons 7 cwts. of coal. If we allow 7 lbs. per hour per horse power as a fair allowance, they should generate heat sufficient for maintaining in motion an engine of 151-horse power. The power required for compressing the air, after making ample allowance for friction and waste, should not exceed 70-horse power, thus leaving a surplus of 81-horse power.

According to M. Bunsen, the temperature which may be attained by the combustion of the gases is 3083 deg., or, if hot air is used for the combustion, 3632 deg. Cast-iron melts at 2192 deg.; and, consequently, the temperature capable of being attained is amply sufficient to melt and work the iron in the more advanced processes.

But the power actually realised, when the combustion of these gases has been effected under the most favourable circumstances, falls far short of the above. The calculations of the chemist on this subject and the results produced in practice are widely different. The power actually obtained is not usually as much as 20 per cent. of the theoretical quantity; while the temperature produced by their combustion is probably under one-third of that given by M. Bunsen. It is certain, at least, that in no instance in this country has a sufficient heat been obtained for the melting of iron, or for any operation demanding a high temperature.

The cause of this great discrepancy between the theoretical estimate of the analytical chemist and the results attained in practice with the gases from blast furnaces, we attribute to the generally limited acquaintance possessed by chemists of blast-furnace operations on the one hand, and the little attention paid by the practical smelter to the most efficient modes of applying the gas to profitable use on the other.

We readily admit that the gases escaping from some blast furnaces may, with proper management, be made to yield $\frac{4}{10}$ths as much caloric as that evolved in the combustion of the fuel; but we dissent from the generally-received opinion that a sufficiently intense heat can be maintained by their combustion for the purposes of the forge, or for the rapid generation of steam. We are aware that on the Continent of Europe the gases have been applied *experimentally* to the melting of iron; but the value of their use thus, on the large scale, has yet to be ascertained. That they have not been yet utilised, notwithstanding the length of time which has elapsed since the first experiments were made, and the favourable opinion generally entertained of their value, appears unaccountable to theoretical writers, and is not unfrequently quoted as evidence of the backwardness of the state of the manufacture in this country, and the disinclination of ironmasters generally to adopt ascertained improvements.

The heat is produced by the combustion of the carbonic oxide and hydrogen. The proportion which these gases generally bear to the entire quantity is 36 per cent. Nitrogen and carbonic acid, neither of which yield heat, are present to the extent of 63 per cent.

If the combustible gases are capable of generating a temperature of 3083 deg. alone, the presence of nitrogen and carbonic acid will reduce it in proportion to the quantity of them present. A certain number of units of heat are generated by the combustible gases, but instead of being concentrated these units are disseminated through a volume of other gases; and in consequence of this diffusion the temperature attained is inferior to that necessary for the manipulations of the forge. The quantity of heat generated remains unaltered; but the temperature attained decreases from 3083 to 1100 deg. The admission of atmospheric air to effect this combustion also augments the volume, and consequently reduces the temperature of the ignited gases still lower; so that the working heat cannot be estimated at more than 900 deg.

This would be amply sufficient for generating steam for the engines and heating the blast; but from the dissemination of the units of heat through such a large volume of gas, the quantity in contact with the plate is small, and the vaporization of the water proceeds at a much slower rate than with the ordinary coal fires.

At the Dowlais works three several experimental trials were made upon the escaping gases; but the temperature attained rarely rose above a dull red heat, and the evaporative power of the boiler, as compared with its performances with a coal fire, was reduced nearly two-thirds.

At the Ebbw Vale works the gases were applied to the engine boilers, and a quantity of steam was thus generated. They have continued to be thus used since 1848, and large sums have been expended in bringing the apparatus to its present state. Yet the heat practically available is insufficient to work the blowing engines, and a large quantity of coal is also consumed for this purpose. The same firm are the proprietors of the Abersychan, Victoria,

Sirhowy, Aberdare, and Abernant works in Wales, in each of which the application of these gases to heating purposes has been carried to a greater or less extent.

At the Victoria ironworks the gases are applied to the boilers of the blowing engine; but the power generated is insufficient, and recourse is had to coal fires to supply the deficiency. The consumption of coal in the grates we were unable to ascertain; but the heat produced by its combustion was evidently causing the greatest evaporation of water.

At the Abersychan works the gases are collected and applied to a number of boilers; but a nearly equal number are fired with coal. Some of the hot-blast stoves are also heated by gas; but the temperature of the air in those heated by gas was under the melting point of lead, whereas in those with coal fires it was above.

At the Sirhowy works the gas is also applied to the engine boiler; but the saving in fuel does not appear great. A number of the boilers were using coal, and although no means existed for ascertaining the exact proportion which the volume of steam produced from the gas-fired boilers bore to that from the coal-fired, yet, judging from the number of boilers which formerly sufficed to keep the engine going when coal only was used, we should conclude that fully one-half of the steam was from the coal-fired boilers.

At the Aberdare furnaces the gases are brought down and applied to the heating of five boilers. But as there are six boilers with coal fires, the insufficiency of the gas alone is very apparent. Prior to the application of gas at these works, six boilers with coal fires sufficed to generate steam for the engines; now there are eleven at work. The consumption of coal is about 14 tons a day, or 6 cwts. per ton of pig-iron made by the furnaces. Now, as 5 cwts. is a large allowance for ordinary engines, the saving in these works must be very trifling indeed.

At the Goloynos works the gas is applied to heating the engine boilers; the saving of coal is reported as considerable; but the consumption in the coal fires maintained averages 3 cwts. per ton of pig-iron. The difference between this and 5 cwts. may be taken as the saving due to the gas.

At the Ystalyfera works a number of the engine boilers are heated by gas, while others are fired with coal. The hot-blast stoves are also heated with gas.

In the other iron-making districts the gases have been applied to the engine boilers and hot-blast stoves, effecting a saving in every case, and diminishing the consumption of coal formerly found necessary for compressing and heating the blast.

To make, however, a change of apparatus practically economical it is necessary not only that a saving be effected, but that the saving be sufficiently great to compensate for the outlay upon the new arrangement. Where the tunnel-head gas is applied to raise steam a larger number of boilers are required than where coal is employed.

At the Ebbw Vale, Abersychan, Sirhowy, Aberdare, Ystalyfera, and other works using the gas, the number of boilers now in use is nearly twice the number which sufficed with coal fires only. The necessity of having a larger number of boilers shows most conclusively that the practically available heating power of the gases is greatly inferior to that theoretically obtained by the analyst.

The diminished evaporative power of boilers heated by the gas is no doubt greatly owing to the incrustation formed on the exterior of the plates. On the flue surfaces of coal-fired boilers a thin covering of soot is deposited, which to some extent interferes with the rapid communication of heat; but with gas this evil is greatly increased, for in a few days an incrustation is formed which at places reaches a thickness of some inches, and, of course, materially affects the generation of steam. It, consequently, is necessary frequently to clean the surfaces of such a boiler.*

The cost of the necessary arrangements for collecting, conveying, and burning the gases, including the additional boiler power and chimney-stacks, amounts to about 1000*l*. per blast furnace, besides considerable current working expenses. To render this outlay of capital profitable, the saving in coal must be large—larger than has yet been accomplished in practice.

Although chemists do not hesitate to state that the gases may be withdrawn from the furnace without disturbing the smelting operations, they are not agreed respecting the level at which it may be done successfully. And we infer, therefore, that it can be best effected at one point only, the position of which remains to be discovered.

In the charcoal furnace it appears that the gases, to be of any value for heating purposes, must be withdrawn from a low level (probably at or near the boshes) where they are richest in carbonic oxide; their entire withdrawal at this level, however, disturbs the operations, by depriving the superincumbent materials of the heat and gaseous carbon. In these furnaces, therefore, only a portion of the ascending column can be withdrawn. It is conceded by chemists that the entire withdrawal of the gas ascending in these furnaces would seriously disturb the operations. The result, then, of the inquiries on furnace gases is merely certain statements that a portion of the gas may be withdrawn at some part of the furnace: but the quantity and exact position for the withdrawal are left undecided. But in the absence of evidence we are unable to accept the statement that while the withdrawal of the whole column disturbs the operations, the withdrawal of a portion is wholly free from any prejudicial effects. For if the loss of all the carbon and caloric of the ascending column is undoubtedly injurious to the operation, the loss of a portion, however small, would be expected to be felt, though in a less degree.

The gas escaping from charcoal furnaces contains a minimum per-centage of combustible gases, and at the top their value for heating is too small to offer inducements for their collection. In the best-regulated charcoal furnaces the carbonic oxide does not exceed 4 or 5 per cent., whilst the carbonic acid forms 30 to 36 per cent. of the whole. In furnaces in this country the quantity of carbonic oxide rises as high as 42 per cent., while the carbonic acid nearly disappears. This abundance of partially oxydised carbon is entirely due to the large consumption of fuel in the upper part of the furnace, of which we shall speak more fully hereafter.

* If a sufficient supply of atmospheric air were admitted, these deposits would probably not be formed.—J. A. P.

But since the gases escaping from the surfaces of the materials in British furnaces contain so large a proportion of carbonic oxide and so little carbonic acid, they are generally collected for utilisation from the throat or its immediate neighbourhood.

Various plans for collecting the gases have been tried; the one which appears to answer best is delineated Pl. XXIX., Fig. 142. The cup, which is a funnel-shaped casting, equal in its largest diameter to the throat of the furnace, and 4 or 5 feet deep, rests upon the top of the furnace by a flange round its outer edge. The orifice at the bottom measures from 3 to 5 feet in diameter, and is closed by a conical casting, with the apex upwards. This casting is suspended by a chain from a lever, which is counterbalanced at the other end. The materials are filled into the cup, and the workmen, by suitable gearing affixed to the lever, lower the cone, and the materials fall into the furnace, and the stopper is restored to its place by the counterpoise on the opposite end of the lever. The circular space around the funnel inside the furnace, forms a chamber for the reception of the gas, from which it is conveyed by brick tunnels or iron piping to the place of combustion.

Where mechanical appliances are employed in filling, this plan is probably amongst the best that can be adopted. It possesses, however, the disadvantage of reducing the available working height of the furnace to an extent equal to twice the depth of the casting at top. The average height of the furnaces where it is in use is 42 feet, consequently the working height is reduced to 34 feet.

Another plan (Pl. XXIX., Fig. 140) which has also been extensively adopted, consists of a lid fitting closely to the furnace; this lid is lifted by means of a counterbalance on each occasion of charging materials. No reduction in the working height of the furnace is caused by this arrangement, but the time during which the throat is open while the cover is being lifted, the materials filled in, and until it is again shut close, is very prejudicial to the quality of the gas. It is commonly stated that no gas passes while the cover is up, but this is an error; the same quantity of gas is evolved from the furnace whether the cover be open or closed, but if it is open a large quantity of atmospheric air also passes into the pipes, increasing the bulk of the unprofitable gases, and thereby reducing the heating power of those that are combustible, as well as endangering the apparatus by causing a great increase of temperature in the pipes. To utilise the gases successfully, it is therefore a matter of the greatest importance that the supply be regular, and not subject either to interruption or variation in quality.

A third plan (Pl. XXIX., Fig. 139) in use at some works is very readily applicable to existing furnaces. An iron cylinder of 6 or 7 feet in depth, and 6 or 8 inches smaller in diameter than the throat, is sunk into the furnace; a flange on the top, which rests upon the brickwork inside the tunnel-head, forms a joint and sustains the cylinder. The annular space between the cylinder and furnace underneath the flange and above the materials forms a chamber for the ascent of the gases, which are conveyed away through a suitable pipe or tunnel.

This plan also has its disadvantages. The duration of the cylinder is subject to great variation. In some cases it is burnt down in two or three weeks, and, under more favourable circumstances seldom lasts longer than a few months. The cost of the cylinder, and the delay and expense attending its so frequent renewal, are formidable items in the working cost of this plan for collecting gas.

This method is also subject to the disadvantage of reducing the working height of the furnace. The cylinder is kept full of materials, it is true, but they receive very little heat while they are in it, as the hot gases are drawn into the outside flues and do not enter the cylinders. It must be conceded that the capacity, and consequently the smelting power, of the furnace is diminished by the space occupied by the cylinder and chamber for collecting the gas. If the cylinder is immersed 7 feet, one-tenth of the capacity of the furnace will be useless so far as the reduction of metal is concerned. The deficiency of smelting power is still greater with the plan first described.

A fourth plan (Pl. XXX., Figs. 145, 146) of collecting the gases is considered by some engineers as the least objectionable. At a convenient depth, generally 8 or 10 feet from the top of the furnace, an annular flue is constructed around the brick lining, with a number of orifices opening downwards into the body of the furnace. This plan leaves the form of the throat and the arrangements for filling unaltered. From the descending direction taken by the orifices communicating with the furnace, they are not liable to obstruction from the materials, and the supply of gas is probably more regular than with either of the other plans.

The admission of atmospheric air in certain proportions to the gases produces an explosive mixture. The pipes, and other connexions, are therefore required to be made air-tight in their joints to prevent the access of dangerous quantities of atmospheric air during the collection and conveyance of the gas to the place of combustion. And to reduce as much as possible the effects of an explosion, large flap-valves, hinged in a sloping direction and kept shut by their own gravity, are placed at short intervals in the pipes or flues for the ready escape of the gases in case of explosion. Yet, notwithstanding these precautions, the shattered brickwork and broken chimney-shafts tell of the destructive force exerted in the explosions occurring even in the best-managed establishments.

To withdraw gas in sufficient quantities, lofty chimney-shafts have been erected at several works, and it is now pretty generally accepted that without such chimneys the principle is not applicable to existing works. The resistance occasioned by the great length of the piping or tunnelling, through which the gases are conveyed to the boilers, appears to necessitate the assistance of an additional draught.

But notwithstanding the general opinion in favour of the collection and combustion of the gases for heating purposes, we question whether any plan with this object can be made practicable without interfering more or less with the operations of a furnace working with a minimum yield of fuel. By the experiments made at the Dowlais furnace we found the consumption of coal to be sensibly increased, while the quality of the iron was deteriorated. In other works, also, we have observed that the consumption of coal in the furnaces has increased, in the words of the attendants, "The furnace does not carry so good a burden;" and also, that the same deterioration in quality has taken place. The advocates for the utilization of the gases will not readily admit these results, but as they are patent to most practical men who have had opportunities of observing the working of furnaces both with and without apparatus for the collection of the gases, we will endeavour to explain the cause of this increased consumption of fuel.

We have already spoken of the injurious effects which follow from the contraction of the throat of the furnace, a rapid draught being created, and a partial consumption of the coal taking place in a region where its combustion produces no useful effect. Bearing in mind, then, that a rapid draught at the surface of the materials, no matter how created or maintained, is injurious to the smelting power of the coal; the fact that the withdrawal of the heated gases, necessitating a greater draught than that usually produced by their natural ascent, will account for the additional consumption. The effect of immersing a cylinder into the furnace, or of applying almost any other mode of collecting, is to reduce the available area for the ascent of the gases, and thus to create a rapid combustion of the upper stratum of coal which is made up by charging a larger quantity. To augment the velocity of the current of gas beyond that attainable by the powerful chimneys already alluded to, the density and volume of the blast have been largely increased in several instances, but this increase of blast, by adding to the rapidity of the draught, has still further augmented the consumption.

The mode of withdrawing the gases through a number of flues entering the furnace at a considerable depth from the top, can hardly be otherwise than injurious to the yield of coal and working of the furnace. This method is in use at several works, but is evidently attended with an increased consumption of coal. The abstraction of the heated gases at a low depth causes a partial combustion of the fuel next to the flues, and deprives the materials above of the heat and carbon of the ascending column. Additional coal is, therefore, consumed in compensation.

But the bad effect is not confined merely to the greater consumption of fuel. The quality of the metal is deteriorated as well. From the comparative coolness of the materials above the flues the conversion of the coal into coke takes place far down in the furnace, where the rapid evolution of hydrogen, watery vapour, and other products of distillation, by taking up caloric, reduces the temperature of the surrounding materials and so disturbs the operations of the furnace. The expulsion of the water and carbonic acid of the limestone also takes place lower down; and the changes which the ironstone undergoes in its descent commence at a lower level, and consequently it is a shorter time under the carburizing influence of the gases and coal.

Effects similar to these result from the withdrawal of the gases from the surface of the materials by means of closed tops. The diminished reducing power of the coal, coupled with the practically reduced height of the furnace, is followed by a corresponding deterioration in the make, quality of the metal, and yield of fuel.

The employment of iron cylinders immersed in the throat of the furnace is attended also by an additional evil where raw coal is used. The parallel form of the sides retains the coal when expanded by heat, and not only is a considerable portion of its power unprofitably expended, but by hanging in the cylinder for periods of two or three hours, forming, as it were, miniature scaffolds, great irregularities are produced in the working of the furnace. At the Dowlais works the heat evolved by the combustion of the coal within the cylinder, together with that produced by the rapid draught in the annular space between the cylinder and furnace, burnt down a wrought-iron cylinder made of $\frac{1}{4}$-inch boiler-plate in 15 or 16 days. Where coke is used as fuel, we have known similar cylinders to last 4 or 5 months; but this appears to be their maximum duration.

After a careful examination of the various modes of collecting the gases escaping from the blast furnaces, in use both in this country and on the Continent, and having witnessed the alterations produced by each on the operations of the furnace, we are of opinion that it is not expedient or profitable to control the escape of the gases. We also believe that not one atom of gas, nor one unit of heat can be withdrawn from a furnace without disturbing the equilibrium of the smelting. This opinion is, we confess, at variance with the statements of Continental chemists. But it must be remembered that the estimates made by those gentlemen of the commercial value of the products of combustion have invariably been drawn from theoretical calculations founded on laboratory experiments, and they also assume that the gases may be withdrawn in quantity without injuriously affecting the smelting. Practice, however, has proved the incorrectness of the latter conclusion. By calculations founded on data equally insufficient, the heat capable of being attained by the combustion of the gaseous products under ordinary circumstances was greatly over-estimated, and in practice the maximum working temperature scarcely reaches a third of the theoretical statement. Altogether, the brilliant anticipations formed of the value of these gases for heating purposes have not been realised, and the policy of collecting them for such purposes may be fairly questioned.

But leaving for a moment the question of withdrawing the gases let us endeavour to ascertain the amount of the saving which would be effected, supposing the entire quantity of coal usually consumed under the blowing-engine boilers could be dispensed with. For the purposes of this calculation we will assume that the Dowlais works will present a fair illustration. The consumption of coal at the blowing engines in those works averages about 6 cwts. per ton of pig-iron. This coal is the screenings from the furnace-yard, and the broken coal produced underground in mining the large coal, and if not used at the engines would be completely valueless. It is estimated by the proprietors as being worth 1s. 6d. per ton; 6 cwts. will consequently be worth $5\frac{1}{2}$ pence, and thus the total saving at that establishment could not exceed this amount per ton of pigs. With the certainty then, that, the saving must be under 6d. per ton, is it good policy to disturb the operations of the furnace, with the certain prospect of adding to their consumption of coal? It is easy to ascertain the value of the saving at the engine boilers, admitting that the application of the gases is successful in generating a sufficiency of steam, but we cannot so readily estimate the effects upon the furnace. There is one point, however, which should be well considered; that is, that while the coal saved from the engine boilers is worth 1s. 6d. per ton, that additionally consumed in the furnace costs from 6s. to 7s. per ton. An additional consumption of furnace coal of no more than 1¼ cwts. per ton of iron, or 3 per cent. on the usual consumption would cost precisely as much as would be saved by the successful use of gas under the boilers. But the extra consumption occasioned by the abstraction of the gases greatly exceeds 1¼ cwts., being from 3 to 4 cwts., or 7 to 9 per cent. So that upon this view of the case by withdrawing the gases and depriving the materials of a portion of their value, a saving of 6d. per ton of iron is accomplished at the engine boilers, but at the expense of 1s. per ton at the blast furnace.

If this question be examined with regard to the return for the capital expended, the benefit to be derived from the use of gas will appear equally trifling. We have already stated that the additional outlay in boilers, piping, and other erections, averages 1000*l.* per furnace; larger sums have been expended, but we will consider this as sufficient. Estimating the make at 100 tons weekly, the annual saving will amount to 5200 sixpences, equal to 130*l.*, a sum not more than sufficient for interest and working expenses, leaving profit out of the question.*

* The experience of the ironmasters of this country is evidently at variance with the opinions advanced by Mr. Truran. The utilisation of the tunnel-head gases has steadily progressed during the last few years, and the blast-furnaces at the Dowlais works have been recently fitted with apparatus of the most complete description for collecting and burning their waste gas.—EDS.

SECTION XII.

ECONOMY OF HEATED AIR AND INFLUENCE EXERTED BY THE FORM OF FURNACE ON THE CONSUMPTION OF FUEL.

The remarkable effects produced by a heated blast in reducing the yield of fuel and augmenting the make of metal in certain localities require some explanation.

The late Mr. Mushet in his papers on iron and steel, Dr. Thomson in his report to the British Association, and Dr. Clark in his paper read at the Edinburgh Society, attribute the inferiority of a cold, as contrasted with a heated blast, to the cooling effects of the former; thus giving rise to the very common impression that the heat maintained at the zone of fusion in the hot-blast furnace is more intense and concentrated than with the cold blast.

This explanation, though generally adopted, is manifestly very far from correct. Every pound of carbon, in burning to carbonic acid, evolves a definite amount of heat. The time occupied in the evolution of this heat will depend entirely on the rapidity with which the air can be brought into contact with the fuel, and the temperature attained will be in direct proportion to the rapidity of combustion. If, then, sufficiently powerful mechanical means are adopted for bringing the oxygen in contact with the carbon, the highest temperature which it is possible under any circumstances to produce, may be maintained in the hearth of a cold-blast furnace. With a dry cold-blast the intensity of the heat attained is evidenced by the rapid reduction of the most refractory ores. How are we to reconcile this attainment of a maximum temperature with the assumed cooling effect of a cold blast? If the cold blast has a cooling tendency, then surely the greater the volume delivered in a given time the more rapid will be the reduction of temperature; but experience testifies to the reverse: an increase of the volume is found to be followed by a corresponding increase of temperature.

Equally unsatisfactory is the explanation that a hot blast is better fitted for supporting combustion than a cold. But before we can allow this assumed superiority we must know in what respect the composition of the hot differs from the cold blast. If hot air supports combustion better than cold the relative proportions of oxygen and nitrogen composing atmospheric air must alter with the accession of caloric; or else the cold air contains some deleterious ingredient which is got rid of by heating. But the relative proportions of these gases are not altered, and whatever substance may be mingled with the cold air exists to the same extent in the heated blast.

The expanded volume of the heated air is supposed to be more favourable to perfect combustion in consequence of the enlarged surface presented by the atoms of oxygen for combining with the carbon. This involves the supposition that the atoms of oxygen are themselves expanded by heat, whereas it is believed that the expansion of gases by heat is due to the greater separation of the individual atoms from each other.

The explanation which we have to offer of the superior effects of a heated blast as contrasted with those of a cold is based upon our practical experience of the working of blast furnaces on both systems. From numerous observations, and the results of several experiments, we are disposed to ascribe the superiority to two separate causes. The first is, that the heat thrown into the furnace along with the blast permits a corresponding quantity of coal to be withdrawn from the burden of materials, and a proportionate reduction in the volume of blast. The effect is seen in an augmentation of the make, but not in any saving of fuel. The second cause is that the reduced volume of blast and the large amount of heat which it carries with it cause a diminished consumption of fuel in the upper parts of the furnace, the result being that a quantity of fuel is saved at the furnace greater than what would be due merely to the caloric introduced by the blast.

In reference to the first-named cause, it is obvious that if the furnace be supplied with a given quantity of heat with the blast the natural result will be a reduced consumption of coal at the top, but this reduction is counterbalanced by a consumption at the blast stoves equal in amount. No coal, then, being saved, the gain is simply limited to an augmentation of make.

The augmentation of make is explained by the well-known fact that a reduction in the proportion of coal to ore is followed by an increased make of iron. This holds good whether the blast be hot or cold, but there is this difference in the systems: With a cold blast the reduction is followed by a change from grey to white in the quality of the iron. But with the hot blast, especially if the ores have a considerable quantity of carbon, either chemically or mechanically, combined with them, such a change does not so readily take place. If, however, the burden is chiefly composed of hematites or siliceous ores, any diminution in the supply of carbon is speedily felt, even with hot blast.

As partly illustrating the foregoing statement, we may mention that the ordinary yield of coal to produce grey iron at the Dowlais furnaces, with cold blast, is 50 cwts. per ton of iron, and the make with this proportion 90 tons weekly. On reducing the quantity of coal so that the yield averages 40 cwts., the make increases to 106 tons, but the quality of the iron is little above white.

Whenever the make is very large we find the yield of coal low. At the Cwm Celyn furnaces the make occasionally reaches 240 tons a week from a single furnace, smelting argillaceous ore, hematite, and cinders, and the yield of coal is as little as 23 cwts. per ton of iron, but the iron is very low in quality, and can only be manufactured into the coarsest varieties of bar-iron.

From this connexion of the make with the yield of coal, elsewhere investigated at greater length, it would appear that within certain limits the total consumption of coal is constant with the same blast, and that the make varies nearly in an inverse ratio with the proportion of coal to ironstone and other materials forming the burden.

If, then, by heating the blast, and so conveying into the furnace an amount of heat available for reducing the ore, we are enabled to withhold a portion of the coal, the make will be doubly augmented—first, by the reducing power of the additional caloric at bottom; secondly, by the reduced proportion the carbon in the materials charged bears to the volume of blast. Estimating the make of iron and yield of coal with the cold blast at 100 tons weekly, and 40 cwts. per ton of iron, respectively, and assuming the saving of coal at the furnace and the consumption at the stoves each at 5 cwts., the increase of make with a hot blast may be easily ascertained. In the first place, taking for granted that the heat evolved by the combustion of the 5 cwts. of stove coal possesses the same reducing power as an equal weight charged at top, the make will be increased by it $12\frac{1}{4}$ per cent. Secondly, from the reduced proportion of coal charged there will be an increase of 14 per cent.; total, $26\frac{1}{4}$ per cent. The increase of make on the substitution of a hot for a cold blast is thus fairly represented; but it will be observed that 14 per cent. of the addition is owing to the diminished proportion of coal. On a cold-blast furnace this diminution would be followed by the same increase in make, although with a falling off in the quality of the metal. Hence the hot blast is only absolutely superior to the cold in respect of make to the extent of the reducing power of the heat thrown in with the blast. However, as this rate of production with a diminished supply of coal is incompatible with the obtaining of grey iron, the volume of air entering the stoves is considerably diminished, so that the make is not in reality more than 8 or 10 per cent. higher than with a cold blast. In Wales, indeed, with the lean argillaceous ores the production of grey iron of a high quality from a furnace on hot blast is very little superior to that from one blown with cold air. In the case, however, of irons requiring only an inferior degree of carburization the make is greatly in favour of the hot-blast system.

The superiority of the hot blast, slight as it is, disappears altogether with certain classes of ores if the quality of the resulting metal is an object. In smelting the hematites, siliceous ores, and some varieties of the argillaceous ore, any reduction in the quantity of coal shows itself by a corresponding deficiency of carbon in the metal. This is not difficult of explanation. By throwing in caloric along with the blast at bottom, a quantity of the coal previously required may be withheld at the top without reducing the rate of smelting; but as the hot blast carries no carbon with it, the gaseous carbon available for combination with the metal is reduced in proportion. If the temperature of the blast were elevated to the melting point of the ore the fuel might be withdrawn altogether, with the exception of a quantity containing sufficient carbon for combining with the oxygen of the ore. But the metal so obtained would be nearly void of carbon. We conclude, then, that for every degree that we elevate the temperature of the blast a certain quantity of coal may be saved from the furnace, but the carburization of the metal suffers, and its quality is deteriorated.

With the carbonaceous ores and some varieties of those of the argillaceous class these bad effects do not follow the reduction of the coal charges on the application of a hot blast.

This is doubtless owing to the large quantity of carbon combined both chemically and mechanically with them. Even if no coal at all were charged, metallic iron of a high quality might be smelted from these ores by the employment of a blast heated sufficiently to melt them, their melting point being, according to our own experiments, between 1300° and 1400°. Besides which, they do not require to be in the furnace so long as other kinds for the production of grey iron. It is obvious, then, that the make may be largely augmented without injury to the quality of the iron.

It is probable that if the requisite heat were communicated to the materials through the medium of the blast alone —coal not being supplied to the furnace at all—the make might be augmented beyond anything attainable under the present system of smelting. Two-thirds of the quantity of limestone at present used is necessary for fluxing the earths combined with the coal. Consequently under this mode of smelting the materials charged into the furnace for the production of a ton of iron would only weigh 37 cwts.—that is, 35 cwts. of ore and 2 cwts. of limestone. The weekly produce of a medium-sized furnace has, we have already stated, reached 240 tons, but the consumption of solid materials exceeded 1000 tons, and the gross weight of melted matter equalled 700 tons. Supposing the materials to consist of fusible carbonaceous ore and a minimum dose of limestone, and the consumption to be equally large, the make of iron under the proposed system would be nearly 600 tons weekly. But taking into consideration the richness of the carbonaceous ore, its comparative freedom from earthy matter, and the low temperature at which it melts, we venture to predict that the time is not distant when a weekly make of 800 to 1000 tons will be as common as 150 to 200 tons under the present system.

The proposal to smelt these ores without the employment of fuel in the furnace may at first sight appear chimerical, but a careful consideration of all the circumstances will probably lead the intelligent observer to a different conclusion. At the end of this section we shall discuss the effects which the altered mode of smelting would produce on the quality of the iron.

Hitherto we have only considered the effects of a heated blast in augmenting the weekly make of metal, under circumstances where its application is not attended with a saving of fuel—that is to say, where the consumption of coal in the heating stoves is equivalent to the quantity saved from the furnace. We will now proceed to examine the superior effect of a heated blast over a cold, as exhibited in saving fuel, that is, where the reduction in the furnace consumption exceeds the quantity of coal burnt in the stoves.

We shall find our most remarkable examples among the ironworks in Scotland. At the Clyde works, where the new system was first applied, the furnace consumption of coke per ton of pig-iron was reduced from 60 to 38 cwts., the consumption in the heating stoves amounting to 5 cwts. of coal. Here was a clear saving of 17 cwts., allowing that the calorific power of the coke was only equal to that of the raw coal, though in practice it is considerably higher.

In this instance the superiority of a heated blast is shown in the most marked manner. 5 cwts. of coal burnt in the heating stoves are of equal value with 22 cwts. of coke consumed in the blast furnace.

No explanation, that we are aware of, has ever appeared of this circumstance—the very different reducing powers of the coal consumed in the furnace and that consumed in the stove; and this result, obtained at the Clyde furnaces, is quoted as evidence of the saving which follows on the use of heated air, and consequently of the immense value of that invention.

On examining this statement, we find that the matter appears to stand thus: the 22 cwts. of coke burnt to carbonic acid in the blast furnace evolve a certain quantity of caloric; and 5 cwts. of coal burnt to carbonic acid on the stove grates evolve nearly one-fifth of that quantity; but as not more than three-fourths of the quantity evolved is absorbed by the blast, it follows that an amount of heat equal to that produced in the combustion of 3.75 cwts. of coal, conveyed into the furnace by the tuyere, is equal in effect to that of 22 cwts. of coke charged into the throat; apparently, then, the caloric conveyed into the hearth is six times more effective in the reduction of the ore than that produced there,by the combustion of the coke.

From what cause does this superiority arise? Can it be that one pound of carbon burnt outside the furnace evolves as much heat as six burnt inside? Or is it that of the six pounds burnt inside five-sixths is consumed at such an elevation, or in such a manner that it renders no service?

We can very well understand that the caloric communicated to the materials through the medium of a hot blast permits the saving of an equivalent portion of coal in the furnace, but in this there is no economy. When, however, we are told that the quantity saved at the furnace-top amounts to six times that expended on the blast, the subject becomes worthy of patient investigation.

Our attention has been directed to this point for some years past, and during our residence at the Dowlais and Hirwain works we endeavoured to collect all the information bearing upon it which these establishments afforded. At the Dowlais works, indeed, the frequent alterations in the burden on the furnaces, mode of blowing, and volume of blast, furnished valuable data for our guidance in this inquiry. Our observations at the Dowlais works alone on the eighteen blast furnaces of that establishment extended over a period of thirteen years. We do not, however, purpose to rely solely on the information collected at the Dowlais and Hirwain works, but, as opportunity may serve, we shall bring forward the results of observations on all the iron-making districts of this country to correct and corroborate the conclusions to which our own practice has led us.

In seeking for a satisfactory solution of the question before us the first inquiry is, what proportion of the carbon charged into the furnace is burnt to carbonic acid in the hearth?

For the complete combustion of one pound of carbon nearly 153 cubic feet of atmospheric air is theoretically required. This is the quantity necessary, supposing that all the oxygen of the air enters into combination with the carbon; but as in practice this precision cannot be attained, we may safely assume 160 feet as a minimum supply.

Knowing, then, the consumption of carbon and supply of air in a given time to a blast-furnace, we can ascertain by calculation how nearly practice assimilates to a chemically correct standard of perfect and profitable combustion.

At the Clyde works, prior to the use of heated air, the weekly consumption of coke, yielding 87 per cent. of carbon, was 375 tons. The furnaces were under blast 156 hours weekly, and the supply of blast averaged, after allowance for leakage, 7140 cubic feet of air per minute. This supply of air was at the rate of 85 cubic feet to each pound of carbon.

After the application of a hot blast, the fuel used was coal, yielding 76.5 of carbon, the weekly consumption averaged 554 tons, the volume of blast remained as before; for each pound of carbon then 67 cubic feet of air was delivered into the furnace.

The four new furnaces at the Dowlais works burn weekly 1033 tons (long weight) of coal, containing above 87 per cent. of carbon. They are under blast 156 hours weekly, and receive during that time upon an average 21,560 cubic feet of air per minute, or at the rate of 90 feet to the pound of carbon.

The fourteen other furnaces at the same works have consumed 3911 tons of coal in a week, with 77,000 cubic feet of blast per minute; for each pound of carbon there were 81 cubic feet of air.

The foundry iron furnace at the new furnaces belonging to the Dowlais Company, blown with heated air, has made as much as 130 tons of iron in a week, with a consumption of 50 cwts. of coal per ton, and a volume of blast averaging 5390 cubic feet per minute. This is equal to 78 cubic feet to the pound of carbon.

The foundry iron furnace at the Hirwain works, blown with heated air, averages 90 tons of pig-iron weekly, with a consumption of 34 cwts. of coke, yielding 94 per cent. of carbon to the ton, and a blast averaging 2541 cubic feet per minute. Dividing the volume of the blast by the weight of carbon consumed for equal times we find that for each pound there is 68 cubic feet.

The six blast furnaces at the Langloan works, Scotland, average 150 tons each, or 900 tons of iron weekly; the average yield of coal is 38 cwts., yielding 76.5 of carbon. The blowing engine delivers 14,824 cubic feet of blast per minute. The volume of blast is at the rate of 44 cubic feet of air to 1 lb. of carbon.

At the Gartsherrie works, Scotland, eight of the furnaces are blown by a single engine, which delivers 24,335 cubic feet of air per minute. The eight furnaces make on average 1120 tons weekly, with a yield of coal of 40 cwts. to the ton. The consumption therefore is 2240 tons, containing 76.5 per cent. of carbon. At 156 hours blowing weekly the supply of atmospheric air is at the rate of 55 cubic feet to each pound of carbon.

Messrs. Playfair and Bunsen in their Report on the Gases of the Alfreton furnace state the consumption of coal, containing by their analyses nearly 75 per cent. of carbon, at

31,200 lbs. per day of 24 hours. The blast to this furnace is stated to have been delivered by a pipe 2.75 inches diameter, at a pressure of $3\frac{1}{4}$ lbs. per square inch, and temperature of 626 degs. Fahr. We have ascertained by experiments on a large scale, that, after allowing for expansion of the air, a pipe of this bore delivers 1020 cubic feet of atmospheric air per minute. Divided by the consumption of carbon in the same time we have 63 feet of air to each pound of carbon.

From what is here advanced it is evident that the quantity of atmospheric air at present thrown into the blast furnace is inadequate to the complete combustion of the carbon of the fuel. For even assuming that all the air discharged by the tuyere pipes is effectually decomposed, and yields up its oxygen to the carbon for the formation of carbonic acid, the quantity is in every instance insufficient. The examples given are not selected on account of their evidently great deficiency, but because we happen to possess accurate data of the consumption of fuel and volume of blast. In the case of the Scotch furnaces the maximum quantity of air stated is scarcely one-third of that theoretically required, and even that is still further reduced by the leakage at the tuyeres. If the deficiency were small, or if in any instance there were an excess, we might conclude that the proportions were as good as could ordinarily be obtained in practice; but when we find that the entire supply varies from one-half to three-fourths of the quantity absolutely required, it becomes important to examine how combustion of the fuel can be effected under such circumstances.

It may be objected that allowance ought to have been made for the carbon combined with the iron, and for that which combines with the oxygen of the ore; but in the furnaces enumerated the ores smelted are the carbonates of the coal formation, and in nearly every instance contain a larger quantity of carbon than is thus absorbed, so that we may fairly treat the carbon in the fuel as so much material for the production of heat by combustion with the blast.

In the instance quoted where the largest proportion of air to carbon obtains the quantity of oxygen is barely sufficient to form carbonic oxide, but the production of this gas in the zone of fusion involves the supposition of a temperature greatly below the melting point of the ore. Besides which the quantity of oxygen received by the Scotch furnaces is not more than the half of that necessary for the production of this gas, and is altogether insufficient to enter into combination with the carbon in any known proportions.

If the volume of blast employed for the respective furnaces were less than that required to produce the maximum degree of heat in the combustion of the carbon present in the hearth, the employment of a larger volume should result in an increase of temperature and the production of a superior iron. But, practically, it is found that an augmentation of the volume of blast beyond the quantities we have quoted (unless accompanied by a corresponding addition to the supply of fuel) produces a result the very reverse. The temperature is reduced, and the iron is of inferior quality. We can then only conclude that the quantity of carbon charged into the furnace is diminished during its descent, and that the difference between it and that ultimately available for combustion may be fairly represented by the difference between the quantity of atmospheric air theoretically required and that actually found sufficient for the working of the furnace.

Calculated on the quantity capable of being burnt to carbonic acid by the oxygen supplied we find that at the Dowlais works, under the most favourable conditions now in operation, only 56 per cent. of the coal entering the furnace evolves useful heat, and at the Langloan works only 27.5 per cent. The remainder of the coal consumed may be considered as altogether unproductive in the operation of smelting.

The assumption, however, that from one-half to three-fourths of the present consumption of fuel is wasted must be supported by other facts. These we hasten to produce, and trust that by their aid we shall be able to establish a connexion between this waste and the saving of fuel on the employment of a heated blast.

From this point, however, the inquiry becomes inseparably connected with the form of the interior of the furnace; and embraces the combined effects of a heated blast, and the form of the furnace on the economy of fuel. For the better elucidation of the subject we will recapitulate various deductions drawn from the proportions detailed in a former Section.

1. For the production of grey pig-iron from the leaner varieties of argillaceous ores, the hematites and silicious ores, the solid materials according to the present system of working must be in the furnace 40 hours.

2. If the descent be accelerated beyond this rate the quality of the resulting iron is deteriorated.

3. If the stated proportion of carbon to ore and flux be diminished the quality of the iron is deteriorated (a reduction from 50 to 42 cwts. of coal resulting in the production of white iron) the make being at the same time increased in nearly an inverse ratio to the yield of carbon.

4. If the volume of blast be augmented beyond that stated, the rate of descent is accelerated, and is followed by the production of a less grey iron, and if largely augmented by the production of white iron, in either case the make is increased.

5. A reduction of the diameter of the throat of the furnace is followed by a deterioration in the quality of the crude iron. But the make in this case is not increased.

Here then, with ores, fuel, flux, and blast, the kind remaining the same, we have a deterioration of the quality of the metal from three very different causes—an increased volume of blast—a reduction in the proportion of fuel—and a contraction of the throat of the furnace. But if examined, each of these causes tends to reduce the quantity of carbon in the zone of fusion, thus producing white iron.

By augmenting the volume of blast the temperature is for the time increased, combustion of the fuel and reduction of the metal proceeds more rapidly, and the descent of the ore and coke is accelerated beyond the rate at which the carbon can be properly taken up by the iron. But the mere acceleration of descent is not the sole cause of the rapid deterioration observed in the quality. The increased volume of blast thrown in augments the volume of the ascending column of heated gases, and of course in the same ratio its velocity. Hence, in the throat, the point of exit, the increased draught is followed by a greater combustion of the easily inflammable coal. It is impossible to say with accuracy what proportion of the coal is thus consumed, but when it is considered that a slight draught is sufficient for the immediate ignition of the coal, and that the heat thus generated, communicated to the ascending gases by expanding their volume, again augments the draught and combustion, the probability is that a moiety of the calorific powers of the fuel is thus unprofitably expended.

A contraction of the throat increases the velocity of the draught in an inverse ratio to the area of the outlet, and is followed by an increased consumption of coal, the increase being nearly in the same ratio as the augmented velocity of the ascending column. This was the case at the narrow-throated experimental furnace at the Dowlais works. And in examining the yields of the various furnaces in that establishment, we find that those with the narrowest throats consume the largest quantity of coal in proportion to the weight of iron smelted. Compared with each other, also, we find that the yield of coal appears nearly determined by the volume of blast delivered and the area provided for its escape at the throat.

The combustion of a portion of the fuel in the throat necessarily supposes that a high temperature is maintained there in coal-fed furnaces. From observation, we are of opinion that, where the throat is one-half the diameter of the furnace, and the blast proportioned to the production of grey iron, the temperature ranges between 900 deg. and 1000 deg. Fahr. In furnaces having a smaller throat the temperature is considerably higher. Doubts may be entertained as to the existence of so high a temperature, but we would simply direct attention to the brickwork of the throat of coal-fed furnaces as conclusive evidence that a very high temperature prevails. From examining twelve of the Dowlais furnaces blown out for repairs after having been in blast for periods varying from eight to thirteen years, we ascertained that the brickwork at the throat is destroyed much more rapidly than the vertical work at the level of the boshes. The diameter of most of them at the top was one-half of that of the body; in these the destruction of the brickwork in the throat was more than twice as great as in the lining above the boshes. In furnaces with narrower throats the depth of brickwork removed was nearly three times as great as at the lowest part of the lining. From the throat the loss gradually diminished in the descent until on arriving at the original level of the boshes it was reduced to a minimum.

The wear or destruction was not so great in the hot as in the cold-blast furnaces. This was no more than we expected. As a rule the materials in the throat of a hot-blast furnace are colder than those in the cold-blast furnace. To understand this apparent paradox it must be remembered that the heat maintained in the throat of the furnace is not produced by conduction from below, but is the result of a partial combustion of the fuel which is governed by the velocity of the ascending current, and that again by the area of escape and the volume of gas. In the hot-blast furnace the volume of gas is less, and consequently the velocity of escape less, in proportion as the weight of blast is less than that thrown into the cold-blast furnace. But the temperature is reduced in a still greater degree. From the heat thrown in at the bottom a smaller proportion of fuel is required to be charged at the top. Carbon, therefore, forms a lesser portion of the whole volume of materials, and consequently the temperature maintained in the throat is not so high. The result being that the superiority of the heated air is seen in the reduced consumption of coals, as well as in the smaller quantity of blast required.

The economy of fuel with the heated blast is doubtless to a great extent due to the comparative coolness maintained in the throat, the consumption of fuel being less in that region than in a cold-blast furnace. If then we could lower the temperature in the throat of the cold-blast furnace, a great economy of fuel would be ensured, and the superiority of the heated blast in this respect disappear. In support of this opinion we may adduce some remarkable effects observed in the working of hot-blast furnaces.

We have frequently noticed that when a furnace which has been working with a heated blast and the accompanying reduced quantity of coal, is suddenly changed to a cold blast by withdrawing the fires from the stoves, the descent of the materials is accelerated. For twenty-four to thirty hours after the substitution of the cold blast the furnace makes more iron with the original burden, and no deterioration is to be seen in the quality of the produce. But after that period the rate of descent is checked and the quality changes; in from thirty-six to forty hours the furnace will have returned to its original rate of working, and the quality of the iron be deteriorated to white. At the end of forty-eight to sixty hours the furnace will have settled down to the usual rate of working with a cold blast, and the quality have finally receded to that produced under ordinary circumstances with the diminished consumption of coal. If the coal is increased sufficiently to keep the furnace with cold blast permanently on the quality of iron it was making before the alteration, the make will be diminished in the ratio that the altered quantity of ore bears to the whole of the materials charged.

When the make with a hot blast has averaged 105 tons a week the immediate substitution of a cold-blast has temporarily increased the production at a rate equal to a weekly make of 115 or 116 tons; but when the increased quantity of coal added as a compensation for the withdrawal of the hot blast has taken effect the make has receded to 96 tons weekly.

With those who have not studied the subject, and noticed the different effects produced on the furnace, the hot blast has the merit of effecting a large saving in the consumption of coal, and augmenting the weekly produce in a remarkable degree; and under circumstances which properly ought never to occur, the hot blast doubtless does effect important changes.

If the heating of the air were the real cause of the larger make and greater economy of fuel, how is it that the make is augmented and the economy greatest on substituting a cold blast under the circumstances we have described? According to the published opinions of the ablest advocates of the hot blast system, the admission of large volumes of cold air should be attended with an immediate reduction of the temperature in the hearth. But the temporary increase of make is direct evidence that the temperature is higher.*

When the whole of the circumstances are taken into consideration we apprehend that the real cause will appear evident. While the furnace is working with the heated blast, the burden having been increased and the quantity of blast reduced, the draught and consequent consumption of coal in the throat and upper part of the body is diminished. Of the coal charged, a greater proportion descends to the hearth and is available for combustion, than occurs with the larger consumption and cold blast. On the substitution of the cold blast an ample supply of carbon is present for the maintenance of an intense heat, combustion proceeds more rapidly, and the quantity of metal reduced in a given time is augmented. But this improvement is local. With the admission of the cold blast the volume of the ascending gases is augmented, and the draught created by the increased velocity of the current causes a partial combustion of the coal in the throat. Hence the proportion of carbon which subsequently descends to the hearth is diminished. The injurious effects resulting from the consumption of carbon are not immediately seen. For the first twenty-four or thirty hours the altered blast is acting on the fuel which had passed the throat while the hot blast was in operation. Directly, however, that the coal that was in the upper part of the furnace at the time of alteration reaches the zone of fusion, both cinder and iron alter in appearance. The former changes from grey to dark spongy or black, and the latter from dark grey to mottled and white.

The conclusion then at which we have arrived, is that the temporary improvement under these circumstances, so much beyond the ordinary performance of a cold-blast furnace, is due to the comparatively greater volume of carbon presented to the blast, and were the furnace so constructed that the coal could reach the level of the hearth, suffering but little diminution by the way, the superiority commonly accorded to the hot blast would no longer exist.

We have stated that for a period of twenty-four to thirty hours after the change the cold blast acts more advantageously than the hot, the make of iron is even greater, while the yield of coal is not only not augmented, but is actually reduced by the amount of the consumption in the stoves while the hot blast was in action. Now as the proportionate quantity of coal consumed in the Dowlais hot-blast furnaces is but three-fourths of that in the cold, the continuance of the furnace on the hot-blast burden for a period of thirty hours demonstrates that at other periods there occurs with the cold blast a loss or waste of fuel equal to one-fourth of the entire consumption beyond that occurring with the heated blast. And as the volume of air delivered into the hot-blast furnace is manifestly incapable of yielding more than nine-sixteenths of the oxygen necessary for the combustion of the coal charged,

* The temporary increase of make, on the substitution of a cold blast on a furnace previously working with a hot one, is known to many furnace managers, but we have endeavoured in vain to obtain from them a rational explanation of the phenomenon. It appears, however, to be unknown to the numerous authors who have written on the hot blast, for we do not discover the slightest allusion to this important fact in any of their papers.

we learn that of the coal consumed by the Dowlais furnaces considerably less than the one-half contributes to the reduction of the ore and flux.

This partial combustion of the fuel in a region where the caloric evolved is of no service, but is decidedly injurious to the ore, is common to all furnaces of the present construction. It is most apparent in coal-fed furnaces, and especially those of Scotland. After what has been stated respecting the Dowlais furnaces, which use a less inflammable coal, the immense disproportion of coal to blast, and indeed to the work performed, which we observe throughout that country, must be apparent even to the student. If more than one-half of the coal used in the Dowlais furnaces is wasted—and no term can be more appropriately applied to the coal which is consumed in the descent—what proportion of the more inflammable Scotch coal can be expected to reach the zone of fusion in furnaces of a construction even more unfavourable to economy of fuel than those at Dowlais?

Furnaces fed with coke are worked with nearly an equal waste of fuel. For though coke is not so readily ignited as coal, the porosity of its structure by offering a large surface of carbon facilitates the partial combustion, and during its descent the loss is little inferior to that with coal.

The waste of carbon in the blast furnace is not confined to this country. On the continents of Europe and America the consumption is equally large. With appliances and a construction of furnace nearly similar to those in use in this country a superior economy of fuel is not attainable at home or abroad. Notwithstanding statements to the contrary we find that the American and Continental furnaces consume as much, if not more, coal and coke than similar furnaces at home, and although the withdrawal of the gases for economical purposes is largely practised, American hot-blast Anthracite furnaces consume from 2 to $2\frac{1}{4}$ tons of an anthracite containing 94 per cent. of carbon, for the production of 1 ton of pig-iron.

But in some of the charcoal furnaces we observe that the consumption of carbon is not thus in excess of the blast. In such there are not the same causes in action for the partial consumption of the fuel during its descent. The width of the throat is large, and the volume of blast on account of the defective machinery employed is very inferior. In proportion to the capacity, the volume of blast is not more than one-half of that employed in the coal and coke furnaces of this country. Under these favourable conditions the ton of iron is made with 18 cwts. of charcoal, but to work to this yield the furnaces are driven very slowly. The draught through the throat is insufficient for the ignition of the charcoal, and nearly the entire quantity of carbon charged descends to the hearth for combustion by the oxygen of the blast.

The remarkable effects produced by a heated blast on coal-fed furnaces are not produced on charcoal furnaces, previously working to the low yield we have named. A saving of charcoal certainly attends the application of a heated blast, but it is not commensurate with the consumption of carbon in the stoves. Where the carbon is correctly proportioned to the volume of blast and the work to be performed a given weight converted into carbonic acid in the furnace is effectual in reducing a greater quantity of ore than the heat communicated to the blast by a similar weight burnt in the stove grates.

To what cause are we to ascribe the inability of the hot blast to economise fuel in the case of charcoal furnaces carrying a high burden?

The structure of the fuel operated on has been considered a sufficient explanation of the widely different results obtained with the heated blast. But apart from the known fact that with the same fuel the cold blast is for a limited time under certain circumstances superior, we do not well see how the temperature of the blast can be beneficial to one and injurious to another coal. It must be borne in mind that whatever fuel is used its temperature is elevated during the descent, and the blast acts on carbon already at a red heat. If a stream of heated air were directed on masses of cold coal, coke, and charcoal of varying qualities, the sudden accession of temperature would have very different effects. On some of the raw coal it would cause a partial coking, on others a total disintegration; on coke it would have little effect from its porosity offering a large surface for the absorption of caloric; on the charcoal from its more open texture still less. But whatever kind of fuel is used in the blast-furnace, at or before its arrival in the hearth, it is converted by the evolution of its gaseous constituents into a porous coke; the softer coals from being coked under great pressure are of a denser structure than they would be if coked prior to their introduction. The difference in the densities of various kinds of coke is met by employing a blast of greater or less pressure. At the zone of combustion, then, the difference in the structure of the respective fuels is not sufficiently great to explain the superiority of the hot blast in particular localities.

Charcoal has the least density of any fuel employed in iron smelting. If the inferiority of the hot blast with this fuel is due to its structure it is but reasonable to infer that with the lightest cokes the saving will be a minimum. But the Scotch coals when coked are probably the lightest of any used in iron-making, and yet it is in Scotland that the application of the hot blast system produces the greatest saving. So that it cannot be the density of the fuel that regulates the economy of the hot blast.

The superior smelting power of charcoal under the circumstances detailed has been explained by a foreign writer, on the supposition that the smaller dimensions of the coal conduce to a more perfect combustion. Instances were quoted, showing that in smelting with anthracite the consumption of carbon is treble that with charcoal. As a remedy for the inferiority of anthracite it was proposed to assimilate its dimensions to those of charcoal by breaking the coal into small pieces of from 1 to 4 cubic inches each. But it is well known that coal thus broken small cannot carry as high a burden in the present furnace as when in larger pieces. Besides, this economy of charcoal is not observable in furnaces having a narrow throat, and driven by a volume of blast, large in proportion to the area for its escape. In the United States, there are numerous furnaces consuming 35 cwts. of charcoal to the ton of iron, or nearly twice the consumption at other furnaces, where the rate of driving is much slower. With similar ores, but different volumes of blast, the consumption of carbon varies from 18 to 35 cwts. This variation in the consumption with different rates of driving is evidence that in the foreign charcoal-furnace, as well as in our own coal and coke fed furnaces, a large proportion of the carbon is consumed during its descent without yielding any beneficial effect.

The greater economy of fuel under certain conditions with a heated blast, the superiority of a cold blast under special circumstances, the heavy burden of ore carried by some charcoal furnaces, and the universal deficiency of atmospheric air for the combustion of the fuel entering the throat, clearly point to a large consumption in the upper parts of the furnace; while the maintenance of a high temperature in the throat, as exhibited by the rapid destruction of the brickwork, can only be accounted for on the supposition that the coal is there ignited and partially consumed. We submit our conclusions to the reader, begging his careful attention to the facts on which they are based.

The rapid combustion of the coal in the throat explains the greater reducing power of a given weight of coal in large blocks, as compared with the same in smaller pieces. At the Dowlais works it is impossible to make foundry-iron with the existing furnaces when the pieces of coal are below a certain size. They contain the same quantity of carbon, and on arriving at the zone of fusion ought to yield nearly the same heat. We are well aware that a blast acting on a number of disjointed pieces does not create so high a temperature as when directed on a single piece; but the greatly inferior power of the smaller pieces in the Dowlais furnaces demands another explanation.

Of the combustion of a considerable portion of the fuel in the vicinity of the throat there cannot be a doubt. The depth of the portion of each piece consumed will be the same whether they be large or small, but from the extended surface presented by the smaller pieces in proportion to their cubic contents, the quantity consumed will be greater in the same ratio. If we allow that the mean diameter of the pieces charged is 10 inches, and that one-half is consumed in the descent, the substitution of others 5 inches diameter will double the surface for combustion, and of the carbon charged fully three-fourths will be consumed before the hearth is reached.

The remedy for this waste is obvious. Let the area of the throat of the furnace be enlarged. With every enlargement the velocity of the ascending column of gases will be decreased in an inverse ratio. The enlargement may be advantageously extended until it equals the diameter at the boshes, from which point upwards the furnace would be cylindrical. The top being from three to nine times the area of the present throats, the rapid draught now maintained will be reduced to a minimum, and the partial consumption of the coal will no longer take place there.

The temperature of the upper strata of materials will be reduced in the same ratio as the draught is diminished in velocity; so that the coal no longer subjected to the high temperature of the throat will absorb caloric more gradually, and will not undergo that sudden transformation into coke which involves its partial combustion. The full calorific powers of the carbon being retained for useful combustion in the hearth, the quantity of coal now used in smelting may in every instance be largely reduced. At works where apparently a marked economy of fuel has been realised, the quantity really necessary for the reduction and carburization of the ore is under one-half of that actually consumed, while in works where an equal economy has not been practised the consumption is from three to four times the quantity required by the ore. In the case of the carbonaceous ores the entire quantity of coal now used may be withdrawn with every advantage to the make of the furnace and quality of the iron produced.

In furnaces so constructed that the carbon of the fuel shall descend for combustion at the tuyeres, the superior economy of the heated blast in certain cases will no longer exist. The cost of the heating apparatus and expense of maintenance will be saved, and the present furnaces with the enlarged throat and a cold blast will smelt a greater weight of ore with a given weight of coal than is now accomplished with the hot blast. There will be greater economy with the cold blast, inasmuch that the entire quantity of caloric evolved during combustion will be available for the reduction of the ore, instead of a portion only, as is the case with the coal consumed in the heating stoves.

With the reduced consumption of coal consequent upon the altered form of furnace the quality of the iron cannot be otherwise than greatly improved. All the coals used in smelting contain sulphur in greater or less quantities, and, not unfrequently, potash, and other substances equally injurious. The quantities brought in contact with the ore will vary with the consumption of coal. If the quantity of coal per ton of iron is reduced one-half, these impurities will be diminished in the same ratio. But if, as in the case of the carbonaceous ores of Scotland, the entire consumption of coal is withdrawn, from 24 to 36 cwts. of sulphur will also be withdrawn weekly.

The ashes of the coal are liquefied by combining with a portion of the lime used as flux. If the coal contain a considerable quantity of ashes the limestone required for its fusion may be equal in amount to that required for the earths combined with the ore. At the Scotch furnaces, when coking was considered necessary to the production of good iron, the consumption of coal averaged 8 tons to the ton of iron. This coal contained above 6 per cent. of ash, principally silica, amounting altogether to nearly half a ton to each ton of iron. For its fusion an equal weight of limestone was required, in addition to that necessary for the ore. On the substitution of the more fusible carbonaceous ore, along with an enlargement of the filling throat, the consumption was reduced to 38 cwts. of raw coal; the quantity of ash was reduced in the same proportion, and the ton of iron is smelted with 5 cwts. of limestone.

In the reports of the British Association the reduced consumption of limestone in the Scotch furnaces is ascribed to the use of a heated blast. It is difficult to see such a connexion between the temperature of the air and the quantity of lime necessary for fusing a given quantity of siliceous earth. It is certain that in Wales the hot blast effects no saving of limestone. It would be more correct to ascribe the reduction effected in the Scotch furnaces to the diminished quantity of siliceous earths requiring a proportionately less weight of limestone for the formation of a fusible cinder.

ADDITIONAL REMARKS ON THE HOT BLAST.

In reference to the important question raised in the foregoing pages, we have some additional observations to offer. If the waste of carbon, which we have described, is really going on in the blast furnaces of this country, how is it that the numerous chemists who have analysed the escaping gases have not drawn attention to the subject? Messrs. Bunsen, Playfair, Ebelmen, Scheerer, and others, have abundantly proved that they contain carbonic oxide—the form in which the carbon escapes—in quantities varying at different furnaces within very wide limits, and in which it forms a proportion by weight ranging from within a fraction to 42 per cent. of all the gases evolved. Now it is evident that if carbonic oxide is a necessary or an unavoidable ingredient, the variation in quantity would not be so great. This has excited attention from some of the analytical chemists, but none of these gentlemen have offered a satisfactory explanation. The size of the furnace, composition, and nature of the ore, fuel, and flux, have been assigned as causes, but if subjected to a practical examination their insufficiency is very obvious. That the dimensions of the furnace and composition of the materials influence the processes going on within cannot be doubted, but there is no connexion between the influences thus exerted and the presence of a large quantity of carbonic oxide in the throat. That is regarded as essentially necessary under certain circumstances to the success of the smelting operation.

In the inquiries which have been made respecting the composition of furnace gases, the object in view in every case has been to ascertain their value for heating purposes. From an examination of the various memoirs that have been published, it appears that the labours of the analytical chemists have been exclusively directed to the composition of the gases, without reference to the arrangements by which they have been produced. Having ascertained the presence of carbonic oxide—a combustible gas—in quantities sufficiently great to be of commercial value, it is considered that a great discovery has been made, a patent is secured, and general attention directed to the caloric which the gas gives out when burnt with air to carbonic acid. Meanwhile, the main point to which attention ought to be directed is entirely overlooked. The presence of carbonic oxide in large quantities in the gases issuing from one furnace, and its absence from those of others, evidently shows inequality in the action of the various arrangements for the combustion of the carbon. If the carbon can be burnt to carbonic acid in one furnace, and all the heat it can produce be obtained at once in the hearth, surely it is much better to seek to obtain a similar result in other furnaces than to allow it to be half burnt in the first instance, and then, after it has left the furnace, to supply an additional quantity of air to bring it to carbonic acid. To completely burn the carbon at first, it is only necessary to attend to the quantity of carbon, the volume and disposition of the blast, and to protect the carbon from combustion in the throat and upper regions. Altogether, we are of opinion that the labour expended by chemists in this instance has been misdirected, and the collection and combustion of the gases is but a clumsy expedient for obtaining some service from the carbon charged in excess of the absolute requirements of the furnace.

As a proof that chemists, in their researches into the nature of the waste gases, have not directed their attention to the causes which conduce to the presence of carbonic oxide, neither Messrs. Bunsen and Playfair, nor the Continental chemists, have given the quantity of atmospheric air delivered into the furnaces under experiment. This omission is fatal to the correctness of any conclusions which these gentlemen have drawn from their observations as to blast-furnace operations generally. A knowledge of the alterations in composition which the ascending column of gases undergoes during its ascent, and of the composition and quantities of the ore, fuel, and flux, to be of very great practical value must be accompanied by the quantity of air consumed. This generally weighs three times as much as all the other materials. But in none of the various inquiries is reference made to the volume of blast, as to whether it is sufficient or not for combustion. Had attention been directed to this important point, the insufficiency of the blast to convert the carbon charged even into carbonic oxide would have been apparent. It seems in each case to have been assumed that the volume of blast was correctly proportioned to the requirements of the carbon.

Analyses, however, are valuable so far as they go, and are remarkably confirmatory of the position we have taken. If the composition of the gases from the Baerum charcoal furnaces be contrasted with that of those issuing from the Alfreton coal-fed furnace, and the sectional form of the two furnaces be compared (Pl. IX., Fig. 60, Pl. XII., Fig. 78), it will be apparent that the form of the latter is the less favourable to economy of fuel; and the analyses prove this to be the case. For while the Alfreton gases are observed to be richer in carbon as they ascend to the throat, notwithstanding that their volume is increased by the carbonic acid expelled from the limestone, and the gaseous products of distillation from the coal, the Baerum gases are decreased in carbon until, at the surface, a given weight of the escaping gas contains one-fourth less than at half the depth of the furnace. This is only as it should be. For the moisture, carbonic acid, and volatile matter evolved from the materials augments the quantity of gas in the higher regions, thereby diminishing the per-centage of carbon. In the Alfreton furnace, however, while the same causes are at work, the opposite result is observed. The combustion of the fuel in its progress downwards through the confined throat is so great that the increased volume of gas contains a larger per-centage of carbon than existed in the lesser volume at half the depth.

We find that a given weight of gas from the Alfreton furnace contains nearly twice as much carbon as the same weight from the Baerum furnace. So that the superior economy of fuel in the charcoal furnace needs no explanation.

SECTION XIII.

ON THE USE OF RAW COAL IN BLAST FURNACES.

The enlargement of the throat of the furnace, advocated in the preceding section, will be attended with another advantage, scarcely inferior to the saving of fuel. It would enable all the coals now employed in iron smelting to be used without being previously coked. At present a few only are considered suitable for use raw; the others have been tried, but, failing to give satisfactory results, have been condemned as unfit for blast-furnace purposes in that state. In this section we intend to examine into the causes which have contributed to the general, though erroneous, opinion that certain coals are more applicable to smelting in their natural state than others.

We shall first briefly describe the characteristics of the principal kinds of coal wrought for iron-making, and then proceed to show that all the varieties are equally applicable in their raw state, and may be so used with advantage to the yield, make, and quality of the crude iron.

The coals used for smelting may be divided into four classes: 1, the bituminous; 2, the semi-bituminous; 3, the semi-anthracite; and 4, anthracite.

Of these the bituminous class is by far the largest. Indeed, with the exception of a number of those in the South Wales basin, all the furnaces in Great Britain are worked with coal of this description. It is distinguished from other kinds by the large quantity of volatile matter in its composition. When slowly heated its bulk is increased from 20 to 35 per cent. In coking the quantity of tarry matter evolved binds the pieces together in large masses, on which account it is sometimes distinguished as caking coal.

The large per-centage of tarry matter in these coals enables the small to be advantageously coked in ovens, a peculiarity belonging only to coals of this class.

The yield of coke from a given weight of coal varies with the character of the coal, the mode of coking practised, and the care exercised during the operation. In the South Wales district the yield ranges from 75 per cent. in the Rhondda Valley to 50 per cent. at the eastern outcrop in the neighbourhood of Pontypool. In Dean Forest, Staffordshire, Shropshire, Yorkshire, Northumberland, and Scotland the coal loses during conversion into coke from 30 to 55 per cent. of its weight.

The semi-bituminous class is a small one, being limited to such seams as are found located between the bituminous coal and anthracite, but partaking more fully of the characteristics of the former. Coals of this kind contain an inferior quantity of tarry matter. When heated the expansion of volume ranges from 5 to 15 per cent. They may be converted into coke, but from the diminished quantity of tarry matter do not cohere in large masses. The yield of coke averages 75 per cent. The small cannot be coked with its natural proportion of tarry matter.

The semi-anthracite class embraces those coals which lie immediately contiguous to the anthracite formation. The per-centage of tarry matter they contain is still less than in the preceding kind. Under the action of heat their bulk is increased 5 to 10 per cent. They may be converted into a coke, but on account of the small proportion of binding matter it is deficient in strength. The yield ranges from 70 to 75 per cent. The small will not bind, and is incapable of being coked into masses, except by the addition of tar.

The anthracite coal is distinguished by its great specific gravity, deficiency of tarry matter, and absence of flame during combustion. When its properties become better understood it will, no doubt, rank as the most valuable kind of coal which this country produces. It expands very little when heated. During the process of conversion into coke a minimum quantity of volatile matter escapes, consequently the yield amounts to from 80 to 90 per cent. From the deficiency of tarry matter the small will not cohere so as to form large coke.

Although we refer principally to the Welsh district, yet as almost every kind of coal is represented there, our remarks will be found to be equally applicable to the other iron-making districts.

We may here observe that when raw coal is charged into a furnace its volatile constituents are driven off by the heat to which it is exposed, leaving behind a porous coke, differing only from the coke prepared in heaps or ovens by its denser structure. This superior density results from the distillation having been conducted under pressure. Whatever kind of coal is used the evolution of its gaseous products is effected in the upper part of the furnace. By the time it reaches the level of the boshes, if not a little earlier, the coal has been converted into a porous coke, the degree of porosity depending principally on the quantity of gaseous matter evolved during the process.

The general composition of the coals in the respective classes may be seen by referring to the analyses in Section I., where each will be found represented. Among the South Wales coals, the Pontypool exhibits the bituminous class; the Dowlais furnace coal, the semi-bituminous; the Hirwain coal, the semi-anthracite; and the Yniscedwyn, the anthracite.

The bituminous coals are coked previous to being charged into the furnace. They have been tried in the raw state, but their tendency to cake and obstruct the blast necessitated a return to coking. Their rapid increase of bulk, when heated at the rate of 20 to 35 per cent., proved a serious defect. When they were precipitated into the hot furnace-throat, the sudden expansion of the masses of coal in a confined space produced obstructions to the descent of the materials. The scaffolds thus formed remained suspended until a partial combustion of the coal permitted the materials to descend.

The semi-bituminous coals are used in the raw state. They are not liable to cake in the furnace, as they contain comparatively little bituminous matter, and expand but slightly when heated. These qualities have been considered a sufficient explanation of their superiority over other coals. Their use is confined to the Rhymney, Dowlais, and Penydarran works, and the supply for each is drawn from the same mountain.

The semi-anthracite coals are coked before entering the furnace. They are employed at the Cyfarthfa, Plymouth, Aberdare, Gadleys, and Hirwain works. These coals have been tried in the raw state, but the results were not satisfactory. At the Cyfarthfa furnaces the experiment of using raw coal was persevered in for some months. The greatest drawback was found to be the accumulation in the hearth of quantities of unconsumed small coal. As lumps only were charged, this constant deposition could only be produced by the splintering of the large pieces, indicating a deficiency of binding matter in the coal. The loss of carbon in this way, and the additional labour entailed, was deemed of greater value than the advantages accruing from using the raw coal, and the use of coke was ultimately resumed.

Anthracite is used in the raw state. For many years attempts were made to smelt with it, but from inattention to its composition and characteristics they were not successful. Latterly, however, it has been extensively used, and although the consumption is still unnecessarily great, its applicability to smelting has been satisfactorily demonstrated.

On reviewing the effects produced in the furnace by these different kinds of coal, we observe that the first requires to be coked because it contains too much bituminous matter; the second may be used raw, the proportion of bituminous matter apparently being favourable; the third must be coked because it contains too little bituminous matter; while the fourth, though nearly devoid of this substance, is used raw.

So, then, if the composition and characteristics of the coal determine whether it should be coked or used raw, we find that coals containing a maximum or minimum per-centage of bituminous matter require coking, while those containing a medium quantity, or are altogether devoid of it, may be used raw.

With the practical smelter, and, indeed, with writers generally, the opinion is current that the comparative failure of the attempts to use the bituminous and semi-anthracite coal in the raw state arose from the peculiar composition of those coals. Having tried the coal raw instead of coked, and perceiving that its use deteriorated the quality of the iron, and was attended with other disadvantages, it was but natural to suppose that it was unfit for the furnace in that condition.

But is it certain that the fault lies in the coal? May not the form of the furnace also affect the result? If raw coal be used, a process formerly performed in the coke-yard is transferred to the interior of the furnace. Is the internal configuration of the blast furnace, as at present usually constructed, favourable to the conversion of the coal into coke with a minimum loss of carbon?

One circumstance that strikes us in connexion with the attempts to use coal raw is that the experiments were invariably made in furnaces built for coke. Generally these had narrow throats, and even with coke the temperature was high. What, then, must have been the temperature on substituting a more inflammable fuel?

With a narrow-throated furnace the inevitable consequence of substituting raw bituminous coal for coke would be a sudden increase of temperature and a partial combustion of the coal. The heat formerly existing may not have been very injurious to the coke, for this substance requires a high temperature for its combustion, which then proceeds slowly. But on the raw coal the effect is very different. Immediately that it enters the furnace the tarry matter ignites, and the coal rapidly expands under the action of heat. The evolution of tarry matter continues, and the masses cohere together, diminishing the area for the ascent of the heated gases. The draught is thus quickened in the available space, and, acting on the surrounding ignited coal, combustion goes on with great rapidity. The expansion of the coal and its cohesive properties cause frequent scaffolds in the throat. These do not subside until a considerable portion of the carbon is consumed. Thus the quantity of carbon retained for combustion in the hearth is not sufficient for the effectual reduction of the ore. The resulting metal is, therefore, of an inferior quality, and, from the irregularities in the working of the furnace, the make is also diminished.

It appears to us that the sole cause of the inferiority of this kind of coal in the raw state is the excessive heat in the upper part of the furnace. Were the throat enlarged, the temperature would be reduced in an inverse ratio to the increased area, and the coal could no longer cake into masses sufficiently large entirely to obstruct the area. With the reduced temperature, the evolution of tarry matter, and the conversion of the coal into coke will proceed more slowly, but, from the slower descent of the materials, the process will not be prolonged to a lower level.

In some furnaces raw bituminous coal is used mixed with coke. By itself it is considered that the coal cannot be used advantageously. But if the raw coal be really prejudicial to the quality and make of iron, it is difficult to see how its partial use can be otherwise than proportionately injurious. However, where raw coal is used we observe that the throats are larger than the average size. We therefore consider that the partial use of raw coal in these furnaces, instead of being evidence of its unsuitability to form the sole fuel, is a proof rather that the dimension of the throat is too small to permit a larger quantity to be used with advantage.

The general proportion in the bituminous coal district for the diameter of the throat is two-fifths only of the diameter of the furnace. Even with coke there must be a large waste of carbon from this cause; but when raw coal is used the consumption of fuel becomes excessive.

The utter impossibility of converting raw bituminous coal into coke in the throat and upper part of the furnace, as at present constructed, otherwise than with a waste of carbon, must be apparent if the intense draught which exists there is considered. We have shown already that in the throat the velocity varies from 47 to 201 feet per second, according to the area provided for its escape. With a throat of two-fifths the diameter of the body the velocity with the volume of blast commonly employed will be nearly 73 feet per second, or 50 miles an hour. For several hours the ignited coal is exposed to a draught little inferior to this in velocity.

How very different is the operation of coking in the yard or in ovens. There the injurious effects of the slightest draught on the quality of the resulting coke are known, being easily seen. Immediately that the coal is thoroughly ignited the draught is diminished and finally destroyed. If it is allowed to continue, the additional loss by combustion of the carbon shows itself in the reduced weight of coke obtained. The principle observed throughout is the ignition and expulsion of the volatile gases at so slow a rate that the carbon shall remain intact.

But in the present blast furnace the operation of coking is attempted on principles the reverse of those adopted in the coke-yard; and the waste of carbon which follows displays itself in the results.

At the Rhymney, Dowlais, and Penydarran works the change from coke to raw coal was made without any attending disadvantage. The kind of coal used at these works expands less in bulk and contains a smaller per-centage of bituminous matter; but the principal circumstance in favour of the alteration was the comparatively large throats at the furnaces in each of these works. The mean diameter is equal to half the diameter of the furnace, consequently the throat is comparatively cool. Scaffolding, however, is not unfrequent in these furnaces; and, even with the advantages accruing from the additional area, the consumption of coal is, as we have shown, fully double that required for the reduction of the ore.

That a wasteful combustion takes place in the throats of these furnaces cannot be doubted if the appearances presented by the coal while uncovered are carefully noted. Immediately that it enters the furnace the small projecting pieces take fire, and in a few seconds attain a white heat. This is speedily communicated to the remainder of the mass already highly heated. The active combustion thus commenced continues until the coal is covered with other materials, when it is deadened, but not destroyed. The great up-draught continues to support combustion, but, as the coal descends, this diminishes in intensity until at the boshes it is at a minimum.

The evils of a high temperature in the throat are equally manifest in furnaces using semi-anthracite coal. Since they are deficient in tarry matter, the liability to cake and obstruct the draught does not exist with these coals; but this very deficiency entails another evil of scarcely less importance. The exterior portions of the lumps decrepitate and crumble off under the influence of the heat into which they are suddenly introduced, and unless the coal is of a very homogeneous structure they are finally split into two or more pieces. The bulk of the small detached pieces is consumed in the throat, but a portion of them descends unconsumed to the hearth, where their presence entails additional labour on the attendants and loss of time in their removal.

These disadvantageous circumstances have caused this coal to be denounced as unfit for use in the raw state, and at the several works we have named coking is deemed an indispensable operation. Yet the decrepitation of the raw coal in the furnace is only evidence that the high temperature suddenly communicated to it is too much for the cohesion of its particles, and not of its being otherwise unfit, if the operation were differently conducted. In the coke-yard this coal is converted into coke with no more than the average loss. What then are the circumstances which prevent it from being coked in the blast furnace? In the coke-yard the temperature of ignition is attained very slowly, being the work of some hours; but in the narrow-topped furnace it is communicated in a few seconds. The violent evolution of gas which then takes place, coupled with the expansion of the outer portions, destroys the cohesion of its particles. The highly bituminous coals are charged into red-hot ovens without apparent injury to the coke produced, but if the same method of coking is attempted with this coal the splintering into fragments and consequent waste of carbon is scarcely less than that produced by the high temperature of the furnace throat.

The obvious remedy for this splintering and weakening of the coal is a reduction of the temperature at the furnace top; and as this can be done only by diminishing the draught, the enlargement would enable these coals to be used raw in the furnace with the best effect.

The successful employment of anthracite coal in the blast furnace dates from a comparatively recent period. In the early part of the present century it was attempted to be used for smelting, but unsuccessfully. The desirability of using it in smelting, however, was apparent, and after repeated failures anthracite is now used with partial success.

When the means by which the iron-smelters in the anthracite districts, in the first instance, sought to solve the problem of smelting with this coal are considered, their insufficiency for the attainment of success is apparent. In the experiments the greatest pressure of blast employed did not exceed $1\frac{1}{4}$ lb. to the inch. With a fuel of such dense structure as anthracite, the weakness of the blast was of itself a sufficient cause for failure. But if to this there be added the disadvantage of employing furnaces constructed for burning the coke of bituminous coal, it is very evident that, however desirous of using this coal the experimenters might be, their arrangements were not such as could obtain success.

The anthracite is still more deficient in bituminous matter than the coals around Merthyr Tydfil, and when it is precipitated into the highly-heated narrow throat, the sudden accession of caloric results in the partial disintegration of the coal. The detached pieces descend to the hearth, and in the early experiments formed an obstacle to success. Up to the present time this accumulation of carbonaceous matter in the hearth is a serious disadvantage attendant on the employment of anthracite.

The furnaces in which the experimental trials were made had the usual narrow throats, but in those recently erected the throats are constructed larger in diameter in proportion to the boshes than in any other furnaces. The general proportion, as will be seen by referring to the plates of blast-furnace sections (Pls. X., XI., Figs. 66, 67, 68, 69), is two-thirds the greatest diameter. This alteration has greatly increased the facility of smelting with anthracite; the temperature in the throat is reduced, and as the coal suffers less in the same proportion, an increased burden is carried. But, as a further reduction of temperature cannot fail to be highly advantageous to the coal, reducing the tendency to splinter and disintegrate, and allowing the entire mass to be converted into a dense coke, the enlargement of the throat to the diameter of the boshes would be productive of great advantage. (Pl. XIII., Fig. 84.)

If reference be made to the proportion which the throat bears to the diameter of the furnace, it will be seen that for every 100 feet of horizontal area in the furnaces in the bituminous district the throat has an area of 16 feet; in the semi-bituminous and semi-anthracite the proportion is increased to 25 feet; in the anthracite to 44 feet. Furnaces with a proportion of 25 feet are unable to smelt advantageously with a coal deficient in bituminous matter, unless previously coked; but when the proportion is increased to 44 feet the pure anthracite itself is employed raw. We have only to go from Hirwain to the Neath Valley to see the beneficial effects on the coal which would follow from an inconsiderable enlargement of the throat.

We have hitherto advocated an increase of the diameter of the throat to equal that of the boshes, which would make the upper portion of the furnace cylindrical; but with anthracite we cannot proceed too cautiously in communicating an increase of temperature. We have no question but that in furnaces for smelting with this coal the enlargement may be beneficially extended until the throat is one-fourth, or one-third, greater in diameter than the boshes. The result of this will be that the velocity of the issuing column of gases will be reduced, and a minimum temperature maintained. The area then allowed for the escape will be four times that now provided.

By a large class of persons engaged in the iron trade it is supposed that anthracite cannot be advantageously used unless with a heated blast. This is an error, and it arose from the defective blowing-machinery originally employed. To show how insufficient the first blasts were, we may mention that there is a patent extant for using a cold blast of more than $2\frac{1}{2}$ lbs. to the square inch with this coal. With a cold blast of this and greater densities large quantities of cold-blast iron have been smelted. But while furnaces having the contraction at top are employed for smelting, the hot blast will be the most economical in the yield of coal. The diminished volume of blast employed consequent on the caloric thrown into the furnace causes a diminished draught, and reduced temperature at top.

The saving attendant upon the advantageous use of raw coal, together with the economy in the consumption of the coal itself, consequent on the reduction of temperature of the furnace throat, will reduce the cost of smelting fully one-half. In the bituminous coal districts of Monmouthshire, the Midland Counties, and Scotland the conversion of the coal into coke is attended with such waste that from $3\frac{1}{4}$ to 4 tons of coal are required for each ton of foundry-iron produced. The proportion of carbon ranges from 76 per cent. in the inferior bituminous varieties, to 92 per cent. in the anthracite. The present system of coking is attended with the combustion of from 10 to 50 per cent. of this carbon. Since the proportion of carbon determines the value of the coal for smelting purposes, the retention and combustion of the entire quantity in the furnace will be attended with a proportionate generation of heat.

The suggested form of furnace will permit of raw coal being used, and, by economising the coke and retaining the entire quantity of carbon for combustion in the hearth, it will render 20 cwts. of raw coal more effective than $3\tfrac{1}{4}$ tons converted into coke, and afterwards consumed in furnaces of the present form.

The widening the top of the furnace, so as to ensure a reduced temperature, will be highly advantageous to smelting with compressed peat. Large tracts of this valuable fuel exist in the vicinity of deposits of the richest iron ores, but hitherto all attempts to use it in the blast furnace have failed. The best specimens contain large quantities of volatile matter; and, unless previously well dried, injurious quantities of water. The rapid evolution of these in the blast furnace of the present form causes a greater or less destruction of the coal, while, from the high temperature maintained, a portion of the carbon is consumed. In the same proportion as the coal is weakened and carbon consumed are its smelting powers reduced, and the yield per ton of iron augmented. And from the moisture and generally large per-centage of ash the increased consumption becomes fatal to the economy of smelting with this fuel. The large residuum of ash requires for its fusion a corresponding quantity of limestone. Hence the quality of the iron is contaminated by the excess of earthy matter present.

With the improved form of furnace the diminished temperature at top would favour the retention of carbon. The fuel also, being subjected to a great pressure long before its temperature is elevated to a red heat, the cohesion of its particles will be ensured, and its ability to stand a blast of the requisite density will be little inferior to that of charcoal.

Under favourable circumstances we have no doubt but 30 cwts. of well-dried peat will smelt a ton of pig-iron.

Although of secondary importance compared with the saving of fuel, the enlargement of the furnace in the manner described will be highly beneficial to the smelting operations, where raw or imperfectly calcined ores are employed. The effect produced on the materials in the furnace by raw or insufficiently calcined ore is that of reducing their temperature by taking up a large quantity of the caloric evolved by the fuel. By this absorption of caloric the water and volatile matters present in the ore are expelled. Time is a necessary element to the perfect calcination of the ore, and if the materials descend very quickly the operation is not completed until they are at a low level, the time allowed for the deoxydation of the ore being, of course, proportionately diminished.

In the wider furnace, however, the descent of the materials in a given time will not be at more than one-fourth of the present rate. In the Dowlais furnaces the materials descend at the rate of 22 inches per hour, but at that part of the furnace where the diameter is largest the speed is reduced to $5\tfrac{1}{4}$ inches. This latter rate will be that with the improved form of furnace, time will therefore, be afforded for the gradual expulsion of the volatile gases and perfect calcination of the ore, in a region where the heat absorbed will not injuriously affect the working operations of the furnace.

Calcination is now limited almost entirely to the carbonates of the coal formation. But a form of furnace in which the water combined with the primary ores, is evaporated in the upper stratum of materials, will greatly facilitate the production of grey iron from these ores.

With raw limestone also the heat taken up by the evolution of carbonic acid and water would be absorbed from the surrounding materials at a higher level, and a superior temperature consequently be maintained in the furnace.

For the carbonaceous ores the suggested furnace would be of very great value. The per-centage of carbon in these ores frequently exceeds that of the metallic iron. With the present system of calcination in clamps this carbon is consumed in an operation where one-fifth or one-sixth of it would suffice. In the wide furnace this ore might be advantageously used in the raw state, and the carbon in combination be made available for the reduction of the iron.

SECTION XIV.

BLOWING-ENGINES.

THE blowing-engines now employed for supplying the blast to furnaces and refineries are generally of an improved construction as compared with those existing at the commencement of the century. They are usually larger, and are worked at higher velocities, with a generally reduced consumption of coal, and require less labour and repairs.

But though unquestionably much improved in their construction, they are, with very few exceptions, greatly behind the requirements of the manufacture. There are in this country about three hundred and ten, and having personally examined the greater number of them, we consider their make and power and the expense of their maintenance inconsistent with the present advanced state of mechanical engineering. A deficiency of power is a defect almost universal. When it is considered that the entire success of the operations as regards quality, produce, and economy is dependent on the blast, the necessity of having superior blowing-engines of ample power and maintained in first-rate working order is apparent. But as ironmasters are not usually practical engineers, most of the faults observed in their engines must be placed to the credit of the makers.

With the majority of engine-makers a blowing-engine is considered as a machine in the construction of which good workmanship and materials are unnecessary. But a greater mistake could not be committed. The limited number of engines of this kind at work may partly account for this neglect, but we apprehend that a want of attention to the great importance of the efficiency of the engine to the success of the manufacture is the principal cause. There are several iron-works in this country where a breakage would probably entail the loss of the furnaces. It is but a short period since an accident of this kind occurred at the Dowlais works to an engine constructed in this manner, which nearly resulted in the setting of the materials in four furnaces. It was only by unremitting exertion and the assistance of a large foundry and machine-shop on the establishment that the furnaces were saved.

In the construction of a blowing-engine the design, workmanship, and materials should be such that the liability to accident and derangement is reduced to the narrowest limits. The utmost regularity in the working ought to be obtained. A blowing-engine differs from all others, inasmuch as it is continuously at work, every stoppage, from whatever cause, being attended with loss; and, assuming that it is of sufficient power, its value to the manufacturer is directly dependent on the time it will work without requiring renewal or adjustment, or any other operation involving a stoppage. In the case of locomotives, marine, and other engines opportunities are afforded for those operations connected with the engine requiring time for their completion, and their service is not directly interfered with; but with the blowing-engine it is different. The blast is on the furnaces for months and years, with only a few minutes interruption weekly, and the full engine power is therefore demanded so long as the furnace is in blast.

A blowing-engine should be able to work a month without stopping, and then require not more than an hour's delay. Once in two or three years a stoppage of a few hours will be required, but as a rule no really efficient engine should need to stop more than thirty hours in a year for current repair. We have found this sufficient, and believe that with care it may be considerably abridged with advantage to the operations of the furnace.

Formerly all the engines were low-pressure and condensing, having an air-pump, cold-water-pump, a nozzle containing five or six valves, and complicated working gear. Engines of this kind are still in use at several works, but when comparatively new they require frequent repairs, of little importance, but still occasioning stoppages of greater or less duration; and after working a few years they cannot be kept in efficient order with less than five or six hours stoppage weekly. From the great number of working parts accidents of a minor description are of frequent occurrence; the sudden cessation of blast on such occasions is attended with greater expense, and more injurious effects on the furnace than stoppages at stated intervals, for which preparation may be made.

The blowing-engines that have lately been constructed are generally high-pressure and non-condensing, and where the latest improvements have been adopted the expansive action of the steam has been made use of with a corresponding economy in the working expenses. The use of high-pressure steam has enabled engines to be constructed with less than one-third the number of working parts formerly required; and with this greater simplicity of the working arrangements the liability to accidental stoppages has been proportionately reduced.

The adoption of the high-pressure principle has resulted in a greater uniformity in the density of the blast discharged by the engine. With the condensing engine the dead stop at the turn of the stroke produced a corresponding effect upon the blast. This has been obviated in a great measure in the high-pressure engine by the employment of a heavy fly-wheel, and with the same number of strokes per minute the stream of blast is greatly superior. For this reason the workmen attending the blast-furnace give the preference to a blast from a high-pressure engine as being the most steady.

The foregoing are not the only advantages of the high-pressure system, and there can be no question but that when the superior reducing powers of a greater density of blast than is ordinarily attainable with other engines is fully appreciated, this description of engine will become general. In the old condensing engine there was a limit to the density of the blast, dependent on the diameter of the steam cylinders. The low pressure of the steam employed, from 3 to 4 lbs. per square inch above the atmosphere, placed the diameter of the blowing cylinder within certain limits. The total mean working pressure on the steam-piston averages about 13 lbs. to the inch, but after deducting friction and leakage the effective pressure rarely exceeded 10 lbs. Hence, in determining the size of the blowing cylinder, engineers were guided by the density of the blast; as much as this was below the available steam pressure, by so much was the area of the blast cylinder larger in proportion to that of the steam cylinder. By common consent the maximum blast pressure was fixed at 2¼ lbs., or one-fourth of the steam pressure; consequently the area of the blowing cylinder was made four times that of the steam cylinder. With these proportions the density could never exceed 2¼ lbs. when the engine was in the best working order. But leakage, a defective supply of steam, and imperfect condensation often reduced it below this, and the mean working effect could not be rated higher than 2 lbs.

The early double-acting blowing-engines were constructed to work at a velocity of 180 to 200 feet per minute. When an increased volume of blast was found beneficial the velocity was increased to 260 and 300 feet per minute, and in some instances to 400 feet. At this velocity the delivery of blast was doubled, but the rapid movement of the engine quadrupled the accidents and delays; in addition to which the greater wear increased the leakage of the pistons and valves, and by giving less time for the condensation rendered the engine less able to maintain the blast at its original pressure.

With the high-pressure system the practical limits to the density of the blast are much wider. High-pressure engines, having cylinders similarly proportioned to those of condensing engines, are capable of compressing the blast to a pressure of 8 to 10 lbs. to the square inch; and from the absence of all injurious concussion they may be driven at double the usual velocity, and the wear and leakage will be less than in the old engines. We have found a velocity of 650 feet per minute to cause less injury to these engines than 250 feet per minute would occasion to a low-pressure condensing-engine.

In point of economy the high-pressure engine merits the preference. In first cost—the engines giving out equal power at the same velocity—the high-pressure engine is nearly one-fourth less expensive than the low, and this where an ample supply of water for condensation is at hand; but where provision has to be made for the supply the difference becomes still greater. But since the high-pressure engine may be safely and advantageously driven at double the speed of the condensing engine, its cost, estimated upon the volume of blast delivered in a given time, will be under one-half that of its competitor.

A comparison of the working expenses of the two systems results greatly in favour of the high-pressure. The consumption of coals, stores, repairs, and labour is from one-fourth to one-third less than with condensing engines of similar date of manufacture. At the Dowlais works the cost of a given quantity of blast produced by four condensing engines is fully twice as great as that of the same quantity from the four high-pressure engines.

Until within very recently, blowing-engines, whether on the high or low-pressure system, were constructed with vertical cylinders and a working beam to communicate the power from the steam to the blowing cylinder, and to afford the requisite movements to the pumps and working gear. In some works recently erected the engine and blowing cylinders are placed horizontally, and the working beam and several other parts required with the vertical engine have been dispensed with. Engines of this kind are at work in several Scotch works, in Yorkshire, Derbyshire, and in Wales. In first cost they are the cheapest of any hitherto erected, but in maintenance they appear to be the most expensive. We are advocates for that measure of simplicity which does not interfere with the efficiency of the engine, but any simplification and reduction in the first cost which entails stoppages and frequent repairs is more than counterbalanced by the ruinous consequences to the blast furnace. The horizontal engines in use are, without exception, more inefficient and expensive in maintenance than the old class of condensing engines. When the essentials of a good blowing-engine are considered their inefficiency ceases to be a matter of surprise.

The horizontal construction was first used in small steam-engines, and since its general adoption in locomotive engines this arrangement has partly supplanted the beam and vertical cylinder engine. With small engines the change has unquestionably been advantageous—a point on which we can speak from the experience obtained in the working of between twenty and thirty erected by ourselves in the last few years; but when applied to engines of the largest calibre disadvantages of a serious character are met with. The unequal wear of the cylinder, and the rapid wear of the piston are the greatest defects of horizontal engines. They exist more or less in all engines having horizontal cylinders, locomotives included, but are most apparent in large engines. In these the bearing surface of the piston, in proportion to its weight, is diminished as the diameter of the cylinder is increased. From this arises the rapid wear.

The duration of the cylinders of horizontal engines before the wear becomes so great as to render reboring necessary depends on the hardness of the metal in the cylinder and piston. Soft metal will require reboring in a comparatively short period. In the case of a 33-inch cylinder engine, made of soft Scotch hot-blast iron, the direct wear after the piston had travelled 70 millions of feet was nearly $\frac{1}{4}$ inch in depth in the middle. With harder metal cylinders of a smaller diameter (18-inch) lasted for nearly 300 millions of feet. Locomotive cylinders average, taking the working of ten engines at the Dowlais works, 350 millions of feet. In these three examples the distance travelled by the piston was distributed over periods varying from four to ten years, so that the necessity for reboring and refitting occurred at only comparatively distant intervals. It remains to be seen how long the steam cylinder of an horizontal blowing-engine could be worked without reboring.

The velocity of the high-pressure engine may be taken as averaging 400 feet per minute, at which rate the piston will have travelled 300 million feet in 17 months, consequently the necessity for stopping, reboring, and a thorough refitting of the engine would occur at intervals of a few months, instead of years. The peculiar circumstances under which blowing-engines work have been altogether overlooked in the application to them of the horizontal construction. It is seen that, measured by the distance travelled by the piston—the only correct index—the wear of the cylinder to an unserviceable point would be accomplished in one-fifth of the time usual with engines of this description applied to other purposes.

This is of itself sufficient to account for the defective performance of this class of engine. But a still greater defect is found to exist in the working of the blowing piston. It is known that in large steam cylinders on this principle the wear is greater than in small engines. What, then, must be the wear with cylinders of 9 and 10 feet diameter? In those blowing-engines which have been erected, it has been found proportionately great. The wear of a horizontal blowing-cylinder is much greater than that of a steam cylinder of like diameter. In the latter case the tallow, or other lubricating material, descends to the lower side, where the rubbing occurs, and is there maintained in a fluid state by the heat of the steam. The blowing cylinder is lubricated with blacklead, or a compound of which blacklead forms the chief ingredient, which indeed falls to the bottom, but on account of the coldness of the cylinder and the passing dust, collects at the ends behind the pistons and does little real service in reducing the friction. This difficulty of keeping the rubbing surface well lubricated is made painfully apparent by the romping noise common to these engines. We have found the vibration occasioned by the friction of the piston, when the engine has been driven at a higher speed than 250 feet per minute, so great as to endanger its stability. With a view to reducing the wear the piston has been made of wrought-iron, and hard steel bars have been fitted into the cylinder. The piston-rod has been continued through the back end of the cylinder, but without any appreciable improvement. A third plan has been adopted and partially remedies the defect—the piston is mounted on small wheels, which roll on the inner surface of the cylinder and reduce the abrasion. All these expedients, however, are so many evidences that the horizontal blowing-engine in cost of maintenance and irregularity in working is really more expensive than condensing or high-pressure engines with working beams. Looking at the inherent defects of all engines on this principle, we do not consider it possible in the present state of mechanical science to construct horizontal blowing-engines, that can successfully compete with those with vertical cylinders.

In the construction of the vertical cylinder-engine there are some points which demand close attention. A very common error is to make the blowing piston-rod too small. Engine makers have assumed that as the pressure on the blowing piston is less than that on the steam piston, a rod of the same tensile strength will suffice. But in this assumption the larger diameter of the blowing piston and the greater leverage which it has to bend the rod has been overlooked. From inattention to this circumstance the breaking of the rod is not an unusual occurrence. The smallest sectional area of the blowing piston-rod should be double that of the steam piston-rod, and one of still larger area is preferable. The vibration of the quick-moving piston-rods in the Dowlais engines is considerable, and eventually diminishes the tensile strength of the iron to the working strain, when fracture takes place.

The area opened by the wind valves for the admission of air to the blowing cylinder cannot be too large, where a maximum working speed is intended. By having a large area and valves in proportion, the duration of the valves will be increased and the working of the engine improved. We have found in practice that the wind valves work silently at a speed of 600 feet per minute, when the aggregate area at each end is one-half the area of the piston. The aggregate area of the delivery valves at each end ought to be not less than one-seventh the area of the piston. Valves of one uniform size throughout should be employed; two thicknesses of leather rivetted together are sufficient, where the seating is crossed by wrought-iron bars, reducing the space between the beats to about six inches each way

The area of the blast pipes should be as large as possible, as a rule not less than one-seventh of the area of the piston, a proportion of one-fifth even would be better, and by acting as a magazine would ensure greater regularity in the delivery of the blast.

A diversity of opinion exists as to the merits of different descriptions of packing for the blowing piston; formerly leather was universally employed, but with the high velocity at which the engines are now driven this packing is not so durable as could be desired. We have adopted hemp and gasket or oakum packing, screwed down with the common junk ring cast in segments for convenience of handling, and found that for durability and cheapness it is unrivalled. The piston goes four or five months without calling for examination, and the packing is renewed once only in sixteen or eighteen months. (Plate XL. Fig. 232).

It is usual to make the beam so that the stroke at each end shall be equal, but we find the working of the engine improved when the stroke in the steam cylinder is longer than in the blowing cylinder. By lengthening the steam cylinder the expansive principle may be applied with the greatest advantage; and in consequence of the continuous action of the blowing-engine, a duty or performance may be realized little inferior to that of the best Cornish pumping engines, and greatly superior to anything attained with the best marine and mill engines.

For attaining a maximum effect the ordinary proportions followed in the construction of engines require to be modified. The area of the passages and valves for the admission of steam should not be less than $\frac{1}{14}$th of the area of the steam piston. In general it is much less, and the consequences are seen in the slow speed at which the engine can be driven. At three engines in the Dowlais works the proportion of the area of the steam valve to the area of the piston is as 1 to 40, 1 to 42, and 1 to 52 respectively. These passages are much too small, and under no circumstances can these engines be made to travel faster than 280 feet per minute. The boiler power is ample for a speed of 500 feet, but from the contraction of the passage the pressure cannot be maintained in the cylinder at high velocities. In the blowing-engine erected during our connexion with that establishment, we made the area of the passage equal to $\frac{1}{12}$th of the piston. This engine attained a speed of 650 feet per minute, delivering more than double the volume of blast it could have done with the usual contracted passages.

As a precaution against accidents and the ruinous consequences they entail, every part of a blowing-engine should be twice as strong as in any other class of engine. In marine and locomotive engines lightness is an object; but here the cost of a few tons of iron is trifling in comparison with the losses occasioned by accidental stoppages. Labour is the most expensive item in the construction, and this is nearly the same whether the engine is lightly or strongly made; so that the additional expense entailed by the extra strength only amounts to the value of the additional material.

The generation of the blast at a cheap rate is an object of importance to the smelter. Coal is, perhaps, the heaviest item in the working expenses, and the consumption of this varies with the efficiency of the engines employed. The least consumption is with the high-pressure beam-engines. To show the room that exists for improvement in the majority of blowing-engines, we give the quantity of coal consumed at different works to generate a given quantity of blast.

Dowlais.—No. 1 blowing-engine, high-pressure, non-condensing: blowing cylinder, 144 inches in diameter; stroke of piston, 12 feet; 19 double-strokes per minute; quantity of air at a pressure of 3 lbs. to the square inch discharged per minute, 51,528 cubic feet. Coal consumed in twenty-four hours, 25 tons; per minute, 38.8 lbs. Quantity of air at a density of 3 lbs. to the inch for each pound of coal consumed, 1328 cubic feet.

No. 5 blowing-engine, high-pressure, non-condensing: blowing cylinder, $144\frac{1}{2}$ inches in diameter; stroke, 9 feet 3 inches; strokes per minute, 13; quantity of air per minute at a pressure of $2\frac{1}{4}$ lbs., 27,476 cubic feet. Consumption of coal, 15 tons per twenty-four hours; per minute, 23.3 lbs. Quantity of air (corrected to a density of 3 lbs. per inch) per pound of coal, 980 cubic feet.

No. 4 blowing-engine, low-pressure, condensing: blowing cylinder, 108 inches in diameter; stroke, 7 feet 6 inches; strokes per minute, 17; quantity of air at a pressure of $2\frac{1}{4}$ lbs. per minute, 16,218 cubic feet. Coal consumed in twenty-four hours, 11 tons; per minute, 17.1 lbs. Quantity of air (corrected to a density of 3 lbs.) per pound of coal consumed, 790 cubic feet.

Hirwain.—Blowing-engine, low-pressure, condensing: blowing cylinder, 104 inches in diameter; stroke, 7 feet 3 inches; strokes per minute, 16; quantity of air per minute at a pressure of 3 lbs., 13,688 cubic feet. Coal consumed, 17.2 tons per twenty-four hours; per minute, 26.5 lbs. Quantity of air discharged at a density of 3 lbs. for each pound of coal consumed, 512 cubic feet.

Corbyn's Hall.—Two blowing-engines, low-pressure, condensing: quantity of air per minute at a pressure of $2\frac{1}{4}$ lbs., 16,185 cubic feet. Coal consumed per twenty-four hours, 13 tons; per minute, 20.2 lbs. Quantity of air discharged (corrected to a pressure of 3 lbs. per inch) per pound of coal consumed, 622 cubic feet.

Gartsherrie.—Blowing-engine, low-pressure, condensing: blowing cylinder, 120 inches; stroke, 9 feet 6 inches; strokes per minute, 16; quantity of air per minute at a pressure of

2¼ lbs., 24,335 cubic feet. Coal consumed in twenty-four hours, 35 tons; per minute, 55 lbs. Quantity of air discharged (corrected to a density of 3 lbs.) per pound of coal consumed, 405 cubic feet.

Monkland.—Blowing-engine, high-pressure, horizontal cylinders: blowing cylinder, 72⅘ inches in diameter; stroke, 9 feet; strokes per minute, 18; quantity of air per minute at a pressure of 3 lbs., 9298 cubic feet. Consumption of coal per twenty-four hours, 15 tons; per minute, 23.3 lbs. Quantity of air discharged, at a pressure of 3 lbs. the inch, per pound of coal consumed, 400 cubic feet.

Wingerworth.—Pair of blowing-engines, high-pressure, horizontal cylinders: blowing cylinders, 48 inches diameter; stroke, 7 feet; strokes per minute, 12; quantity of air per minute at a pressure of 2¼ lbs., 4221 cubic feet; consumption of coal per twenty-four hours, 6.5 tons; per minute, 10.1 lbs. Quantity of air discharged (corrected to a pressure of 3 lbs. the square inch) per pound of coal consumed, 313 cubic feet. Direct action revolving-engine, high-pressure steam, working fans: quantity of blast generated at a pressure of 1¼ lbs. to the square inch, 4200 cubic feet per minute; consumption of coal, 8.6 tons in twenty-four hours; per minute, 13.4 lbs.; quantity of air discharged (corrected to a pressure of 3 lbs. the square inch) per pound of coal consumed, 166 cubic feet.

These quantities show that the cost of generating the blast, measured by the consumption of coal, is much less with one class of engines than with the others. The great superiority of the high-pressure beam-engine, using the steam expansively as is done at the Dowlais works, is very apparent in the following tabulated statement of the performance of the foregoing nine engines:

CONSUMPTION OF COAL IN DIFFERENT BLOWING-ENGINES.

Name of Works.	Description of Engine.	Cubic feet of blast discharged at a pressure of 3 lbs. for each pound of coal consumed.
Dowlais	High-pressure beam	1328
"	" "	950
"	Low-pressure condensing	790
Hirwain	" "	512
Corbyn's Hall	" "	622
Gartsherrie	" "	405
Monkland	High-pressure horizontal	400
Wingerworth	" "	313
"	High-pressure rotary	166

From this it appears that the mean duty of the high-pressure engines is 1154 cubic feet; of the low-pressure condensing-engines, 560 cubic feet; and of the high-pressure horizontal, 356 cubic feet. The rotary engine and fan-blast may be considered as the least effective form in which the power of steam can be employed.

These quantities agree nearly with the average consumption of the Dowlais engines, of which we annex a tabular statement:

BLOWING-ENGINES, DOWLAIS WORKS.

No. of Engine.	Description of Engine.	Diameter of blowing cylinder in inches.	Cubic feet of air discharged per minute.	Pressure of blast maintained.	Consumption of coal per twenty-four hours, in tons.	Consumption of coal per minute, in pounds.	Cubic feet of blast discharged at 3 lbs. pressure per pound of coal consumed.
1	Condensing.	57.¾	11070	2¼	8.0	12.4	800
2	"	108.⁷⁄₁₆	17226	2¾	11.5	16.0	797
3	"	100.	16350	2¼	11.5	19.0	681
4	"	108.	16218	2½	11.0	17.1	790
5	High pressure.	144.⅜	27476	2½	15.0	23.3	980
6	"	122.	20097	2½	13.0	20.2	850
7	"	144.	28476	2¾	17.0	26.4	906
1	"	144.	51528	3	25.0	38.8	1323

While established in the Dowlais works we made a series of experiments on the blowing and other engines, with a view of ascertaining what proportion of the power yielded by the steam pressure was absorbed by the engine in overcoming its friction and *inertia*. For this purpose we took indicator diagrams of the various steam and blowing cylinders, and by comparing the horse-power exerted on the steam piston with that given out on the blast piston we ascertained with considerable correctness the per-centage absorbed by the engine.

In the following table we have furnished the results obtained from these diagrams, as far as they relate to the blowing engines:

TABLE SHEWING THE POWER ABSORBED BY FRICTION, &c., IN THE BLOWING-ENGINES AT THE DOWLAIS WORKS.

No. of Engine.	Diameter of steam cylinder.	Mean working pressure on steam piston in pounds per square inch, by indicator.	Horse-power exerted on the steam piston.	Mean pressure of the air on the blowing piston.	Horse-power given out by the blowing piston.	Horse-power given out by the blowing piston for 100-horse-power exerted on the steam piston.
1	41	11.7	133	2.30	119	89
2	50	11.8	190	2.42	172	90
3	50	11.0	196	2.15	154	78
4	54¼	10.83	195	2.30	162	83
5	54	10.0	306	2.24	268	88
"	36⁷⁄₁₆	21.0	—	—	—	—
6	40	23.0	272	2.33	240	88
7	53	—	368	2.54	321	87
1	55	—	696	2.60	600	86
Total	. .	. . . . .	2356	. . . . .	2036	86.4

In connexion with this subject, we have drawn up a table of the dimensions of the principal parts of the blowing-engines at the Dowlais works. The large size of these engines —averaging as they do more than 250-horse-power each—their low consumption of coal, and the generally cheap rate at which they are worked, will probably render the information interesting to engineers employed in iron-works.

The sizes of the cylinders will be ascertained by referring to the preceding tables:

DIMENSIONS OF THE BLOWING ENGINES AT THE DOWLAIS WORKS.

Engine.	Date of construction.	Length of stroke, in feet and inches.	No. of strokes per minute.	Diameter of steam piston-rod, in inches.	Diameter of blowing piston-rod, in inches.	Diameter of air-pump, condensing engines, in inches.	Diameter of end gudgeons in beam, in inches.	Diameter of main gudgeons in beam, in inches.	Depth of main beam in middle, in feet and inches.	Thickness of plate of main beam, in inches.	Length between extreme centres, in feet.	Aggregate area of the wind valves, in square feet, at each end of blowing cylinder.	Diameter of blast main, in inches.	Area of blast main, in square inches for each square foot of area of blowing piston.	Diameter of crank shaft, in inches.	Diameter of crank pin, in inches.
		ft. in.							ft. in.							
1	1790	7 6	19	4½	5	29	4	8	3 8½	1⅝	25	11	24	10.8	—	—
2	1800	7 6	18	4½	5	33	5¼	7½	4 0	2	25	18	28	9.6	—	—
3	1817	7 6	20	5	6	34	5½	8	4 3	2	25	14	24	8.4	—	—
4	1824	7 6	17	5½	6¼	36	5½	8	4 0	2$\frac{1}{16}$	25	18	28	9.6	—	—
5	1828	9 3	13	6	2 of 6	—	7	12	4 6	3	34	20	42	12.2	12	7½
6	1836	8 0	16	6¼	6¾	—	6	11	4 9	2½	25	21	30	8.7	12	6
7	1839	9 0	14	6	8½	—	6	13	5 9	2¾	28	47	60	15.0	16½	10
1	1850	12 0	19	6¼	9	—	6½	13½	6 6	3½	41	56	60	15.0	18½	10½

DIMENSIONS OF THE BLOWING ENGINES AT THE DOWLAIS WORKS—(*continued*).

Engine.	Diameter of fly-wheel, in feet and inches.	Sectional area of rim, in square inches.	Capacity of forces being that of the steam cylinder, one will be	No. of boilers.	Description of boilers.	Diameter of boilers, in feet.	Length of boilers, in feet.	Diameter of tube, in feet.	Pressure of steam on the boilers, in pounds per square inch.	Aggregate area of fire-grate to boiler, in feet.	Aggregate heating surface of boilers, in square feet.	Superficial surface of fire-grate, in feet, for each horse-power given off.	Superficial feet of heating surface, for each horse-power given off.	Consumption of coal per square foot of grate per hour, in lbs.
	ft. in.					ft. in.		ft. in.						
1	—	—	174	3	Tubular.	6 9	36	3 9	12	90	1728	.75	14.5	8.2
2	—	—	219	4	"	6 6	38	3 9	14	120	2355	.70	13.7	9.0
3	—	—	283	4	Cylindrical.	6 6	36	—	11	176	1440	1.14	9.3	6.0
4	—	—	279	4	Tubular.	7 0	42	4 0	15	128	2528	.79	15.6	8.0
5	15 0	144	270	5	"	7 0	42	4 0	50	160	3410	.60	12.9	8.7
6	16 0	144	130	4	"	7 0	36	4 0	60	124	2167	.51	9.0	9.7
7	22 6	192	220	5	"	7 0	42	4 0	52	180	3410	.56	10.6	8.8
1	20 0	216	230	6	"	7 0	42	4 0	55	216	4092	.36	6.8	10.7

The consumption of stores at the blowing-engines, forms a considerable item in the working expenses. We are acquainted with engines where it is from twice to thrice the necessary quantity. Subjoined is a table of the consumption after some years of retrenchment:

MANUFACTURE OF IRON.

Consumption of Stores at Blowing Engines, Monthly.

	Olive oil, in quarts.	Seal oil, in quarts.	Tallow, in pounds.	Engine yarn, in pounds.	Hemp, in pounds.	Flax, in pounds.
Dowlais, No. 1	6	4	68	100	8	2
2	6	4	68	100	8	2
3	6	4	68	100	8	2
4	6	4	68	100	8	2
5	8	8	112	100	8	4
6	6	8	80	80	8	4
7	8	8	80	80	8	4
Hirwain, No. 1	14	7	133 } 25 }	120	87	30

In addition to the foregoing goods, the first seven engines consumed monthly, 158 lbs. of new brass, and returned to store 143 lbs. of old; 41 lbs. of valve leather; 24 tons of miscellaneous castings; 18 tons of sheet-iron, afterwards returned as old iron; 2½ tons of wrought-iron, and smaller quantities of other goods.

SECTION XV.

REFINING.

This is a process commonly used in the Welsh ironworks, and, to a certain extent, in the other iron-making districts of this country. In the manufacture of the finest qualities of wrought-iron it is universally adopted, but with the inferior kinds it is not so much employed as formerly.

The refinery furnace (Pls. XLI.—XLIII.) usually consists of a strong cast-iron framework, surmounted by a short brick chimney. The bottom frame rests on a brick or masonry bedding, upon which is laid a floor or hearth of dressed sandstone, 10 or 12 inches thick. At each side and at the back, within the vertical frames, cast-iron water-blocks are fixed, and a cast-iron damplate in front, the whole forming a quadrangular space about 4 feet square inside, by 15 or 18 inches deep. Above the side blocks, and resting on a ledge cast for their reception, are fixed tuyere plates, 2 to 3 inches thick, having openings for the insertion of the water tuyeres, and bolted fast at the ends to the vertical frames. The space between the tuyere plates and the top frame which carries the chimney is fitted with stout cast-iron plates, bolted at the ends to the vertical frames. In front, resting on the damplate, it is usual to have a dust-plate for the convenience of filling and working the fire. At a height of a few inches above this plate in front, and also above the rear water-block, cast-iron doors about $2\frac{1}{4}$ feet high are hung to the side frames. Through these doors the working operations are carried on.

At a sufficient distance below the inside floor of the refinery, and a few inches in advance of the damplate, the casting bed or pig-mould is constructed. A brick, or, what is better, a cast-iron cistern, about 30 feet long, 4 feet wide, and 2 feet deep, forms the substructure. The casting bed is composed of thick cast-iron blocks, about $3\frac{1}{2}$ feet wide, the same in length, and 6 or 8 inches thick, having flanges at each side to rest on the edges of the cistern underneath, and sloping flanges on the upper surface, to restrain the fluid metal within the desired limits. When in working order the cistern is filled with water to within an inch or two of the mould blocks, and is maintained at this level by a small stream, the superfluous water escaping by an overflow notch. The jointing of the mould blocks to each other is done with care, that no metal may penetrate into the cistern below; a thin stratum of fire-clay between them generally suffices for this purpose. The blocks are maintained in close contact by stout clamps taking hold of corresponding snugs cast on the sides of the moulds.

The mould blocks are also made with a flange running down the centre, dividing the plate of metal into two widths; and to reduce still further the labour of breaking it up they are sometimes constructed with longitudinal grooves for receiving the metal, the dimensions and length being very similar to those of the moulds prepared in the dust-bed of the blast-furnace for forming the original pigs.

The blowing arrangements usually consist of two or three small nozzle pipes at each side. Each pipe is furnished with a suitable stop-valve for regulating the supply of blast. The connexion between the metal nozzle pipe and the fixed blast pipe containing the valves is generally made by a leather bag fastened at the ends around the pipe by screw clamping-glands. The leather bags, however, may be dispensed with, and their place supplied by telescope pipes having a cup-and-ball joint as a provision for any variation that may be required in the lateral and vertical direction given to the blast. This mode of connexion has been in use at the Dowlais works in sixteen refineries for about fourteen years. Its first cost is somewhat higher, but it has been found much less expensive in repairs and renewals than the common leather connexion.

Refineries are also constructed with a single pipe at the back; the framework, water-blocks, mould, and other parts, are then of a lighter description, and the fire is altogether of much smaller dimensions. Other refineries are constructed with two, and sometimes three, pipes at the back. They are known as single refineries, while those having two sets of pipes, one on each side, as in the fire we have described, are known as double refineries. The double fires are generally blown with two or three pipes on each side, but four may be seen at some works.

Refineries are also distinguished as melting-down and running-in fires. The former melts cold pigs from the blast furnace, old castings, and scraps, while the latter works on hot fluid metal run direct from the blast furnace.

The melting-down refinery is usually in a building by itself at some distance from the blast furnace. The running-in fire is erected immediately contiguous to the blast furnace, from which the crude iron, on being tapped, flows into it. This mode of working was first practised at the Dowlais works. It has since been adopted at other works with a considerable saving of coal.

The operation of refining crude pig-iron is conducted nearly as follows: The floor of the fire is strewn with some broken sandstone, and a fire is lit in the centre. A quantity of coke is filled in, and a light blast directed upon it. A charge of pigs, scraps, or broken castings is next placed on the ignited coke; a fresh charge of fuel is heaped on the pigs, and the full power of the blast brought into action. The weight of pig-iron or other metal charged will vary with the size of the fire, but may be taken at 2 tons, and the coke for the same at 5 cwts. An intense heat is soon produced; the broken sandstone on the floor melts, and glazes the surface of the hearth. In the course of about an hour the metal begins to melt, dropping through the coke to the hearth; in about two hours or two hours and a half the whole of the iron is melted and lies under the coke. The blast is still kept up, fresh coke is added, and the metal heaves and boils from the evolution of gases. The process is continued until the whole being sufficiently decarburized, the fluid metal is tapped into the cast-iron mould-bed. To render it more easy of removal from the mould, small dams of cinder are placed across at convenient distances, thinning the plate metal at such places sufficiently to render its separation easy.

The iron and cinder escape together from the refinery into the mould, but from its inferior specific gravity the great body of the cinder rises and collects on the surface of the plate. This separation of the metal from the cinder is stimulated by throwing water on the fluid metal immediately that the entire charge has left the refinery. The sudden cooling caused by the water renders the metal very brittle, and facilitates its subsequent breakage into pieces fit for the puddling process.

The time occupied in the operation of refining each fireful will average about three hours. White forge-iron is not blown so long as grey pigs; the latter often require three and a half to four hours to be properly refined. Castings take still longer; the large and irregularly-shaped pieces to be melted frequently require nearly twice the usual quantity of blowing to effect their reduction.

With the running-in refinery the operation is different, since the metal is charged, or more correctly speaking run, into the fire in a fluid state; hence the time occupied in melting it is saved. These fires are consequently enabled to refine a larger quantity in a given time, and are also worked more economically in their consumption of labour and fuel than the others.

A few pounds of the cinder from previous refinings are added in operating upon such irons as are smelted with less than the usual proportion of cinder in the blast furnace. By the addition, in moderate quantities, of a good cinder the work is hastened and the yield of iron improved. In this, as indeed in every other operation, the presence of cinder in moderate quantities is highly beneficial; when it is produced in small quantities the operation becomes more difficult, the quality variable, and the yield generally bad.

The bottom of the hearth, from the intense heat of the fire and the force of the blast being directed on it, is burnt away in a short period, and usually requires repair once a week. Brick bottoms are used at some works; and the practice of repairing the hearth by covering it with a course of bricks weekly is also practised to some extent. For durability, however, a sandstone bottom of millstone grit is superior to all others.

For conveying the blast into the hearth small wrought-iron tuyeres are used, having their smaller orifice $1\frac{1}{4}$ or $1\frac{3}{8}$ inches diameter, and the larger $3\frac{1}{4}$ or 4 inches. A $\frac{1}{4}$ inch or $\frac{3}{8}$ inch pipe is screwed into the upper end as an inlet pipe, and a similar one as an outlet for the water. The inlet pipes are connected with a small cistern, placed three or four feet above the tuyere; the outlet pipes discharge the water into the side blocks, from which it enters the rear block, and finally is conveyed by a small pipe to the cistern under the mould-bed.

The nozzles of the blowing pipes, in double refineries, where four are employed, are usually $1\frac{1}{2}$ inch diameter, or if of another section, are equal in area to a circular pipe of this size. A pipe flattened at the point, so as to increase the horizontal surface of action, is considered by some refiners as superior to the circular form. The angle which the direction of the issuing blast makes with the bottom is a matter of some importance. We have obtained the best results when the line of the blast makes an angle of 38 deg., and the angle enclosed by the two streams of blast 105 deg., the meeting-place of the streams being continued their direction by two lines being at the upper surface of the hearth.

THEORY OF THE REFINING FURNACE.

The operation of refining is a combination of chemical and mechanical processes, whereby the metallic alloy is deprived of a portion of the extraneous matters contracted in the blast furnace. The crude iron contains various substances in mixture; generally the most important consist of carbon, silicon, and aluminium, as will be seen by referring to the analyses in a proceeding section. It is the province of the refiner to extract from it the larger portion of these impurities preparatory to its conversion into malleable iron.

For this purpose the crude iron is fused in the refinery fire, along with coke or charcoal, as before described, and there kept at a liquid heat for a short period by means of numerous small jets of air. In the blast furnace the atmospheric air delivered through the blast pipe is required for the maintenance of combustion. In the refinery the blast answers a double purpose. It creates and maintains an intensely high temperature, fusing the crude iron with great rapidity, and promotes the rapid oxydation of the impurities. But in this process a considerable quantity of metal is also oxydised, and this, in combination with a portion of earthy matter, forms the refinery cinder. Hence, of the oxygen of the blast delivered into the refinery the larger volume unites with the carbon of the fuel, forming carbonic acid, and ascends into the atmosphere—a minor volume combines with the metal oxydised, forming oxide of iron (still another portion unites with the carbon contained in the molten crude iron, forming also carbonic acid, and escaping in a similar manner), while the remainder unites with the other substances, forming silica, alumina, &c. The separation of the various impurities is further facilitated, as in the hearth of the blast furnace, by mechanical subsidence. Specifically lighter than the metal, they float on the surface, united in definite proportion with oxide of iron, and to a partial extent protect the lower stratum from further oxydation during the process.

The decarburization and consequent refinement of the crude iron may be effected by fusion and oxydation in reverberatory furnaces without the intervention of a blast; but, since the blast expedites the operation, and results in a superior yield for the same degree of refinement, it is generally preferred.

The fracture of the refined plate metal when cold is white and dense at the bottom, but is of a honeycombed or cellular structure at top. The depth of the honeycomb is affected by the quality of the iron and length of blowing. If the metal is from ordinary forge pigs, and the blowing has been conducted an average time, the depth will be from 1 to $1\frac{1}{4}$ inch; but if the plate is from good grey pigs, it probably will not exceed $\frac{1}{2}$ inch. By the reduced depth of the honeycomb and the bright silvery lustre presented by the metal, the general quality of the pig-iron used in its manufacture may be pretty accurately determined.

The make of a running-in refinery is nearly the same as that of a blast furnace in the same district. It has increased and kept pace with the increased make of the furnace, so that from 25 to 30 tons—the make with single fires at the beginning of this century—it has increased to 150 and 160 tons with the present double refineries. The make of a melting-down refinery at the present day will range from 80 to 100 tons weekly, but if working on all grey iron it will seldom exceed 80 tons; and by using old castings of considerable bulk this make may be reduced to about 50 tons. The refineries, however, are under blast only five days weekly, consequently during the time they are working they can produce refined plate metal much faster than the blast furnace can supply the crude iron.

The consumption of crude iron per ton of refined metal at the running-in fires averages 22.3 cwts. when refining common forge-iron, and 22.1 cwts. when working grey iron of superior quality. In the melting-down fire the yield on each is about $\frac{5}{16}$ of a cwt. higher.

The direct loss or waste of metal in the refining process is not great. The 22.3 cwts. of crude iron produce 1 ton of metal, and on an average 3 cwts. of cinder, containing from 56 to 60 per cent. of iron. Hence, of the consumption of 22.3 cwts. of iron 21.8 are obtained in plate metal and cinder, showing a loss of but 57 lbs. per ton. This would be still further reduced if the whole of the cinder could be collected, but a portion is carried up through the chimney before the ascending blast in the form of small hollow globules.

All the varieties of crude iron smelted with a hot blast lose more in refining than those smelted with cold blast. The cause of this is probably that they contain a greater quantity of earthy matter, and melt at a lower temperature than cold-blast irons. The consumption of crude iron per ton of refined metal averages 36 lbs. per ton more with all the varieties of hot-blast irons.

Crude iron smelted from a burden composed largely of cinder is refined with a greater waste, for though cinder is beneficial when present in moderate quantities, in excess it proves injurious to the yield and quality of iron. Hence a large addition of cinder in the blast furnace is generally followed by bad refinery yields.

The consumption of coal in the form of coke varies with the description of refinery, quality of coke, and quality of crude iron. In the running-in fire working forge iron, the consumption of the dense coke prepared from bituminous coal will be about 4 cwts. per ton of metal made; with grey iron the consumption will rise to about 5 cwts. In the melting-down refinery the consumption will be about $6\frac{1}{4}$ and 8 cwts. respectively. If the coke is of a weak friable character and of a low specific gravity the consumption will be much greater, and with such coke the waste of crude iron in the process will also be increased.

The consumption of blast is small compared with the consumption at the blast furnace, but is sufficiently high for the perfect combustion of the carbon charged. When refining forge iron in the running-in fire it is about 94,000 cubic feet per ton of metal made, or by weight 3 tons nearly. The quantity of carbon being estimated by the weight of the coke we find that the air necessary for its combustion is 69,000 cubic feet, leaving an excess of supply of 25,000 cubic feet. A portion of this combines with the carbon of the metal while the remainder escapes undecomposed. If we allow that the metal is deprived during the process of carbon amounting to 2½ per cent. by weight of the whole, which is very near the actual loss, we shall find that the quantity of air thus absorbed will amount to 17,200 cubic feet, leaving 7800 cubic feet, or one-twelfth of the quantity used, as waste. With grey iron the consumption will be nearly 110,000 cubic feet per ton.

In the melting-down refinery the quantity of blast is increased proportionately to the larger consumption of coke. The average consumption in these fires for forge iron is 136,000 cubic feet, and for grey iron 153,000 cubic feet.

The density of the blast employed is generally equal to that blown into the furnaces in the same establishment. Refineries are worked with a pressure of 1¼ lb. to the square inch, but this may be considered a minimum, from 2 to 2¼ lbs. being more common. The qualities of the fuel require to be taken into consideration here as in the furnace; a weak coke carrying a lighter blast than one of a denser description. But the range in pressure is not so great with fineries as with furnaces. The blast being directed upon the surface of the metal in the hearth of the finery, an excessive pressure will be attended with greater waste of metal. Hence the refiner prefers a blast of 2 to 2¼ lbs. per square inch, and endeavours to throw this as much on the surface as possible. The spread of the blast is considered of more importance in the decarburization than great density.

At the Dowlais works refining has been conducted for some years with raw coal, but we are unable to discern any real advantage from its use in preference to coke. The substitution was made at a time when the supply of coke was inadequate to the demand, and in the absence of any great drawback raw coals were afterwards adopted at other refineries. But after an experience of some years, however, we consider that coke of a good quality is far superior to any raw coal for refining purposes. The heat produced by raw coal is not nearly so intense or concentrated as with coke, and much of that which is generated does not produce any useful effect. The yield of coal is about one cwt. higher than is required with coke. Looking at the greater calorific power of coal over coke this increase of consumption with raw coal requires some explanation. In the blast furnace where raw coal has been substituted for coke, the consumption of coal has been reduced, but this has not occurred at the refinery. We must look to the more rapid and superficial operation of this process for a solution of this apparent anomaly.

Raw coal when charged into the blast furnace undergoes a distillation in the upper part, and is thus converted into a coke more or less dense according to its original constituents and the weight of the superincumbent materials. The temperature of the throat through which it enters the furnace is low compared with the temperature in the zone of fusion, and the transition from the lesser to the higher temperature occupies from thirty to forty hours, during rather more than one-half of which time the process of distillation is in slow operation. The coke on its arrival in the zone of fusion is composed of nearly pure carbon—by the escape of its gaseous constituents the solid coal is converted into a cellular mass—the surface area of the carbon presented to the oxygen of the air for combustion is immensely increased, and the requisite volume of atmospheric air being brought into contact with it, a maximum temperature is attained. But in the refinery the case is very different. The coal is precipitated into an intense heat without any previous preparation. A rapid distillation is the result; a portion of its volatile constituents are violently expelled, partially breaking it up, and the coking is still incomplete when the coal arrives before the blast. In the blast furnace the time permitted for the transformation into coke averages twenty hours—in the refinery from the time it is charged to its combustion is scarcely the same number of minutes. As a consequence of this rapid action the coal is but superficially charred, and the surface of carbon exposed to the action of the oxygen of the blast is limited. The absence of the conditions essential to a rapid combustion for the creation of an intense heat accounts for the inferior reducing power of the raw coal in the refinery.

In practice the finer complains of the difficulty of getting a good heat on the iron, and when it is melted, this difficulty continuing, obliges him to blow longer with coal than with coke. The make of the refinery is consequently reduced while the labour is increased. As some compensation for this reduction of make, which, measured by the time the refinery is under blast, may be taken at 10 tons per week, and for the additional labour with coal, the rates paid the workmen are considerably lower than for coke.

Anthracite coal has been used in refining, but its proper management in this process is not generally well understood. This coal, from its small proportion of bituminous matter, is liable to splinter and disintegrate when suddenly exposed to a high heat. Attention, therefore, should be directed to remedy this defect. At the Ystalyfera works anthracite has been partially charred in ovens and conveyed to the refinery while yet hot. This preparation has enabled anthracite to be used for refining with considerable success. An arrangement superior to this, however, might be adopted. In a suitable chamber, fitted with a small blast pipe contiguous to, but three or four feet higher than the refinery hearth, the coal might have its temperature gradually elevated to prepare it for the intense heat of the refinery into which it could be drawn as required. By regulating the blast the distillation in the supplementary chamber may be conducted at a rate most advantageous to the structure of the coal and the object in view.

A difficulty is experienced in refining all the classes of iron smelted from carbonaceous ironstone, most perhaps with those from Scotland. The cause of the uniform inferiority of these irons in the refinery is a matter of uncertainty amongst ironmasters. To form a correct opinion of its origin we must look to the characteristics of the iron from the carbonaceous ironstone—these are fluidity at a low temperature, an excessive quantity of carbon in combination, and as a necessary consequence of the richness of the ore in metallic iron a small proportion of other substances. . Either of these characteristics alone necessitates the subjection of the iron to a longer blowing, and results in an increased consumption of fuel, blast, and labour, and greater waste, consequently we may conclude that where all of them are found together the difficulty of refining will be proportionately increased.

From the low melting temperature of this iron the ordinary heat of the finery would result in a large oxydization of the metal. This is avoided as much as practicable by keeping the heat lower; but the operation is prolonged, and is attended with a considerable though smaller waste of metal. The excess of carbon mechanically combined with the metal is removed only by bringing into contact with it a proportionately larger quantity of oxygen by the blast—involving at the low working heat a prolongation of blowing. The small per-centage of silicon and aluminium causes the iron to work drier, and to correct this defect a quantity of cinders are added to protect it, and otherwise improve its quality for the forge.

Yet after careful arrangements, and the employment of the best workmen, the refining of these irons is attended with great loss of metal. The general consumption of pigs per ton of refined iron is 24 cwts. the excess being nearly twice as great as with grey iron from argillaceous ores. This added to the larger consumption of coal, and the reduced make has operated greatly against the manufacture of bars from this kind of iron. So great is the waste in the Welsh works, partly caused however by the workmen being long accustomed to iron melting at a higher temperature, that the Scotch pigs are not unfrequently charged into the blast furnace and there melted along with the local ironstone in preference to working them directly through the refinery. By this mode of working their decarburization is affected in the blast furnace instead of the refinery through which they afterwards pass in mixture with the iron smelted from the ironstone. The loss by this double refining cannot be accurately ascertained, but from calculations we find the yield to be between 24 and 25 cwts.

This iron is also refined in conjunction with that from the local argillaceous ironstone in the proportion of one-fourth or one-fifth. By admixture in this way the yield is better than when it is refined by itself, but the decarburization is not so complete, and the average quality of the plate metal produced is inferior.

Iron smelted with caustic lime as flux is refined with greater difficulty than such as is smelted with raw limestone. The presence of the carbonic acid of the limestone appears to have considerable influence on the fluidity of the iron both in the blast furnace and refinery. In its absence the crude iron is thick, runs in a sluggish stream, and in the refining fire requires longer blowing to raise the cinder and bring out the cellular structure. The cinders are thick and whiter than usual. Still the metal from furnaces fluxed with caustic lime is superior to the other for the rolling mill, the ultimate quality being considerably improved.

A hot blast has been tried at the refinery, but without any appreciable advantage. The heated blast, as we have already explained, possesses a penetrating power inferior to that of the cold; and in the decarburization of the metal (though the extended surface presented by the oxygen of the air is advantageous) the weakness of the blast was found to be prejudicial to the yields. For the refining process, a blast of given density is absolutely necessary if the decarburization is to be effected with economy of metal and carbon. The pressure of the hot blast being equal to that of the cold, its intensity at a given distance from the nozzle of the blast pipe is diminished in proportion as its volume is augmented by heat. Hence, to produce an equal effect the nozzle would require to be brought much nearer the surface of the iron, thereby contracting the working surface of the blast, and increasing the burning and wear of the blocks and tuyeres.

The effects of the hot blast in reducing the consumption of coal in the blast furnace are generally cited as a reason for its adoption in the refinery. But we have already shown how greatly these effects have been exaggerated by all writers on ironmaking, and we would now add that the application of the hot blast to refining has hitherto effected no saving in coal; indeed, the yield was rather worse, the diminished decarburizing power of the blast apparently more than compensating for its lesser absorption of heat.

The addition of limestone during refining is attended with beneficial results to the quality of the metal when the crude iron has been smelted from lean argillaceous carbonates of the coal formation. The quantity which may be used with advantage is between 25 and 30 lbs. per ton. It should be broken small. Where a larger proportion has been used, the manufactured iron has a red short tendency. The lime may also be added by impregnating the coke with caustic lime to the amount of 15 or 18 lbs. per ton of iron. With lime, the cinder which collects on the iron in the fire is white and thicker than usual. This alteration in the cinder entails a longer blowing, but the beneficial results will generally compensate for this additional expense.

Whether lime be added in the shape of limestone or caustic lime, the improvement in quality is very marked, and is probably due to the union of a portion of the sulphur in the iron with calcium. It is generally known that the lean carbonates of the coal formation, abounding largely in silica, produce finished iron of a cold short character. The addition of lime appears to neutralise this tendency, and if not carried too far the opposite extreme, red shortness, is avoided.

The addition of potash to iron in the refinery appears to deteriorate the general quality. In experiments where 6 lbs. per ton was charged, the tendency of the metal, whether to hot or cold shortness, was heightened by the use of this substance.

From the intense heat to which they are subjected the duration of the principal parts of the refinery is short. The side and rear blocks will be so much melted away after refining about 2100 tons as to require renewal. The pig-mould will generally remain in a working condition twice this period, but the tuyere-plates, damplates, and other small castings, are frequently rendered unserviceable before 1000 tons have been refined. The consumption of new castings in replacing those burnt and worn out, including also the breaking up of the metal, averages 12 lbs. per ton of iron refined.

The breaking-up of the refined plate metal into pieces of a convenient size for the puddling furnace is done with heavy two-handled sledges, (see Pl. XLIV., Figs. 252-3). There is a fact in connexion with the duration of these sledges which is worth recording—those cast from cold-blast iron will break nearly twice as much metal as those from hot-blast iron.

The refining of the crude iron has the effect of depriving it of a portion of the carbon, silicon, aluminum, and other substances, which may be mixed with it. The proportion which the quantity removed bears to the whole, has never been satisfactorily ascertained; but it is directly dependent on the quality of the ore and the duration of the process. As a general rule, the longer the metal is exposed to the blast the greater is the improvement in the quality; but the process may be unnecessarily prolonged. By shortening the time of blowing refined metal may be obtained with a very small proportion of the impurities removed. For some purposes such iron is preferred to that containing less cinder. The quality of the original crude iron also may be such that the refined metal will contain a considerable proportion of cinder. For though the presence of cinder in quantity is usually considered as evidence of inferiority, it is well known that in the manufacture of malleable iron the most successful results are obtained when the metal, by freely yielding a fluid cinder is protected from oxydation during the process. Hence, in refining, the object is not so much to deprive the iron of the cinder (except in cases where this is of a prejudicial quality).

If depriving the iron of earthy matter were the chief object in view in refining, the grey varieties, having the smallest quantity, would be refined with the least trouble instead of the greatest. The proportion of carbon principally determines the facility with which the operation may be conducted. If the quantity combined with the metal is small, the refining will be quickly done with a minimum consumption of crude iron and fuel, but if large, it is just the reverse.

The average quantity of carbon in crude iron is supposed to be near 4 per cent. In the refining this is reduced about one-half—the other half combining with the oxygen of the air and escaping in the form of gas. With chemists a difference of opinion exists as to the relative proportions of carbon in the white and grey varieties of crude iron. By some it is maintained that the white contains the largest quantity, while others contend that the grey is richest in this substance. Without going into an explanation of the many conflicting statements which have been published on this point, we will content ourselves with stating that the consumption of carbon in the blast furnace, in proportion to the weight of the melted products obtained, influences the time required for the subsequent process of refining. If it be large we have found the iron refine with difficulty, but if the minimum proportion, the same result is obtained with comparative ease. An addition to the usual proportion of coal in the blast furnace is immediately made known to the refiner by the longer time occupied in the decarburization. With this evidence we are of opinion that the white contains the least carbon. An exception, however, must be made in the case of white iron from blast furnaces consuming a maximum proportion of carbon. This variety of white iron we are inclined to consider as richer in carbon than any other, though apparently the poorest. It takes the longest blowing, and this we attribute to the large quantity of carbon in chemical combination.

There are circumstances connected with the refining of crude iron for which we must confess we are unable to afford a satisfactory explanation. The weight of the products obtained exceeds the weight of the metal charged by nearly 8 per cent. Although attention does not appear to have been directed to it, we find a similar circumstance occurs at other works and the same difficulty is experienced in accounting for the excess.

If this excess occurred for a month or shorter period we should be inclined to attribute it to an error in the accounts, but since it appears to have existed at all times in refining, we must look to some other cause for a solution. We cannot do better in illustration of the subject than give the following weights as having occurred in practice. By dealing with large quantities distributed over long periods, the liability to error is reduced, and the excess is proved to be a permanent and not a merely temporary occurrence, as we at one time imagined.

Consumption and yield of iron at thirteen refineries for a period of 2½ years—130 weeks' working:

	Tons.
Crude iron delivered to refineries	149,461
Castings used in repairing ditto	859
Total iron delivered	150,350

Against this consumption there was the following produce of iron in refined metal and cinders. We have estimated the cinders to yield 60 per cent. of iron—when smelted alone in the furnace they gave:

	Tons.
Refined metal	134,314
Cinders produced, 28,250 tons, yielding at 60 per cent.	16,950
Total iron produced	151,264

Thus showing an excess of 914 tons of iron received from the refineries above the quantity delivered. To what source can we attribute this excess? Instead of being accompanied by a waste of metal, the refining process apparently augments the production. The increase is at the rate of .6 per cent. nearly.

But the gross weight of the products obtained is greatly in excess of the weight charged:

	Tons.
Crude iron charged	150,350
Products obtained:	
Metal	134,314
Cinders	28,250
	162,564
Excess of products over crude iron charged	12,214

The excess of .6 per cent. on the production of iron appears trifling in comparison with this excess in the whole products obtained. The residual earths of the coal may account for a portion of this. For the refining of this metal, 47,009 tons of coal were used; estimating that they contained 2.1 per cent. of earth, 987 tons are accounted for; the siliceous sandstone used in forming the bottoms may also add 335 tons, but there still remains 10,892 tons.

The quantity of oxygen combining with the iron to form in the cinder a protoxide will be about 5700 tons, leaving 5192 tons unaccounted for.

The composition of the cinders may be easily obtained with sufficient accuracy. By adding the iron and oxygen together we obtain 22,650 tons of protoxide, leaving 5600 tons for the earths in the cinder. The cinder is consequently composed of 80 per cent. of protoxide of iron and 20 per cent. of siliceous earths. The difference in the composition of crude and refined iron is seen in the following table, according to the analyses of a French iron by a Continental chemist:

	Carbon.	Silicon.	Phosphorus.	Iron.
Crude iron	3.	4.5	0.2	92.3
Refined metal	1.7	.5	—	97.8

Admitting the correctness of these analyses we will apply them, to the Dowlais irons, which do not differ greatly in the quality of the earthy mixture.

By refining it appears that iron is deprived of 4 per cent. of silicon; on the foregoing quantity of refined metal this will amount to 5372 tons, which is augmented by the ashes of the coal and siliceous sandstone of the hearth to 6694 tons. Hence we have the following products:

	Tons.
Refined metal	134,314
Iron in cinders	15,950
Oxygen in combination with ditto	5,700
Siliceous earths in cinders	6,094
Total	163,058

This is 1102 tons in excess of the quantity actually realised, showing that the deprivation of silicon is not so great with the Dowlais as with the French iron. The first three quantities are certain, but the fourth may be modified. If we suppose the iron to be deprived of 3.2 instead of 4 per cent., the quantity by the analysis would agree with the products in practice.

Thus the excess of 5192 tons is not accounted for by analyses. On the supposition that the per-centage of iron in the cinder has been overstated the apparent excess of iron produced over that charged might be explained, but the refinery cinder of these works is known to yield 60 per cent. of crude iron, and though a reduced yield would account for the disappearance of 914 tons of iron, the excess on the gross products obtained would not be affected.

In the conversion of the 150,350 tons of crude iron into 134,314 tons of refined metal, 32,906 tons of carbon were consumed. May not a portion of this carbon have combined with the refined iron? Chemists have hitherto been unable to determine the quantity of carbon combined with the metal in pig-iron, what evidence have we that the proportion of carbon is not *increased* by the refining process. An addition of 3 per cent. would account for the large excess of the products over the iron charged.

SECTION XVI.

BOILING AND PUDDLING PIG IRON.

In converting the crude iron of the blast furnace into malleable iron, upon an extensive scale, two modes of procedure are open to the manufacturer:—Either to refine the crude iron in the finery fire, and then pass it through the puddling process; or, to put the crude iron through a modification of the puddling process, understood in the trade by the term "boiling." Each method possesses certain advantages, but where quality is the sole consideration the process of refining and puddling is entitled to the preference. We may state, however, that upon the merits of the two systems ironmasters do not generally agree. By some the boiling process is held to be fully equal and more economical than refining and puddling; on the other hand, it is maintained that boiled iron is more subject to be red short. In several works both methods may be seen in operation, but where this occurs we have noticed that the larger quantity of iron is first passed through the refinery. Hence, in such instances it would appear that while boiling a certain quantity of pigs is considered advantageous, it is not desirable that the manufacture of the entire quantity of crude iron should be conducted in this way.

We are of opinion that boiling may be practised to a limited extent with most kinds of iron, though it is more applicable to some than others. Before entering, however, into the merits of the respective systems, we will describe the furnace employed and the process followed at the majority of the Welsh works.

The furnace for boiling pigs (Pl. XLIV., Figs. 259-262) is constructed with an outside framework of cast-iron plates, about 12 feet long, 5 feet 6 inches wide inside, and 6 feet high. Of this height 9 or 10 inches will be below the floor line of the forge. At one end the side plates are bolted to an iron framing, carrying the chimney stack, at the other they are attached to a cross plate of lesser depth, below which an ash-pit is formed, 2 feet deep, and of nearly the same length and breadth as the iron frame-work. The fire-place is generally of such a size that the superficial area of the grate shall be from 8 to 12 feet, varying with the quality of the coal to be employed. Three or four inches above the level of the bearing bars of the grate there is fixed horizontally a cast-iron plate, nearly equalling in width the distance between the side plates, and extending from the fire-place to the stack framing. This is supported at short intervals by stout bearing bars, resting on angle-pieces, bolted to the side plates. Upon this plate, which is called the bottom, a fire-brick furnace is built. The breadth is about 3 feet 9 inches at the fire end, and it runs parallel for about two-thirds of its length, when it begins to diminish, till at the stack end it is contracted to 16 or 18 inches. The arched roof above the bottom is about 27 inches high at the fire end. It falls throughout its length usually, but in all cases a sharp descent occurs close to the stack, where the under side of the roof in the narrow flue is brought down to within 10 inches of the level of the bottom; from this point it is carried level for 9 or 10 inches to its junction with the vertical flue of the stack.

The length of the fire-place having been determined, a brick bridge, 14 or 15 inches thick, is built on the extreme end of the bottom plate, and carried up to within 10 or 12 inches of the roof. At the stack end, where the furnace is contracted to its narrowest dimensions, a second bridge of fire-brick, about 9 inches in thickness and 10 or 12 in height, is built to restrain the metal from flowing into the flue. When finished the body of the furnace measures about 6 feet long, 3 feet 9 inches wide, by 2 feet high to the centre of the roof. On one side a doorway, about 16 inches square, is formed, for charging and working the crude iron. The height of the bottom of this doorway above the bottom plate is of some importance. The average height at several works is 10 inches, the lowest being 8 and the highest 11 inches. As the height of this doorway is determined before casting the side plates, it regulates the height of the bottom, and also of the roof of the furnace, especially at the end next the stack, where the general rule is to have the under side of the arch level with the lower side of the doorway.

The metal forming the lower edge of the doorway is subject to wear by the constant pressure and friction of the iron working-bars of the puddler; to prevent this as much as possible a loose plate, about $1\frac{1}{4}$ inches thick, is bolted on to it, which can easily be renewed when necessary. The cast-iron door is lined inside with fire-brick, and is made to slide up and down between strong cast-iron flanges by means of a rod connected to a counter-balanced lever. For the convenience of working, and for the protection of the puddler from the intense heat, a small slit, about $3\frac{1}{2}$ inches wide by 5 inches high, is left in the under side of the door; through this the working operations are principally carried on. To prevent the sides and upper edge of this slit from being enlarged by constant wear, the metal around it is hardened by being cast in metal chills.

This, the working door, is situated rather nearer the fire bridge than the flue. In the wall left on the side of it next the flue a second doorway of smaller dimensions than the working door is used for charging the metal, where this is done before the previous heat has been withdrawn. This charging door is usually about 10 inches by 13 inches, and 12 or 13 inches above the bottom plate, having a lever and balance-weight for lifting it similar to the working door. Both are often used in boiling furnaces, but generally a single door suffices. In puddling furnaces, however, they are generally adopted.

A doorway, about 10 inches by 10 inches, is also left opposite the fire-place; it has a cast-iron mouthpiece, but no door, the mode of firing rendering this unnecessary. At the stack end a small aperture, about 4 inches by 6 inches, is provided for the escape of any cinder that may pass over the bridge into the flue. A small fire is kept burning over this aperture, in a grate secured to the outside frame of the stack, to keep it open for the passage of the cinder, and to maintain the latter sufficiently fluid.

The chimney-stack is built of fire-brick. For the generality of forge coals it is 30 feet high above the cast-iron framework, or altogether 36 feet. The interior flue is made about 24 inches square, but at its junction with the roof of the furnace it is contracted to about one-third of this area. This contraction is regulated partly by the skill of the workman, but principally by the qualities of the coal. The size of the flue in this place we have seen as small as 17 inches by 9 inches, with a coal approaching nearly to the character of anthracite. With a more inflammable coal it has been 18 inches by 18 inches. The chimney walls are usually built 1½ brick thick for 14 feet, 1 brick for 10 feet, and half a brick the remaining 6 feet. The intense heat in the chimney destroys the lower courses in a comparatively short period. To facilitate the repairs of this part a lining half a brick thick is carried up, without binding with the other work, for about 20 feet. When necessary this is drawn down and rebuilt without interfering with the stability of the stack.

The top of the chimney is surmounted with a light cast-iron frame-work fitted with a damper for regulating the draught. This damper is opened and shut by a lever, from which an iron rod or chain descends to the workmen below. A different mode of regulating the draught is sometimes adopted, but of this plan we shall have to speak hereafter.

The effects of the expansion and contraction of the brickwork by the alternate heating and cooling are provided against by numerous iron binders built in, the projecting ends of which are punched or cast to receive vertical wrought-iron rods, which are keyed up tight against the brickwork by iron wedges at their backs. Unless the light chimney-stacks were well bound together they would not long remain upright under the straining to which they are subjected. Imperfectly bound stacks may be seen in every work inclining at angles more or less dangerous to their stability. The chimney-stack delineated in Pl. XLVIII., Fig. 275, is bound with more than two hundred separate pieces of wrought and cast-iron.

The immense strain exerted by the expansion of the brickwork of the roof has also to be met by a number of strong wrought-iron bolts at the top and bottom of the side plates. For ordinary furnaces these should not be more than 2 feet 6 inches apart when the bolts are 1¼ inch square. The plates may also be strengthened by vertical ribs on the outside face; if this be done the risk of their breaking in the middle—a very frequent occurrence—will be nearly removed. In some works—Cyfarthfa for instance, the binding is composed of wrought-iron looped straps at top and bottom with vertical connecting bolts, also of wrought-iron; by this arrangement the direct strain on the side plates is greatly reduced and their durability consequently increased.

The plate in which the doorway for feeding the fire is situated, commonly called the stock-hole plate, is the least durable of the whole. The stock-hole is usually a square with sharp angles; after a few weeks, sometimes only a few days, the plate breaks across one or more of these angles. This is doubtless caused by the unequal expansion and contraction of the surface, but a remedy has not yet been discovered. The angles have been rounded off without effect. In other cases wrought-iron looped clamps have been cast in the metal across, and at right angles to the general direction of the fracture but without adding greatly to the durability.

The process of "boiling" is thus conducted:

The bottom of the furnace is covered with some broken cinder—from previous workings—and mill scales, and a fire is lit in the grate. In from ten to twelve hours with new furnaces (five or six is sufficient with old), the interior of the furnace will be at a white heat, the cinder melts, and flowing over the bottom protects it from the fused iron and intense reverberatory action of the roof, and fills any crevices in the edges of the brickwork; the draught is now slacked a little, about 30 or 40 lbs. of cinder are charged at the flue end, and the quantity of pigs to be operated on—technically called a "heat"—generally $4\frac{1}{4}$ or $4\frac{1}{2}$ cwts., is charged in pieces of convenient size—30 to 40 lbs. is best, and the more uniform the better. The charge is distributed upon the bottom of the furnace and the doors closed, the admission of cold air is prevented by throwing a little small coal or cinders around its edges, and filling up the notch with a lump of coal, covering it with a small iron plate. The damper is opened to its full extent, fresh fuel is added in the grate, and the fire is strongly urged. From the peculiar form of the roof the heated products of combustion are deflected on the pigs, and the extremity of the roof being placed low they are compelled to pass in close contact with the entire charge.

In about a quarter of an hour after charging the puddler throws in about 60 or 80 lbs. of the cinder expelled by the rolls from mill bars; where these cannot be obtained recourse is had to the cinder from rolls, rolling puddled iron bars. The cinders which are drawn from under rolls working on boiled iron are of inferior quality, and are never used in the boiling furnace if others can be procured. They contain a larger per-centage of silica and are less fluid; the time occupied in the boiling process consequently is lengthened whenever they are used, and it is believed with some reason that the quality of the resulting iron is inferior.

When the pieces of pig approach a red heat the puddler directs his attention to their position; those in the coolest parts of the furnace are shifted forward to the hottest, and *vice versâ*, the object being to bring the different pieces simultaneously to the melting point. Unless this is accomplished the waste of iron and loss of time will be considerable.

The working door is now made fast by tightly wedging it into the frame. In from twenty-two to twenty-five minutes after charging, dependent in great measure on the quality of the coal, the edges of the pigs begin to melt, in another five minutes they are softened and apparently adhere to each other and the bottom. The puddler now raises them, and turns them over to expose them equally to the heat and prevent their adhering together, which would obstruct their melting. At this stage it is common to charge two or three lumps of coal next to the flue bridge, and about 15 lbs. of cinder for the protection of the brickwork in this quarter. Thus far the fire has been urged to its utmost power, the second hand adding fresh fuel every few minutes and maintaining a clean grate and free draught.

In thirty minutes from the time of charging the iron is all melted, and the most laborious operation of the puddler commences. He puts in the rabble, and rakes up the fluid iron fore and aft, and raises the lower portions to the surface. At this point the energies of the puddler and his second hand are taxed to their utmost, both labouring at the raking up and stirring of the metal.

The fluid iron boils violently and rises spontaneously nearly to a level with the lower edge of the door; its surface is dotted with innumerable eruptions, caused by the escape of gaseous matter. In five or six minutes after the boil begins the damper is partially lowered, checking the draught and reducing the heat within the furnace. The effect of this reduction of heat is immediately seen; the iron becomes evidently thicker and more pasty; now, too, it adheres to the tools, and has to be removed by a hammer. The raking up of the metal from the bottom is continued unceasingly; the small door is opened, and the parts next the flue turned over along with the rest.

This working of the boiling metal continues for about eighteen minutes, at the end of which time the fluid iron has the appearance of a quantity of dirty snow. The continual raking motion has resulted in the evolution of the carbon and the separation of the iron from the cinder, which now flows over the bottom apparently as fluid as water.

The period for balling up now arrives; a few pounds of wet scales from the cooling bosh are thrown in. Their introduction causes an immediate reduction of temperature, which is increased by the puddler towards the end of the period of pasty condition desired. After eight or nine minutes' raking of the iron, now in the condition of pasty lumps, but which require to be constantly stirred to keep them from running back to the form of boiling iron, the puddler commences to form the puddle-balls. The number of these depends on the iron charged and the ability of the workman. Five or six is usual, but seven or eight may be seen brought out. The puddler commences by raking together such a quantity of the pasty iron as he conceives will suffice for a ball, and placing it a little aside in the furnace. He then proceeds with the remainder in a similar manner, keeping the iron together, and shaping his balls by the help of the leverage which he has with the iron bars, the slot in the door acting as a fulcrum. When the balls have been roughed out the damper is nearly closed. This is done so that in the finishing of the balls the heat may not be such as to soften them and cause an unnecessary waste of iron.

The puddle is now ready to "come out," the wedges around the door are driven back, and the balls drawn. This occupies about four minutes. From charging the first piece of pig to the extraction of the last ball the time occupied will average, with good workmen and a fair coal, one hour and twenty minutes; but with inferior workmen and a less inflammable coal, one hour and fifty minutes is about the average. If it is performed in eighty minutes, as we have described, a puddler and his second hand will easily boil eight heats in the twelve hours, producing, with charges of 4¼ cwts. each, 32 cwts. of boiled iron bars daily, or 9 tons 8 cwts. weekly, making, for the entire weekly produce of the furnace, working night and day, 18 tons 16 cwts.

On the withdrawal of the balls a quantity of cinder will remain on the bottom. A portion of this is tapped below the working door before charging a fresh heat. This cinder is produced by the oxydation of the iron and metalloids in alloy; it contains a large portion of silica, and, if not frequently renewed, will ultimately contain so large a quantity as to render it unfit for the protection of the iron. By tapping and replacing it by other cinder from the mill rolls, the puddler prevents the increase of silica, and insures a fluid cinder rich in iron.

Boiling crude iron direct from the blast furnace is practised to a limited extent. By operating on fluid iron the coal consumed in melting the cold pigs, amounting to one-third of the entire consumption, is saved, and the certainty obtained that all the iron is perfectly melted before the boiling commences, thereby insuring the greatest uniformity in quality. Yet notwithstanding the acknowledged superiority of the boiling process in direct connexion with the blast furnace and the period which has elapsed since the system was first adopted, the number of furnaces working on this plan is not large. The necessity of re-constructing the forge and bringing it inconveniently close to the blast furnace, is a great objection to its extensive use in existing works, while in the erection of new ones the contracted space permitted for carrying on the operations of the blast furnace is a disadvantage. The huddling together of the boiling furnaces, so that they may be as near as possible to the fall, operates against the success of this mode of working, in close weather. A puddling forge cannot be too open in summer time. Suspension of operations through the exhaustion of the men, produced by the heat evolved by the blast and adjacent boiling furnace, is a common occurrence in these forges, and exists to a greater or less extent in some others.

A species of double furnace (Pls. XLV., XLVI.) is used in several works with a marked improvement in the yield of coal. A fire-place of large dimensions is provided, and the body is made wider than in single furnaces. A working door is made at each side, and two puddlers work at the same time. Twice the usual quantity of pig-iron is charged. In all other respects the operation is conducted as in single furnaces. It is difficult, however, to get the puddlers to work well to time. Unless this be done, no advantage is realised over the single furnace. The two men must bring their heats to the respective stages simultaneously in order to render these furnaces profitable. If one be kept waiting for ever so short a period by the other the loss in iron more than counterbalances the reduced consumption of coal. This difficulty of obtaining men who will work thus in concert has operated against the general use of double furnaces. Were it not for this circumstance they would entirely supersede the single furnace. In the double furnace, working hot crude iron, the consumption of fuel is under one-half of the quantity required with single furnaces working cold iron.

The puddling furnace differs but slightly from the boiling furnace. With a few trifling alterations in the interior, principally confined to lowering the flue bridge, which, in the puddling furnace, is seldom more than 6 inches high, and raising the bottom to within 8 inches of the door, the boiling furnace is equally well adapted for puddling.

The process differs from boiling in the absence of the swelling and violent agitation of the fluid iron. The general charge is $4\frac{3}{4}$ cwts. of broken refined metal to a heat. In boiling it is usual to withdraw the finished balls before charging a fresh heat, but in puddling the refined metal is charged through the small door next the flue, at the point when the metal has arrived at the pasty condition. The reduction of temperature consequent on the introduction of a body of cold metal has then no sensible effect in retarding the progress of the operation. The metal is consequently exposed to the furnace flame for a period of fifteen to eighteen minutes before the withdrawal of the heat under operation, and when drawn it is forwarded into the body of the furnace which has been already elevated to a dull red heat. The damper being opened, a sharp heat is obtained, and in from ten to twelve minutes the metal is melted, and the operation of puddling commences. The same incessant raking motion by the puddler, relieved occasionally by his second hand, is practised as in boiling, and is followed by the separation, in a great measure, of the iron from the cinder. Finally, it is brought to the same pasty condition, and balled up.

From the time of charging to the extraction of the last ball, the puddling process occupies about one hour and twenty-five minutes; but as the iron is charged fifteen minutes before the extraction of the previous charge, the time actually occupied in working each heat is one hour and ten minutes. With inferior workmen it averages one hour and thirty-six minutes.

The presence of sulphur, and of several metals, including copper, lead, and zinc, retards the puddling process. If any of these are present in considerable quantity, the iron cannot be brought to a pasty condition for balling up, all the efforts of the puddler are thrown away, and the heat eventually has to be raked out. Crude iron rarely contains either of these metals in injurious quantities; but when they obtain admission, the pasty character of the mass is destroyed, and the further conversion of cast into malleable iron is totally prevented.

The yield and general quality of several kinds of iron are frequently improved by the addition, during the process of conversion, of a mixture composed of ground magnetic oxide or a rich hematite, caustic lime, and a minimum dose of black oxide of manganese; the quantity added may amount to 5 or 6 per cent. by weight of the charge. The operation is facilitated and the malleablization greatly increased by their employment, which we attribute to the oxygen of the ore and the caustic lime uniting with the carbon and sulphur of the metal.

The time and labour expended in working the superior qualities of iron are greater than that required with the inferior kinds. The grey varieties will require twenty to twenty-five minutes longer in "coming to nature," as the working puddler terms it, the point from which the balling-up process may be said to commence. The cause of this longer time appears to be that the larger quantity of carbon in the metal requires for its evolution longer exposure to the oxygen of the passing current of air, and repeated manipulation to facilitate its escape.

In the working of iron from carbonaceous ironstone, smelted in the manner now practised at Scotch works, the labour is very severe. This metal melting at a low temperature and containing the largest per-centage of carbon, is brought to the malleable state with the greatest difficulty. Its extreme fluidity, the absence of a good cinder for its protection, and the frequent presence of sulphur, lengthen the process, add to the waste, and reduce the quality.

Puddling hot iron direct from the refinery has also been practised, but it is doubtful if the advantages from this mode of working can ever be such as to cause its extensive adoption. The crude iron, after being refined, is run into a puddling furnace and worked in the usual manner. The invention is a very old one, having been first tried nearly half a century ago. A due separation of the metal from the cinder of the finery appears to be the principal difficulty in this mode of working. In the ordinary finery the metal and cinder escape together from the hearth, but by this plan the metal only is allowed to enter the puddling furnace, the cinder being obtained in a separate running. Close attention is required to be paid to the separation; if cinder enters the furnace along with the metal, the conversion into malleable iron is rendered more difficult, while the escape of metal along with the cinder results in a direct loss.

Puddling with steam has been several times experimentally tried. The original experiments were made at the Dowlais works, where the plan was in operation at several furnaces for some months. The invention was considered at the time to be a decided improvement, producing a superior quality of iron and a larger quantity weekly. The steam was brought down to the surface of the iron by a row of vertical telescopic pipes passing through the roof of the furnace, their depression and elevation being under the control of the puddler. On the withdrawal of the heat, the steam was directed on the fluid-cinder until it was cooled down to a pasty consistency, when it was raked up against the back, sides, and bridge of the furnace to fill up any cavity that may have been burned during the working of the heat. This operation on the cinder, enabling it to be used instead of clay or limestone, was considered a decided improvement to the quality of the iron, a less quantity of earthy matter combining with it during the puddling.

After an extensive trial, however, it was discovered that the advantages were not commensurate with the expense of applying and maintaining the apparatus. As the value of the invention was practically tested before the patent was secured, its abandonment shortly afterwards may require some explanation.

In the first experiments made, the value of the discovery was considered as established by the large produce obtained from a furnace working on this plan, amounting to 28 tons weekly, by the improvement discerned in the quality, and by the capability of substituting the cinders treated with steam for the clay and limestone previously used for repairing. When applied, however, to a considerable number of furnaces, the average weekly produce was not greatly in excess of that obtained before its application, the average quality was not superior, while the substitution of the cinder for other materials could not always be depended on. Having witnessed the whole of these experiments, we are of opinion (and that opinion is unshaken by the apparent success attending the plan in some recent trials), that the success which was ascribed to the use of steam, was entirely due to the superior abilities of the workmen at the furnaces selected for trial. In this we are borne out by the observation of subsequent years. We do not consider a measure of success attending any mere experiment of a few weeks' duration in such an operation as puddling as trustworthy evidence of the value of an invention. There are workmen who with certain qualities of iron will bring out nearly the weight charged and obtain from a furnace 28 or 30 tons, whilst others are working with a loss of 1¼ cwts. to the ton, and are unable to make 20 tons of inferior bars weekly. Hence, in experiments requiring manual labour for their successful performance, we are disposed to make large deductions from published reports for the superior skill of the workmen selected.

A steaming apparatus combined with a blast has been used experimentally. The more rapid decarburization of the metal, by passing a current of hot air over it, has also been tried and abandoned. Improvement in quality and other advantages were expected to follow from its use, but were not realised in practice.

The employment of a heated blast directed in minute jets on the surface of the iron was also tried, but eventually given up, as causing an excessive waste by the increased oxydation of the metal.

In the early puddling furnaces the body between the ash-pit and the stack was filled up nearly to the level of the intended bottom with cinder or other material; above this a sand bottom was made on which the puddling was conducted. The sand bottom, however, gave way to the iron bottom, now universally adopted in preference to any other. For boldness and originality the idea of using a thin plate of cast-iron as a bottom for a furnace constructed expressly for melting crude iron has not been equalled, but without it the puddling process could not have attained its present high state of perfection. Next to the invention of puddling we look on the iron bottom as the greatest improvement effected in the operation of converting cast into malleable iron bars.

While sand bottoms were used the yield was extravagantly high, the consumption of coal in the furnace was great, and the resulting bar-iron, through mingling with a portion of the siliceous bottom, was inferior in quality. This inferiority would have been more apparent but for the employment of the ponderous forge hammers of that period. A portion of the cinder was expelled during the violent hammering to which the blooms were subjected; but as a quantity of the metal was also detached the improvement was not effected without great waste of iron. Formerly the ton of puddled bars was made with a consumption of 30 cwts. and sometimes as much as 36 cwts. of refined metal. With the present furnaces it is done with about 21 cwts., and as there has been no sensible reduction for the last twenty-five years, we must consider the substitution of iron for sand bottoms as having principally effected this great reduction.

The portions of the furnace exposed to the intense heat, and the action of the fluid metal, unprotected by cinder, are rapidly burnt away. For repairing, fire-clay is largely used in several Welsh works, while in others, calcined forge cinders are successfully employed. Cinder, when the calcination has been carried so far as to convert it into a refractory silicate of iron, is undoubtedly the best material. It does not appear, however, from experiments, that all forge cinders are equally applicable to this purpose. Such as contain a large quantity of metal, and a sparing quantity of silica, cannot be used with the same success as leaner cinders. Limestone is frequently used in boiling furnaces by the puddler in preference to any other material.

To increase the durability of the brickwork, hollow metal troughs, protected in front by a thin facing of brick, have been used with partial success. By means of a current of air circulating through them the work is kept comparatively cool. This plan has been several years in operation at the Dowlais works. The principle has been carried so far as to substitute water for air, by lining the sides and bridge of the furnace with hollow castings connected with each other containing water in circulation; greater durability was obtained, but the difficulties in the way of applying this element successfully were found too great in practice. The numerous contractions in the pipes connecting the various pieces, and the liability to leakage at the joints, render the plan an extremely dangerous one. In an experimental furnace erected with water boshes, a temporary stoppage of the water, was followed on its readmission, by a tremendous explosion, carrying away the roof and entirely demolishing the furnace. The intense heat which is communicated to the metal, if unprotected by the current of water for a few minutes only, results in the instantaneous production of volumes of steam greater than the exit-pipe can carry away in the time.

It is a matter for serious consideration whether the employment of air or water boshes is attended with any real advantage, supposing that no difficulty occurred in their application. Contrivances of this kind are usually proposed on the score of greater economy in some material. In the case of the boiling and puddling furnaces they effect a saving in the wear of the brickwork, rendering the interior of the furnace more durable, and consequently enabling the furnace to be worked with less repair; by repair we allude to such as is effected by the puddler with clay, calcined cinder, or other materials—all of which are more or less injurious to the quality of the bar-iron produced. The direct saving in brickwork may be ascertained, but the value of the improvement in quality cannot be so easily appreciated; against these advantages there must be placed the absorption of heat by the boshes.

On this point we may remark that in patents connected with the working of iron an utter ignorance of the simplest principles of ironmaking may often be seen. It is not confined to the theoretical inventor alone; the practical engineer may often be seen securing to himself an invention which, on investigation, proves to be worse than useless. This is the case with water boshes and numerous other cooling contrivances employed in the iron manufacture. In a puddling or other furnace a great heat is required to be generated quickly, and maintained with the least consumption of coal. The escape of caloric, otherwise than over the metal under operation, should be prevented by using in the construction of the inner lining as perfect a non-conductor of heat as may be available for the purpose. Fire-brick is the only material obtainable in sufficient quantity at a cheap rate. Where a thickness of nine or ten inches is employed, the heat escaping through the brickwork is not great. For this reason the furnaces are built and roofed with fire-brick, which generally lasts from three to four months in working condition. Where iron boshes are employed the temperature of the walls is brought down by the ready conduction of heat, and as a current of air cannot absorb the caloric as fast as it is communicated by the iron a current of water has been used. The principle of economising the heat evolved by the fuel is thus altogether abandoned, and facilities are afforded for its escape. In all estimates, then, of the advantages derivable from water boshes, the loss incurred by the escape of caloric in the water must be taken into consideration, as well as the loss of metal displayed by inferior yields. In the case of a blast furnace we have already seen that the heat absorbed and carried away in the water requires the expenditure of from 7 to 12 tons of coal weekly. By measuring the quantity of water, and taking its temperature before and after entering the furnace, the quantity of coal which is consumed in elevating it to the higher temperature may be readily ascertained.

The consumption of iron to produce one ton of puddle bars by the boiling process varies with the quality of the pigs, and to some extent with the quality of the coal. The yield of good forge pigs smelted from a high burden we find to average 21 cwts. 3 qrs., with a forge of puddlers of average ability; with less able men in other forges, working under precisely similar conditions, the yield has been 22 cwts. 3 qrs. 14 lbs. If the conditions are very favourable and the puddler skilful, the ton of puddle bars can be produced from 21 cwts. 1 qr. of pigs.

The yield of the iron from carbonaceous ore is probably worse than that from any other description. From the working of the large forges at the Monkland and Dandyvan works, we find that the consumption of pigs in these establishments in the boiling process averages 23 cwts. 3 qrs. 19 lbs. per ton of puddle bars.

The ton of puddled bars may be produced by the puddling process with a consumption of 21 cwts. 1 qr. of refined metal. This is the average consumption in a forge of sixteen furnaces worked by men of fair average ability. All circumstances being favourable, a ton can be produced with 20 cwts. 3 qrs. of metal. But taking the average of eighty-five furnaces over twenty-two years, we find the yield to average 21 cwts. 1 qr. 20 lbs.

The consumption of coal is subject to similar variation with a bituminous coal yielding much flame; the consumption with superior workmen will average 14 cwts. per ton of boiled iron bars. With a less inflammable coal it will rise to 18 cwts., and with the coals mined on the edge of the anthracite basin 22 cwts. is near the average. The weekly consumption of coal at the furnace is nearly the same, whatever varieties of iron may be under operation, so that with the kinds most difficult of conversion the yield per ton is increased in the same ratio as the make is reduced. Inferior puddlers will burn 4 to 5 cwts. per ton more than able men. The double boiling furnace effects a considerable saving of fuel if successfully managed. The yield of coal is nearly one-fourth less than with single furnaces.

The consumption of fuel in puddling refined metal is smaller than with pigs. With coal of good quality and suitable for the purpose the ton of puddle bars is produced with a consumption of 10 cwts. only; proceeding, however, to the semi-anthracite coal district, the consumption rises to 17 and 18 cwts. per ton.

A more perfect combustion of the coal, resulting in a slight reduction in the quantity used, has been produced by introducing into the fire-place above the fuel atmospheric air for burning the gaseous products. This invention requires closed ash-pits for its successful application; the air supplied to the coal above and below the bars is heated in flues underneath and at the sides of the furnace. The mixing of the gases and air is effected by a perforated divisional bridge through which the heat passes to the body of the furnace. Irons melting at a low temperature have been worked with a considerable saving of fuel, but with the harder kinds the obstructions caused to the draught by the bridge renders the furnace less manageable, and the loss in the yield of iron is of far greater value than any saving of coal.

The horizontal area of the chimney-flue at the junction of the stack with the furnace is mainly dependent on the character of the coal. With the highly bituminous varieties, which swell considerably during their combustion, and by lying close in the grate cause an obstruction to the draught, the flue in this place—or, as it is termed by builders, the "take-up"—is made about 18 inches square; the grate measuring 2 feet 8 inches by 3 feet 9 inches. This is at the rate of 32 inches of flue to each superficial foot of grate. At the Hirwain works, where the coal is of a semi-anthracitic nature, producing little flame, and increasing very slightly in bulk during combustion, the take-up is 17 inches by 10 inches, for grates 2 feet 4 inches by 3 feet 5 inches; equal to 21 inches to each foot of grate.

The area of the take-up is regulated also by the skill of the puddler. A good workman will prefer it contracted; but an inferior hand desires an increased area. To a workman less skilful in the manipulation of the iron, the enlarged area affords greater control over the draught, but at the expense of the iron under operation, a portion of which is thus oxydised and lost. The maintaining of the take-up unaltered is considered of the first importance with puddlers, and where it is constructed of fire-brick its enlargement after a week's work requires that it should be taken down and renewed. Sandstone, from its greater durability, has been adopted at some works. If the take-up be not reconstructed of the original size, the yield of metal becomes worse as the area is enlarged. Hence, with a forge of good workmen, we find that as the time approaches for repairing, the yield of iron per ton is augmented.

The area of the grate is dependent, in a great measure, on the quality of the coals. At the Hirwain forges an area of 8 feet is adopted as sufficient with their coal; but at the other forge belonging to the same works, and working iron from the same blast furnaces, we find the grates averaging 10 feet in area. From the very different qualities of the coals, however, the lesser area of grate at Hirwain burns a greater quantity than the large grates at the Forest works, although the area of the take-up in the latter furnace is nearly twice that in the former.

The make of a boiling furnace is dependent on the skill of the puddler, the quality of iron operated on, and the general character of the coal. Where these are favourable the weekly make will not fall short of 21 tons, and the average may be estimated at 18 tons. This, however, is greatly above the production in some districts. The Staffordshire furnaces, for instance, do not usually average more than 10 tons weekly.

The lesser make of the Staffordshire furnaces may be explained by the shorter time they are at work, and the slower rate of working practised by the puddlers. In the Welsh district, with an abundant supply of the raw materials, iron and coal, the furnace is under work one hundred and forty hours weekly, the only stoppage being four hours on Saturday evening and the whole of Sunday. In Staffordshire the furnaces are lit on Monday evening and let out early on Saturday, the working period seldom exceeding one hundred and four hours weekly. From keeping the furnaces longer at work each week the Welsh ironmasters are enabled to turn out a comparatively large quantity of iron with a limited number of furnaces. The yield of metal is believed to be improved, while there can be no question but that the yield of coal is considerably diminished. A certain quantity is expended every week in getting up the heat. The consumption in this way for each ton of iron will be in an inverse ratio to the weekly make.

The make of the double boiling furnace averages 36 tons weekly. Working on hot iron from the blast furnace the make is as high as 46 tons weekly. Similar furnaces at the Chillington forges, Staffordshire, produce about 28 tons weekly.

The make of puddling furnaces, working on all refined metal, depends very much on the skill of the puddler. With first-rate workmen, and iron and coal favourable, the produce will reach 28 tons; with inferior hands the make will be about 21 tons. Taking the average of eighteen years' puddling, we find that the make of puddle bars from five forges was 23 tons per week for each furnace at work.

SECTION XVII.

HAMMERS AND SQUEEZERS.

THE puddle balls are delivered by the helper puddler to the shingler, who shapes them into blooms preparatory to passing them between the puddling rolls.

The operation of blooming was formerly performed with heavy hammers; these consolidated the balls by repeated blows and expelled a large portion of the cinder. During the hammering the bloom was placed endways, receiving a couple of blows in that position to "upset it," or condense the particles of metal longitudinally. It is generally considered that where quality is an object, no substitute has been discovered for the hammering. But in yield, the principal object looked to in the manufacture of much of the bar-iron of the present day, the modern reciprocating squeezer is superior.

The substructure of a forge-hammer (Pls. LXII., LXIII., Figs. 392-407), usually consists of a solid timber bedding, containing from 1000 to 1500 cubic feet of oak, capped by a cast-iron bed-plate measuring about 24 feet by 7 feet, and weighing from 10 to 12 tons. Two standards, weighing about three tons, for carrying the helve are fixed on the bed-plate in strong jaws, and a third, also of nearly equal weight, for carrying the cam-ring shaft. The helve is T-shaped in plan, and measures about 8 feet long by 6 feet wide at the centre of vibration, and 2 feet deep by 12 inches wide in the middle. It weighs from 5 to 7 tons. At one end it has a recess for receiving the hammer-face, which measures 18 inches square at the lower side. Standing on the bed-plate, under the centre of the hammer-face, is the anvil-block, weighing from 5 to 6 tons, having an anvil-face on its upper side similar to the hammer-face. The helve and its hammer were lifted by a revolving cam-ring, 5 feet in diameter, having wipers or catches on its circumference; these caught in the point of the helve, lifted it up, and passing around, permitted it to fall again on the bloom under operation.

The great strength of these hammers, and the weight of the blows given, may be partly understood from the weight of the castings used in the construction of one of medium size: Bed, 11 tons; helve standards, including brasses, 3 tons; helve, 5 tons 10 cwts.; hammer-face, 15 cwts.; anvil-block, 5 tons 10 cwts.; anvil-face, 16 cwts.; standards under cam-ring shaft, 2 tons 10 cwts.; cam-ring shaft, 12-inch bearings, 2 feet 4 inches diameter in the middle, 7 tons; cam-ring, 4 tons 5 cwts.; four wipers, 24 cwts. . total, 41 tons 10 cwts.

When not working, the helve was propped up clear of the cam-ring on an iron bar made to fit under a projection cast for that purpose. The puddle ball having been placed on the anvil-face, the helve is lifted off the prop by a boy holding a small iron block underneath the point, and so bringing it within the action of the wipers; the prop being withdrawn, the helve descends on the ball to be lifted again by the succeeding wiper. The height of the lift depends on the relative position of the helve and cam-ring, and provision is made in the standards for any alteration that may be deemed necessary; for a hammer of the dimensions described, the lift would average 16 inches. The gearing on the cam-ring shaft in connexion with the engine or other prime mover, is proportioned to 18 or 19 revolutions of the cam-ring per minute; consequently, with 4 wipers in the cam, the number of blows ranges from 72 to 76 per minute. The puddle balls receive from 15 to 25 blows, occupying from 18 to 30 seconds, to convert them into blooms.

The squeezer has now almost entirely supplanted the hammer in the forge. Its first cost is not half so great, the cost of maintenance is diminished in a similar ratio, and if the quality of the iron treated is not improved, the quantity produced is greater. The squeezers commonly employed have a reciprocating motion, and are distinguished as single and double-ended. The single have but one anvil and hammer (Pl. LIII., Figs. 304, 305; Pl. LV., Figs. 320-330), the double have two hammers and two anvils. (Pl. LXI., Figs. 387-391.)

For a double-ended squeezer, the cast-iron bed-plate is laid on two longitudinal balks of timber; it measures about 20 feet by 5 feet, and weighs 6 tons. On one end strong standards, having heavy brasses, are securely fixed to it for carrying a dip crank. Near the centre, two other standards firmly secured to the bed-plate, carry the squeeze arm. This consists of a V-shaped lever moving on a centre gudgeon, one of its ends being connected by a sweep-rod to the crank. Recesses are cast in it to receive hammer-faces, 3 feet long by 1 foot 6 inches wide. On the bed-plate a strong horizontal frame carries the two anvil-faces, each measuring 6 feet by 18 inches. When the lever is mounted and in a horizontal position, the inside end of each hammer-face will be 5 inches, and the outer end 16 inches from the anvil-face. If the crank has a 16-inch stroke, these distances will be diminished to 4 and 11 inches respectively at the bottom centre, and increased to 6 and 21 inches at the top centre.

The weight of the various pieces composing a double squeezer, such as we have described, may be stated as follows: Bedding, 6 tons; crank-shaft standards, 2 tons 10 cwts.; crank, 12 cwts.; standard under anvils, 4 tons; centre standards, 2 tons 16 cwts.; squeezer arm, 3 tons 5 cwts.; anvils, 1 ton 16 cwts.; hammers, 14 cwts.: total castings, 21 tons, 13 cwts.

The puddle ball is delivered by the helper puddler to the shingler, who moves it forward on the squeezer anvil until it arrives in contact with the hammer-face. At each stroke of the squeezer-arm the ball is flattened by the pressure, and a portion of the cinder expelled; during the up stroke it is turned over by the shingler towards the fulcrum of the arm, where it is reduced to a bloom about 5 inches in diameter by 18 inches long, after having received in its progress from 15 to 20 strokes. The upsetting is performed at the extreme end of the squeezer, where its elevation above the anvil gives sufficient height for the bloom to be set up on end and pressed.

The squeezer-crank revolves from 45 to 80 times per minute, according to the speed at which the rolls are set; the last is a high speed; 56 to 60 revolutions is more advantageous.

The time occupied in squeezing each ball averages 25 seconds when the crank revolves 60 times per minute, giving 25 blows altogether to each bloom.

The hammering and squeezing processes differ from each other, inasmuch that in the former the ball is shaped by the impact of the descending hammer; whereas in the latter, the object is attained by simple pressure. In erecting a hammer, the chief requisites are a foundation that shall withstand the concussion, and machinery capable of lifting and supporting the helve at the rapid rate of working practised. For this purpose the castings are made very heavy, and weigh as we have already stated above 40 tons, of which nearly 19 tons are in motion. In the construction of the squeezer, the tensile strength of the cast-iron employed is severely tried. The crank and centre standards, sweep-rod, and squeezer-arm are subject to enormous strain, and require to be made proportionately strong. From the experience obtained in the working of nine puddling forges, we learn that the aggregate sectional area of the crank standards in their weakest place should not be less than 136 inches; the centre standards, 212 inches; and the wrought straps on the sweep-rod, 12 inches.

With the weights and proportions given, the duration of the respective moving parts we find to be as follows, for a forge of sixteen furnaces: Squeezer-arm, 10 months; anvils, 6 months; hammers, 11 months; cranks, 3 months; brasses to cranks, 3 weeks. The duration of the hammers and anvils may be increased by casting in them a small wrought-iron pipe bent in a serpentine form for keeping them cool by a current of water, and thus preventing the adhesion of the cinders. The inlet and outlet pipes of the hammer are brought over the centre gudgeon where the vibration is least, and united by a flexible connexion to other pipes. By using water in circulation through them, the hammer and anvil will work nearly twice the usual quantity of iron before requiring renewal.

Motion is usually communicated to the squeezer by coupling the crank direct to the end of the bottom roughing-roll of the puddling train; in a few works shafting, independent of the rolls, is employed, and the squeezer driven at a reduced speed. The strain is taken off the rolls in this arrangement, but the greater number of bearings in motion and the additional spur gear increases the resistance to the working of the forge, and probably balances any advantage that might otherwise accrue from a separate connexion.

The connexion of the squeezer-crank with the end of the roll ought at all times to be made by means of a connecting-spindle, as long as circumstances will allow. Connecting direct to the roll end is objectionable, though it is generally done; the lifting of the squeezer-crank causes the roughing-rolls to wear unequally, and throws an unnecessary strain on the necks. By employing an intervening spindle this is avoided, and the durability of both rolls and crank is increased. Greater facilities are also afforded by this arrangement for changing rolls, and the stand for the rougher is made more durable by keeping the squeezer farther off. In a forge where the cranks were connected by crabs directly to the roughing-rolls, placing a short spindle between increased their average duration from six weeks to five months.

Various modifications of, or substitutes for, the common lever squeezer have been brought out from time to time, and used to a limited extent. The first in the list was an American invention. It consisted of a circular cast-iron well, containing a revolving cylinder of equal depth, placed eccentrically; the least distance between the two was equal to the diameter of the finished bloom, while at the widest the breadth was equal to the diameter of the largest size ball. Motion having been communicated to the inner cylinder by strong bevil gearing in connexion with the engine, the ball is placed in the machine, the inner cylinder, armed with short teeth on its circumference, seizes it, and during its revolution, by a combined squeezing and rolling motion, the ball is reduced to a bloom of the desired dimensions, and delivered at the opposite side to the rougher.

This machine is, taken altogether, a specimen of great ingenuity, but in practice the bevil gearing and the liability to derangement are great drawbacks to its employment; besides which no effectual means are provided for the upsetting of the bloom, an operation which cannot be dispensed with if the quantity is to remain unimpaired.

An apparatus of a similar kind working vertically is also in use in a few works (Pl. LXIII., Fig. 408). The revolving cylinder is mounted on two strong cast-iron frames, between which a semi-cylindrical casting is fixed eccentrically to the cylinder. The conversion of the ball into a bloom is effected in the same way as with the American machine, and is subject to the same defects. In one erected at the Plymouth works an attempt was made to manage the upsetting by means of side blocks acted on by springs; self-feeding and delivering machinery was also provided, altogether it probably was the most complete of its kind. Its working, however, was not satisfactory and the reciprocating squeezer, formerly employed, was restored to favour.

In another substitute for the ordinary squeezer, the blooming of the ball is accomplished by passing it between three eccentric rolls, which during their revolution, by compression, extend it laterally to the size for the rougher. The three rolls work on bearing brasses in a strong framing fitted with adjusting screws, and are coupled together by nuts and spur gearing.

There are some features common to all the substitutes yet offered for the common squeezer which have not been sufficiently considered by their inventors. Their first cost is from four to ten times as great; and the effectual upsetting of the bloom is accomplished only by using complex machinery. This large outlay for an apparatus which at best does no more than the simpler machine, is an important consideration with ironmasters. With the greater first cost, occasioned by the numerous working and wearing parts, the cost of maintenance is increased in nearly the same proportion. Generally speaking, too, the improved squeezers are not erected without several portions having been turned and fitted; in the event of breakage considerable delay must therefore necessarily occur in the replacement of such parts. The common squeezer, except turning the crank journals, has no fitting work whatever in its construction, and in the event of a part breaking may be got to work again in from two to three hours at the outside.

In one respect, however, the patent squeezers are certainly superior. With the reciprocating machine, if the metal in the ball appears to have been insufficiently worked by the puddler the shingler lets it stand a few seconds before squeezing. In the revolving squeezer, however, no exception is made on account of the condition of the iron, all is treated alike. The properly-worked iron passes through safely, but the labour of the inferior hand, too friable to stand the rolling motion, is torn to pieces. Hence with these squeezers the iron is required to be worked with great care or the yield is very bad—a check is thus obtained upon the men.

When the entire forge is composed of good hands, and the quality is desired to be good, the work produced will be equal, but not superior, to that produced with like care from the common squeezer. Where, however, the forge is made up of mixed hands the yield is considerably against the improved squeezers.

The proprietors of these machines state that they effect a great improvement in the quality of the iron over that produced by the old squeezer. This is very far from correct. No squeezer can improve the quality of the iron. The quality is dependent on the iron used and the ability of the puddler. If the crude iron is bad, and the puddler an indifferent hand, no squeezer ever invented can improve the quality of his work.

There is, then, this difference in the working of the old and improved squeezers, the common squeezer can shingle any description of iron successfully, but the patent squeezer can only work advantageously on well-wrought iron of superior quality. This capability on the side of the common squeezer is a great advantage to the manufacturer of the lower qualities of bar-iron.

SECTION XVIII.

PUDDLING ROLLS.

The puddle ball having been shaped by the shingler into a bloom of suitable size for the grooves of the rolls, the rougher now takes it in hand. The bloom is passed through the largest groove of the roughing rolls, then through the next smaller, until its sectional diameter is sufficiently reduced for the roller, who shifts it to the finishing rolls, and after passing it three or four times between the rolls, through as many different grooves, produces a finished puddle bar.

Two pair of rolls form the puddling train (Pls. LIII.-LX.), one pair for roughing down the bloom, the other for finishing it into a bar. The grooves used in the roughing pair are either oval, gothic, or diamond-shaped; generally the first two or three grooves are gothic and the other diamond. The finishing rolls are usually turned with grooves to produce flat bars from 3 to 7 inches wide by $\frac{1}{4}$ inch to $1\frac{1}{4}$ inches thick. For the narrow bars a pair of finishing rolls will contain a sufficient number of grooves to work iron of two widths; but for the wide bars a pair of rolls are required for each width. In some Scotch forges we observe the train composed of three pair of rolls, one for roughing and two for finishing; one of these being for narrow and one for wide bars. The employment of the second pair of finishing rolls can be attended with no advantage commensurate with their first cost, and the power expended in driving them. The single pair of finishing rolls is much simpler, and having fewer connexions there is less liability to derangement. Whenever a different width is required, the rolls may be changed in the space of thirty-five to forty minutes, and in the puddling forge, with good management, a large quantity may be rolled of each size.

In small forges and where room is an object, the roughing and finishing grooves are sometimes seen in the same pair of rolls, which are then made proportionately longer. This arrangement may be advantageous under certain circumstances, but the greater weight of rolls required to be kept in stock, and the necessity for changing such heavy rolls for every alteration of width, are objections to this plan.

The durability of the necks and brasses is greatly increased by using cinder plates. A narrow groove is sunk in the body of each roll close to the ends, and a thin wrought-iron plate inserted before lowering the top roll. (Pl. LVI., Figs. 331, 348.) By this means the cinders which otherwise get into the bearings, and grind away both iron and brass, are excluded.

The bottom roughing-roll is provided with a serrated fore-plate and rest (Pl. LX., Figs.

377-379, 381); the bottom finishing with rest and wrought-iron top and false guides. (Pls. LIX., LX., Figs. 370-375, 380.) Where water-power is employed, and there is no danger of the guides being drawn in, single guides cottered down to the rest, as in the Cyfarthfa forges, may be used. (Pl. LVI., Figs. 346, 347.) With loose guides, the catches of the coupling-crabs are constructed so that if the motion of the engine be reversed the train of rolls is disconnected. Unless this provision were made, the entrance of the cold iron guides on the backward motion would be followed by a breakage.

The puddling rolls are generally 18 inches diameter by 3 feet 6 inches long between bearings; necks, 10 inches diameter; length of roll over necks, 6 feet 6 inches. A pair will work about a month without cleaning, and will be worn out, body and flutes, in four or five months. The immense strain on the standards when rolling comparatively cold iron requires them to be of great strength. The aggregate area of metal in the two standards to each pair of rolls should be in the weakest place not less than 230 inches; and the pinion standards should be of nearly equal strength.

The puddle bar after leaving the rolls is taken by boys to the cutting-shears, which in well-arranged forges are placed opposite the finishing rolls. The general practice is to shear the bars hot, but when the lengths and sizes for the mill piles are not known, the old plan of dragging them out to the bank and shearing cold is followed. Stronger shears are then required, and the labour is performed by men.

The speed of the puddling rolls ranges from 35 to 80 revolutions per minute. The Staffordshire and Derbyshire forges probably work at the lowest speed of any in this country. The Welsh forges are driven from 50 to 80. The speed preferred by the workmen, and which is found most advantageous with all but very red short metal, may be placed at 56. But if the iron be very red short, a higher speed is attended with less waste. The shears may be driven at the same rate as the rolls when the latter do not exceed 56 revolutions per minute; but when they run faster, the shears should be geared so as not to exceed this number of cuts per minute.

At a speed of 80 revolutions per minute, the bar travels at the rate of $4\frac{1}{4}$ miles per hour, and at this rate the workman must follow; at a speed of 56 per minute, the bar travels at the rate of 3 miles per hour.

We subjoin in the following tables the principal dimensions of such parts of the machinery as demand special care in their construction; they are taken from forges which have been at work some years:

PUDDLING ROLLS.

DIMENSIONS OF ENGINES AND MACHINERY AT PUDDLING FORGES.

Name of Works.	Description of Engine.	Diameter of cylinder, in inches.	Length of stroke, in feet.	Number of strokes per minute.	Diameter of crank-shaft bearing, in inches.	Diameter of crank-pin, in inches.	Diameter of driving-wheel at pitch-line, in feet.	Width of teeth on face, in inches.	Thickness of rim of wheel, in inches.	Number of teeth in driving-wheel.	Pitch of teeth in driving-wheel, in inches.
Dowlais, 1......	Low-pressure condensing beam	45	7.0	22	13.5	7	12.6	15	4.3	102	4.5
2......	" " "	36	7.0	22	12.0	7	13.6	15	4.7	102	5.0
3......	High-pressure, beam "	42	6.0	20	15.5	8	15.0	19	5.0	128	4.5
4......	" horizontal	37	7.0	23	13.5	6	13.6	15	4.7	102	5.0
5......	" vertical	26	4.0	30	10.0	4	11.5	12	3.8	96	4.5
Hirwain	Low-pressure	30	6.0	20	11.0	5	15.8	14	3.0	120	5.0
Forest	Water-power	—	—	—	10.0	—	19.0	14	3.0	144	5.0

DIMENSIONS OF ENGINES AND MACHINERY AT PUDDLING FORGES—(continued).

Name of Works.	Diameter of spur-wheel at pitch-line, in inches.	Width of spur-wheel over flange, in inches.	Thickness of rim of spur-wheel, in inches.	Diameter of fly-wheel shaft bearings, in inches.	Diameter of fly-wheel, in feet.	Section of metal in rim of fly-wheel, in square inches.	Number of teeth in spur-wheel.	Revolutions of fly-wheel per minute.	Number of trains driven by engine.	Revolutions of rolls per minute.
Dowlais, 1......	5.2	21	—	12.0	15.5	144	42	53	2	53
2......	4.3	21	—	12.0	16.0	144	33	68	2	68
3......	4.9	24	—	12.0	18.0	144	42	61	2	61
4......	4.3	21	—	12.0	15.3	144	33	71	2	71
5......	—	17	—	8.5	12.0	108	25	114	2	—
Hirwain	—	20	3	9.5	16.0	144	26	—	1	—
Forest	—	20	3	9.5	16.0	144	26	—	1	—

DIMENSIONS OF ENGINES AND MACHINERY AT PUDDLING FORGES—(continued).

Name of Works.	Diameter of shear-spindles.	Revolutions of shear-spindle, and cuts of shears, per minute.	Weight of engines, framing under the level of the crank-shaft.	Number of boilers.	Description of boiler.	Surface of boiler exposed to the heat of fire.	Area of fire-grate.	Consumption of coal per twenty-four hours.	Pressure on boilers, in pounds per square inch, above atmosphere.
Dowlais, 1......	8	54	46	3	Cylindrical.	1900	142	9.5	22
2......	10	22	48	3	"	1134	156	9.5	22
3......	8	41	216	3	"	1100	142	10.0	50
4......	8	59	94	4	"	1296	220	14.0	62
5......	8	57	22	2	"	648	112	8.0	75
Hirwain	—	—	37	—	—	—	200	9.0	7
Forest	—	—	43	—	—	—	—	—	—

SECTION XIX.

HEATING OR BALLING FURNACE.

THE conversion of the puddle bars into the various forms of finished iron met with in commerce is done by heating them in furnaces, commonly called "balling furnaces" (Pls. LXV., LXVI., LXVII.)—but, perhaps, "heating furnaces," the name by which they are distinguished in some works, is more appropriate—and afterwards rolling them out into bars, or plates, of such sections and dimensions as may be desired.

The heating furnace is very similar to the puddling furnace; it has a chimney of like dimensions, but is generally 8 or 9 inches wider and 2 feet longer, for working the larger sizes of iron. The area of the fireplace averages 12 feet. The cast-iron bottom is placed 13 or 14 inches below the working door, and on it a sand bottom is laid, falling from the door, both towards the back of the furnace and towards the flue. Between the body of the furnace and the fireplace a bridge, 9 inches thick, is carried up to within 14 inches of the roof; and at the stack end the sand bottom is gradually rounded off to meet the floor of the flue. The iron bottom is not indispensable, though generally used. If the bridge be carried up from the bottom of the ash-pit, the inside space may be filled up with any convenient material to a level for the sand bottom. A stock hole and working door complete the heating furnace.

A number of puddle bars of a suitable length, generally from 3 to $4\frac{1}{2}$ feet, are placed together to form a "pile," the sectional dimension of which varies with the size of iron ordered, from 3 inches to 10 inches square. If the piles are made 3 feet 6 inches long and 7 inches wide, by 8 inches high—a common size for railway bars and the larger kinds of merchant iron—the baller charges four at a time for a heat, by placing them singly on a flat iron bar, called a "peeler," and sliding them into the furnace, taking due care not to displace the arrangement of the bars. When charged the four piles will lie nearly across the furnace, radiating from the door, the ends towards the back lying 6 or 8 inches lower than those nearest the door.

A little fine coal is thrown around the door, to exclude the cold air, and the damper opened to its widest extent. The grate is cleaned, fresh fuel added, and the fire urged to the production of an intense heat. After charging, the baller's chief occupation is watching the piles, and turning them so that they may be heated equally, and be brought to a welding heat in the least time. When this point is approached, a portion of the iron becomes oxydized, and, combining with the earthy matter, it forms a cinder, which flows over the surface of the pile, and protects it for a brief period from the further action of the air. If the operation be prolonged, the flow of cinder ceases, and the iron suffers from the oxygen of the air, losing its tenacity and property of welding.

A "heat" such as we have described will be ready in sixty minutes. The piles are then grasped by a pair of heavy tongs, and dragged on to a carriage for conveyance to the rolls. The drawing out, charging a fresh heat, and repairing the bottom, will average sixteen minutes per heat. Piles of this size weigh about 4 cwts. each. At this rate, a heating furnace will work 36 piles in the twelve hours, or 83 tons of iron per week.

For the smaller sizes of merchant bars the piles are made about 18 inches long, 3 inches wide, and 2¼ to 3 inches thick. The heat is composed of 16 or 18 piles, which take from twenty-eight to thirty minutes in reaching a welding heat. The time occupied in drawing out the heat, recharging and repairing, averages twenty-one minutes. A furnace upon piles of such a size working at this rate heats about 31 tons weekly.

The smallest sizes of bars are rolled from solid bolts of manufactured iron, termed "billets," measuring 12 to 20 inches long by 1¼ to 1¾ in their diameter. Smaller heating furnaces are employed, and from 25 to 30 billets are heated at once. To economise time and reduce the waste of iron, which otherwise would be very great with the smallest sizes, cold billets are charged nearly as fast as the hot ones are withdrawn. Furnaces working on billets for guide iron, heat from 15 to 25 tons a week, according to the size of the finished bar.

The loss of weight during the heating process is dependent chiefly on the skill of the baller. With care and a fair average quality of iron the loss will not exceed 80 lbs. per ton on the large piles, 130 lbs. on the smaller sizes, and 210 lbs. on the guide-rolled iron. The yield or consumption of puddle iron to produce one ton of finished iron is ordinarily much greater than this, but having accurately weighed the iron before and after heating, we find that perfectly sound bars may be produced with a loss no greater than that we have stated.

The consumption of coal in heating the large size piles averages 7 cwts. to the ton of iron charged; in the smaller sizes, 10 cwts.; and in the smallest merchant bars, 13 cwts.

The formation of the pile, in the arrangement of the pieces, their size, weight, and quality is a subject of much importance in the manufacture of sound bar iron. The form of the finished bar, and the purpose to which it is to be applied, require to be carefully attended to in the piling, together with the local character of the iron about to be employed.[*]

---

[*] The principal purpose to which puddle bar is now applied is the fabrication of railway bars. Of late years English railway companies have been in the habit of minutely specifying the qualities of the iron, its arrangement in the pile, length and thickness, and mode of working. The railroad engineer, whose acquaintance with the manufacture must necessarily be limited, dictates to the experienced manufacturer the plan to be pursued in the manufacture of the rails. A superiority in quality is supposed to be ensured by these precautions. Railway companies, however, commit a great error when they undertake to define the section of pile and mode of rolling.

In the first place, by specifying that certain proportions of No. 2 and No. 3 iron are to form the pile, they treat the local appellations of Nos. 1, 2, or 3 as defining irons of particular quality and value, instead of being, as they are, simply convenient terms used by the manufacturer to distinguish iron that has been rolled this number of times. The quality of the iron is modified, but not determined, by the number of reheatings and rollings. The No. 2 of one manufacturer may surpass in strength, fibre, and other qualities the No. 3 of other makers; and, in the fabrication of railway bars, might be quite as advantageous as that of the higher denomination. But the railway companies require the extra process to be gone through, which entails so much additional

A rail pile for the common qualities of rails is usually composed of a bottom piece of No. 2 iron 6 or 7 inches wide, by 1 inch thick, on which 18 or 20 pieces of puddle iron 3 to 3½ wide by ¼ thick are placed, capped by a second piece of No. 2 iron of the same size as the first. If intended for flanch rails, square bars of soft iron are added to the plate of No. 2 to form the flange. The iron for these bars is worked for the purpose from a burden containing little or no red ore or refinery cinder. Thin and broad flanched rails cannot be worked unless attention is paid in the piling to ensure the presence of a very soft tenacious iron in the flange. The greater diameter of the rolls at the body of the rail dragging the thin portion through, throws a strain upon the flanges in the finishing grooves sufficiently great, sometimes as to tear them off. In heating, also, care is required that the pieces to form the flange are not over-heated.

If the rail is large, or the metal unequally distributed, the process of shaping is frequently commenced in the pile, which is made of a diminished width at the head.

For the double-headed, the bridge and some other varieties of railway iron, a common pile is made. Such a proportion of superior iron being used as the specification requires or the manufacturer deems necessary. A portion of the centre is frequently made with pieces of rails cut into short lengths for remanufacture. From their irregular section, however, they do not work in well with flat bars; and to render the pile more solid puddle bars are rolled of such a form as will, when combined with the rails, leave the smallest interstices.

In the manufacture of merchant iron of No. 2, or common quality, the pile is composed entirely of puddle bars laid one on the other. For larger piles, and where the width greatly exceeds the height, a double row of bars is employed; in all cases the pile is rectangular.

The piles for No. 3 iron are made in the same manner, but with No. 2 iron instead of puddle bars. The superiority of No. 3 to No. 2 is consequently due to the additional re-heating and rolling, by which the fibre and general quality of some irons are considerably improved.

In the manufacture of particular orders, in order to develop the fibre as much as possible, the pile is made short and thick, so that in the subsequent great elongation by rolling the iron may become of a dense fibrous character. For this purpose the short thick pile is evidently superior to any other form, but in consequence of its requiring a longer time to heat, the outside gets burnt before the interior is brought to a welding heat; the manufactured iron consequently is not equal to that produced with a larger pile—it is rarely sound in

expense that the superior No. 3 cannot then compete in price with the inferior. Consequently, by specifying the number of the iron to be used the railway companies unintentionally secure for themselves the inferior rails which they are anxious to avoid.

In the second place, when a specification of the iron to be used accompanies the order for the rails, their production is reduced to a mere contract to supply rails according to such specification, and the manufacturer is, consequently, relieved of any responsibility as to the fitness and sufficiency of the iron for the purpose intended. The manufacturer prefers working with a specification, because if the manufactured bars wear badly, or otherwise prove defective, he is absolved from the consequences.

The Continental railways, constructed under the superintendence of local engineers, adopt a more rational course. They stipulate that the finished bar shall bear certain tests without injurious deflection, or opening of the fibre, leaving the quality of the iron used and mode of working to the judgment of the manufacturer; and he, by contracting for certain qualities in the finished bar, is compelled to use such iron as will ensure their presence.

the centre, and its tensile strength, if tested, will be found to have suffered by the over heating of the external parts.

In the manufacture of large bolts, the pile is sometimes made of a number of bars of a wedge-like section arranged radially around a central bar, forming a cylinder, kept together by thin iron bands. This is heated in the balling furnace and rolled into a bolt of the desired diameter and length. By some mechanical engineers this mode of piling is supposed to ensure a more solid bolt than the ordinary rectangular pile of flat bars. In practice, however, we find it difficult to produce a sound bar from a pile of this kind. Since the centre bar can only receive its heat by conduction from the radial bars, it cannot reach a welding heat till long after the outer parts, and the pile is generally drawn before the centre has arrived at a proper temperature. The result is that in passing through the rolls the radial bars are firmly welded to each other at their circumference, but very rarely throughout their entire depth; the central bar is elongated with the rest, but is not welded to them. Having watched the manufacture and subsequent working of several large bars on this plan, in no instance when the iron came into the smith's hands did we find the centre welded to the exterior bars. In a shaft so made, a severe twist disconnected the piece and displayed the centre bar detached from the other part. For piston rods and other purposes where the tensile strength alone is brought into use, the imperfect weld is not generally noticed; but in four piston rods which broke under our immediate observation, the separate existence of the centre bar was evident.

In piling, care should be taken to have the various pieces forming the pile of the same thickness as nearly as may be practicable. If they differ greatly, both the risk of unsoundness and the loss of iron during the heating will be increased. The thinnest pieces are hot first, and if the pile is drawn at once the weld with the thick bars is rarely sound. On the other hand, if the pile is retained in the furnace until the thick pieces are properly heated, the thinner are over-heated, deprived of the protecting cinder, and weld with difficulty. Sufficient attention is seldom paid to this point in the manufacture of railway and other bars. We consider it to be the cause of more than one half of the lamination observable in our railway iron. Our opinion is founded on the wear of rails which were manufactured from various qualities of iron, and rolled in different ways, and afterwards subjected to very heavy traffic under our immediate observation. By experiments on a large number of railway bars, piled in various ways, we found that in more than two-thirds of them the weld of pieces above the medium size was imperfect. It is not just to blame the manufacturer for this imperfect weld under the present system of defining in the specification the sizes of the iron. It is scarcely possible to produce a sound rail when bars of very different thicknesses are required to be used.

By repeated trials we have found that to heat a pile 6 inches thick, composed of 2 widths and 10 thicknesses of puddle iron, 3 inches by $\frac{1}{2}$-inch, in an ordinary balling furnace so that the whole was brought to a welding heat, required on an average fifty-two minutes. We further ascertained that to heat a pile of a single width of puddle bars in the same furnace and exposed to a similar temperature required twenty-seven minutes, and smaller sizes in the same proportion. By these and other experiments, we ascertained that the time required for heating a pile or mass of iron was nearly in the same ratio as its thickness. Hence the necessity for building the pile of pieces of the same thickness. In a smith's fire, or in a forge working on uses the difference in the thickness of pieces of iron to be welded together is allowed for by partially heating the thicker piece before the other is charged; a mode of working inapplicable to the rapid rate of execution practised in rolling mills.

For some kinds of iron faggoted piles are employed; these are formed in different ways, often by making a box pile of iron plates and filling the interior with clippings of plates, old chains, or other scraps. They are heated and then rolled, or what is preferable, hammered well under a heavy hammer, and reheated before being rolled. Hammering improves the quality of scrap iron.

Angle iron, tramplates, and T iron, are usually rolled from piles having a portion of the puddle bars (or No. 2 iron if for best qualites,) cut into short lengths, and laid across the pile. If for angle iron the top and bottom pieces are laid longitudinally, and the centre of the pile built of layers of transverse and longitudinal bars alternately. The power of the iron to resist a lateral strain is increased by cross-piling, and its structure is rendered more homogeneous.

Bars for manufacture into tin plates are required to be of good quality, seldom under best cable; the piles are usually made as for ordinary bars, but some manufacturers require them to be built with layers of bars laid crosswise. Plate iron which is to be manufactured into hollow ware and Birmingham goods, known by the rollers as "blackplate," is piled in a similar manner. Large quantities of tinned iron plates have been made from rail ends and mill crops, but such plates cannot be moulded into the more intricate forms of tinware.

Boiler plates, if manufactured of best iron, are invariably rolled from piles having alternate layers laid crosswise. A cheaper method is now extensively adopted: it consists in hammering two blooms together and rolling them direct into a plate. As the blooms are void of fibre, the extension in both directions in rolling results in the production of a plate equally strong in either direction. The quality, however, is no higher than No. 2 iron. For boiler plate, it is impossible to exercise too much care in the selection of the crude iron, as well as in the subsequent stages of the manufacture.

We are of opinion that cross-piling to a greater or less extent is advantageous in the manufacture of railway bars. In some experimental trials made with bars rolled from piles having one or more cross layers the stiffness was materially increased, and the metal when broken for examination, had the appearance of cast-steel. By attention to the position of the cross pieces in the pile, rails were made from a single quality of iron, on one side soft and porous, while the other side was hard and crystalline.

MILL HAMMERS.

Hammering certainly improves the quality of bar iron. The rapid consolidation under the blows of a heavy mill hammer expels the cinder while the iron is at a sufficiently high temperature to permit its escape. If the hammering be omitted, the pressure exerted on the pile in rolling forces out a portion, but in consequence of the reduction of temperature in the last grooves, the remaining cinder is wrapped up in the iron. Hammered iron is more homogeneous, has a greater specific gravity, and is superior in point of strength. In the manufacture of the best qualities of iron, this operation should never be omitted.

The mill hammer (Pl. LXIV.) is very similar to the forge hammer, but for a mill working the larger sizes of bars, the helve weighs from 7 to 8 tons. The hammer-face, which is cast fast to the helve, measures 4 feet by 18 inches; the anvil-face is made 4 feet by 2 feet. With the heavy gearing necessary, the mill hammer and connexions will weigh nearly sixty tons. The pile receives from 12 to 20 blows, occupying from 10 to 18 seconds.

The steam hammer has been employed in some mills, but for the ironmaster's purposes, it possesses no superiority over the common hammer. Where a great range in the force of the blow is required the steam hammer stands unrivalled, but in manufacturing bar iron the blooms are required to be hammered with the same force throughout. Hence the steam hammer is comparatively little used in the manufacture; it is found that a mill hammer costing only one-fifth or sixth as much, is equally efficient.

ROLLING BARS.

The train of mill rolls for large iron consists of two pairs; one for roughing, about 6 feet 6 inches long by 22 inches diameter; the other for finishing, about 3 feet 6 inches long by 18 inches diameter. The standards, spindles, and connexions, require to be as strong as those of the puddling train. The finishing roll standards are furnished with several adjusting and tightening screws for setting and maintaining the rolls in their position. Motion is communicated to the finishing rolls by a pair of pinions and leading spindles; from the bottom finishing roll a coupling spindle communicates motion to the bottom roughing roll, and by nuts keyed on the ends of the pair to the top roughing roll. Driving the roughing rolls by connexion with the bottom finishing roll only, permits of larger roughing rolls being used at any time, an advantage in rolling large orders.

Railway bars are rolled with rolls having flat and edge grooves alternately. The pile is first passed with the bars of which it is built on their flat; in the next the pile is turned on its side and passed through with the bars edgeways. The first four or five grooves are flat-bottomed, diminishing slightly in width as they deepen, that the pile may freely deliver itself during rolling. The sides and bottom are notched to catch the iron; but if large rolls are used, the necessity for notching—an operation on the rolls which should at all times be avoided—is much reduced. For the ready admission of the pile, care is taken in turning the rolls that the width of the first groove is greater than the width of the pile; and that in the succeeding grooves the breadth is not less than the height of the groove through which the pile has just passed. The flat and edge system of rolling is probably the most expeditious mode that can be adopted. The pile requires less handling by the roughers, is lifted more readily by the hookers, and at all times lies flat on the rollers of the rest. Diamond-shaped grooves were formerly much used in rail rolling, and the gothic form was also used, but to a less extent.

Merchant bars are rolled with roughing rolls having flat and edge grooves, but the diamond or the gothic form produces a superior bar. The first is usually a flat-bottomed groove followed by others of a diamond or a gothic section. Grooves of the last-named form are deemed superior, and are generally used in roughing rolls for both light and heavy merchant bars. Bolts cannot well be rolled without the gothic grooves. In their formation the same principle is followed as in the flat and edge—the breadth of a groove is made greater than the height of the preceding one.

In the roughing rolls of the guide train, flat, gothic, and diamond grooves appear on the same roll, and frequently others of an oval section are added. The billet or pile to be rolled and the class of order in hand determines the kind of grooves to be used.

The finishing rolls of a rail train are turned with five or six grooves, the smallest or finishing groove being the section of the rail when hot. The allowance to be made for contraction in cooling depends on the rate of working, and the local character of the iron; from $\frac{1}{14}$th to $\frac{1}{12}$th is sufficient with iron from argillaceous ironstone, the rolls making 85 to 90 revolutions per minute. Flange rails are certainly the most difficult of manufacture.

Finishing rolls for flat bars are made with flat-bottomed grooves, but from the necessity of delivering the iron freely their sides are not parallel—the bottom of the grooves is narrower than the top. In consequence of this tapering form, the sides of the finished bar are not perfectly square. The deviation from a right angle is diminished by reversing the bar and passing it through with the upper side, the widest, down in the bottom of the groove. In thin bars this defect in form is scarcely perceptible, but in the thickest it is very apparent.

Square bars are produced with rolls having diamond-shaped grooves sunk on their surface. At the bottom the two sides of the groove form a right angle—continuing so for about half the depth, when they spread out from $\frac{1}{12}$th to $\frac{1}{8}$th of the diameter of the bar, across the angles. In the construction of the finishing rolls for square bars the same principle is followed as in the formation of the gothic grooved roughing rolls, the depth of the hole formed by the junction of the rolls being less than the width of the succeeding smaller hole. This, in short, may be stated to be a fundamental principle of rolling. The breadth of the groove is at all times in excess of its depth; if the two dimensions were equal it would be impossible to reduce the pile as is now done from a square of 6 inches to one of 2 inches. To arrive at the reduced dimension the pile is passed in succession through a number of grooves each of a sectional area less than the preceding, but of less dimensions in one direction only. The rolls compress the iron only in a vertical direction; they exercise no power laterally, consequently the reduction is thrown on the bottom of the groove. At each rolling the depth of the pile is diminished, and in order that the iron may be compressed every way, the pile is turned partly round at each succeeding groove so that the horizontal becomes the vertical dimension, on which the pressure acts. The difference in section between successive grooves is technically termed the "draught."

In rolling squares the bar is passed through two or three grooves in the finishing rolls gradually diminishing in size before entering the last. A portion of the reduction is effected in the finishing rolls, the bar in each succeeding groove being turned over one side of the square; through the last groove the bar is passed two or three times, turned a quarter round at each time in order to ensure a perfectly square bar. If passed through only once, as in the previous grooves, the finished bar would possess nearly the same section as the groove, which is of a diamond form.

Large bolts are rolled with grooves approaching a semicircular section. At the bottom they are formed to the radius of the bar which they are intended to produce; at the surface of the roll the width is increased from $\frac{1}{12}$th to an $\frac{1}{8}$th over that due to the diameter of the bar. The horizontal extension of the grooves being nearly similar to that in rolls for square and gothic bars. The rolling of bolts of a large size is probably one of the most laborious operations connected with the rolling of iron. The bar is passed five or six times through the last groove to produce the requisite section. The lateral extension of the grooves produces an oval bar, which is placed in the finishing groove with its largest diameter vertically. It has a strong tendency during the rolling to turn on its axis to the horizontal position; and to prevent this the end is tightly grasped with several pairs of heavy tongs held by the roller and his assistants, and maintained in the vertical position until it has passed nearly through the mill, when it is released. In the next rolling it is turned partly round, still further to reduce the inequality in its diameter caused by the peculiar form of the groove. This rolling through the last groove is repeated until it is ascertained by a gauge that the bolt is of a truly cylindrical form throughout.

The smaller bolts are produced in a different manner. The iron is reduced by passing through a series of diamond and oval grooves until of an oval form, equal in sectional area to that of the bolt to be produced. Grooves of a semicircular section are turned in the surface of the finishing rolls forming when combined a circular hole. The bar is inserted between iron guides, which maintain it in the vertical position while the rolls violently compress the iron to the cylindrical form, no further rolling being required. (Pl. LXXIII.) Great nicety is required in proportioning the oval to the circular groove. If the area of the former be in excess of the latter, the iron is forced out at the junction of the rolls, forming a fin at each side of the bar. On the other hand, if it be inferior in section the iron when compressed will not fill up to complete the circle.

Guide rolling appears to be confined to the manufacture of bolts under five-eighths of an inch diameter; for larger sizes it is rarely used. The great alteration of section effected at once when the iron is comparatively cold doubtless deteriorates the quality. It is only superior iron that can successfully stand under the crushing action of the rolls in reducing the oval to the circular section. Inferior iron rolled with guides into inch bolts is deemed greatly inferior in quality to that rolled in the ordinary way by hand.

Small merchant bars are usually rolled of a great length where a sufficiency of power exists for the purpose. Formerly 20 feet was considered sufficient, but now 50 feet is not an unusual length. The bar is subsequently cut into two or three pieces. The rolling of long bars is advantageous in many respects: the yield is better, the loss from crop ends is less as the length is augmented; the make is increased, while the labour expended remains nearly the same.

The diameter of the top roll for squares and bolts is greater than that of the bottom roll in the proportion of 61 to 60. This larger diameter of the top roll is necessary to throw the iron down on the guides. The number of revolutions per minute being the same, the circumference of the upper roll travels over a greater distance in the same time. This tends to deflect the point of the bar. In the roughing rolls the diameter of the top to that of the bottom one is as 51 to 50. Rolls for flat bars are turned with a similar difference in their diameters, the measurement being taken at the portion of the roll which compresses the iron. In the turning of rail rolls the increase is made on the mean diameter of the roll at the working surface.

The speed of the mill rolls varies greatly in the different iron-making districts. The English mills are driven at a much slower rate than the Welsh. In Staffordshire and Yorkshire 60 revolutions per minute may be considered the maximum velocity at the rail and large mills. In Wales very few of the mills are driven at a less speed than 70 revolutions per minute, while the majority are kept running at from 100 to 110. At the latter speeds the circumference of the rolls travels from 515 to 576 feet per minute. But when they are rolling large bolts the speed is reduced. While the bar is in the finishing rolls the speed is less than one-half of that for rolling rails. The smaller merchant-iron mills, having 12-inch rolls, are driven from 110 to 130 revolutions per minute, or from 346 to 408 feet. Guide rolls 8 inches diameter, 220 to 280 revolutions, or 460 to 586 feet per minute.

The character of the iron is to be taken into consideration in setting the speed of the rolls. If it be of a red short nature a maximum velocity is necessary in order to produce flange rails sound on the surface; but if cold short, a reduced velocity may be used. In Wales, at those works where boiling the pig-iron is largely practised, and the red short tendency of the iron is further heightened by a double heating, the rolls are driven at the highest practicable working speed. In rail mills, as at present constructed, there is a limit to the speed attainable; if it be exceeded, the time lost by the roughers and roller in seizing the bar is more than that saved by the higher velocity. As a general rule inferior qualities of iron work best with a high speed; at low speeds they are seldom worked successfully. Superior qualities, however, may be advantageously worked both at high and low speeds.

We have seen excellent cable iron rolled at 35 revolutions per minute; and 45 to 50 revolutions is about the average speed at mills working entirely on the best qualities of iron.

In ordinary mills the rolls are driven constantly in the same direction, the bar being lifted over the top roll back to the roller to enter the next groove. A few instances have occurred where the motion of the rolls has been reversed, and the bar passed back through the rolls in the succeeding groove. The advantages which result from the reversing motion are not very apparent. It is applicable only to mills running at a very slow speed. The sudden reversal of those driven at 100 revolutions would be quite impracticable. It is a question if the time lost in the reversing is not equal, even if it does not exceed, that lost in passing the bar back over the roll. The number of men employed at a train is increased rather than diminished, while first cost and the liability to accident is increased by the additional spur gearing required.

From the mill rolls the bar is taken to the cropping shears (Pl. LXXIX., Figs. 345, 346), or, if the end is to be perfectly square, to the circular saw. (Pls. LXXVII., LXXVIII.) The cropping shears are usually employed in cutting mill bars and small merchant-iron, but for the larger bolts and squares, for the heavier description of merchant bars, and for railway bars, the saw is now invariably employed. The strain in shearing small rods while they are hot from the rolls is not great, and is frequently performed by light hand-shears made principally of wrought iron. Larger sizes require stronger shears—those for mill bars and the general run of merchant iron weigh about 3 tons. They are furnished with steel knives from 12 to 16 inches long; the heat of the bars softens the steel and renders it necessary to change them every few hours. The knives for bolts and squares are provided with semicircular and triangular notches to receive the bar; without this provision the end of the soft bar would be flattened by the pressure of shearing. Heavier shears still are required for cold shearing. The quality of the iron is more apparent and the cut cleaner when performed on the cold bar with sharp knives. The heavy cropping shears, capable of shearing cold iron 6 inches by 1 inch, weigh with their connexions from 15 to 20 tons.

The employment of saws dates from a comparatively recent period. In the manufacture of railway bars the necessity of an apparatus for cutting the ends perfectly square soon became very apparent. The circular saw for cutting iron bars is made either of steel or wrought-iron plates about one-tenth of an inch thick, and 3 feet 6 inches to 4 feet 6 inches diameter. (Pls. LXXVII., LXXVIII., Figs. 528—537.) It is mounted on an iron spindle and stiffened for the major part of the diameter by stout iron plates. A saw-bench, with friction rollers, stops, and adjusting screws, and slides for moving it backwards and forwards, is fixed in a line parallel to that of the axis of the saw. Its upper surface is level with the mill floor, and 2 inches distant from the lower edge of the saw. The saws are driven at a high velocity by belts and spur gearing from the engine. A speed of 1300 revolutions per minute is not too great. In Staffordshire a single bench, with a saw at each end, and cutting both ends of the bar simultaneously, is very generally used. In the Welsh mills two saws are mounted on a spindle about 4 feet long, and a bench provided at the outside of each. The axis of the saw is placed at right angles to the centre line of the rolls, and the nearest bench is usually placed at a distance of 25 or 30 feet from them, in a line with the finishing groove. The bar having been drawn from the roll on to the first bench, with one end projecting beyond the inside saw, is held in its position by a stop, the bench is moved laterally until the saw has completely severed the projecting end, when it is drawn back sufficiently to allow the bar to be moved lengthways on to the further bench, which is provided with an apparatus for adjusting the length. The movement of the outer bench against its saw completes the cutting of the bar, which is then withdrawn to the hot filer.

In the cutting of some rails great nicety is required in the length, and allowance has to be made for the contraction of the iron in cooling. If the bars were cut at one uniform temperature the allowance for contraction could readily be ascertained, but from the different temperatures at which they are cut, provision has to be made in the screw stop for frequent small variations. With two benches outside the saws great nicety may be obtained in the cutting to length. With the single bench between the saws, cutting both ends at one movement, the same exactitude of adjustment cannot be obtained; and if cut singly the absence of the fixed screw stop for adjustment causes much uncertainty.

Saws worked by an emission engine on the same spindle have been erected, and, under certain circumstances, are superior to those driven by belt and gearing. Where the saws are constantly at work the latter mode of driving is preferable, though expensive, if they are situated far from the engine; but where they are only occasionally used the ordinary steam saw is probably the cheapest. It can be erected at a comparatively trifling expense at a considerable distance from the boiler. In the one, heavy shafting has to be maintained in motion through the day, consuming power and stores; in the other, the steam is thrown on only when required. But during the time it is in operation the consumption of power by the steam saw, measured by the steam used, is immensely greater than by the saw driven by belts and gearing: so much so that its greater consumption of steam, when working continuously, more than counterbalances its low first cost.

If the benches are good, working freely and steadily, and the saws are truly set, revolving at a high speed, the end of the rail when steadily and slowly cut, will have a polish equal to that produced by a smooth file. With less efficient benches, saws out of truth, and too rapid work, the ends will be rough and serrated. Grinding has then to be employed to obtain the desired finish.

The saws are cut with very coarse teeth on their edge, which are sharpened after twelve or twenty-four hours' work, according to the number of cuts made in the day. Steel saws will cut from 600 to 700 bars before sharpening, but iron saws will not cut more than the half of this number. To keep the teeth from being softened by the heat, the lower edge of the saw dips in a bosh containing cold water when working. Files are sometimes used for sharpening, but when several saws are at work a more expeditious mode consists in punching out a triangular piece with a powerful press. The saw is placed on a revolving table, level with the top of the die block; the table is furnished with an adjusting screw by which the circumference of the saw is brought into the required position with the punch. This done, the operation of sharpening is very simple, the saw is carefully turned round by hand the breadth of a tooth at each stroke of the punch. The punch shears off at one cut what the file does in ten or twelve, but care should be taken that the saw is not advanced so near to the punch that it should cut away more than is necessary to restore the original angle of the tooth.

Cutting with the cleft and sledge is still practised to a limited extent. The end of the bar is brought to a red heat, and placed in a heavy block cast with the half profile of the section at the bottom of a slot; a loose piece with the remainder of the profile on its under surface is placed on it and keyed down tightly on the bar. When thus held firmly, with the cast-iron in close contact with the rail at the line of separation, the cutting may be performed with considerable neatness.

Rails are also cut cold by powerful vertical shears, a very complete specimen of which may be seen at the Cyfarthfa works. The block carrying the cutting knife is actuated by a cam shaft revolving at a height of 7 or 8 feet from the floor, and slides between planed guides set vertically in the side frames. The fixed knife or die-block is bolted fast to the bottom framing by countersunk pins; an opening of the precise form of the section of the rail is made in its centre to secure the end of the bar to be cut. The rail is placed on rollers on a turn-table level with the opening in the die-block, and its end put through, when the vertical block and knife in its descent shears it off. The first cut is seldom clean. To regulate the thickness of the succeeding cuts a screw-adjusting apparatus is provided at the rear, by which the quantity taken off and the polish given to the rail may be accurately determined. The cold shearing of rails is advantageous in one respect; they are cut at the same temperature, hence, greater accuracy in the length is obtained.

For cutting cobbles, large scraps and other bars of heavy section, a very powerful shears is constructed with an eccentric cam at foot. (Pls. LXXVIII., LXXIX., Figs. 538—544.) The block carrying the cutting knife slides vertically in guides; it rests directly on the cam, and is elevated by it at each revolution. In the heaviest shears of this class bars 5 inches square are cut with the greatest facility.

The crop ends of the rails are sometimes reheated and wrought into small bars; at other times they are combined with puddle iron, which has been rolled of a suitable section, and remanufactured into rails; but a difficulty usually arises in the piling from their irregular section. To reduce them to a more suitable form they have been compressed under powerful squeezers, or passed between suitably grooved rolls to consolidate them, or passed under revolving cutters, by which the projecting flanges have been sheared off. The description of rail end to be wrought should be taken into consideration in selecting the apparatus; in each case the operation is performed while they are yet hot from the saws. Flange rails are wrought most advantageously in rolls, having such grooves that by passing through three or four the flanges are turned over on the body of the rail end, which is then of a form favourable for piling. For bridge rails the cutters appear to be the most advantageous. These are made of wrought-iron and steel combined, about 18 inches diameter, driven at 35 to 40 revolutions per minute. The rail crop is inserted in the guides, drawn forward by the revolving cutter which shears the flanges from the body. In piling the strips of flanges are placed inside the rail, filling up the hollow, or they may be piled separately.

PLATE ROLLING.

The rolling of boiler plates is conducted on different principles to that of bars. The plate rolls are of a plain cylindrical form of the same diameter throughout, and to increase their durability are invariably cast in thick iron chills, by which the surface of the metal has nearly the hardness and brittleness of cast-steel. The standards are made of cast-iron, often with large wrought-iron screws reaching up through them from the bottom, and provided with large nuts on the top riders. (Pl. LXXVI., Figs. 512, 513.) Levers are commonly employed to balance a portion of the weight and to lift the top roll completely if necessary.

The pile for plates is made wider, shorter, and generally thinner than the piles for bars. It is taken to the heating furnace and passed sideways between the rolls, then endways, changing the direction at each rolling until the plate is reduced to nearly the desired thickness and size, when it is handed over to the finishing rolls. The dimensions and thickness are now roughly ascertained, guided by which the roller passes it between the rolls endways or sideways, according to the direction in which the greatest elongation is required, taking care, however, that the elongation in both directions is such that when reduced to the gauged thickness the finished plate may be sufficiently large to cut to the dimensions ordered.

In making the best boiler plates the piling and rolling require to be carefully adjusted to each other. The length and breadth of the pile should bear the same proportion to each other as the like dimensions of the plate to be rolled. The bars composing the pile should be equally distributed, across and along the pile. If care be now taken in the rolling the plate when extended to its full dimensions will be equally strong in every direction.

Boiler plates too commonly are stronger in one direction than another. Experiments have been made to determine the strength of boiler-plate iron, and a considerable difference is observable between the weights necessary to pull asunder strips cut across, and those cut lengthways of the plate. The iron has the least strength when pulled in a direction at right angles to the greatest distension by rolling. Where the variation in strength is considerable it is conclusive evidence that the plate has been improperly manufactured.

In a published account[*] of some experiments by an eminent engineer, the strength of the plate is stated to have been greatest when pulled at right angles to the grain of the iron. This is an error, and probably arose from a mistake as to the direction of the grain. A mere inspection cannot determine the direction of the grain of the iron in boiler plates. The form of the pile, position of the iron in it, and the direction of extension at each successive rolling require to be noted during the manufacture, otherwise we are unable to say in what direction the grain lies. It is in the power of the roller to produce from a given pile, plates having the grain of the iron at right angles to their length or running parallel to it.

[*] Mechanics' Magazine, vol. liv.

He can also vary the direction of extension so as to produce from a pile built with the grain of the iron disposed in one direction, a plate void of fibre and equally strong in every direction.

Long plates for ship-building generally have the grain of the iron running with the length, but by an alteration in the pile they may be rolled with little fibre and nearly uniform strength. In long plates, however, it is not in the power of the roller to change the direction of the fibre. The rolling is more like that of bars, and the extension is greatest longitudinally, hence in this direction the fibre will lie. If piled with the greater portion of the iron across the pile, the extension of these pieces laterally neutralises the tendency to form fibre.

Tinned iron plates are rolled in a similar manner, and the same attention is demanded to ensure the production of an uniform strength and quality.

FLUES, DAMPERS, AND BOILERS.

Balling and puddling furnaces are sometimes built with dampers at the bottom of the chimney stack. (Pl. XLVIII., Fig. 279; XLIX., Fig. 284.) When in a vertical position the damper door fills up the opening in the brickwork leaving an unobstructed passage for the draught; when let down it rests against the opposite side of the flue, in a diagonal direction; it completely closes the flue and opens the portion of the stack above it to the atmosphere. The damper is in such cases placed above the "take up," immediately on the iron framing under the brickwork of the stack. In width it is about one inch less than the flue, at the bottom it is hinged to a small frame built in the brickwork, and is opened and shut by a lever and balance weight. The back, which is at all times open to the atmosphere, is made of cast-iron, protected from the intense heat in front by a covering of fire-clay adhering to spikes cast on the under side of the damper.

The chief objection to this plan of damper lies in the cooling of the stack, by the ascent of a column of cold air when the draught of the furnace is shut off. The stack is cooled down, and on again opening the damper the reduction of temperature is felt in the inferior draught, a longer time is required for bringing the heat to a welding point, attended with an increased consumption of coal and an inferior make and yield of iron.

The economical application of the waste heat from puddling and balling furnaces has received much attention from ironmasters, but it is questionable if the subject is rightly understood by the majority of those interested. A common plan of economising the heat is to place a vertical boiler between two or more furnaces, the steam being generated by the heat escaping from them. In other establishments a powerful chimney is used to draw down the products of combustion from four or five furnaces under a large boiler. A third plan is to form the lower portion of the stack into a small vertical boiler and central flue, fitted with safety apparatus, feed and steam-pipes.

That sufficient steam can be obtained from boilers so situated to work the engine without the aid of fire for the purpose is well known. It is a question, however, whether the saving in engine coal is not balanced by the increased consumption of furnace coal. On two occasions experimental trials were made at the Dowlais works with boilers attached to heating furnaces, for several months on each occasion. The results with these boilers were such as we anticipated: the weekly make of the furnace declined, while the yield of iron was augmented. The consumption of coal in the furnace grate per ton of iron was greater than was formerly required for the furnace and engine together, and owing to the longer time occupied in the heating, and the inferior temperature attained, the quality of the iron was deteriorated.

In Staffordshire and Derbyshire numbers of boilers may be seen attached to the old furnaces, but it is a significant circumstance that in no instance did we see them applied in the recently erected furnaces in the same works. Consequently we infer that they are not found so economical as is generally supposed.

If the conditions essential to the successful working of heating furnaces be considered, the impolicy of attaching boilers to them is made apparent. The rapid draught necessary to the production of an intense heat can be produced only by a chimney stack of the requisite height, maintained at a comparatively high temperature. If it be cold, the drawing power is reduced to a minimum; at the high temperature of the heating furnace it is at a maximum. Place a boiler or other ready conductor of heat in the stack, and the temperature is reduced, the draught lessened, and the heat in the furnace lowered. If the boiler be placed very near the furnace, say immediately on the cast-iron framing of the stack, the temperature of the furnace is still further diminished. By the quick absorption of heat so near the body of the furnace, the temperature necessary for working the iron is maintained with difficulty. Where the temperature is produced by a draught, we cannot maintain an intense heat in one part of the furnace immediately contiguous to another part comparatively cold. The cold body has the greatest affinity for caloric, and by the continued absorption the final heat of the working parts of the furnace is rendered inferior to that due to the caloric generated in the fire-place.

It should distinctly be understood that the heat escaping up the chimney is the motive power which creates the draught. Deprive the ascending current of its heat, the draught is destroyed; diminish it by a portion only, and the velocity of ascent is diminished in the same ratio. And it should also be remembered that a sharp draught and an intense heat are indispensable in working to a good yield of iron. The saving of the entire engine coal, if attended with a triflingly greater yield of iron, may be productive of loss instead of profit. The great difference in value of the two materials consumed requires to be taken into consideration. The iron in the forge and mills may be estimated at the present time as worth 5l. per ton. The coal is probably worth about 6s. 6d. per ton. The yield of engine coal where firing under the boilers is practised averages 2½ cwts. to the ton; the saving of coal, then, may amount to 10d. per ton. But 18lbs. of iron is of equal value with the coal; and if the yield of iron is only this much more, there is no real saving. In practice, however, we find the yield to be from 40 to 60 lbs. in excess.

SECTION XX.

POWER ABSORBED IN THE DIFFERENT OPERATIONS OF IRON MANUFACTURING.

In the course of experiments having for their object the economical application of power in iron-works, we ascertained that the amount absorbed in the various operations was nearly as follows:

Smelting Lean Argillaceous Ores.—For compressing the blast to a density of 3lbs. on the square inch—55-horse power per 100 tons of iron smelted weekly, or, allowing for friction and leakage in the engine, 66-horse power. The horse power being 33,000lbs. lifted one foot high per minute.

Smelting Carbonaceous Ores.—For compressing the blast to a density of 3lbs., 22-horse power per 100 tons smelted weekly, equal to 27-horse power, including friction and unavoidable loss.

Refinery.—For compressing the blast to a density of 2¼lbs. to the square inch, for refining forge iron in the running-in fire—13-horse power for every 100 tons refined weekly, equal to 16-horse power, including friction and waste.

Puddling Forge.—No. 1. For driving a puddling train, consisting of a pair of 18-inch finishing rolls, a pair of roughing rolls, a double-ended squeezer, and two pairs of cropping shears at 55 revolutions per minute, rolling bars 3 inches by ¼ inch, puddled from refined metal.—Power expended in keeping the trains and machinery in motion—41-horse power. Additional power, when in full work, rolling and squeezing at the rate of 300 tons weekly, representing the mean force exerted in shaping the iron—34-horse power. Total power absorbed—75-horse.

No. 2. For driving puddling train, with rolls and squeezer similar to the above, but running at 82 revolutions per minute, and rolling bars 3 inches by ¼ inch, from boiled pigs. Power absorbed by the engine and machinery—17.5-horse power.—By the roll train running light—28.5-horse power. Total power absorbed by engine, machinery, rolls, and squeezer running light—46-horse power. Additional power absorbed when rolling and squeezing at the rate of 360 tons weekly, representing the force expended in shaping the iron—67.5-horse. Total power expended—113.5-horse power.

Rolling Mill.—No. 1. For driving rail train, consisting of a pair of 18-inch roughing rolls, a pair of finishing rolls, and intermediate pinions worked by a horizontal high-pressure engine, with cropping shears, eight straightening presses, and saws in connexion,—the speed of rolls being 85 revolutions per minute, and rolling T rails. Power absorbed in driving engine, rolls, and all the machinery light—71-horse power. Additional power absorbed when rolling—168-horse power. Total power driving rail train, capable of making 600 tons of rails weekly—239-horse power.

No. 2. For driving 18-inch bar train, consisting of a pair of roughing rolls, a pair of finishing rolls, and cropping shears. Power absorbed by the engine and machinery for three such trains when running light, including power absorbed in driving four rail presses and pair of saws—52-horse power. Power absorbed by each train of rolls when running light—21-horse power. Additional power absorbed by trains respectively, when rolling $1\frac{1}{4}$ inch bolts—29.5-horse power; when rolling $1\frac{1}{4}$ inch squares—29.5-horse power; when rolling 4-inch by 1-inch flats—102-horse power. Gross power consumed in driving the three trains and machinery loaded—276-horse power. Total power, including engine and machinery, absorbed by train of bar rolls rolling flats—149-horse power.

No. 3. For driving 12-inch bar mill, a pair of roughing and a pair of finishing rolls, with engine and machinery, at 140 revolutions per minute, light—26-horse power. When rolling bolts and squares additional—23-horse power.

No. 4. For driving 12-inch train, consisting of a pair of roughing and a pair of finishing rolls, driven at 110 revolutions per minute by independent engine, rolling flats, $1\frac{1}{4}$ in. by $\frac{1}{4}$ in. —32-horse power.

No. 5. For driving a train of 8-inch merchant bar rolls, consisting of three roughing, three ovals, and a pair of finishing rolls, working at the rate of 220 revolutions per minute. Power expended in maintaining engine and machinery in motion—17-horse power. Power absorbed in running train, light—24-horse power. Additional power when rolling $\frac{3}{8}$ in. flats— —21-horse power; when rolling $\frac{1}{4}$-inch flats—14-horse power. Gross power expended when rolling $\frac{1}{4}$-inch flats, 55-horse power.

No. 6. For driving 8-inch train similar to the above, with separate engine and machinery, when rolling squares and bolts—61-horse power.

No. 7. Power absorbed in driving a pair of rail saws, 4 feet 6 inches diameter, 820 revolutions per minute—11-horse power.

A fair approximation to the power employed in manufacturing iron may be obtained by taking the engines at the Dowlais works, and multiplying their power by the annual make of iron.

The power given off by the Dowlais engines in 1855 was nearly as follows:

	Horse Power.
5 Blowing engines	2154
10 Forge and mill engines	2165
2 Engines turning rolls and shearing iron	35
4 Pumping engines draining coal and iron ore workings	496
16 Engines winding out of pits	1134
2 Engines grinding clay for fire-bricks	70
14 Incline and other engines	665
11 Locomotive engines about the works	590
Total horse power	7309

The number of blast furnaces being eighteen, this gives 408-horse power for each furnace.

SECTION XXI.

SUNDRY NOTES ON IRON-MAKING.

FIBRE.

THE fibre observed in bar iron is developed in the rolling mill. In the fracture of a puddle ball when cold we observe the iron in the form of large grains, separated from each other by a thin film of agglutinating matter. During the process of shingling these are brought close together, and when the bloom leaves the hammer they form a compact mass, about 5 inches diameter by 16 inches long. This bloom is extended in length, by being repeatedly passed through the puddling rolls, to a bar about 12 feet long, but is reduced in section from 20 inches to 2.2 inches; each particle of iron is consequently elongated to nine times its former length by the reduction in section. The fibre developed in the puddle iron is of limited extent, and the presence of much of the original cinder is seen in the fracture.

The puddled bars being cut into short lengths and formed into a pile, the pieces lying longitudinally, the development of the fibre is heightened by a second rolling. If a pile 6 inches wide by 6 inches high and 2 feet 6 inches in length is made of 3-inch by $\frac{1}{4}$-inch puddle iron, and rolled into a bar 2 inches square, it will measure about $21\frac{1}{4}$ feet long. The section of the pile, composed of 16 pieces of puddle iron, is reduced by rolling to a bar of 4 inches section. As each piece of puddle iron was formerly 20 inches in section, the square bar contains the same number of particles of iron in each inch of its section as existed in 80 inches of sectional area of bloom from under the squeezer or hammer. Hence, the fracture of the bar produced from puddle iron is more dense, the fibres are more strongly developed and finer, and the presence of cinder is less apparent, from the quantity expelled during the second rolling.

If square bars of No. 2 iron are cut and built into a pile of similar dimensions, reheated and rolled to a bar of similar cross dimensions, the particles of iron in each inch of section will be 720 times as many as in the same area of the original bloom. The fibres are observed to be more numerous, forming as it were, exceedingly fine threads. The expulsion of an additional quantity of cinder has left the iron more pure, as is proved by its greater specific gravity, and by the multiplication of its fibres; its tenacity is likewise increased.

But the fibre thus obtained by the repeated rollings may be neutralized, or even destroyed, at any stage by alteration in the mode of rolling. If common puddle iron is cut into short pieces, and a pile built with these pieces laid crossways, with only sufficient metal lengthways at the bottom to retain them in their position while being heated, and is then rolled into a bar of the same dimensions as in the other case, the iron will be utterly void of fibre, and break with nearly the same brittleness, though offering a greater resistance than cast-iron, from which it differs in appearance only by its superior whiteness and the fineness of its particles. By piling the common No. 2 iron in a similar manner, and rolling at right angles to the fibre, a bar is produced equally devoid of fibre, possessing the same brittleness, but greater purity.

By constructing the pile with a portion of iron laid in each direction, the finished iron will be fibrous on one side and brittle on the other. If the several layers are thin, and cross each other, the tendency to form fibre in one is neutralised by the other, and the extra process of heating and rolling, though improving the quality, will not, in this case, increase the fibre of the iron.

If the bloom from the shingler is slabbed down between cylindrical rolls, varying the direction of the rolling each time, the slab produced is devoid of fibre, but presents on fracture a scaly appearance. If this be reheated and rolled into a thin plate in the same way, the iron is equally void of fibre, but the fineness of the scale is increased. This plate being cut, piled, reheated, and rolled in the same manner into a finished plate, is still void of fibre. The thready appearance observable in bar iron is wanting, but in its place we have a laminated fracture. The original particles of iron, which, in the case of bars, are elongated in the direction of the length, are now compressed into flat scales.

Plates made from piles of No. 2 bars, laid alternately along and across, are nearly devoid of this laminated fracture. For its production the bloom requires to be rolled between cylindrical rolls offering no opposition to the extension of the plate in any direction. If rolled from cross-built piles plates are nearly alike devoid of the fibrous and laminated structure. Thus, we are enabled to judge from the fracture of the iron the manner in which a boiler plate has been manufactured.

The greater value, for numerous purposes, of iron rolled from piles having a portion of the bars laid at a right angle to the others, is not generally understood either by the manufacturer or consumer. Such iron is harder, denser, and possesses greater tensile strength than iron otherwise prepared. Fibre is generally considered an indication of strength, and in the ordinary way of manufacturing, the quantity of fibre developed does determine the value of the iron. For it can only be produced by repeated rollings and the expulsion of the extraneous matter combined with the iron. But while the presence of fibre is an indication of superior quality, we cannot accept it as a measure whereby to estimate the quality of bar iron generally. Iron may be of an excellent quality and yet possess no fibre. If the fibrous character determined the strength of the iron, steel, the purest form in which iron exists in commerce, instead of being the strongest, would rank as the weakest. Iron manufactured from cross-laid piles possesses many of the properties of steel. It is hard, the structural arrangement of the iron is more dense, and the specific gravity is superior to that of iron rolled from piles built in the ordinary way. The strength is increased in the same, or a greater, ratio than the specific gravity. Hence, for boiler plates and other purposes, iron manufactured in this manner, though devoid of either fibre or laminæ, possesses a greater tensile strength, and consequently should have the preference.

The superior density of the iron thus made is easily explained. In the ordinary way of rolling the extension is in one direction only; the original fibres are lengthened at each rolling, and no resistance is offered longitudinally to the degree of extension. In the bar manufactured from the cross pile the pressure exerted by the rolls acts endways on the portion placed across the pile, compressing the iron to one-third of its former length. The density appears to be greater than is due only to the pressure on the cross-piled portion, and is probably the effect of the interlacing of the fibres in the bar when at the half-finished stage. The difference in the iron produced from ordinary piles and that produced from cross piles is very similar to the difference observed in iron drawn out by a continuous hammering in one direction and that produced by alternate extension and compression by turning the end. To produce a dense solid iron the upsetting is absolutely necessary.

In the puddling forge the good effect of the upsetting on the bloom is fully acknowledged. If the quality of the iron is thus early improved by pressure in this direction, it is very evident that a repetition of the upsetting process at each subsequent rolling will result in a corresponding improvement. The upsetting in the mills, however, is best performed, as we have shown, by so disposing the greater portion of the iron that it may be thus acted on by the rolls.

Fibre is produced by rolling or hammering the iron when hot, and by no other means. But the fibrous character of malleable iron may be destroyed while hot by altering the direction of elongation, and while cold by hammering, concussion, and vibration.

IMPROVING THE QUALITY OF CAST AND MALLEABLE IRON.

Various modes of improving the quality of bar iron, by the addition of various metals or oxides at one or other of the stages of its manufacture, have been devised. In all propositions, however, for the improvement of malleable iron by the incorporation therewith of foreign ingredients, it should be borne in mind that while it is possible thus to improve a single characteristic, the inevitable result is to lower the general quality of the iron so treated. In seeking to improve the general quality it should be distinctly understood that a *bonâ fide* improvement can result only from the abstraction of an injurious alloy; or the substitution of a less for a more injurious mixture; or from the addition of metal of a quality superior to that of the iron under treatment. But under no circumstances whatever can the mere addition of substances or metal, of inferior qualities, improve the general qualities of the iron, which are heightened and developed with every degree of refinement, and debased with every adulteration.

The list of substances capable of being mingled or alloyed with iron is large, but their employment as a means of improving the general quality is invariably attended with contrary effects. The presence of carbon, by lowering the temperature of fusion, increases the fluidity of cast metal; but the qualities of hardness and tenacity are reduced in nearly the same ratio. Silicon, in quantity, seems to impart additional hardness, but is attended with an equally great deficiency of tenacity, and materially impairs the ability of the metal to withstand crushing and abrading forces.

The tenacity of cast-iron of a low specific gravity, and consequent inferior quality, may be improved by remelting and incorporating in it wrought-iron scraps of a superior tenacity. But the improvement in quality by this treatment nearly disappears when the cast-iron is of a high specific gravity. And of the improvement occurring to irons of low quality, debased by the presence of an excess of carbon, by far the largest portion is due to the increase of density and consequent greater purity which follows on the partial oxydation of the volume of carbon during the operation.

The superior strength of air-furnace castings is generally acknowledged by iron founders; but the common explanation of its being due to a greater homogeneity, consequent on the remelting of the crude iron, is we consider altogether erroneous, and has arisen from a deficiency of experimental researches on the subject. We have found that the simple operation of remelting invariably increases the density and tenacity of crude irons of grey quality, the improvement being greatest with those containing the largest volume of carbon; and that a second remelting results in a further increase of these qualities, which continue to augment with successive remeltings until the iron has attained a high degree of refinement and increased its tensile strength by fully one-half. The number of remeltings necessary to the development of the tensile powers of the metal, varies with, and is directly proportionate to the volume of carbon to be liberated, but may be largely reduced by prolonging the period during which the molten iron is exposed to the decarburizing influence of the reverberated gases. With white irons from blast furnaces consuming a minimum quantity of fuel, the improvement is not so marked. Containing a lesser volume of carbon, with a greater quantity of metalloids more difficult of oxydation, the act of remelting is attended with a larger waste of metal in proportion to the volume of impurity removed. Since, therefore, the maximum tenacity is not attained with a single remelting, and microscopic examination fails to detect any irregularity in the structural arrangement of the blast-furnace iron, we conclude that the superiority of air-furnace castings is principally due to the greater purity of the metal, which necessarily results from remelting.

But while maximum tenacity is attained only by remelting and mechanical subsidation, the operation results in a corresponding deprivation of fluidity, and the iron so treated, after the third or fourth fusion, is not adapted for small castings, or the filling of sharp angles in larger ones. And with a succession of remeltings, all cast irons, especially the hot blast varieties, and such as have been produced from a burden composed wholly or partly of hematite, are subject to unequal contraction in cooling, sinkings on the surface, and, where the pieces are angular and of large dimensions, they are rarely solid throughout.

Iron possesses the greatest density and tenacity when pure; the presence of any other metal or matter in mixture or alloy reduces its density, and diminishes in a more rapid ratio its tensile strength. The crude iron of commerce ordinarily contains about 80 per cent. by volume of metallic iron, and 20 per cent. of impurity uniformly specifically lighter than pure iron, and possesses a very low degree of tensile strength. The extent to which this property is deteriorated by the character and volume of the alloy, is a subject of paramount importance to the manufacturer and consumer of iron, but one on which hitherto, owing to its costliness and the extreme delicacy of manipulation demanded in the inquiry, no adequate experiments have been made. By a limited series, we ascertained that the tenacity in the various stages of manufacture was nearly in the ratio of the tenth power of its specific gravity; and that the final resistance offered by the iron when converted into blister steel and severely hammered to a specific gravity of 7.92, the tensile strength averaged 84,000 lbs. to the square inch. The dependence on, and direct connexion of the tenacity and general good qualities with the specific gravity is not generally admitted, though in the practical operations of the manufacturer its existence is everywhere manifest. The production of a superior iron possessing great tenacity but of a low density is impracticable: inferior density is invariably accompanied by weakness. But while there is this inseparable connexion between superior tenacity and a high density, through design or inattention the quality may be impaired without sensibly altering the density. And whilst this mode of estimation correctly determines the development of tenacity, we would remark that the results obtained with one kind of iron are not applicable by comparison to another kind.

THE DIFFERENCE CONSTITUTING CAST AND WROUGHT-IRON, AND THE WELDING PROPERTY OF METALS.

Cast-iron, it is generally supposed, differs from malleable iron in the difference in the degree of purity; the greater volume constituting cast-iron, the lesser volume malleable iron; and a further diminution resulting in the production of steel. But while the purifying effect of the processes of converting cast to malleable iron, and the necessarily greater purity of the latter must freely be admitted, there are reasons for believing that malleability is not produced by, or dependent on, a given degree of purity, but results from the action of mechanical agency on the mass under operation, whilst at a certain temperature and possessing an agglutinating character. Crude iron may be refined by fusion and subsidation, yet retain all the essentials of cast metal, and be utterly devoid of malleability. Large quantities of malleable iron are being made containing a greater per-centage of foreign matter than crude iron of other makes; the conversion of this latter, however, into malleable iron, though possessing a minimum volume of impurity, can only be accomplished by the deprivation of a portion of the admixture resulting in the production of an iron of greater purity than the former. From this we conclude that the greater purity of malleable iron from a given source, compared with that of the crude iron, accompanies, rather than is the cause of the malleability, which arises from the manipulation to which it is subjected during manufacture.

All metals are malleable to a greater or less extent, but the degree of extensibility as well as the temperature at which it may be effected is not alike, and in the same metal varies with the degree and character of the alloy. Cast-iron though usually considered a brittle substance possesses extensibility, when its reduction of temperature from the liquid state has by prolongation been imperceptibly lowered; but if the temperature has been suddenly brought down by contact with cold metal or any other ready conductor, it is incapable of extension. Where the mass is large, the central portion, losing its caloric at a slower rate, will often be found to a degree malleable, while the outside is deficient of this property. And in the case of horizontal castings of considerable thickness, it is observed that the surface possesses a malleability of which the lower portion is wholly destitute. Difference in composition cannot account for this loss of malleability; for we have no evidence of the mere circumstance of losing its caloric more rapidly causing an alteration in the relative proportions of the mass, though it may affect the character of the mixture. But annealed iron possesses the malleable property only within a limited range of temperature; heated to about 400 degs. it disappears, and does not again reappear below the fusing heat.

In this respect we see a complete difference in the character of the malleability in crude and finished iron; for while in the former the property is diminished and ultimately destroyed with the infusion of caloric, in the latter it is augmented, and attains a maximum development after absorbing a sufficiency to reduce cast-iron to the liquid form.

The malleability of wrought-iron is developed only by dexterous manipulation, while crude iron possesses a degree of plasticity in its semi-liquid state, and unless immediately subjected to the action of the rolls or hammer, reverts to its normal condition of brittleness. By the rapid application of a varied pressure on the mass while it is in the plastic condition, the agglutination of the atoms of iron is effected, and during the subsequent elongation of the mass by pressure, they are extended longitudinally, until through loss of heat the ductility of the mixture is destroyed and their continuity broken. Crude cast-iron is incapable of extension by the mere infusion of caloric; the atoms of iron roll on each other, and the foreign matter or cinder is deficient of the agglutinous character necessary to the development of the malleable property. After being subjected to an operation whereby the atoms are agglutinated and extended, the mass, by the aid of heat, may be extended indefinitely; but below a certain temperature, the brittleness of the mixed material limits the range of extension. The metallic iron possesses superior absorbent and retentive powers during the process, and its ductility is comparatively unimpaired by the loss of heat; the cinder, on the other hand, possesses inferior powers, and with the escape of caloric loses its plasticity, becomes excessively hard and brittle, and if the extension of the iron by lateral pressure be continued, the compression of the atoms of cinder into the softened iron destroys its tenacity, and renders it either of a red or cold-short quality, according to the volume of extraneous substances and temperature of solidification.

Wrought-iron is distinguished from other metals by the facility with which two or more pieces may be united together and retain unimpaired their tenacity. The property of welding on the addition of heat belongs to all metals, whether cast or malleable, but is most apparent in iron. It is produced by the infusion of caloric until the iron and metalloids of the entire mass are softened, and the surfaces to be united, reduced to a semi-liquid state. The comparatively large quantity required to liquify wrought-iron, enables the softening and partial fusion to be successfully conducted. Cast-iron and other metals may be united by fusion, but during the accession of caloric, owing to the lesser quantity required and the inferior melting temperature, only a momentary period elapses between the softening and complete liquefaction of the entire mass treated, and the rapidity also with which it escapes, does not permit of the manipulation necessary to the effectual consolidation of the pieces. In the case of cast-iron, the difficulty is increased by the large volume of matters in alloy: melting at various temperatures, the mass is not equally and simultaneously heated; brought in contact with each other, the union of the pieces is obstructed by the different conditions of temperature presented by the respective constituents.

The interposition of foreign matter by impairing the agglutinous character of the mass prevents the complete union of the pieces. The fumes of metals oxydizable at an inferior temperature also interfere with the union; if present in sufficient quantity, they alter the character of the iron from its usual tenacity, and ductility to the opposite extremes, and destroy the welding property. Compound metals having an ingredient which sublimes at a temperature lower than the fusing point of the most refractory, cannot be united by welding; the vapours of the inferior metal interpose and prevent the agglutination of the atoms.

MANUFACTURE OF WROUGHT-IRON DIRECT FROM THE ORE.

The production of wrought-iron direct from the ore—the original mode of manufacturing—has engaged the attention of numerous practical and scientific men, and is practised to a limited extent abroad; but the attempts made to reinstate it in this country have hitherto been, commercially speaking, unsuccessful; and though the ores and fuels we possess are unquestionably superior to the foreign for this purpose, fusion in the blast furnace, and conversion into malleable iron by the puddling process, is pursued with all the bar iron now manufactured.

The conversion direct into malleable iron dispenses with the blast furnace and appendages, and the intermediate processes of refining and puddling, and if successful should result in the production of a finished bar of superior quality, with a smaller consumption of

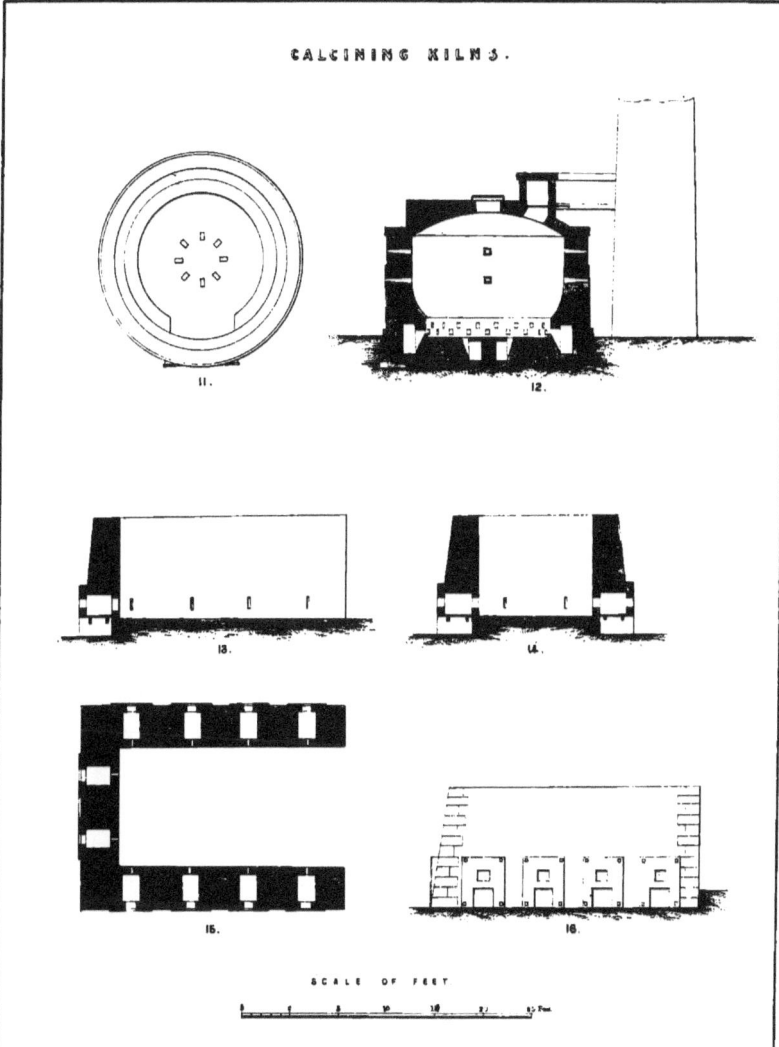

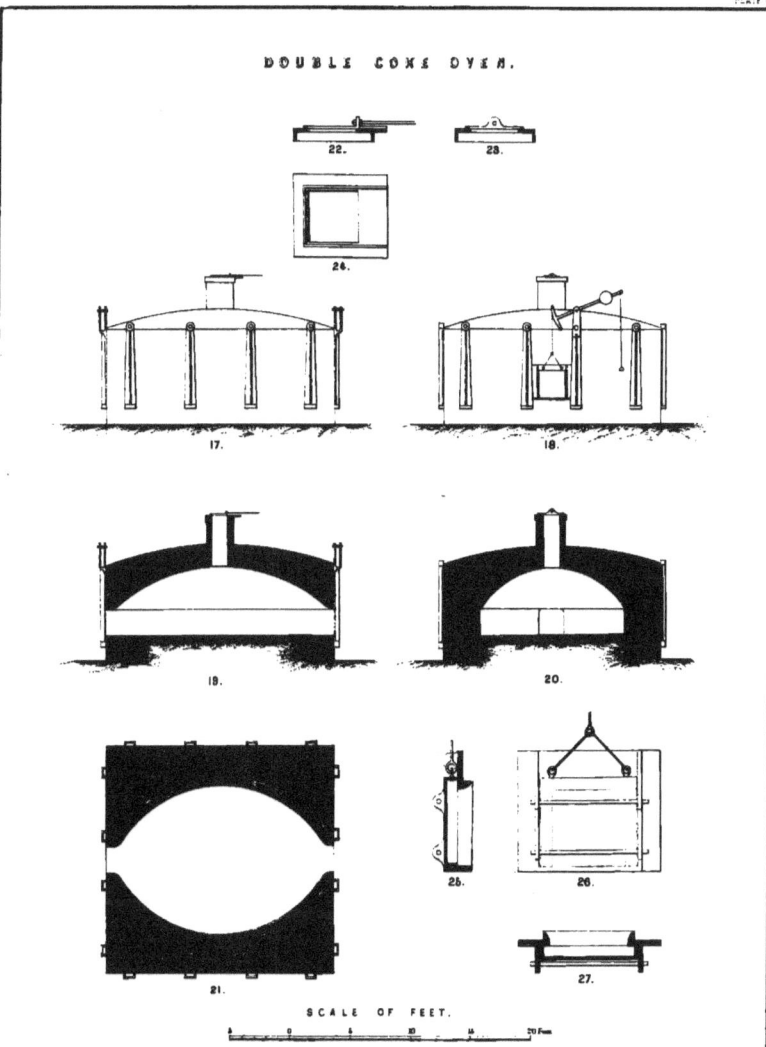

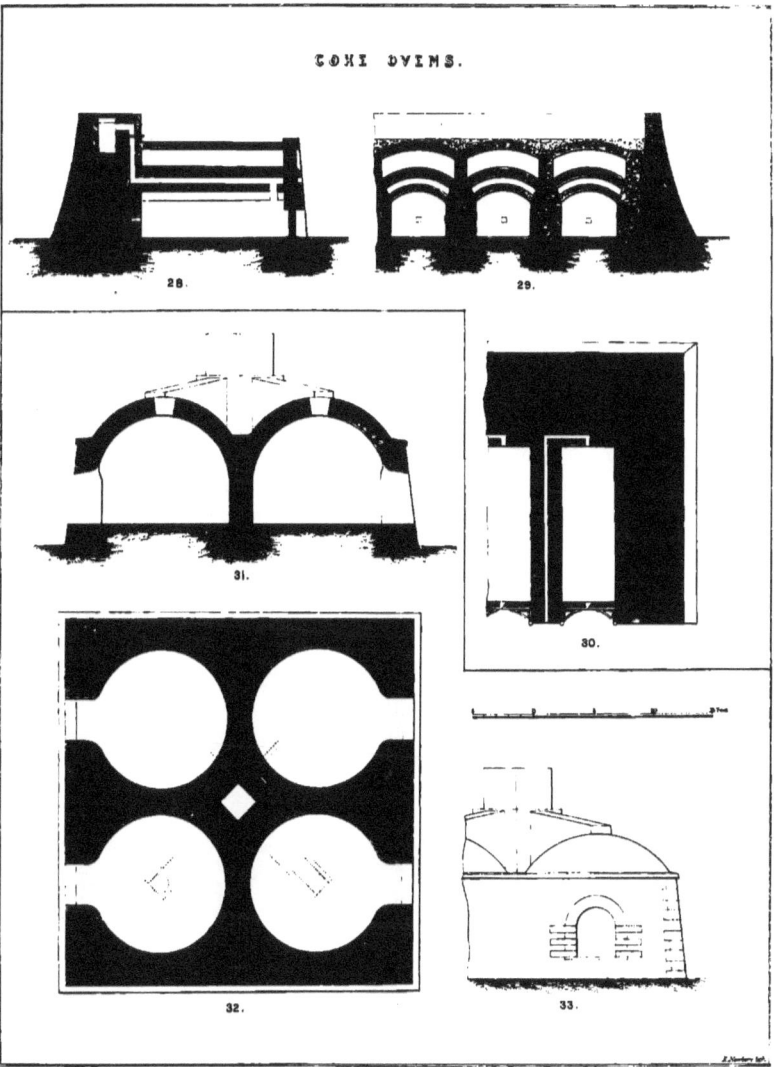

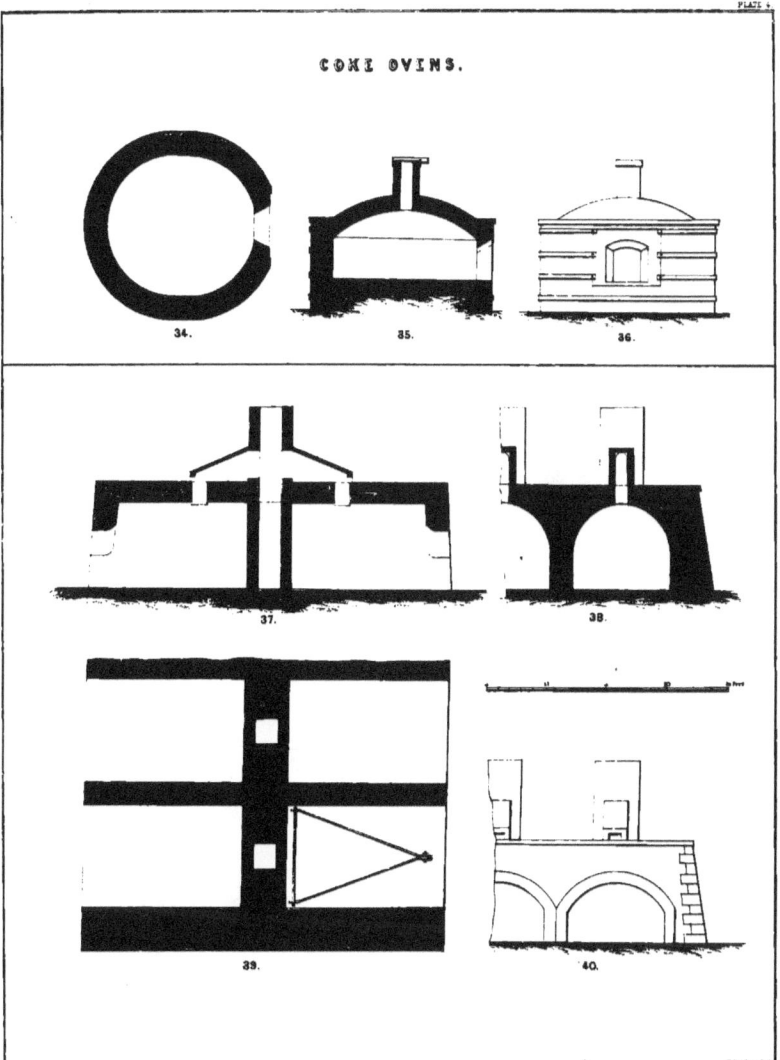

COKE OVENS.

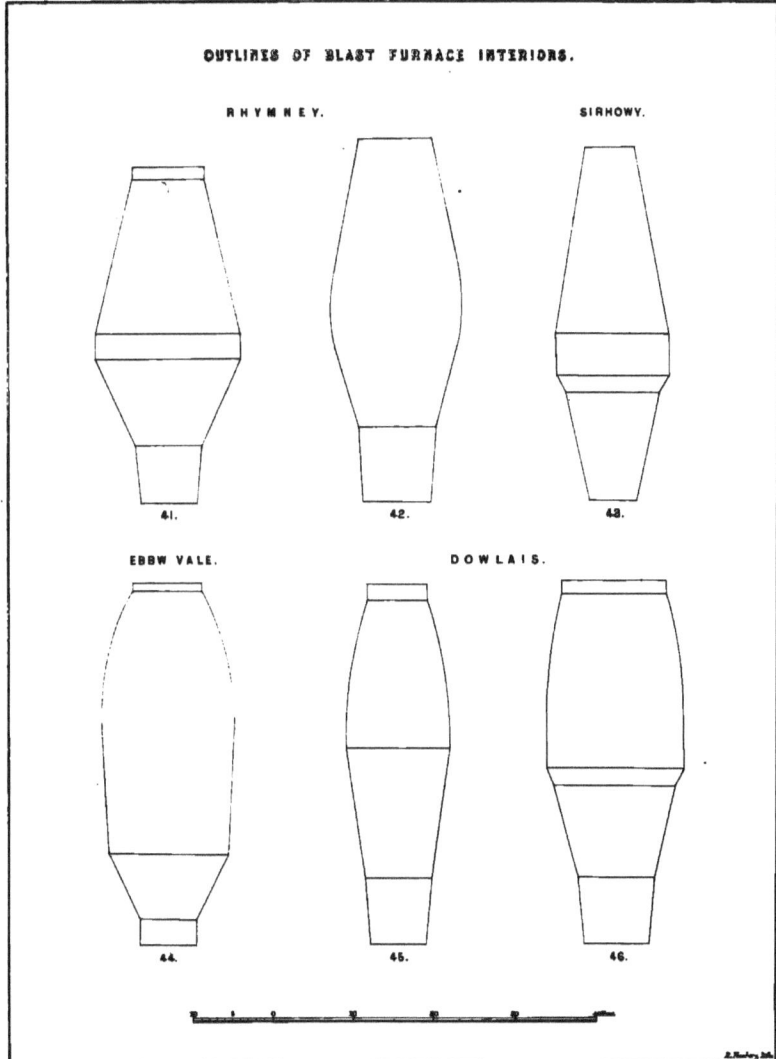

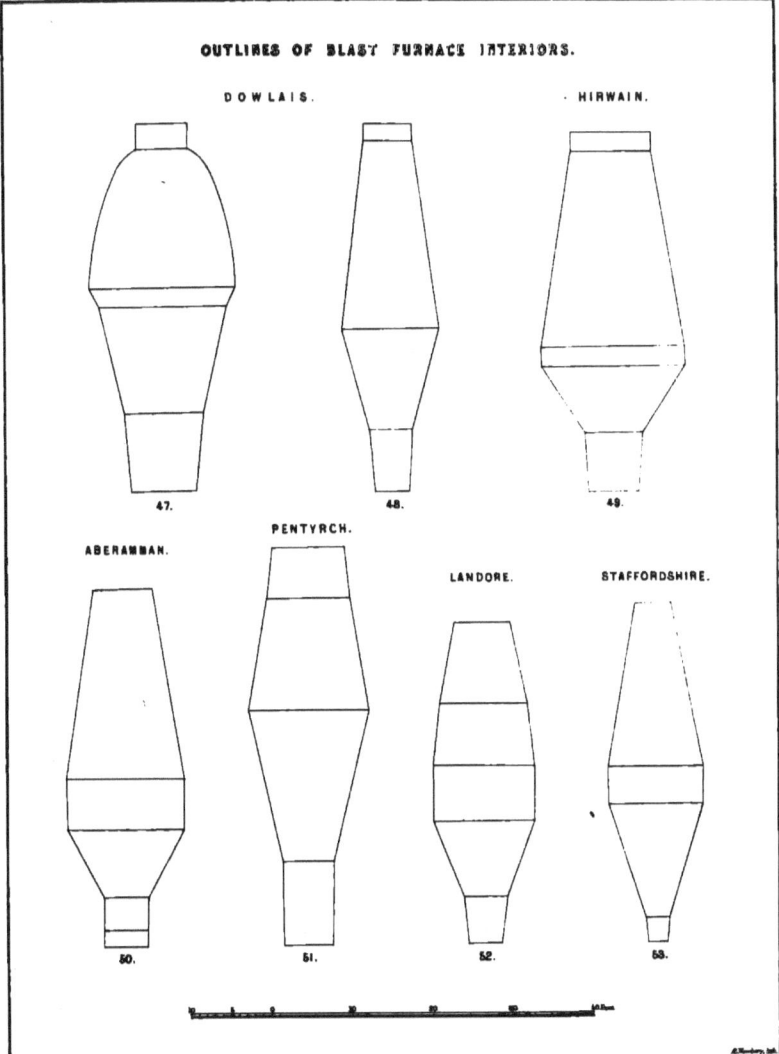

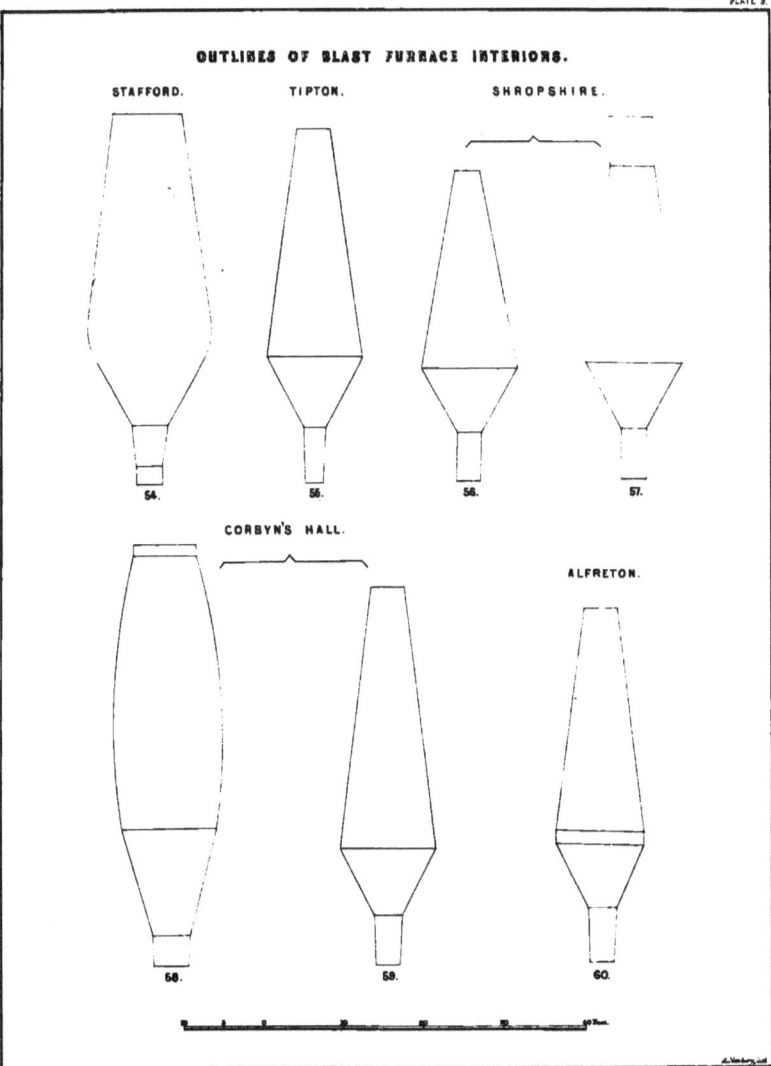

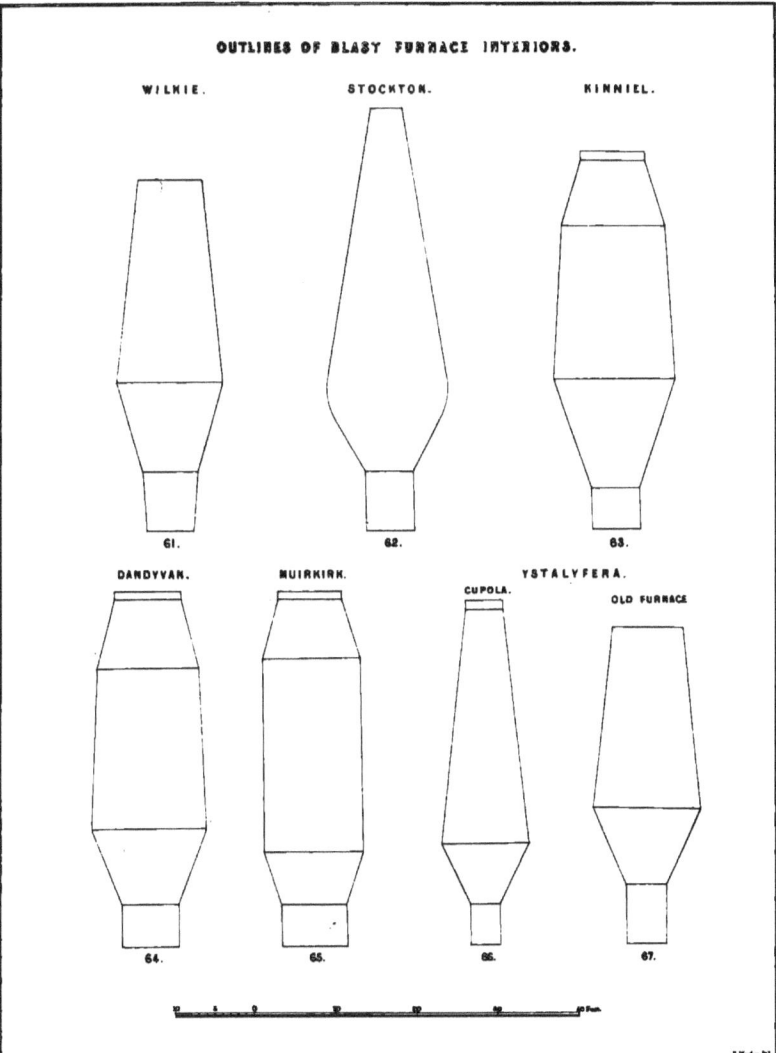

OUTLINES OF BLAST FURNACE INTERIORS.

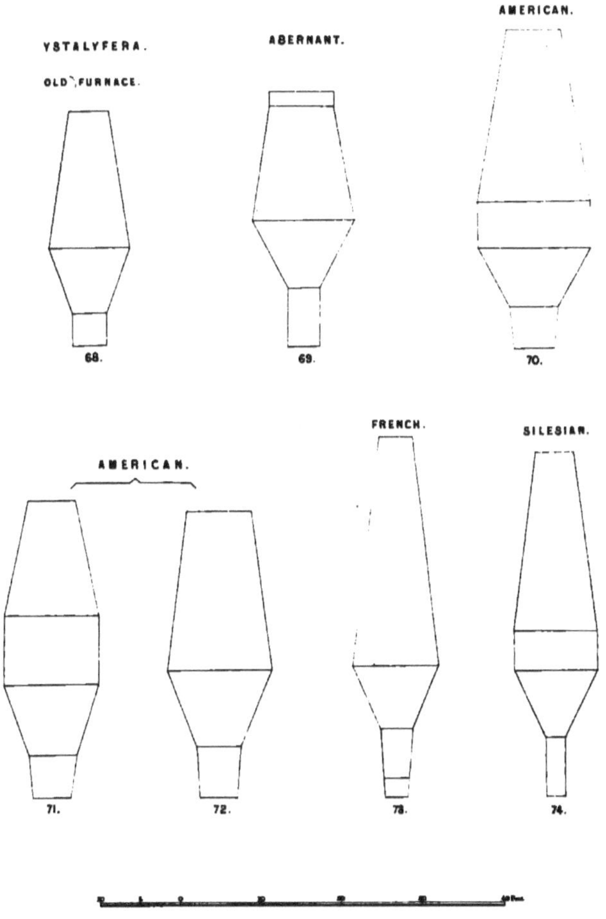
YSTALYFERA.
OLD FURNACE.
68.
ABERNANT.
69.
AMERICAN.
70.
AMERICAN.
71.
72.
FRENCH.
73.
SILESIAN.
74.
10 5 0 10 20 30 40 Feet

E & F N Spon, 16 Bucklersbury London.

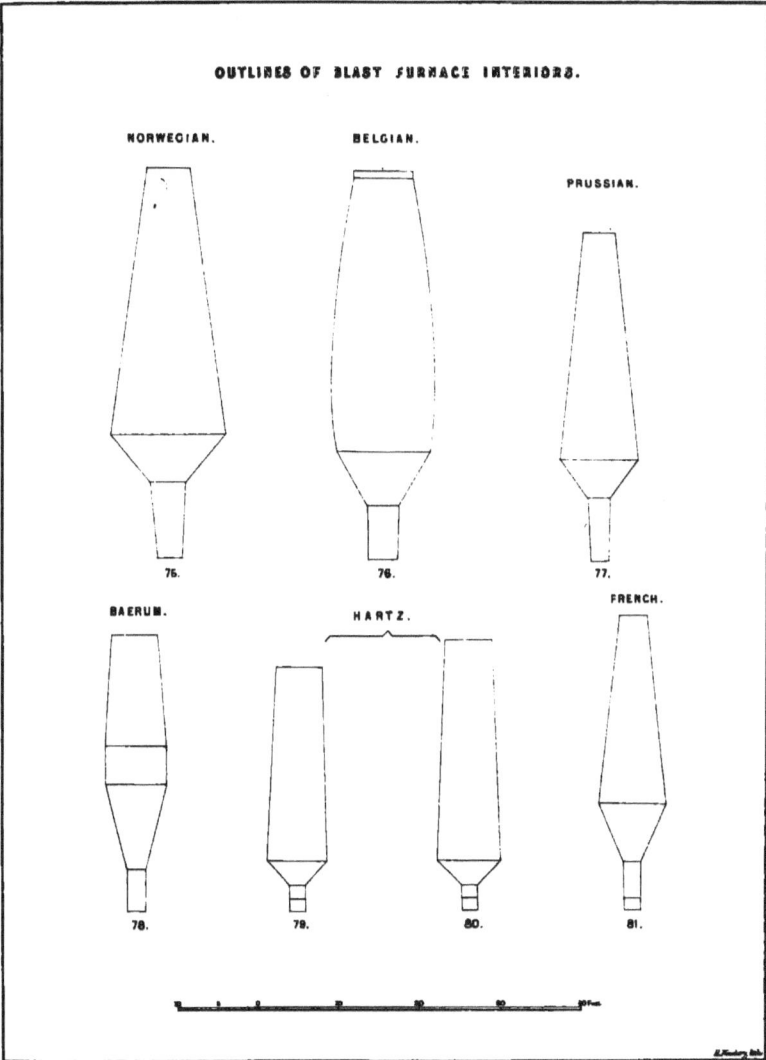

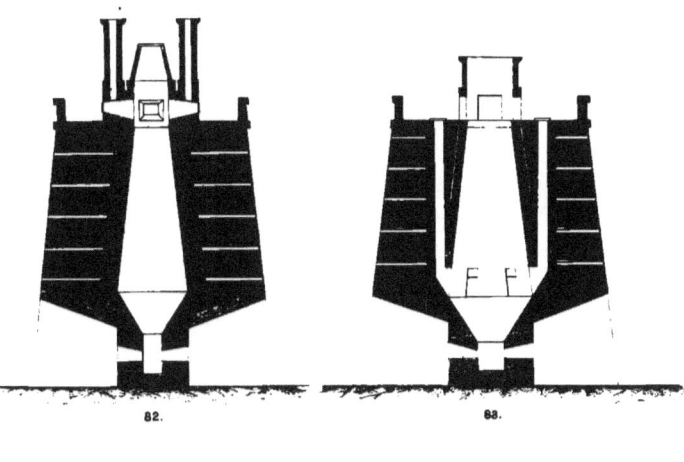
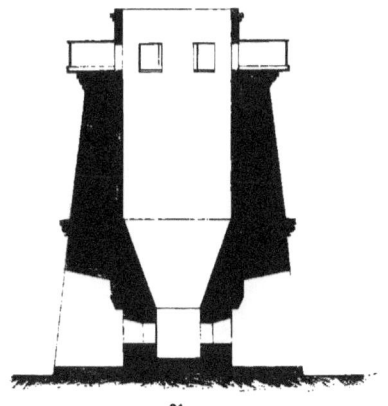

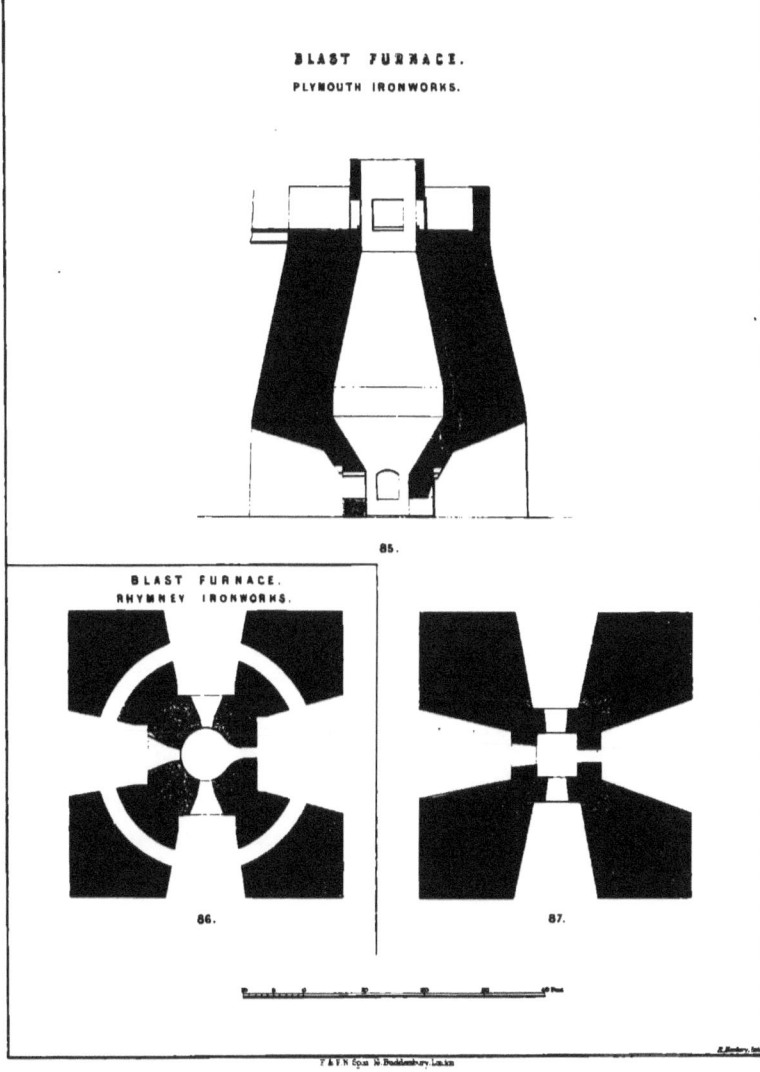

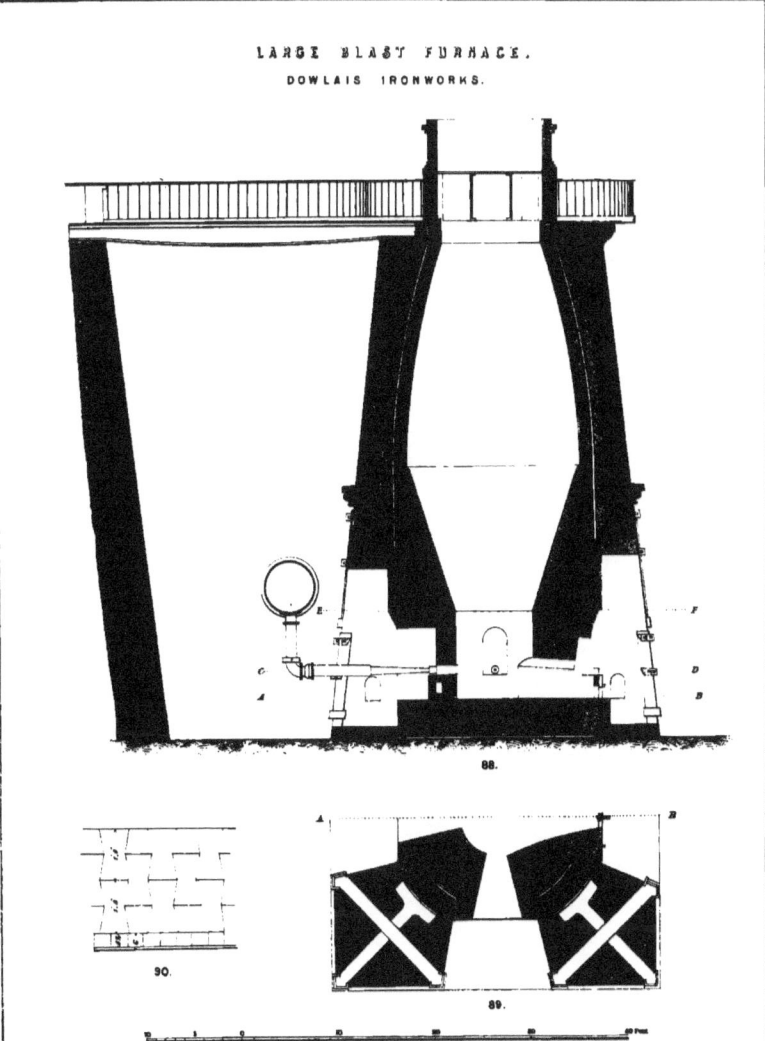

LARGE BLAST FURNACE.
DOWLAIS IRONWORKS.

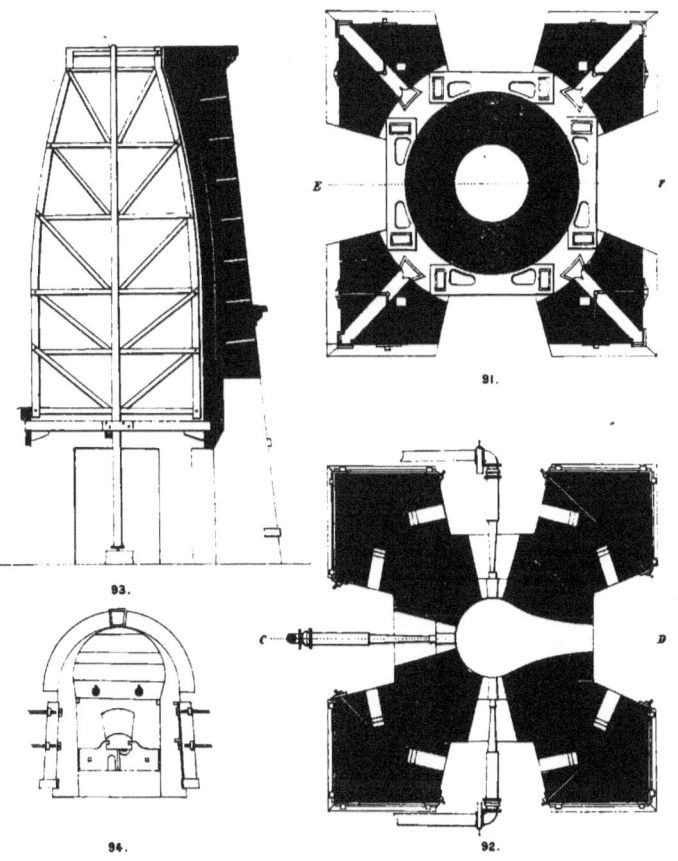

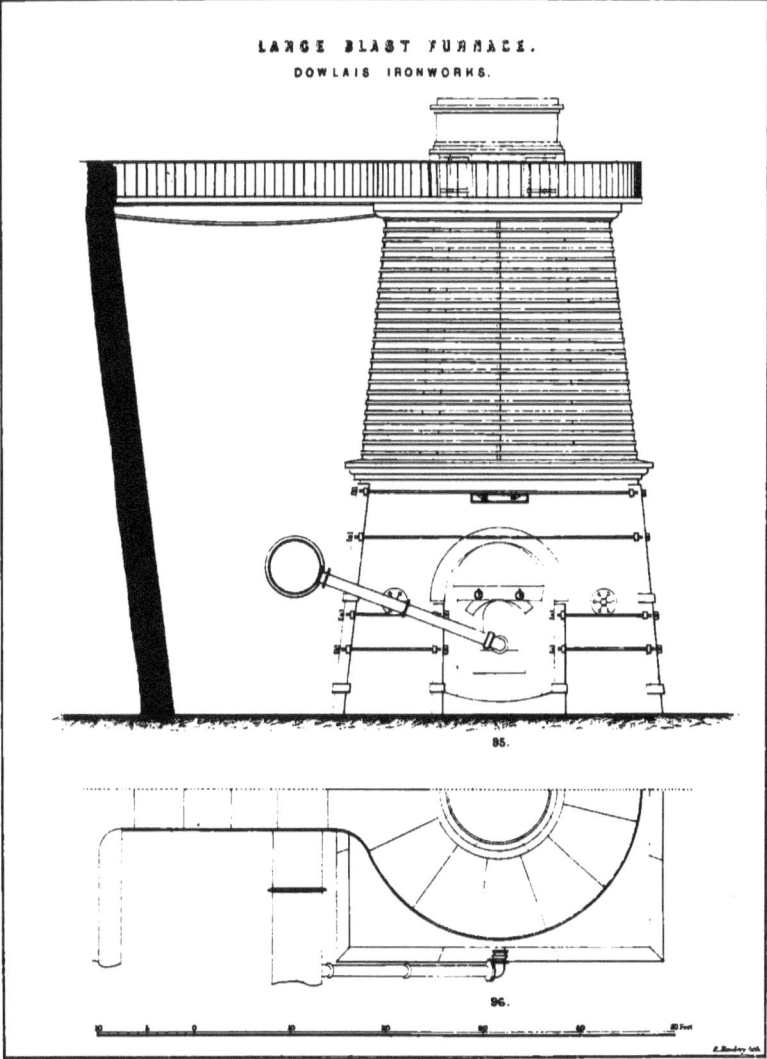

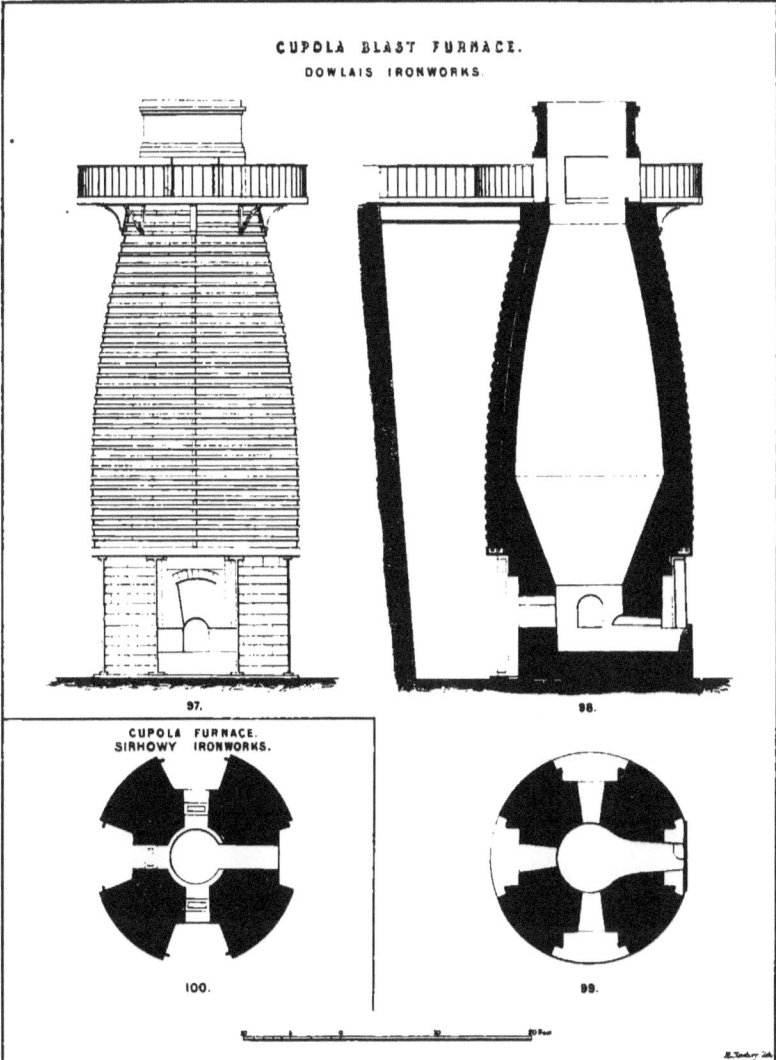

BLAST FURNACE.
ABERAMMAN IRONWORKS.

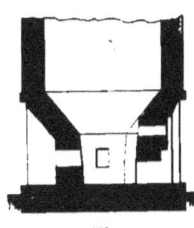

108.

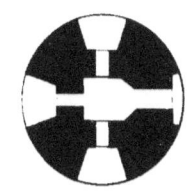

104.

BLAST FURNACE.
YSTATYFERA IRONWORKS.

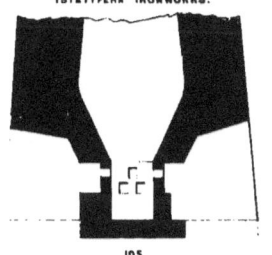

105.

BLAST FURNACE
TREDEGAR IRONWORKS

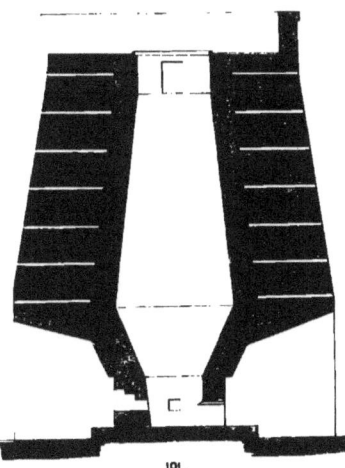

101.

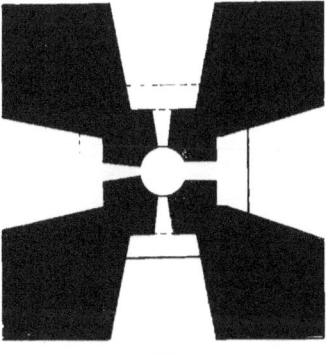

102.

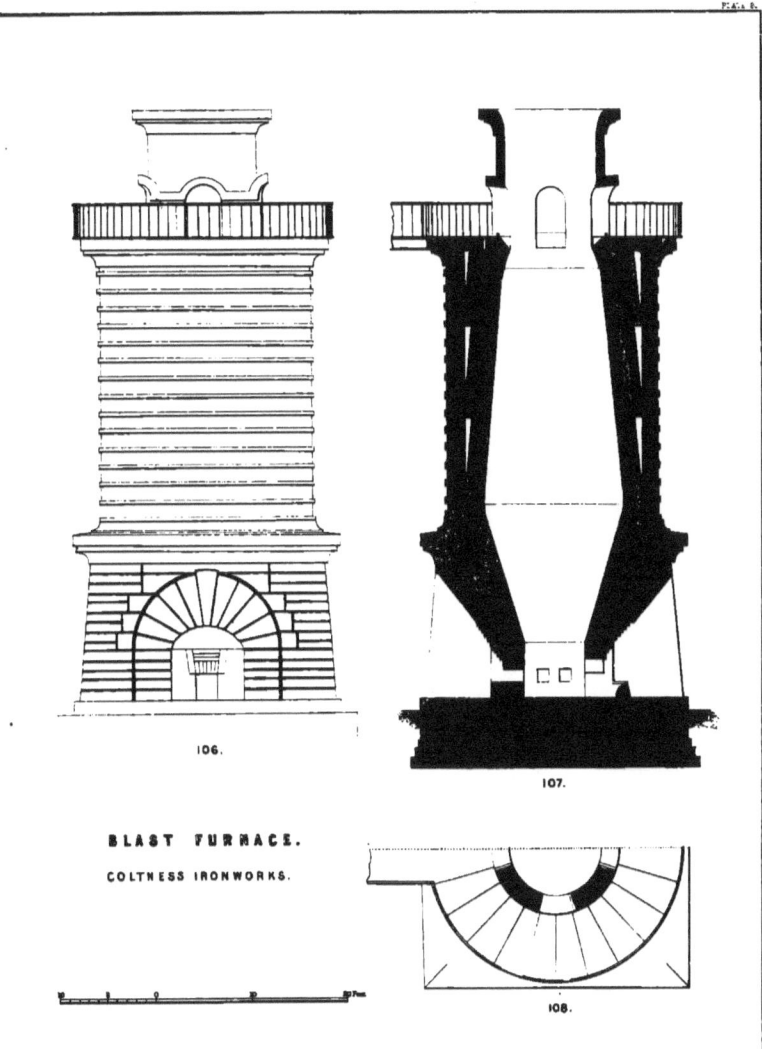

106.

107.

108.

BLAST FURNACE.

COLTNESS IRONWORKS.

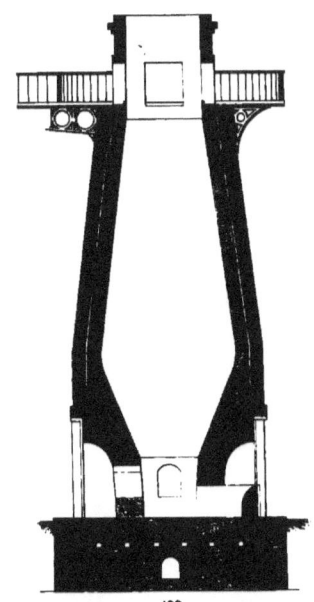

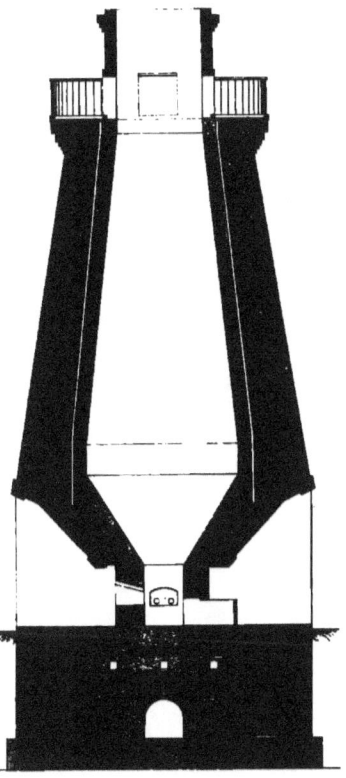

109.

110.

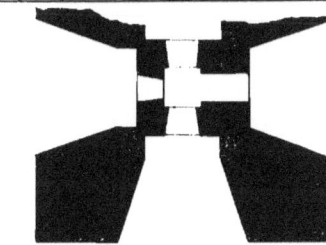

111.

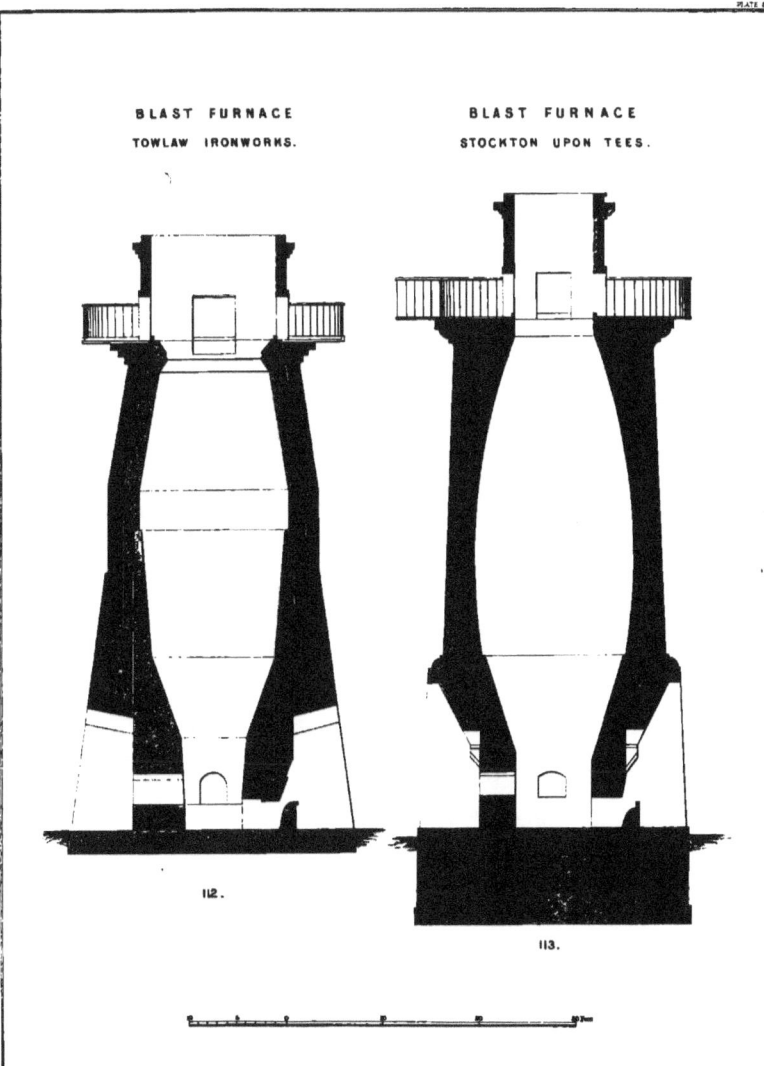

WATER BALANCE FURNACE LIFT.

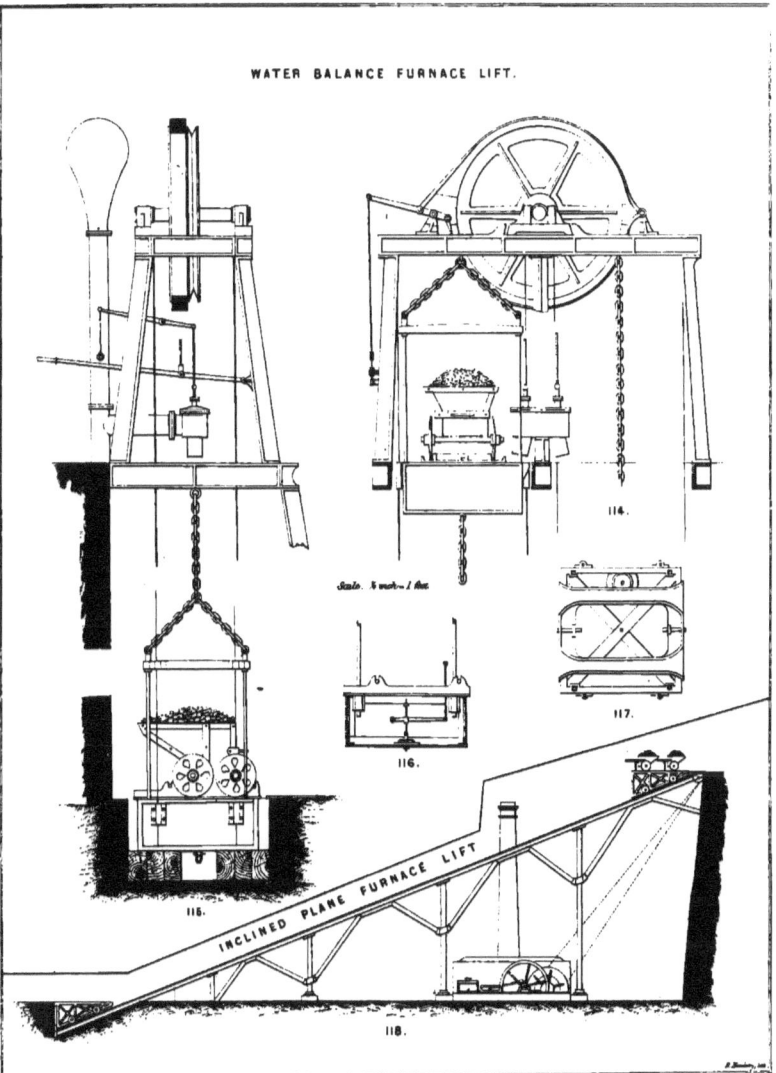

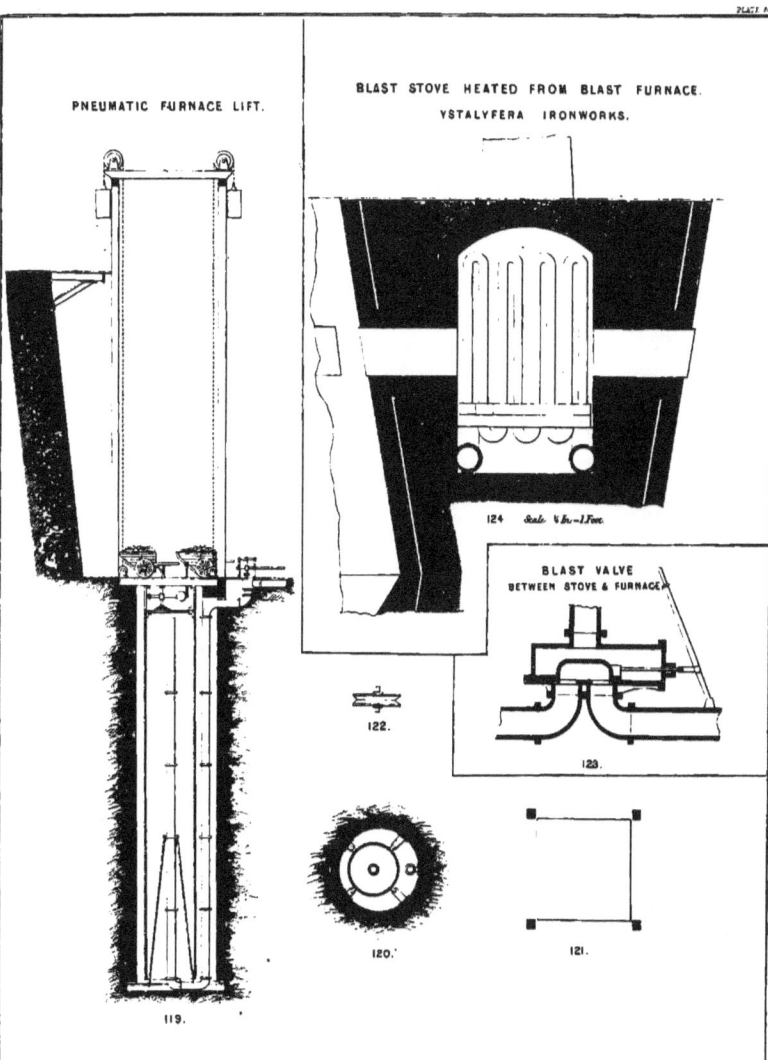

BLAST STOVES.

SOCKETS FOR STOVE PIPES.

127.

128.

Scale ½ In. = 1 Foot

PENY DARRAN IRONWORKS.

126

DOWLAIS IRONWORKS.

129.

125.

BLAST STOVE.
DOWLAIS IRONWORKS.

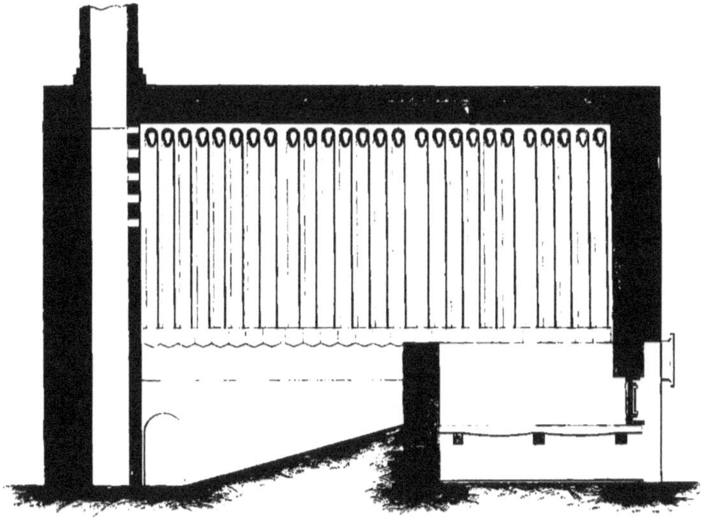

130.

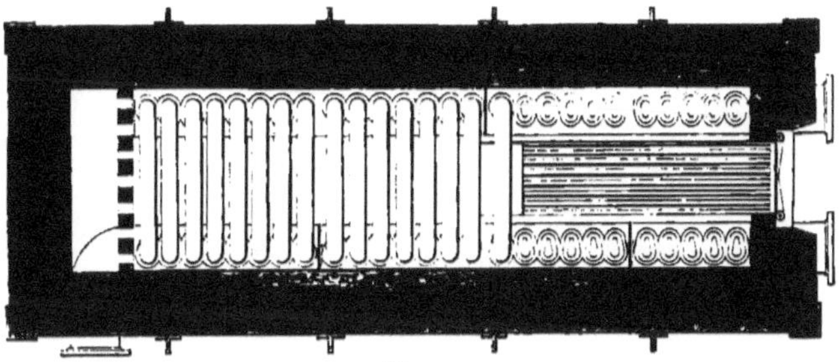

131.

Scale ¾ Inch = 1 Foot.

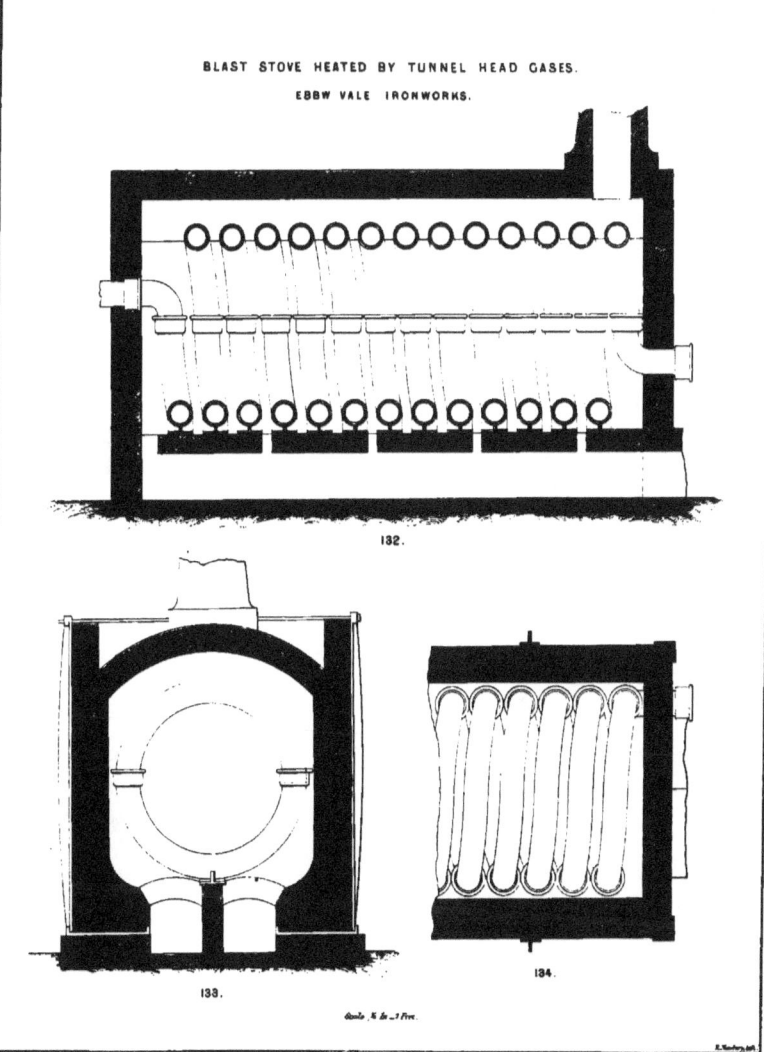

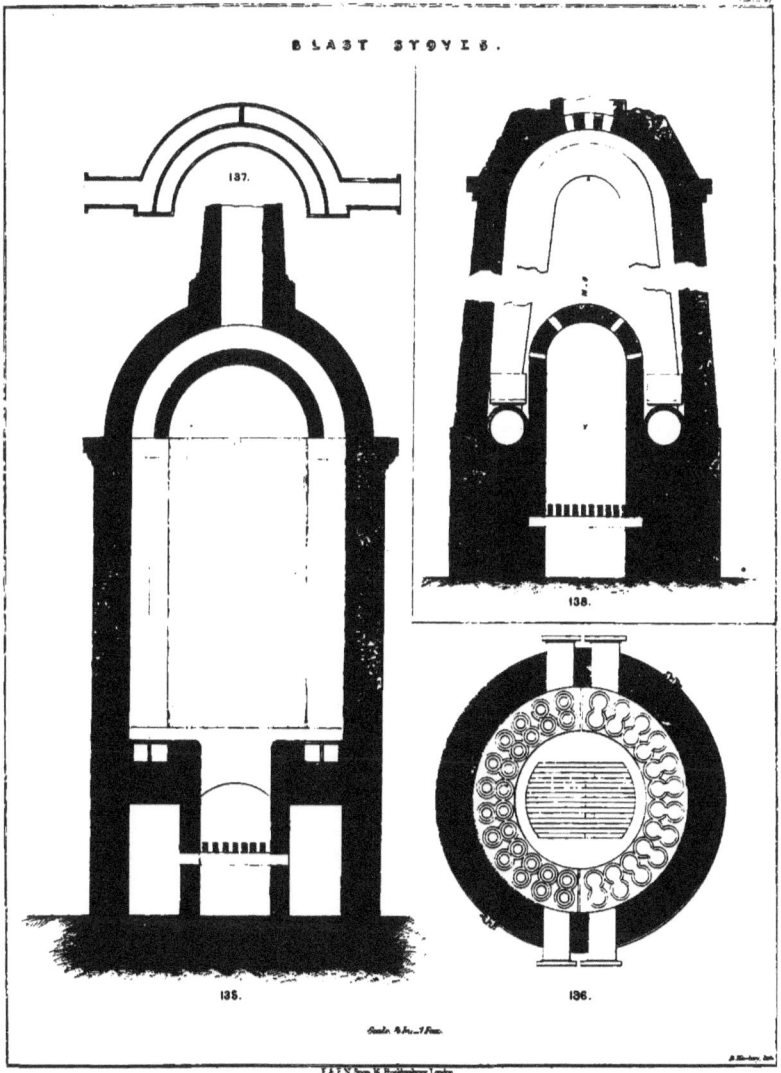

DETAILS OF BLAST FURNACES.
MODES OF COLLECTING FURNACE GASES.

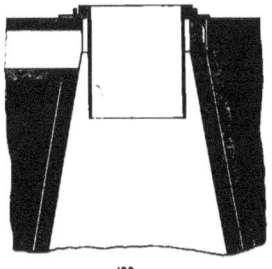

139.

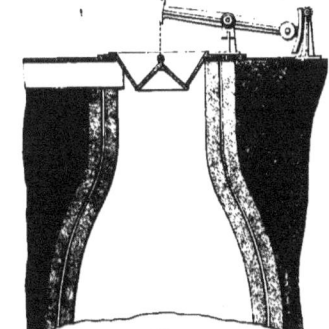

142.

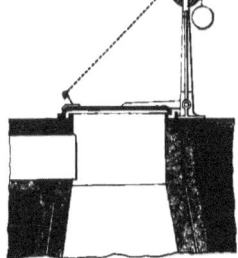

140.

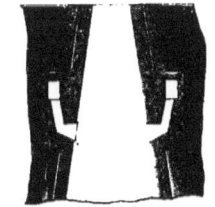

143.

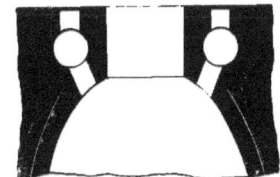

141.

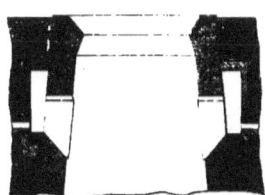

144.

Scale ¾ In. = 1 Foot.

DETAILS OF BLAST FURNACES.
CAST IRON CURBS AND DOOR FRAMES FOR CHARGING HOLES.

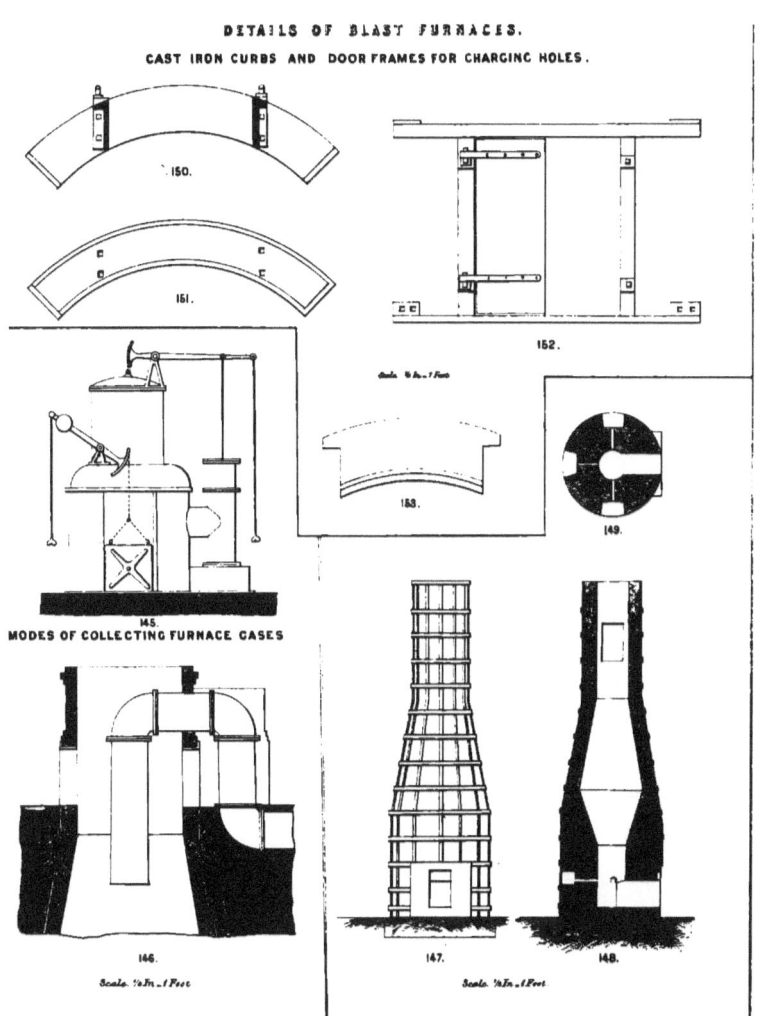

145.
MODES OF COLLECTING FURNACE GASES

DETAILS OF BLAST FURNACES.

BLAST STOP VALVES.

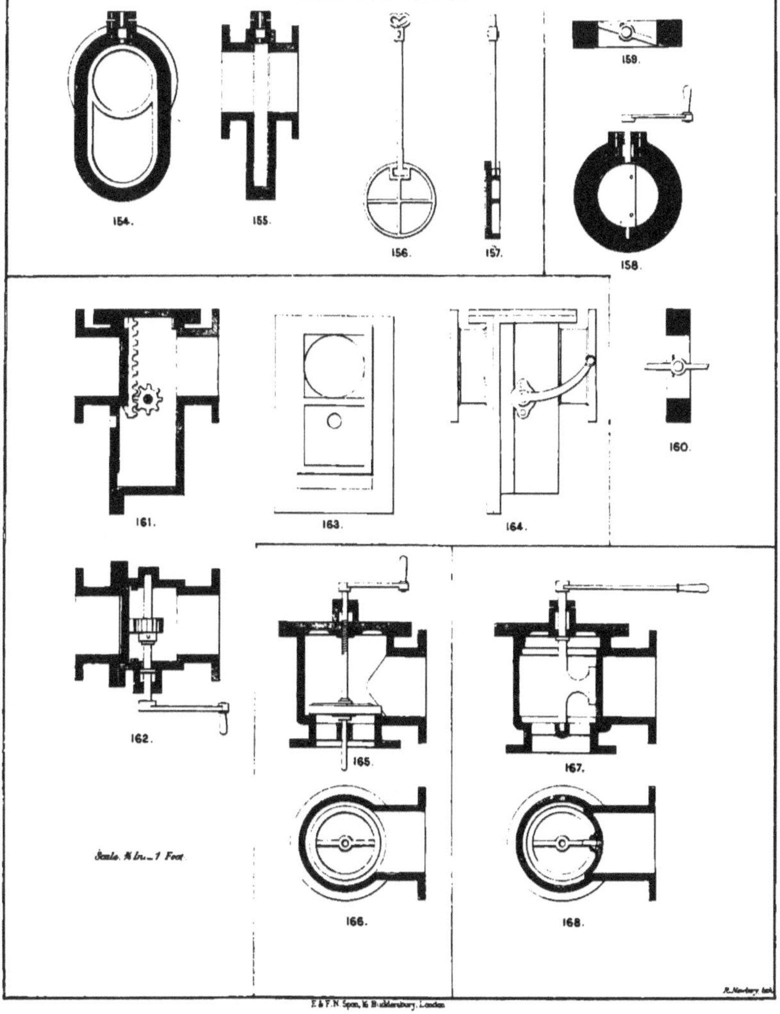

E & F. N. Spon, 16 Bucklersbury, London

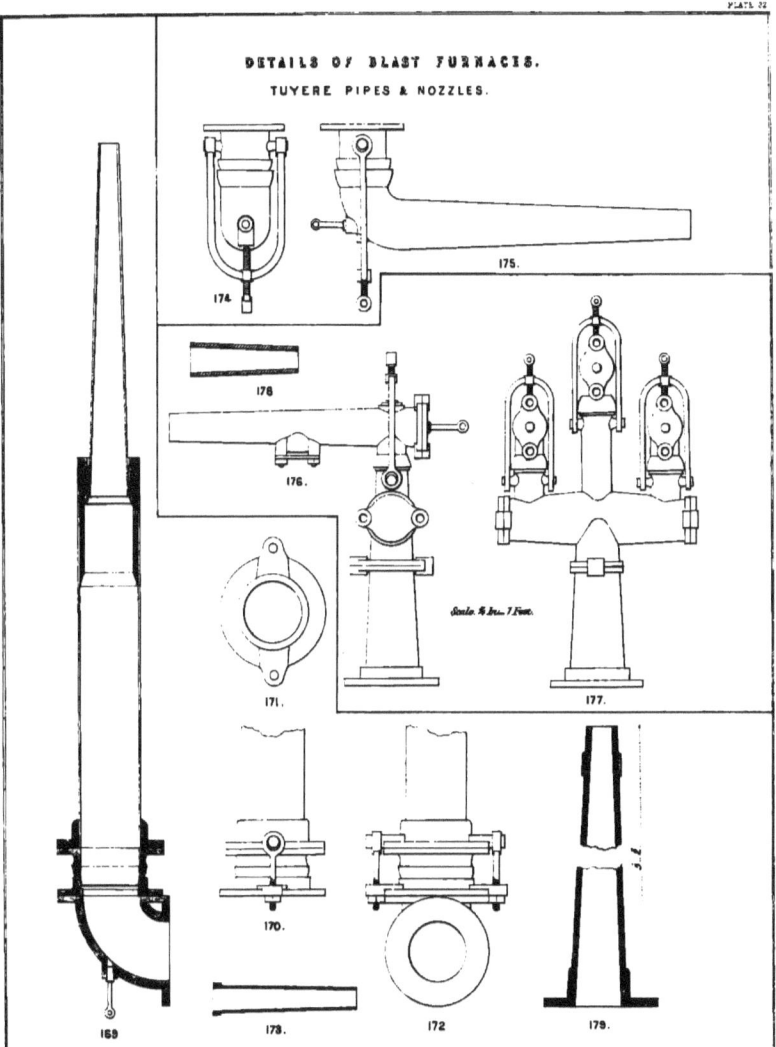

DETAILS OF BLAST FURNACES.
TUYERE PIPES, WATER TUYERES & BREASTS.

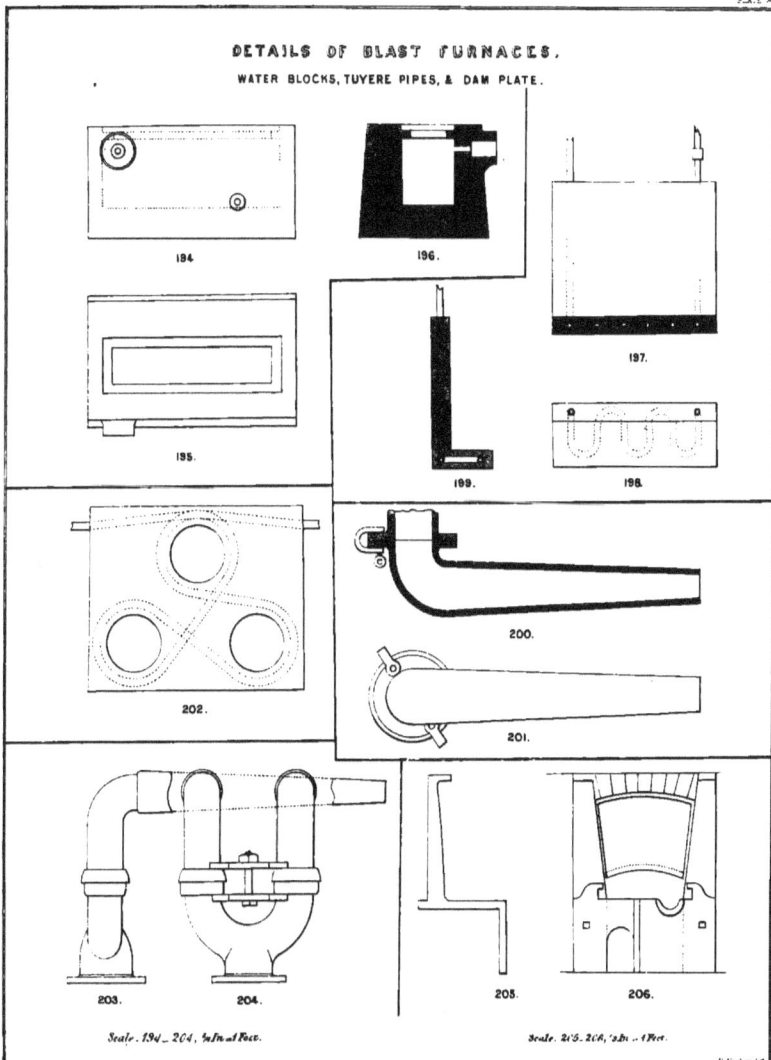

DETAILS OF BLAST FURNACES.
WATER BLOCKS, TUYERE PIPES, & DAM PLATE.

DETAILS OF BLAST FURNACES.
CHARGING BARROWS.

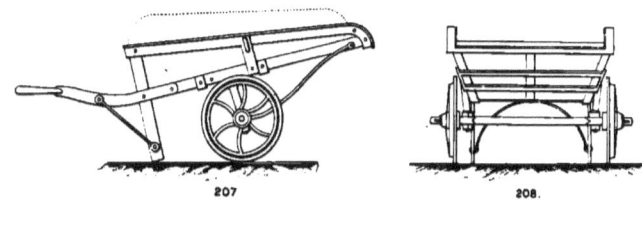

207. 208.

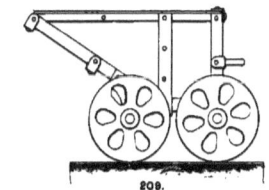 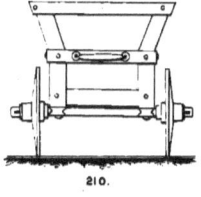 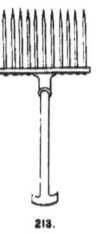

209. 210. 213.

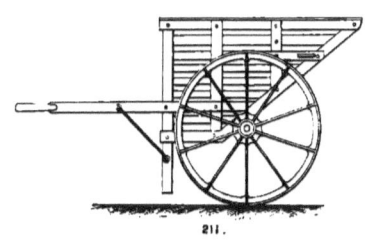 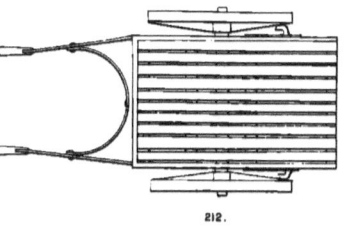

211. 212.

Scale. ½ In. = 1 Foot.

DETAILS OF BLAST FURNACES.
PLAN OF CINDER FALL, TOOLS &c.

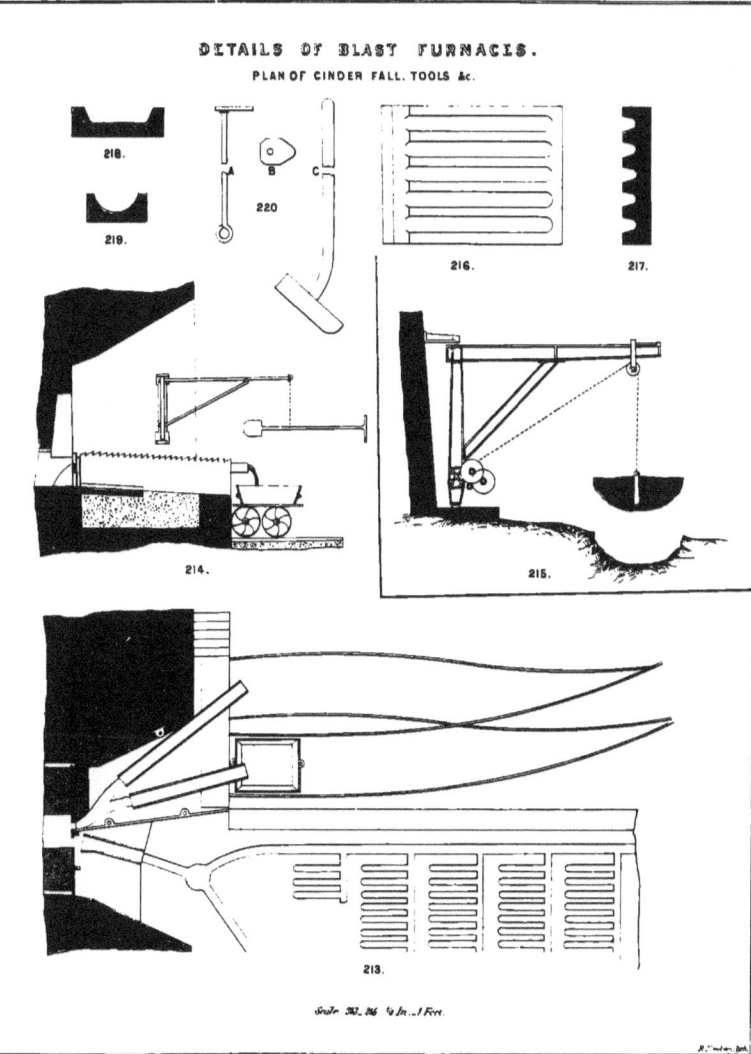

DETAILS OF BLAST FURNACE.

CINDER TUBS AND FURNACE IMPLEMENTS.

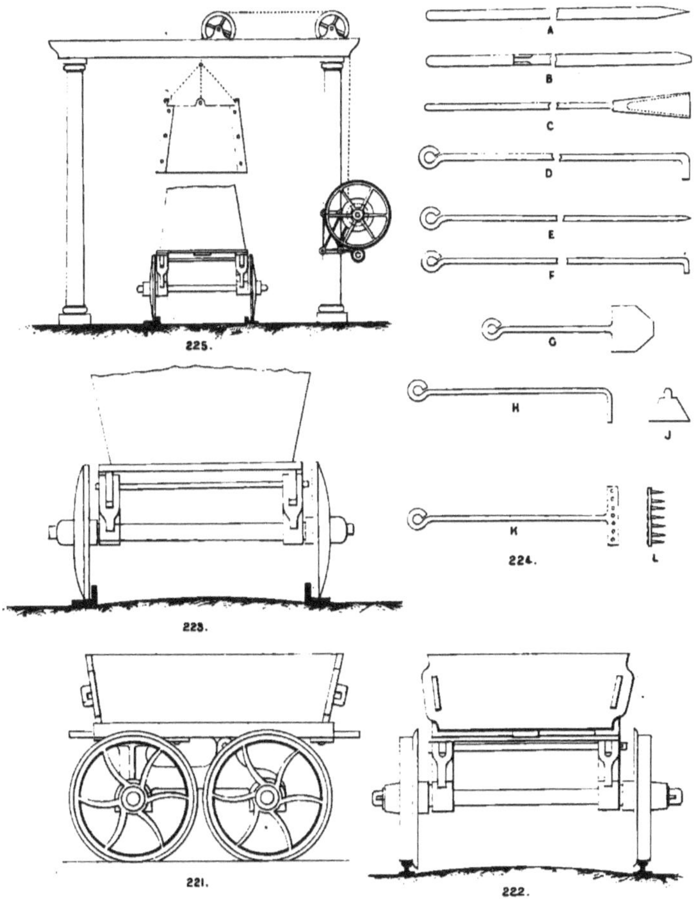
A
B
C
D
E
F
G
H
J
K
L
224.
225.
223.
221.
222.

Scale 221 — 223. ½ In. = 1 Foot.

R. Newbery, lith.

E. & F. N. Spon, 16, Bucklersbury, London.

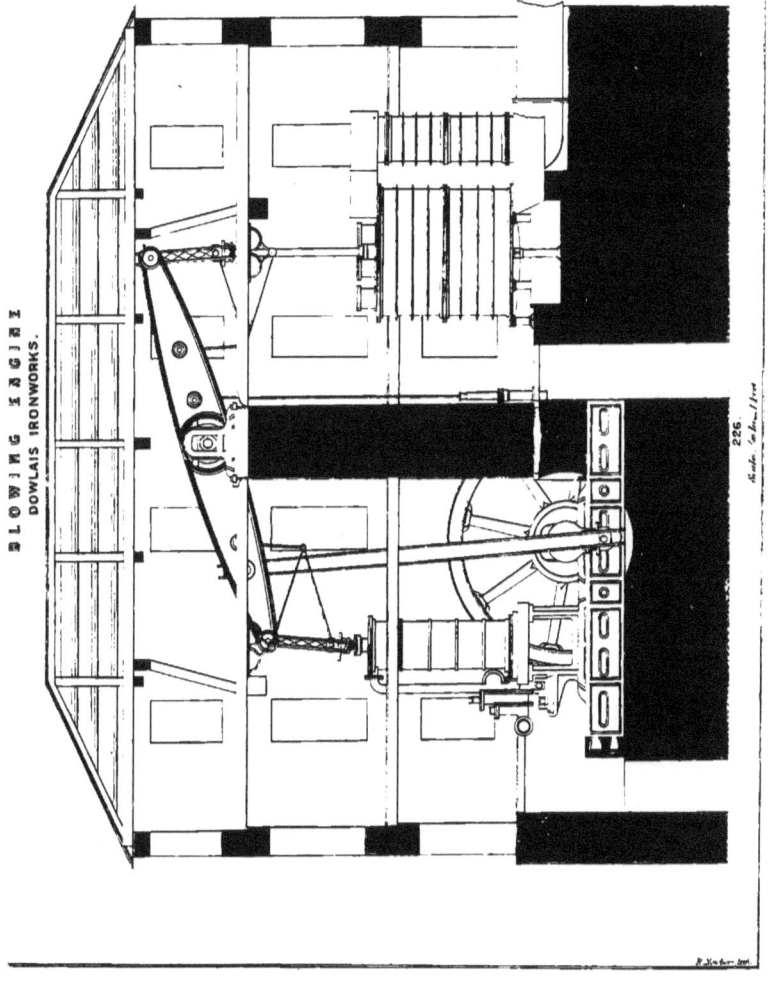

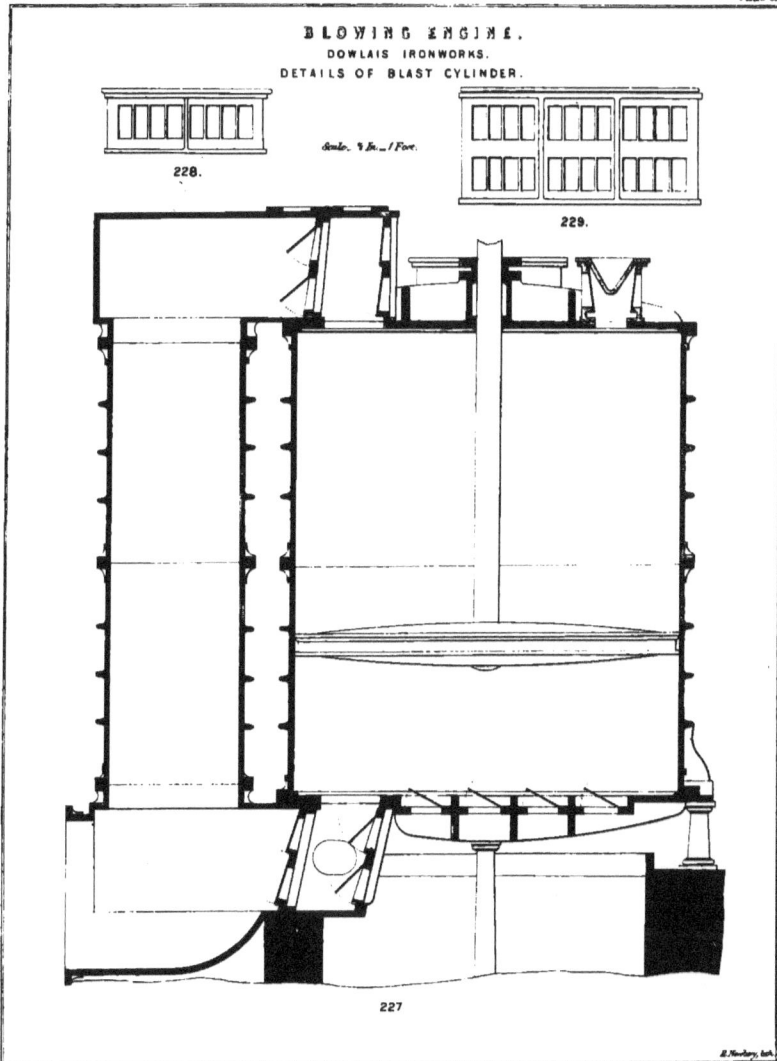

BLOWING ENGINE.
DOWLAIS IRONWORKS.
DETAILS OF BLAST CYLINDER.

BLOWING ENGINE.
DOWLAIS IRONWORKS.
DETAILS OF BLAST CYLINDER.

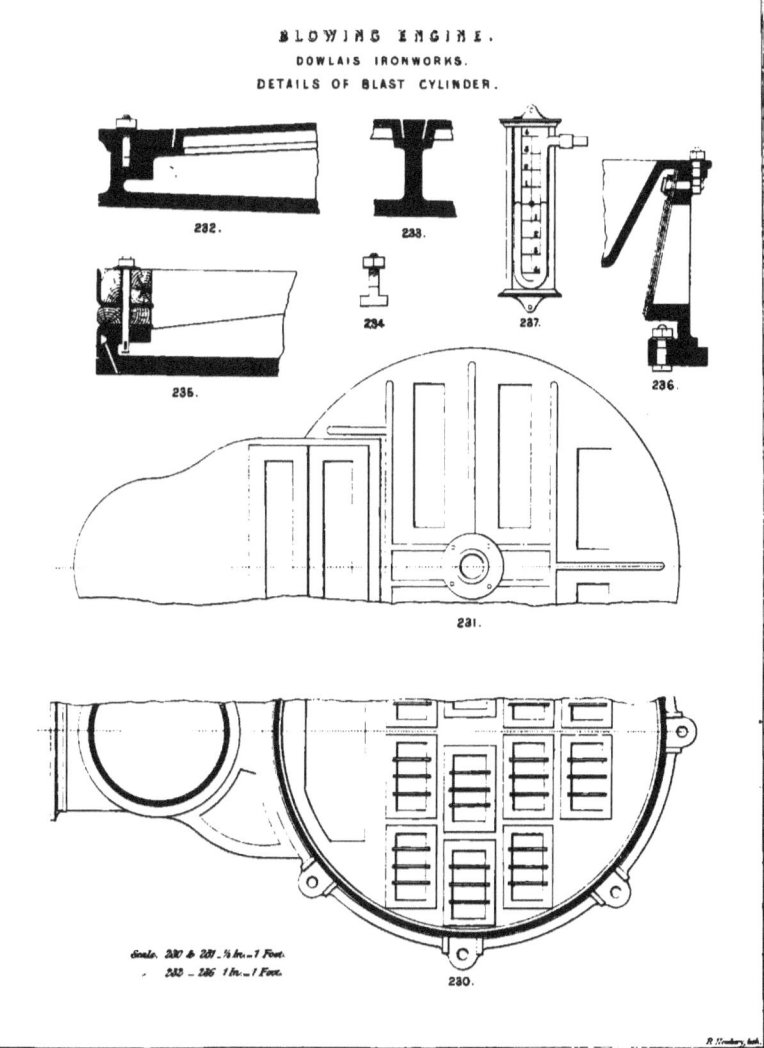

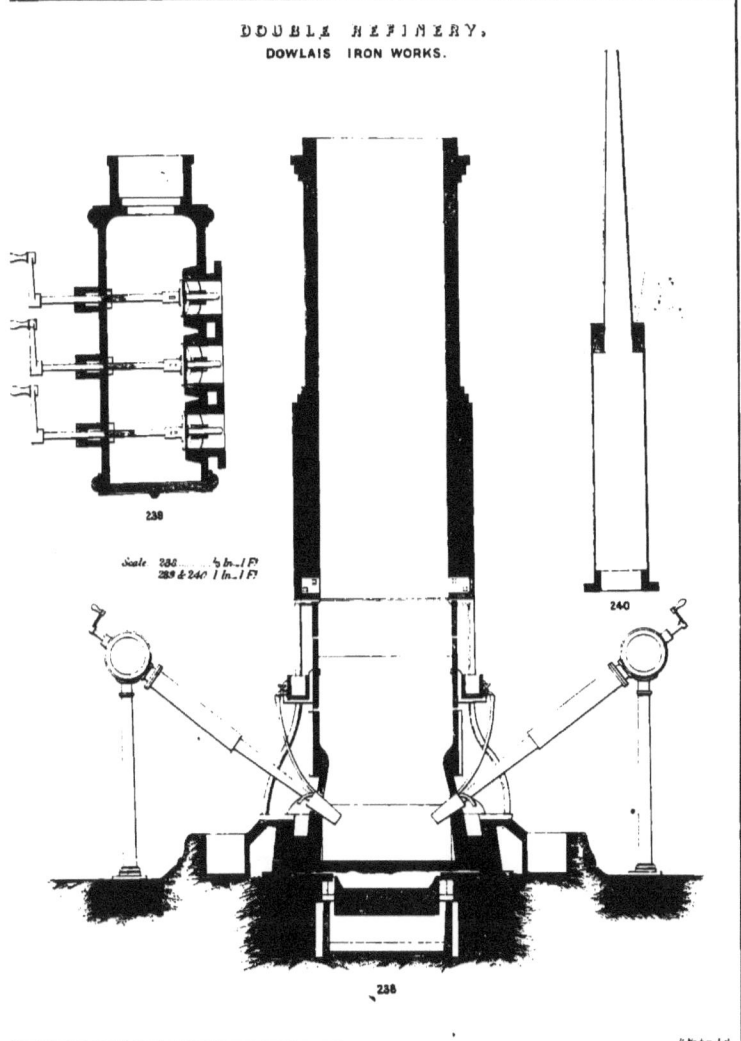

DOUBLE REFINERY.
DOWLAIS IRON WORKS.

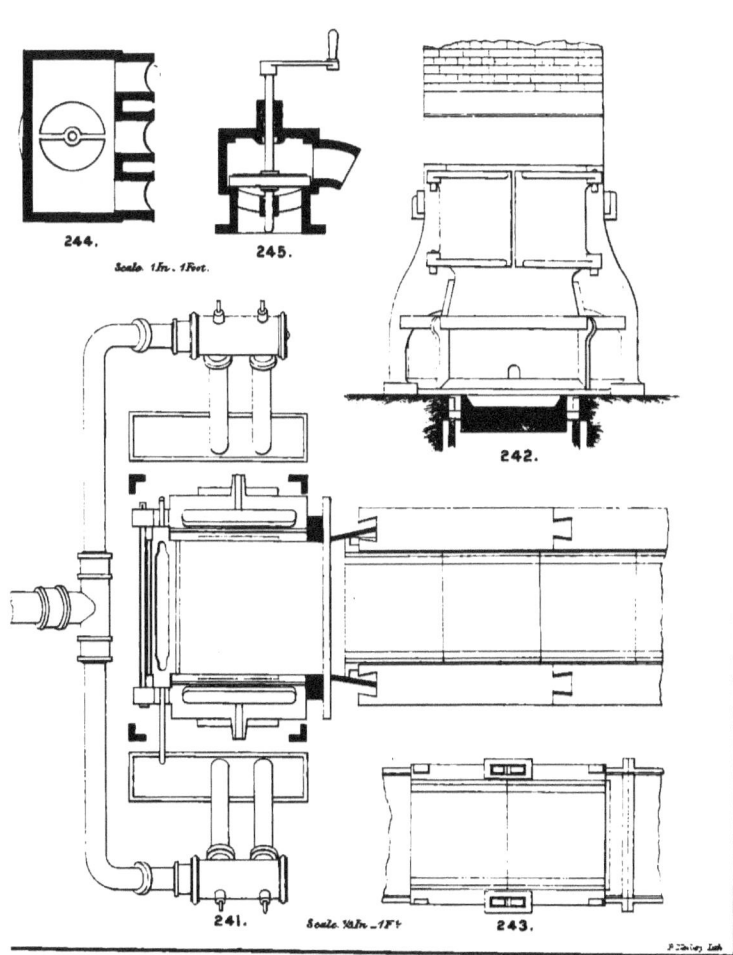

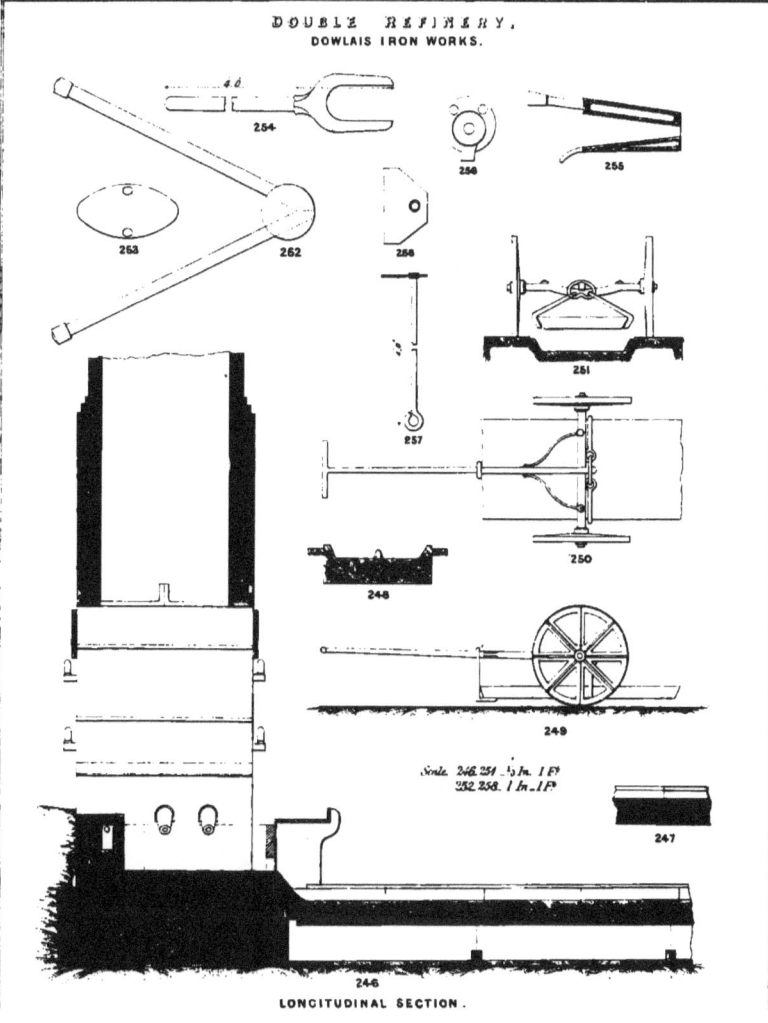

DOUBLE REFINERY,
DOWLAIS IRON WORKS.

LONGITUDINAL SECTION.

BOILING FURNACE.

Scale ⅛ In.= 1 Ft.

261.
262.
260.
259.

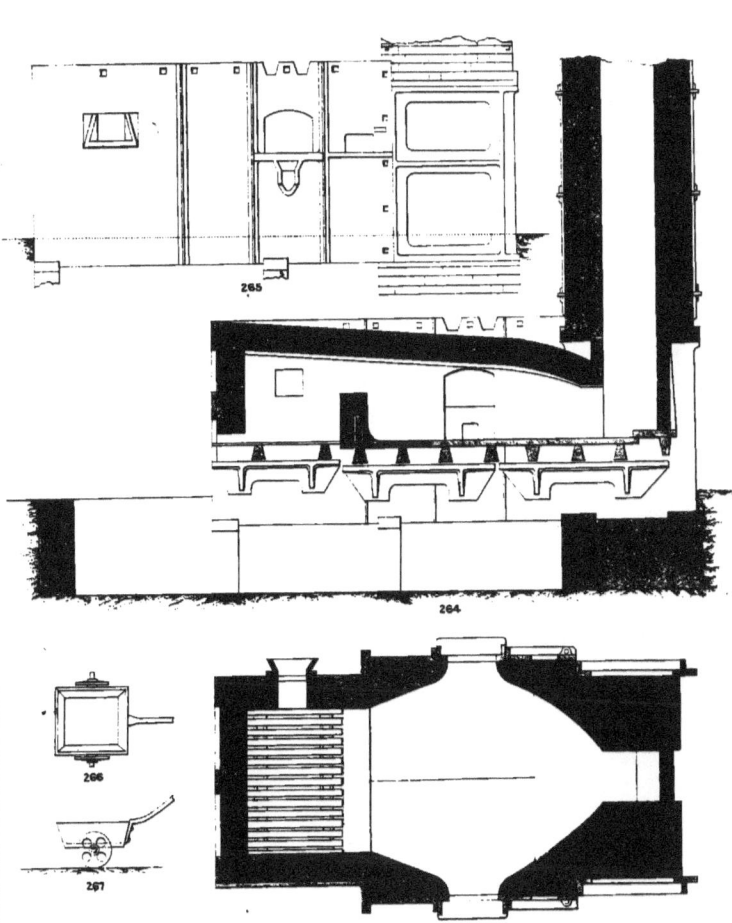

DOUBLE PUDDLING FURNACE.

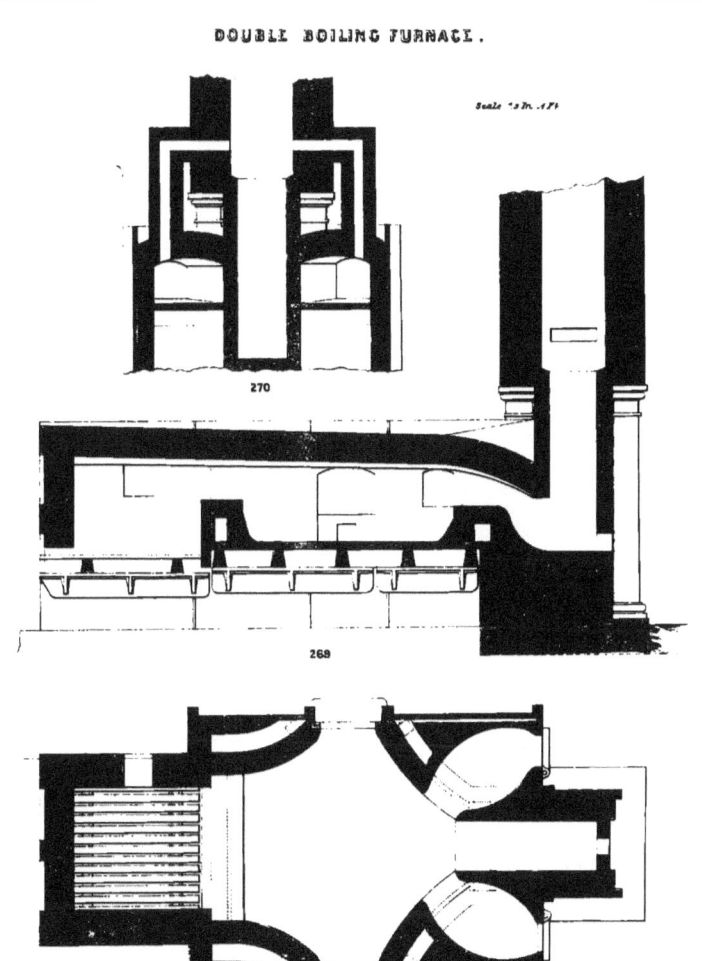

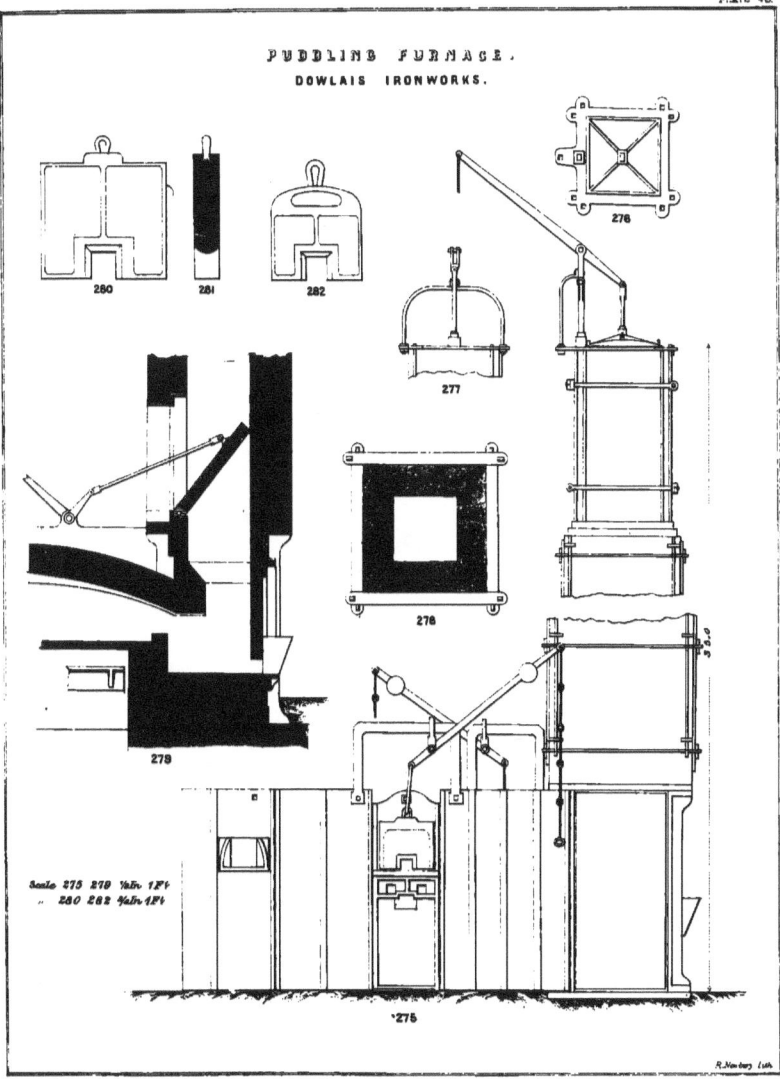

PUDDLING FURNACE.
PLYMOUTH IRONWORKS.

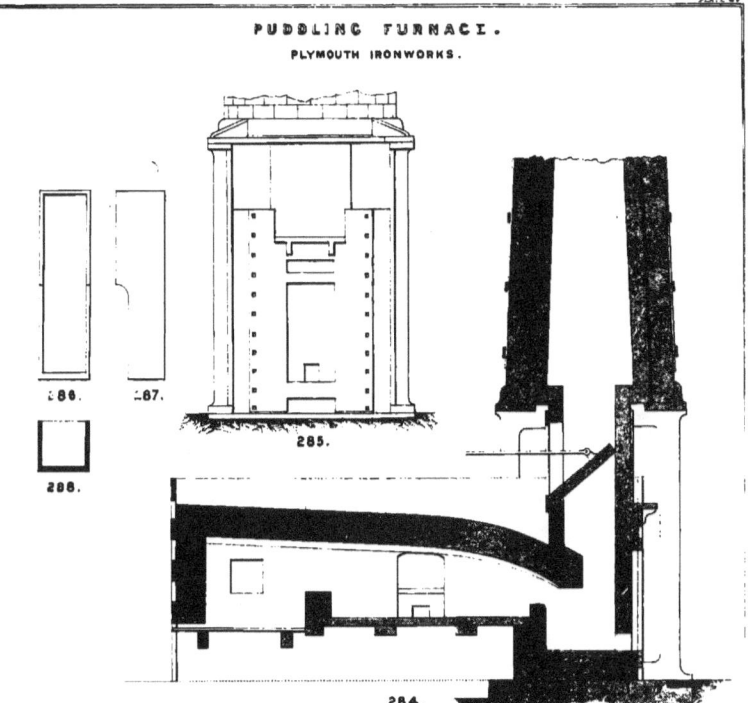

285.

286.   287.

288.

284.

Scale ½ In =1 Foot

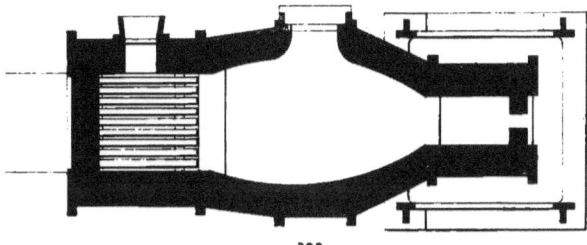

283.

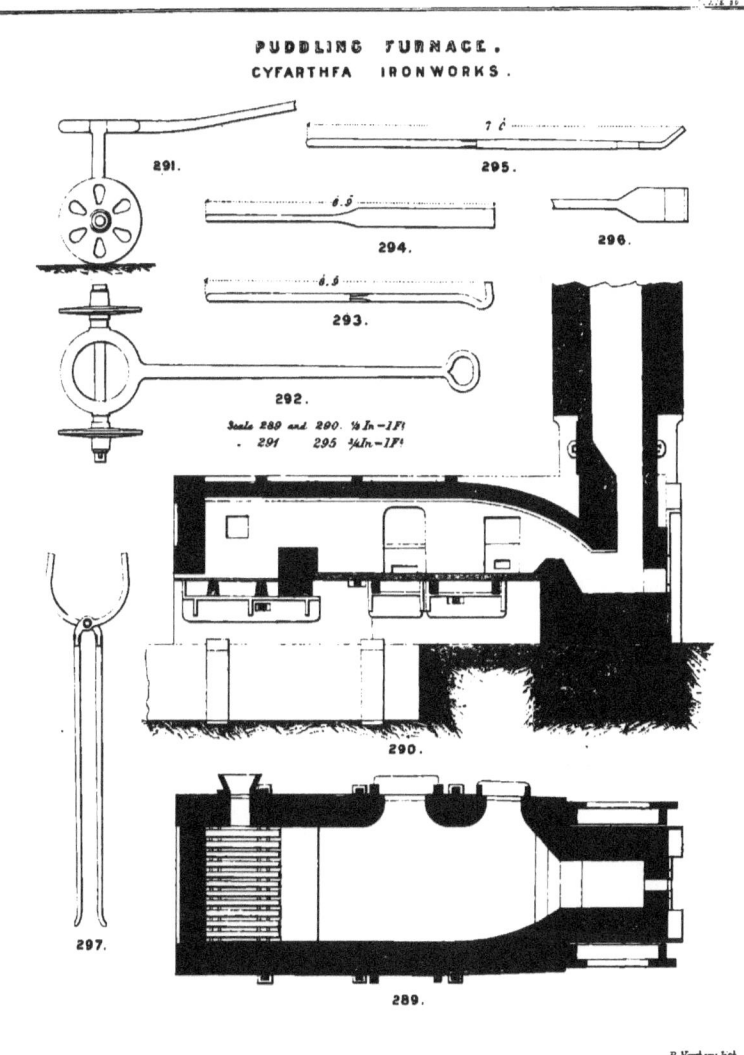

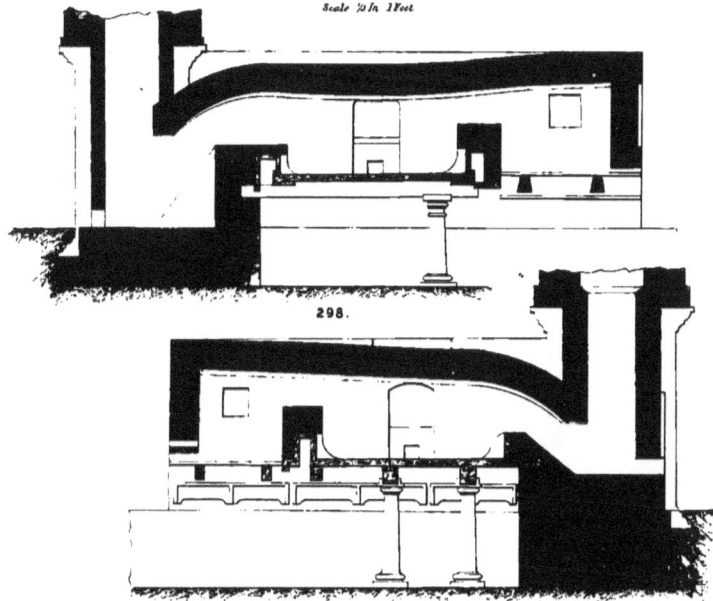

298.

299

300.

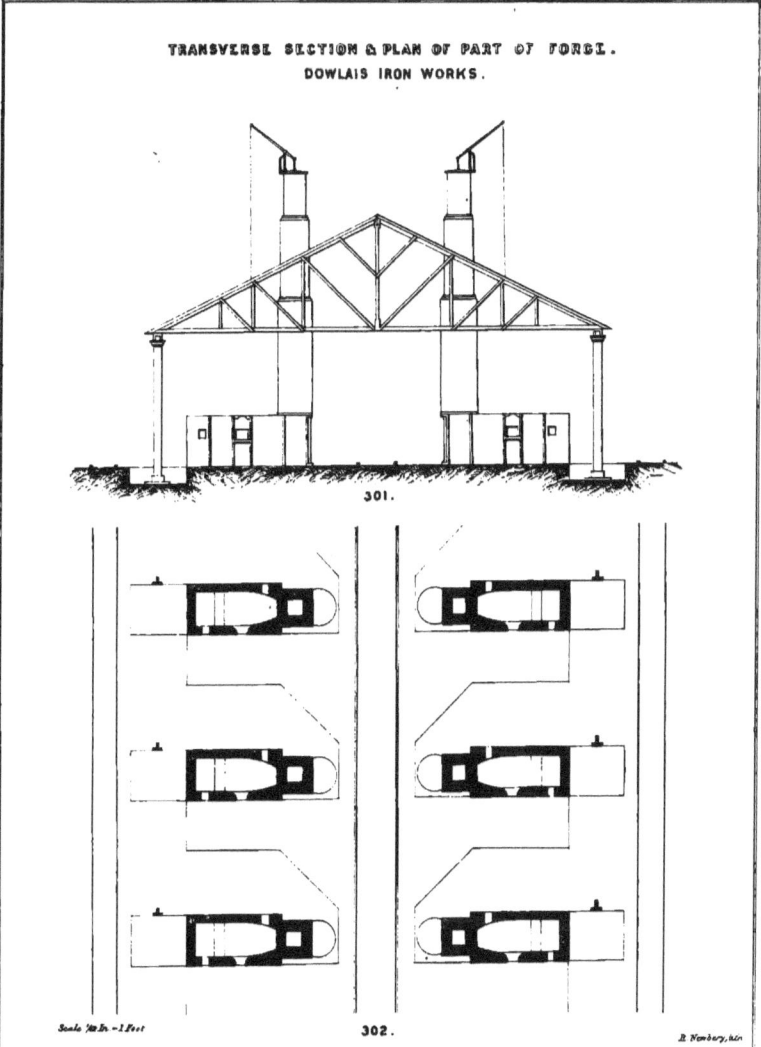

PLATE 60

FORGE TRAIN & SQUEEZER.
CYFARTHFA IRONWORKS.

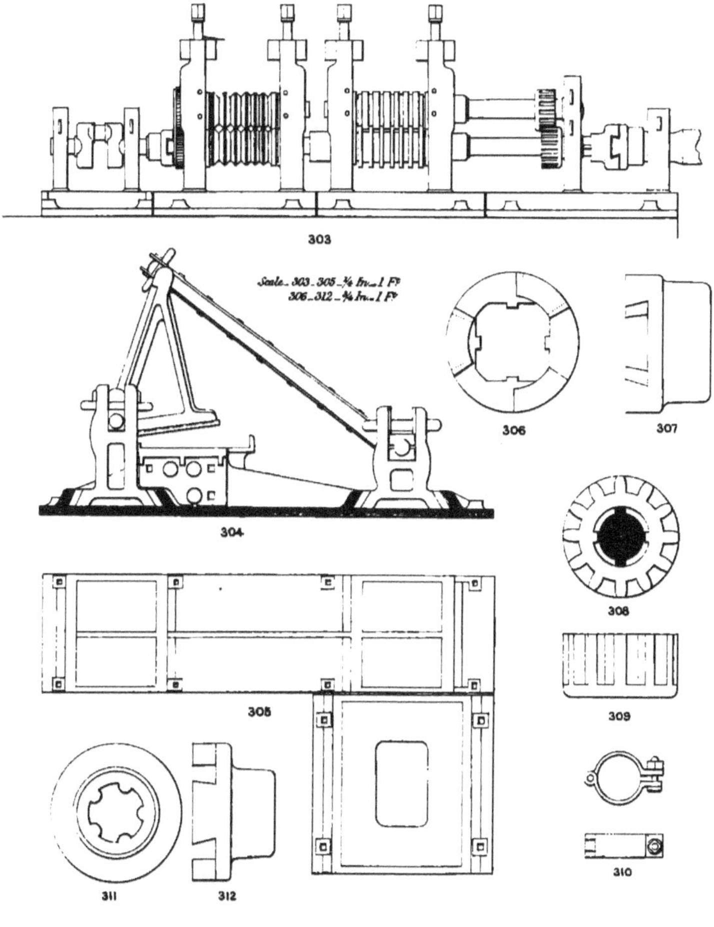

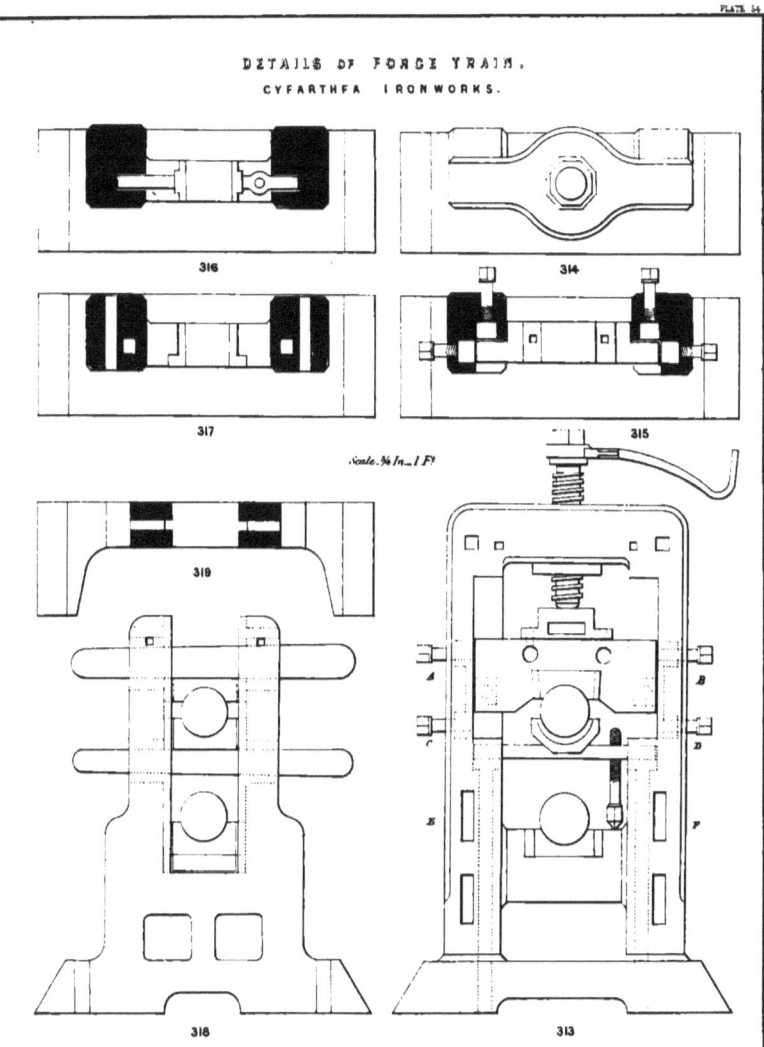

DETAILS OF FORGE TRAIN.
CYFARTHFA IRONWORKS.

DETAILS OF FORGE TRAIN.
CYFARTHFA IRONWORKS.

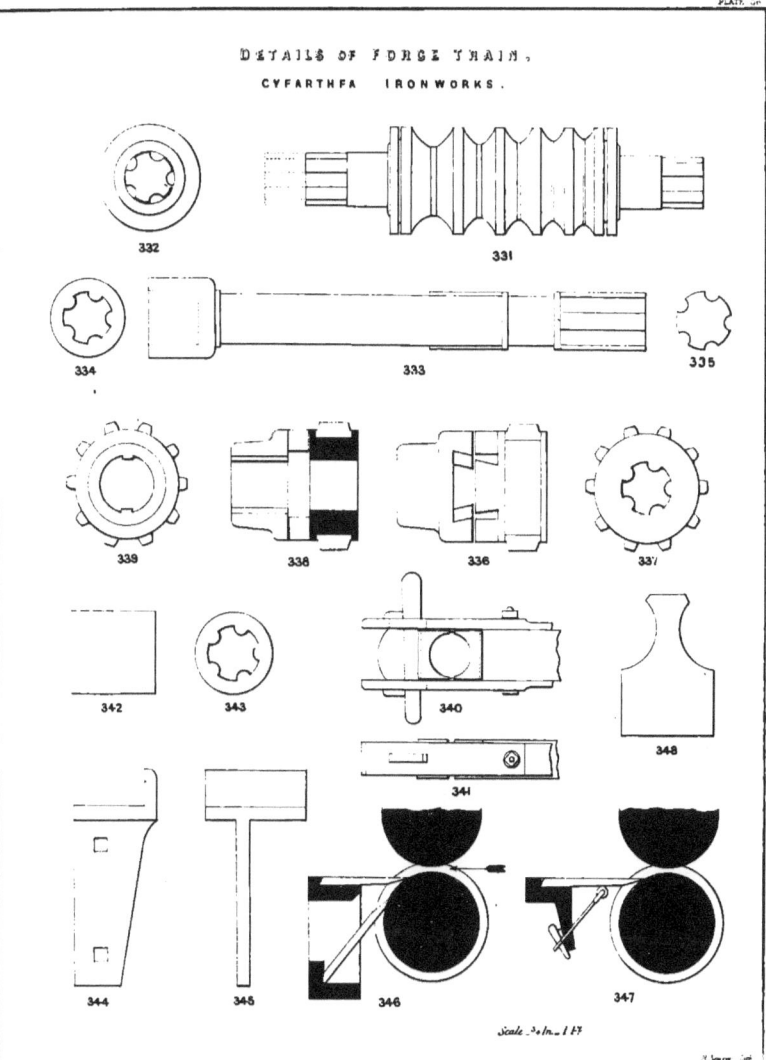

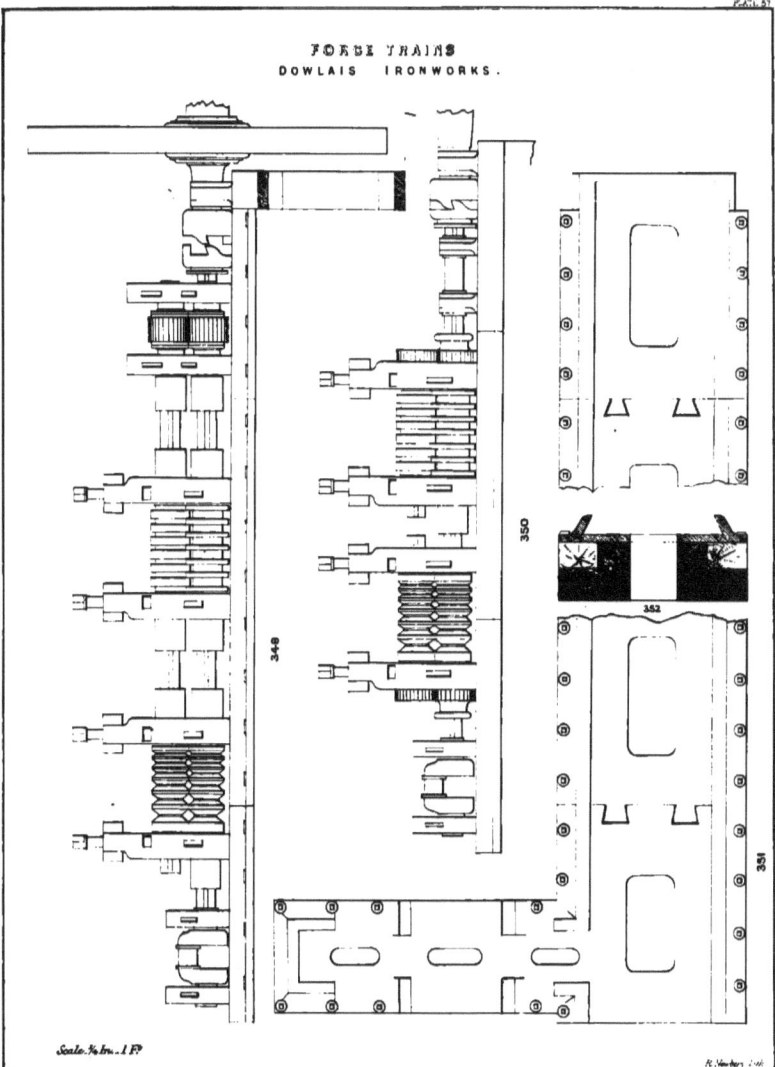

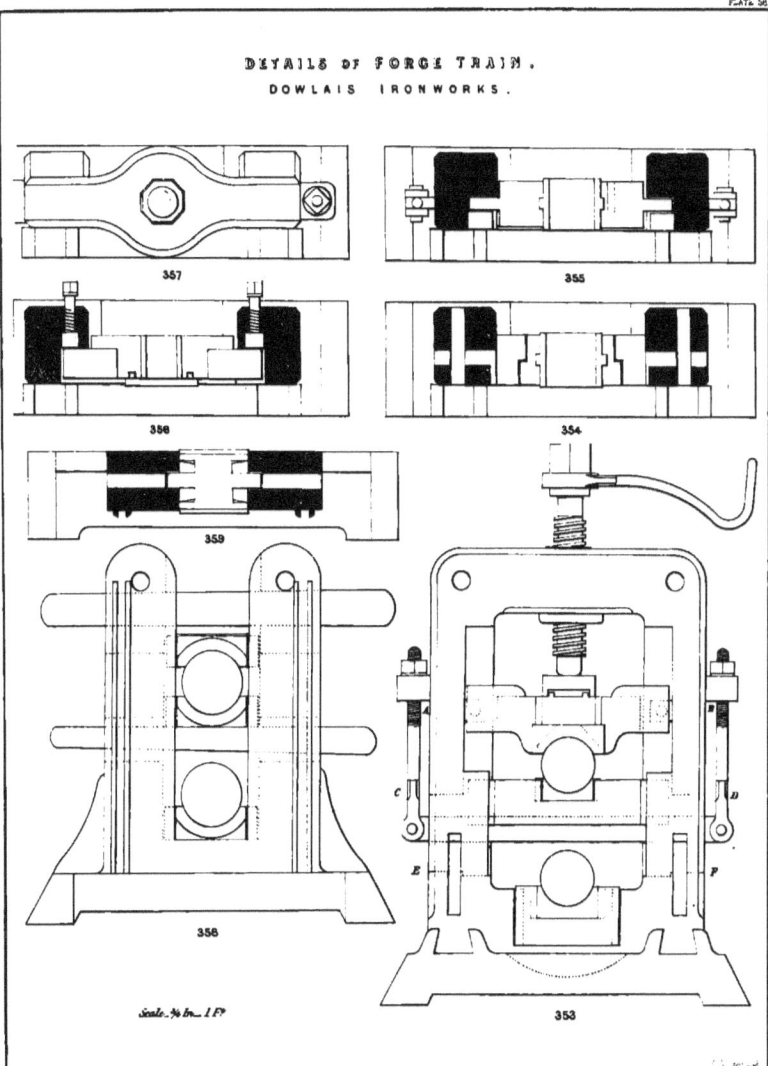

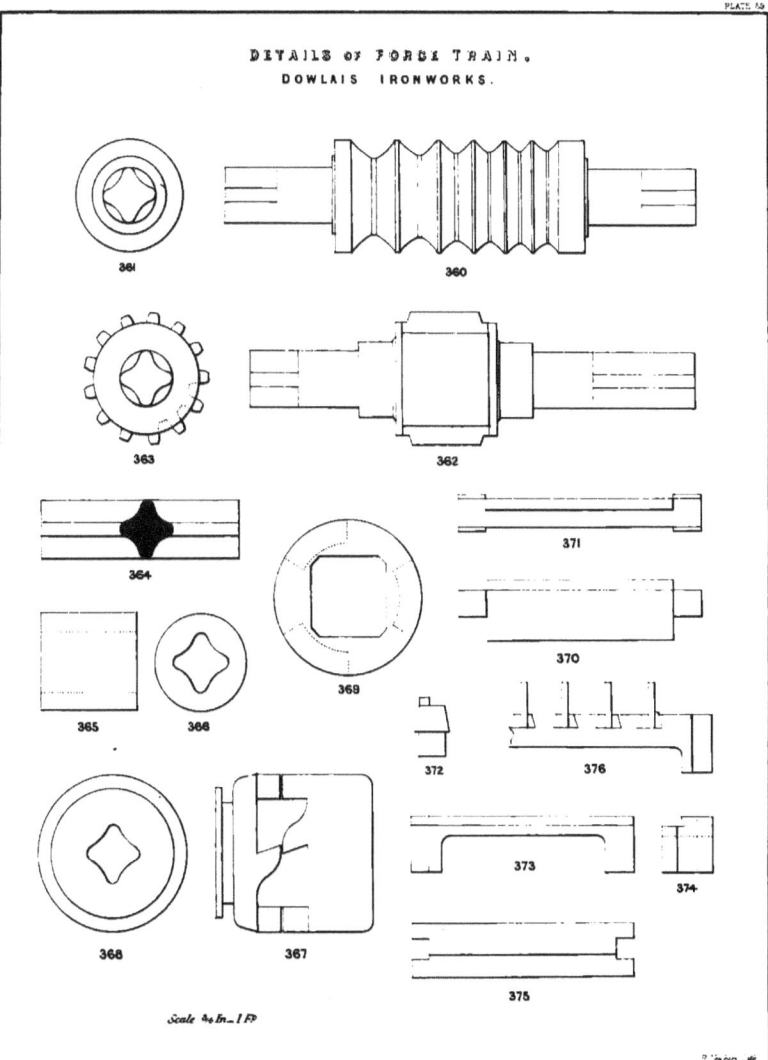

DETAILS OF FORGE TRAIN.
DOWLAIS IRONWORKS.

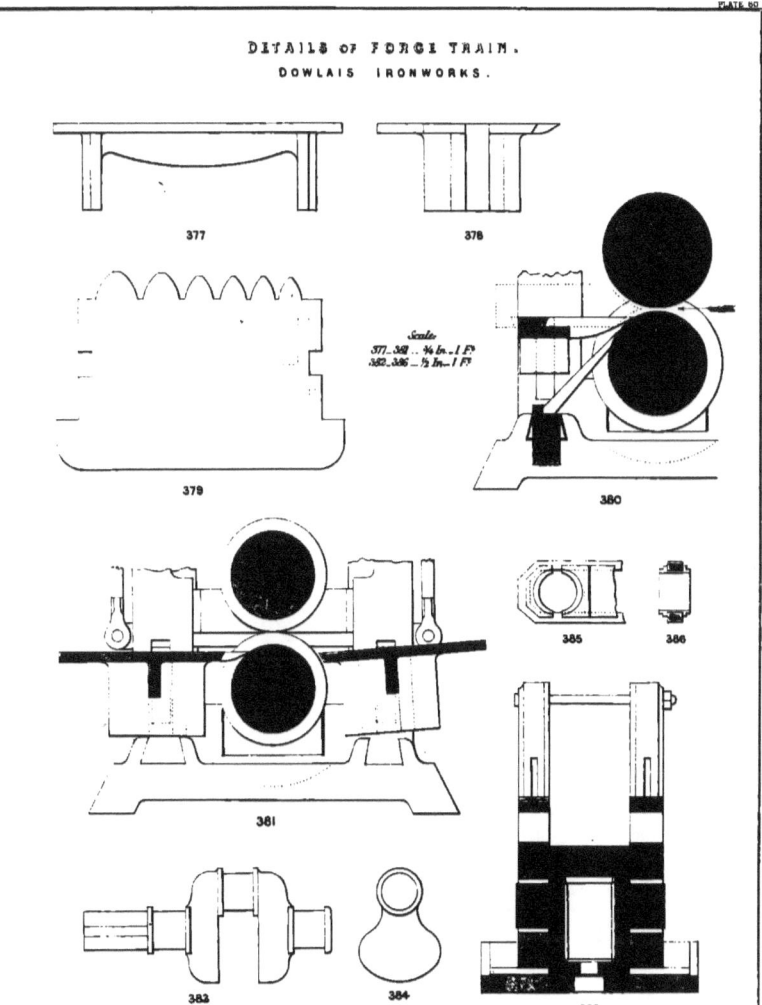

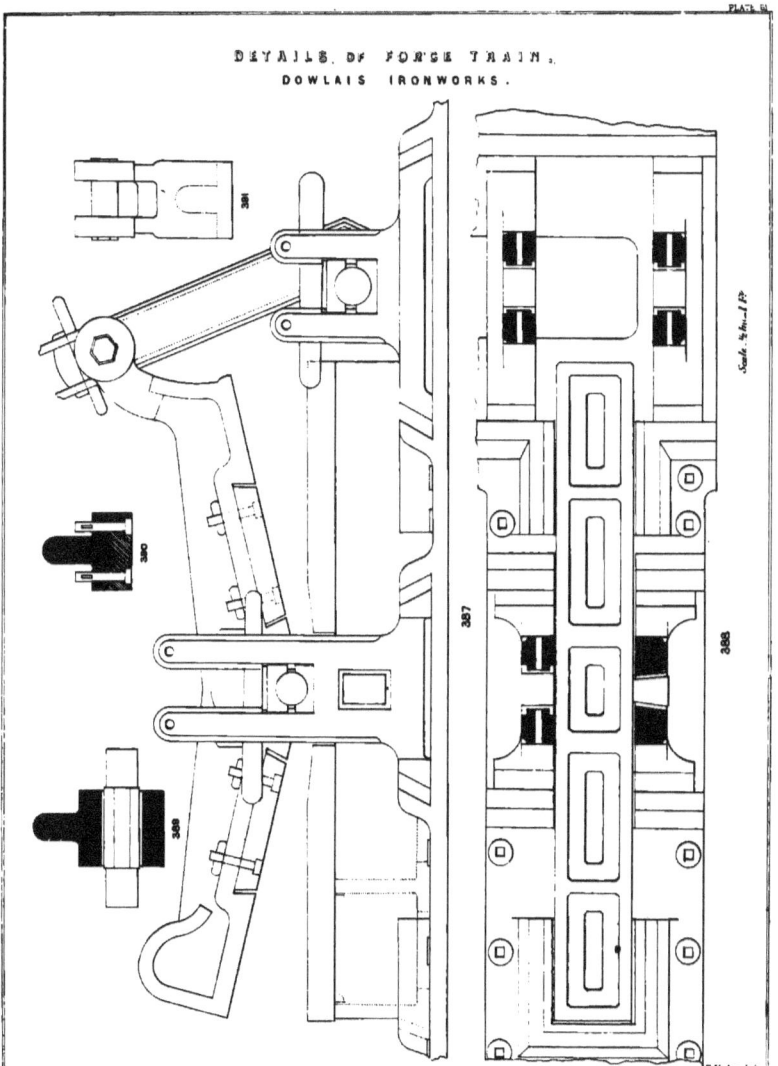

DETAILS OF FORGE TRAIN,
DOWLAIS IRONWORKS.

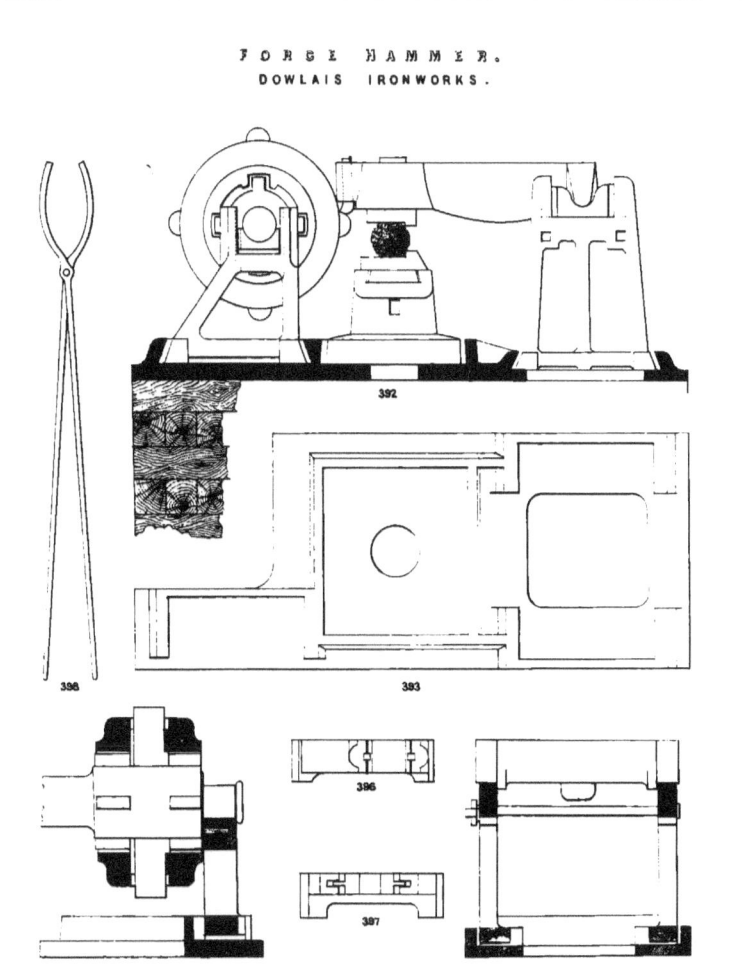

FORGE HAMMER.
DOWLAIS IRONWORKS.

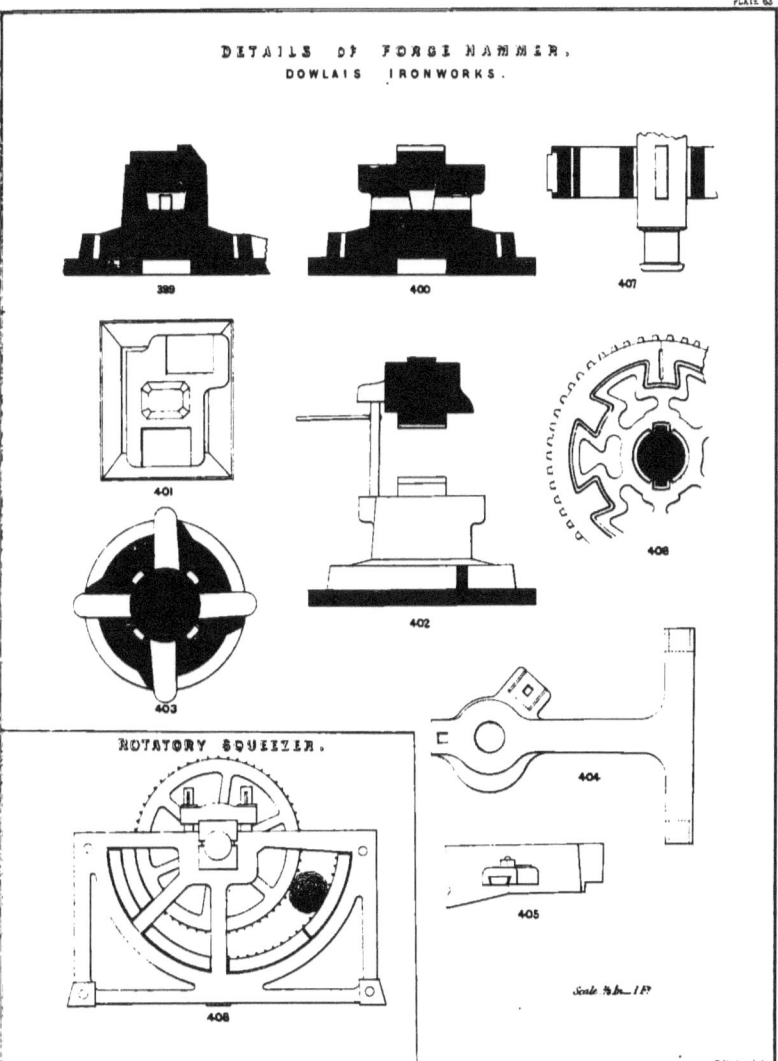

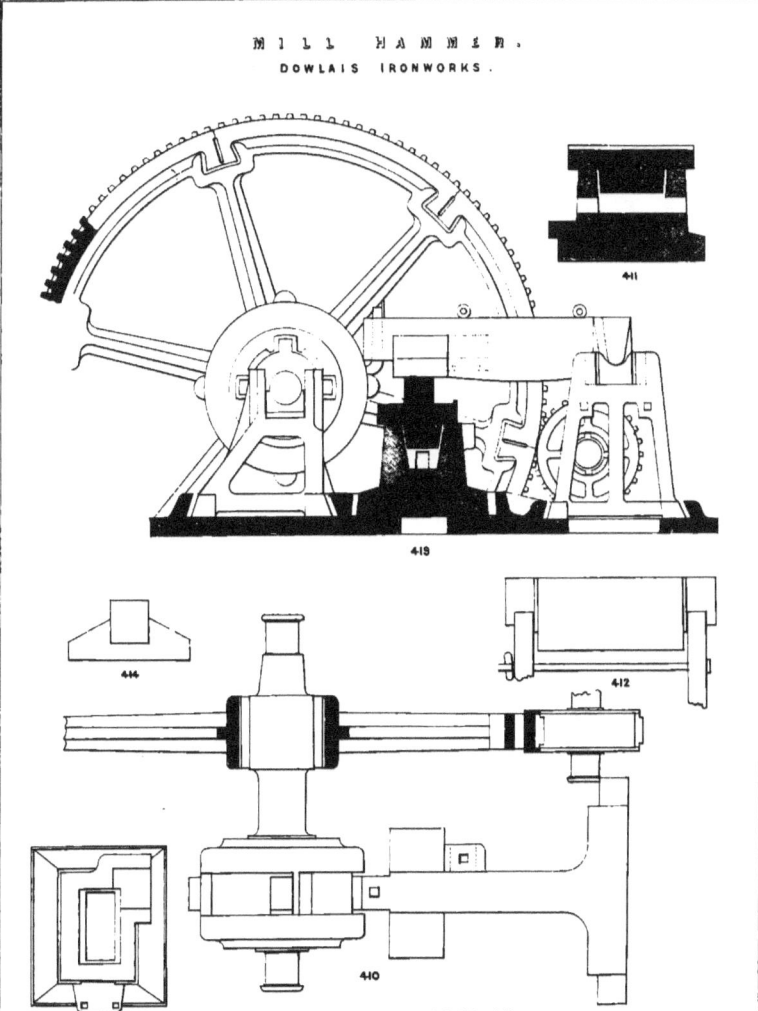

MILL HAMMER.
DOWLAIS IRONWORKS.

HEATING FURNACE.
FOREST & CYFARTHFA IRONWORKS.

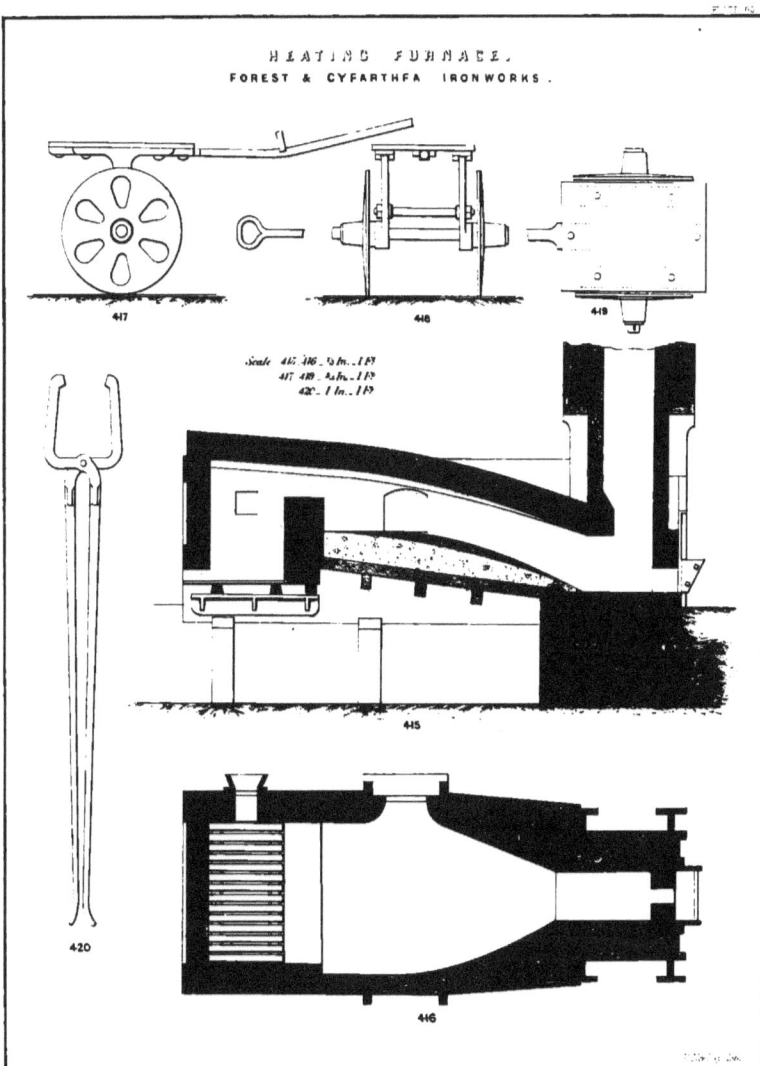

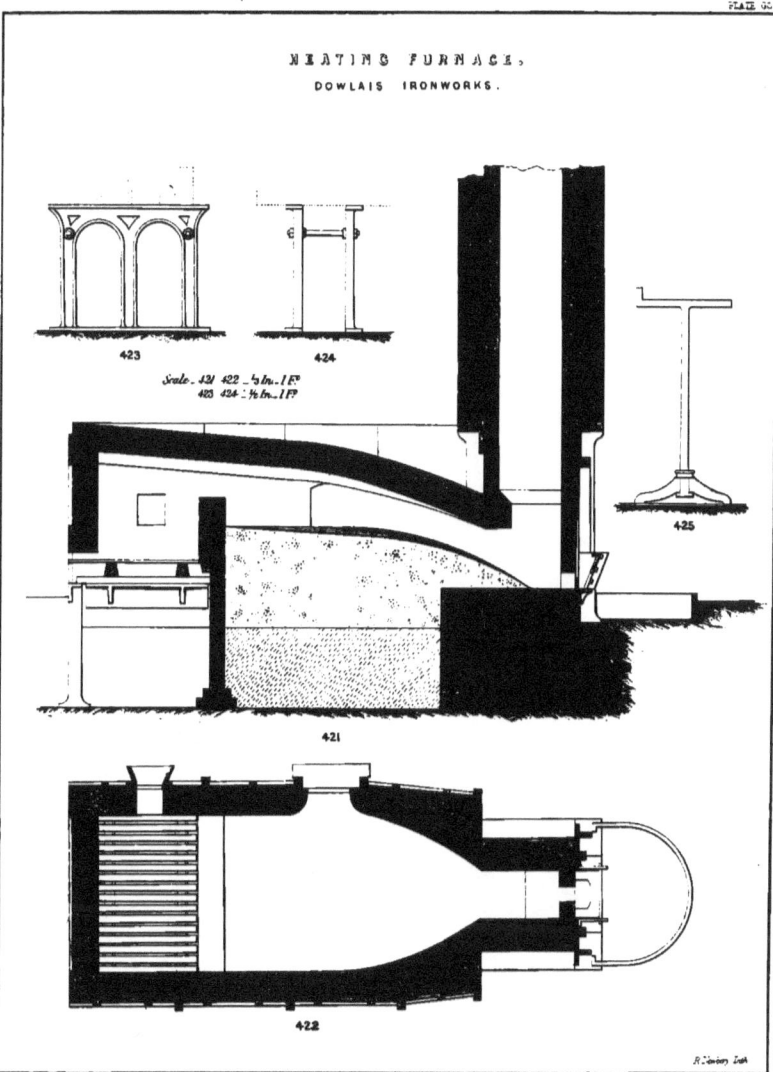

HEATING FURNACE,
DOWLAIS IRONWORKS.

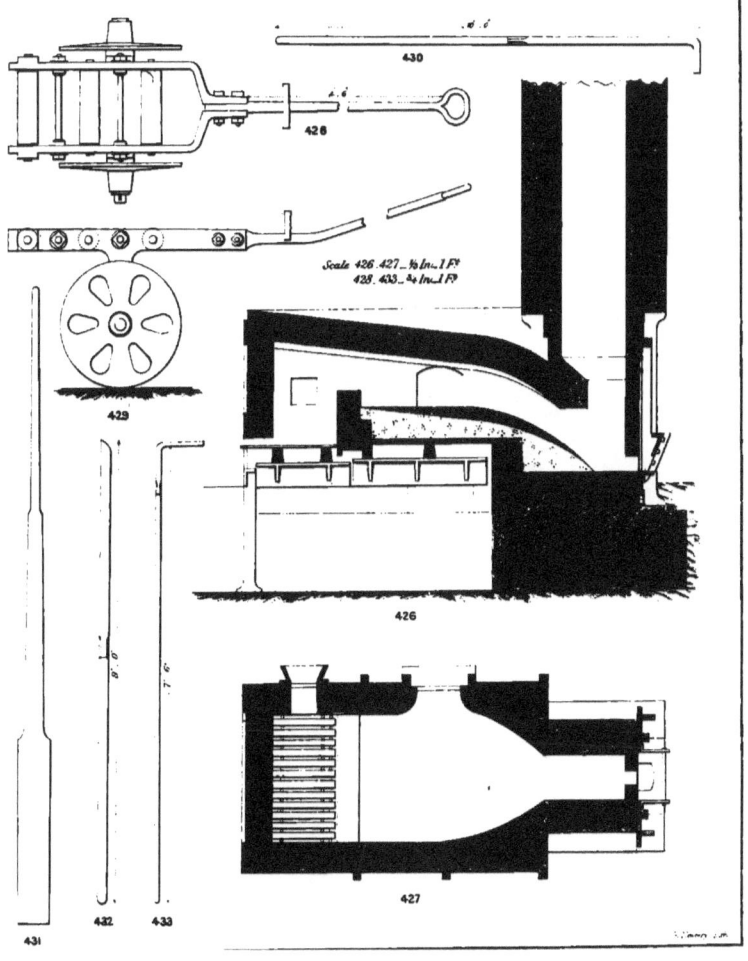

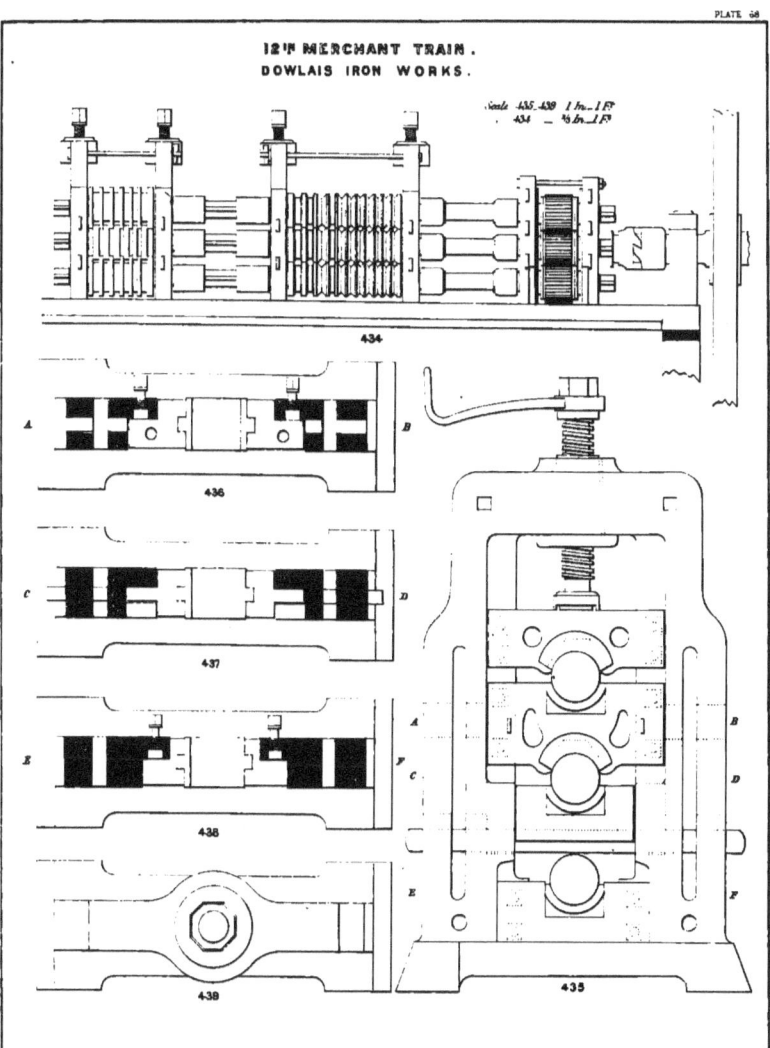

DETAILS OF 12" MERCHANT TRAIN.
DOWLAIS IRON WORKS.

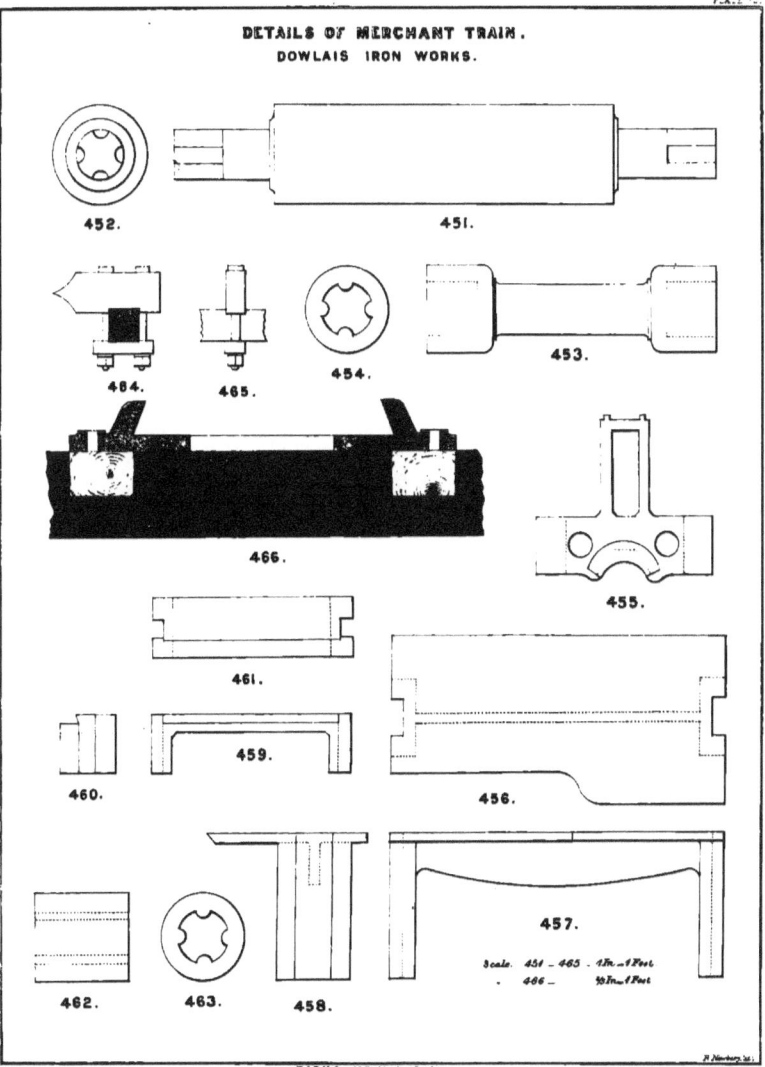

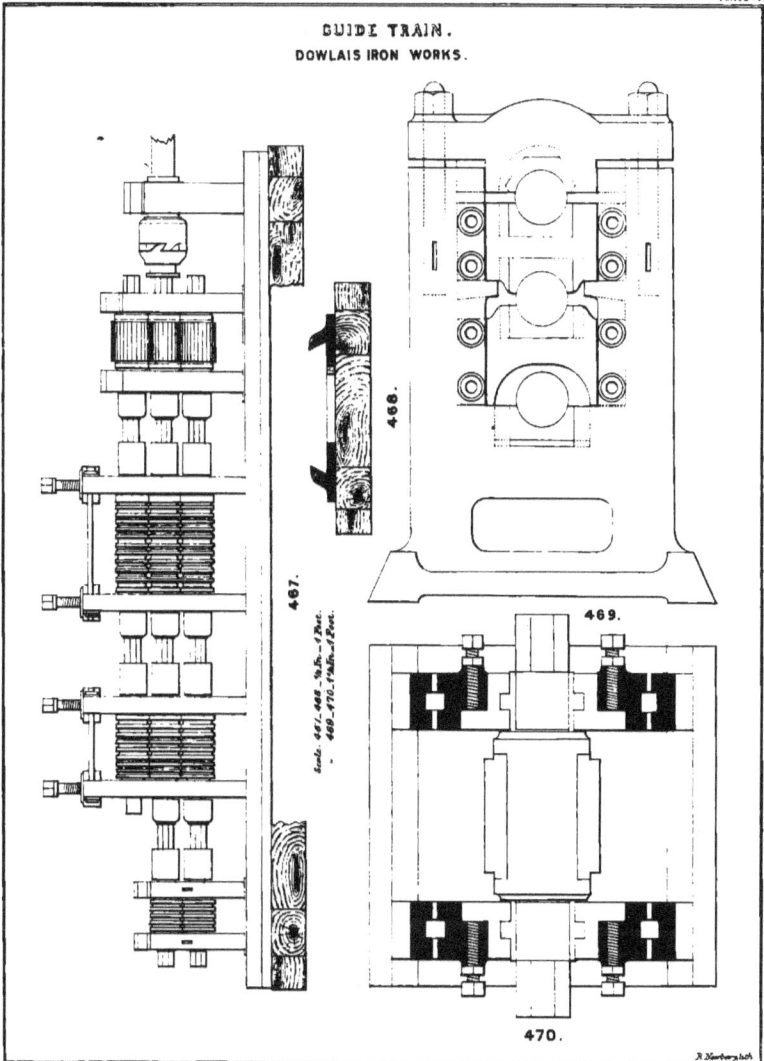

DETAILS OF GUIDE TRAIN.
DOWLAIS IRON WORKS.

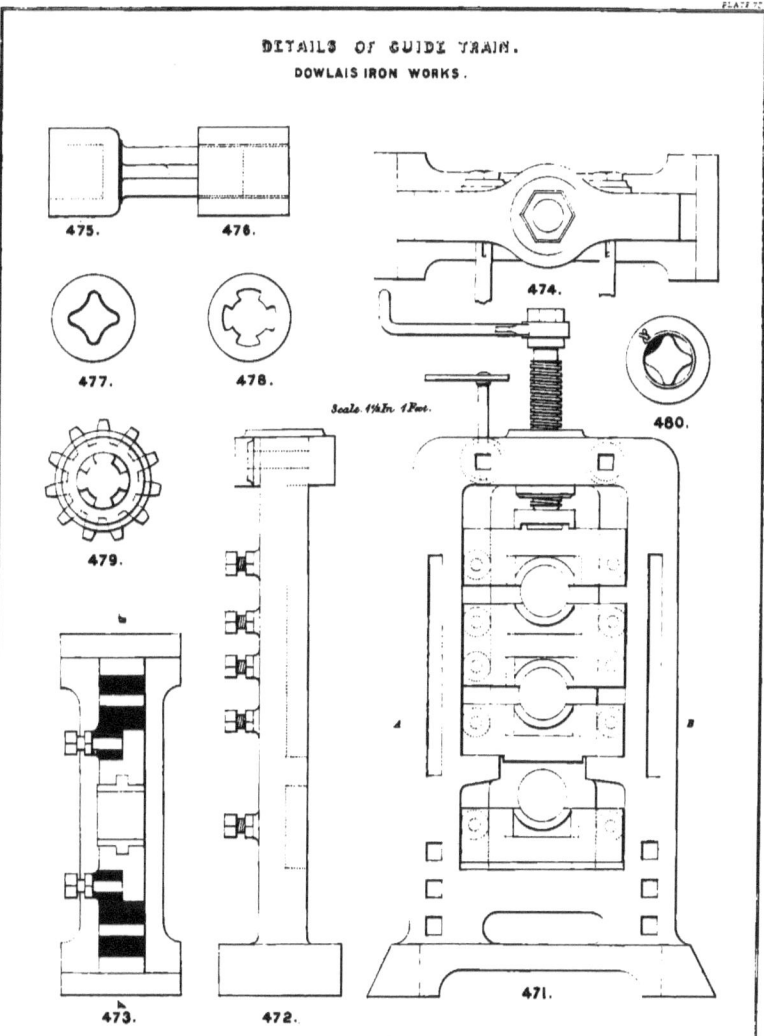

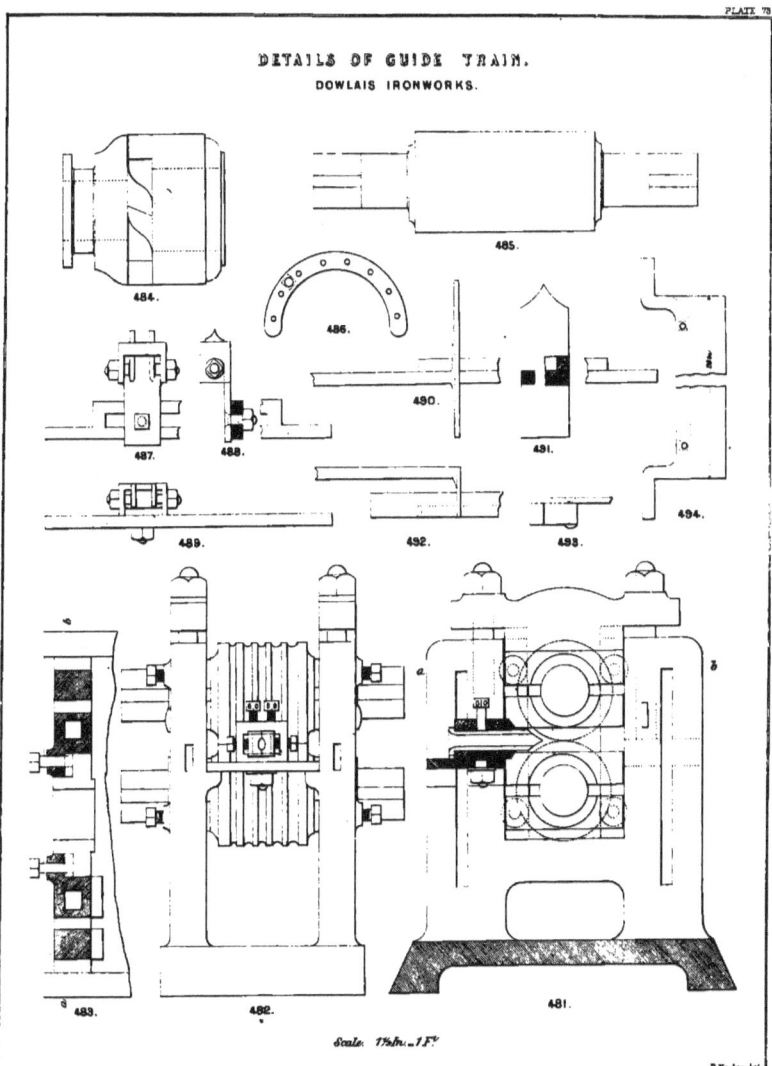

DETAILS OF GUIDE TRAIN.
DOWLAIS IRONWORKS.

Scale: 7½ In. = 1 Ft.

SLITTING MILL.

DOWLAIS IRONWORKS.

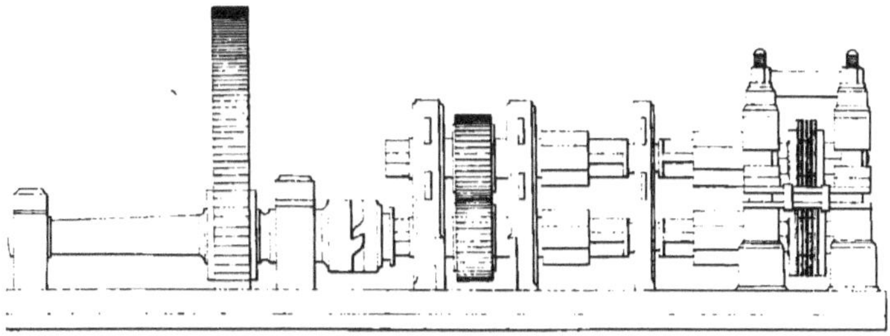

495.

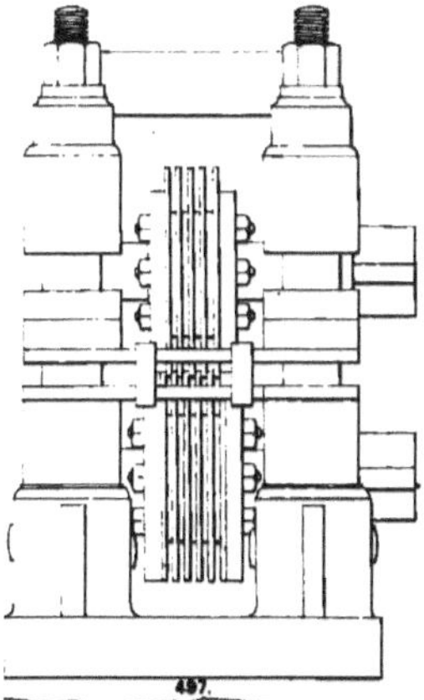

497.

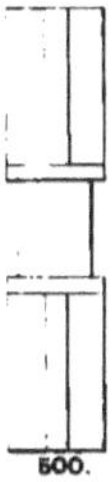

500.

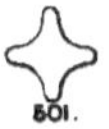

501.

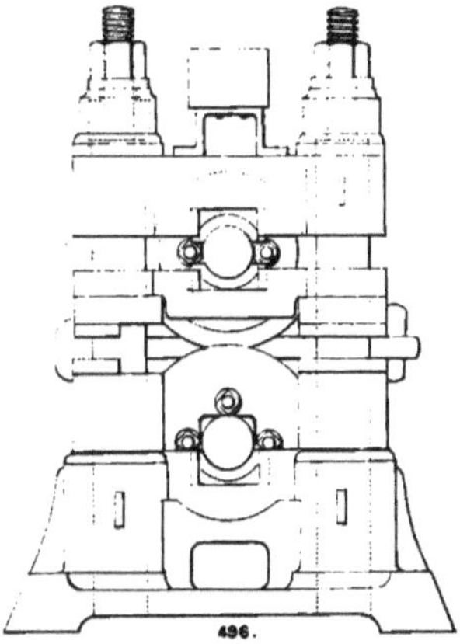

496.

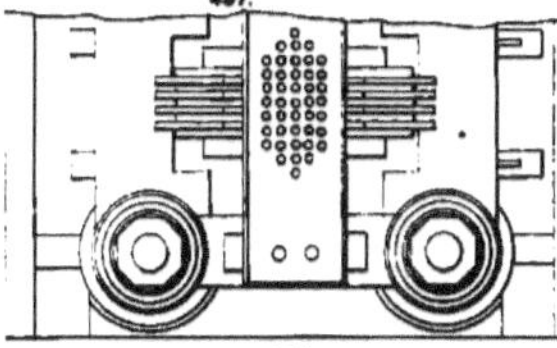

498.

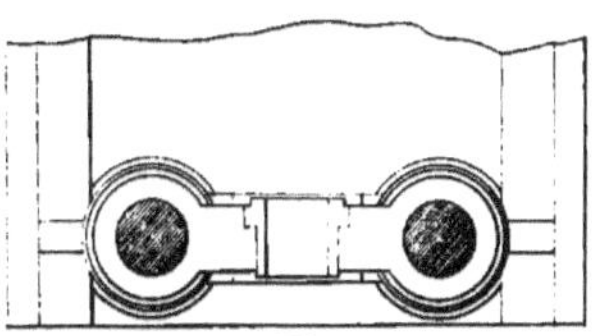

499.

Scale 496 - 501 1 In. - 1 Ft.
495 ½ In. - 1 Ft.

R. Newbery, lith.

E & F. N. Spon, 16 Bucklersbury, London

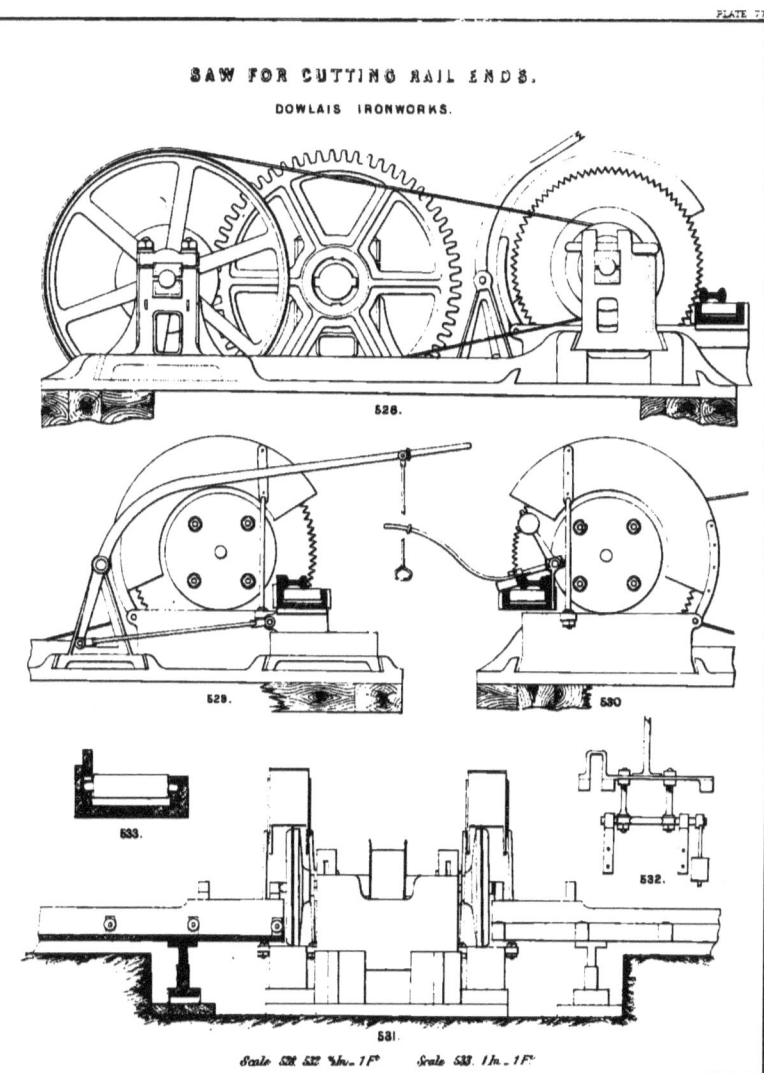

SAW FOR CUTTING RAIL ENDS.

DOWLAIS IRONWORKS.

DETAILS OF SAW.
DOWLAIS IRONWORKS.

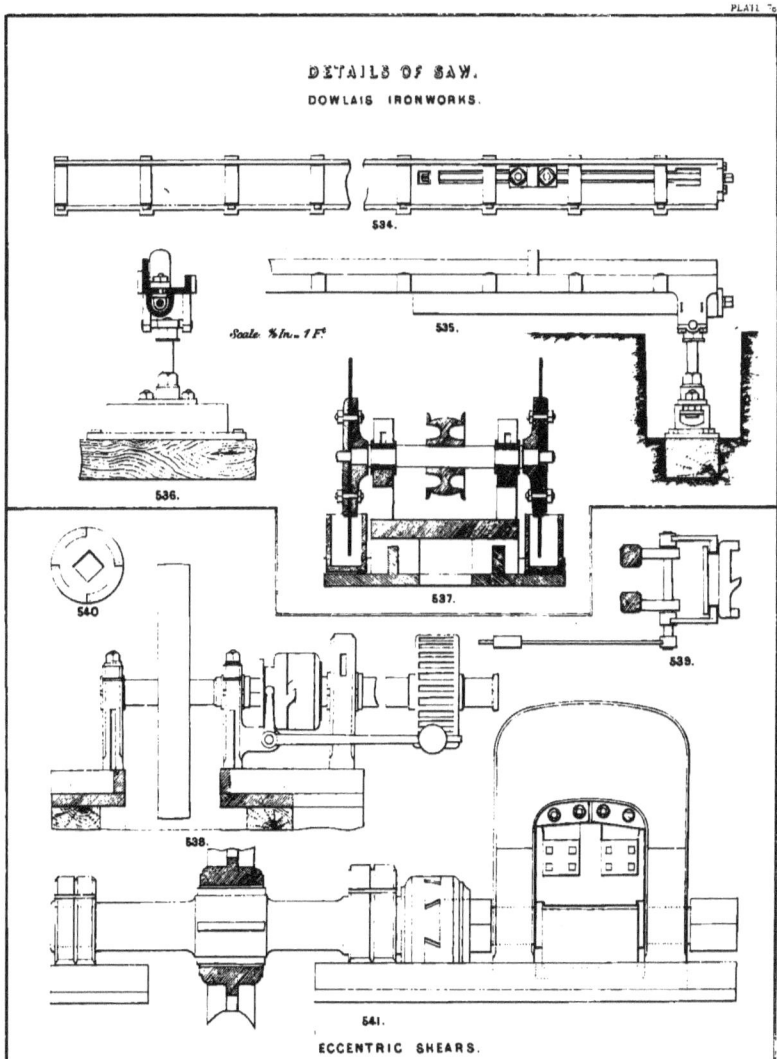

ECCENTRIC SHEARS.

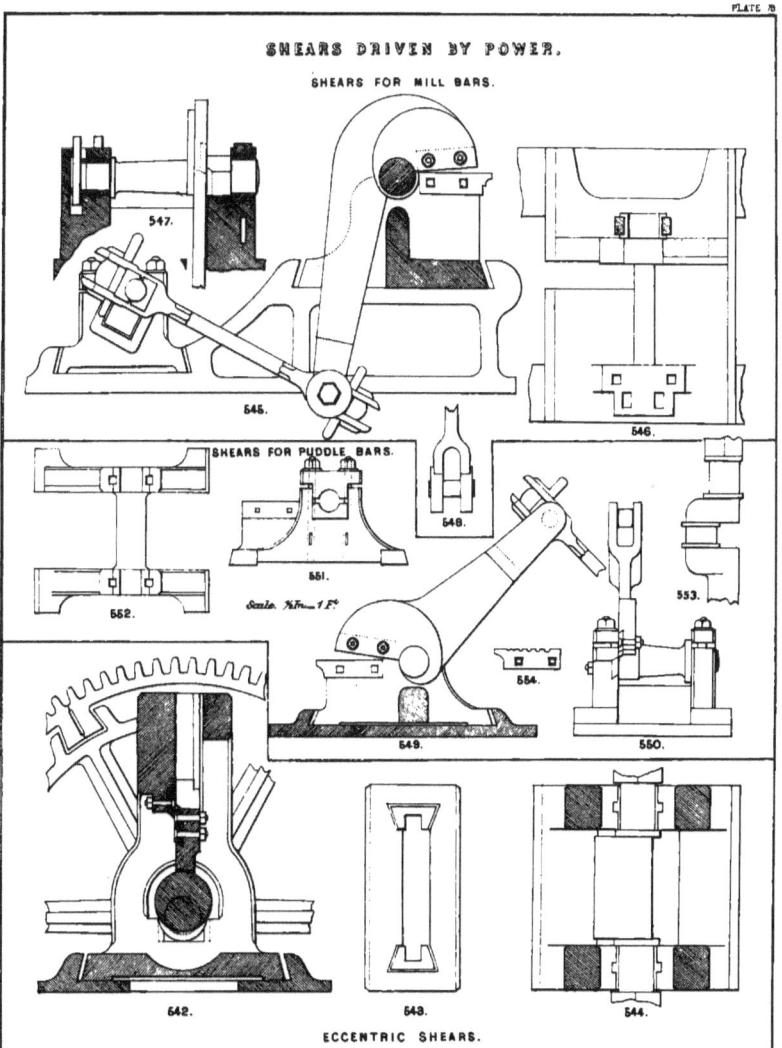

RAIL STRAIGHTENING PRESS.
CYFARTHFA IRONWORKS.

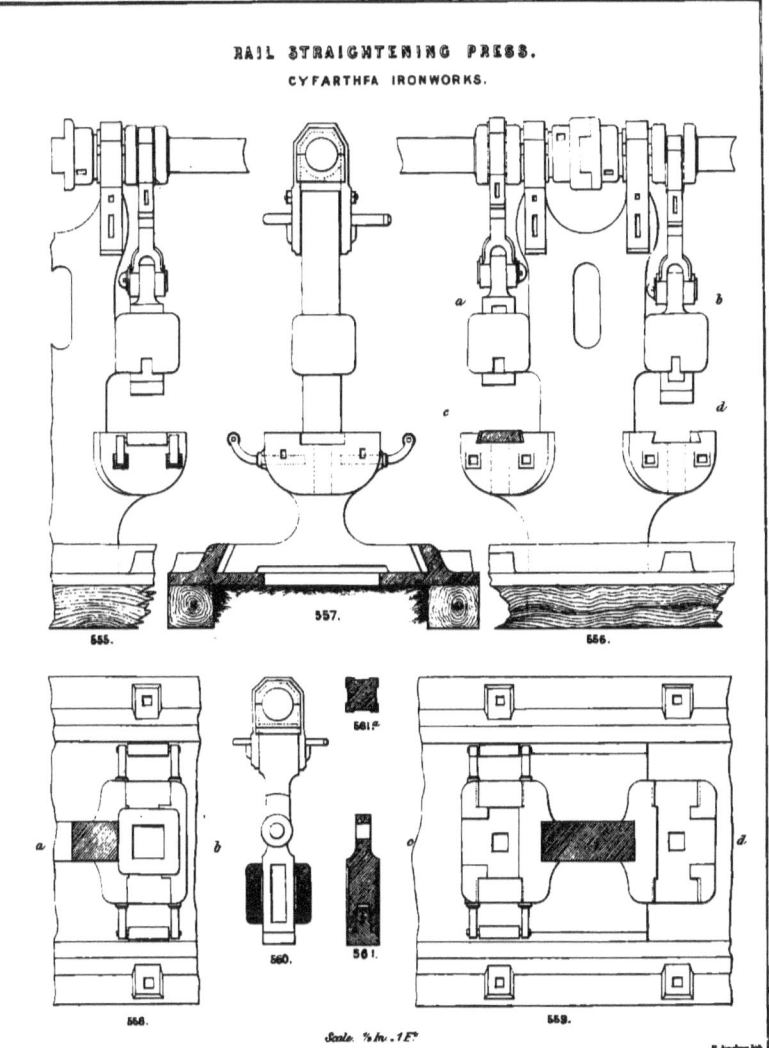

RAIL STRAIGHTENING PRESS.

DOWLAIS IRONWORKS.

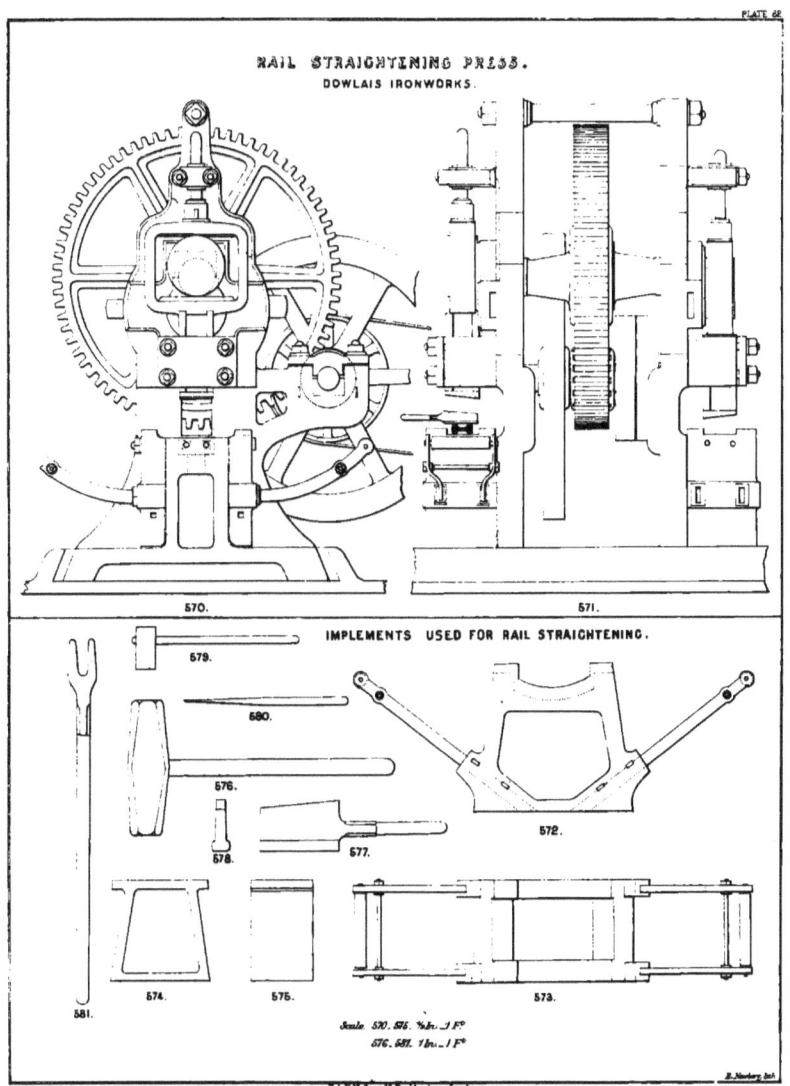

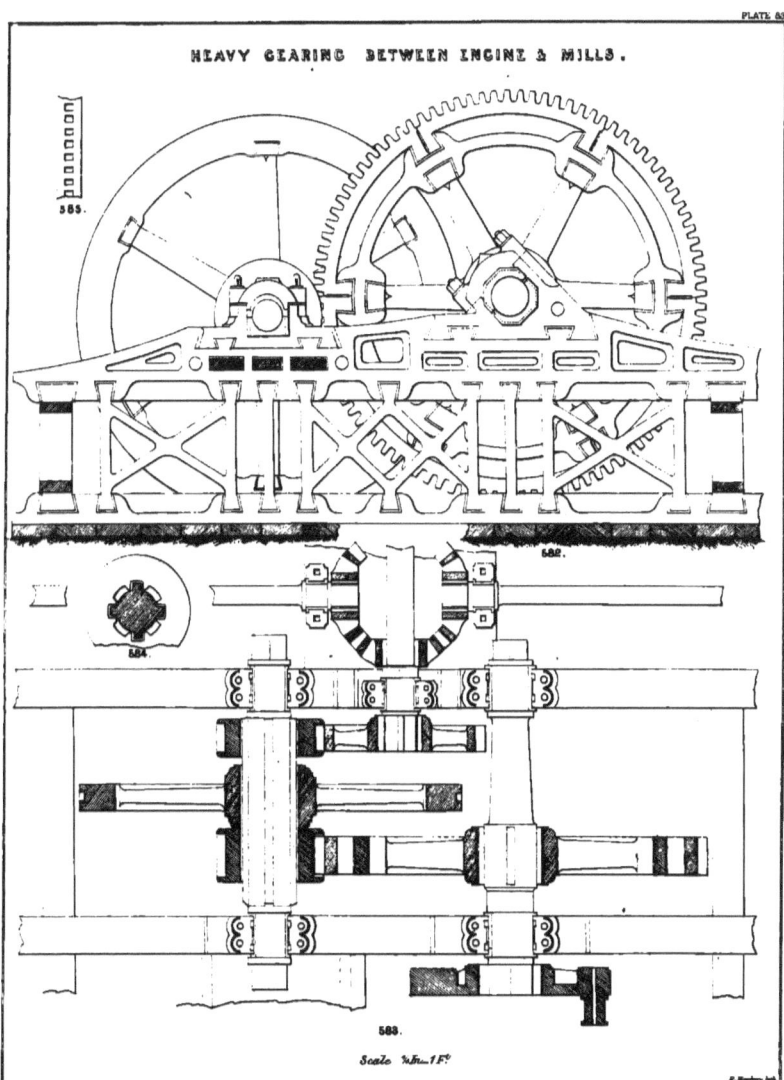

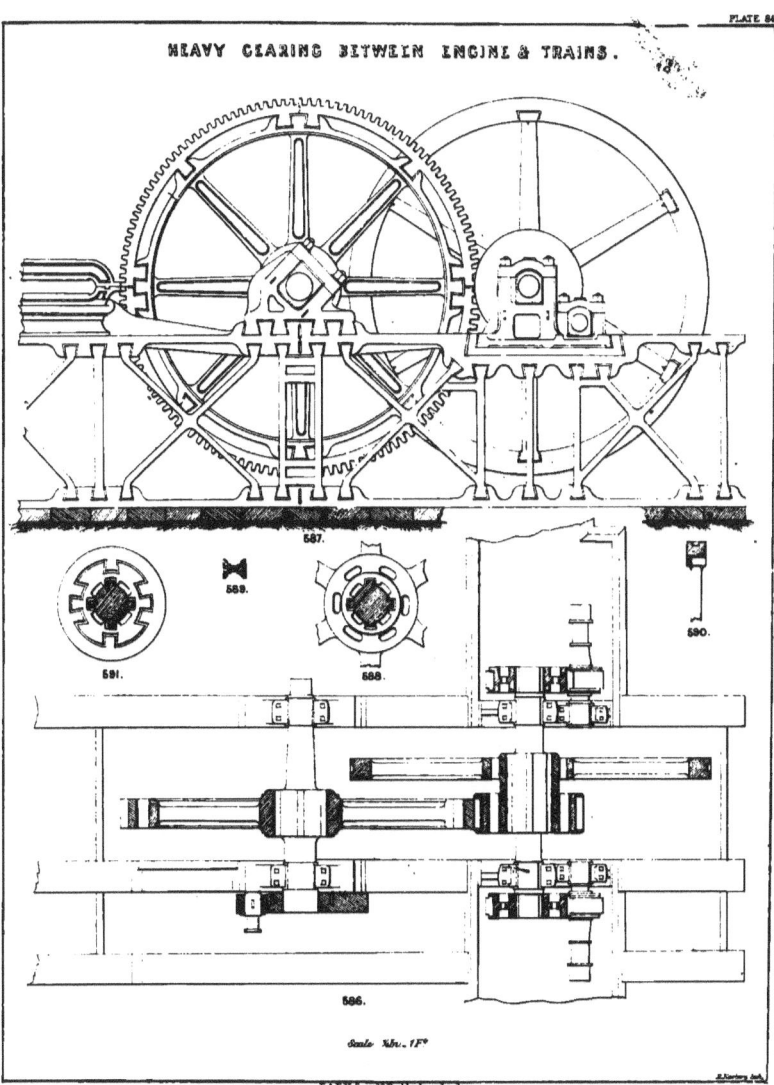

LIST OF BOOKS

PUBLISHED AND SOLD BY

E. & F. N. SPON,

16, BUCKLERSBURY, LONDON.

ANCIENT ALPHABETS.

The Book of Ornamental Alphabets, Ancient and Mediæval, from the Eighth Century, with Numerals, including Gothic, Church Text, (large and small), German, Italian, Arabesque, Initials for Illumination, &c., &c., for the use of Architectural and Engineering Draughtsmen, Illuminators, Masons, Decorative Painters, Lithographers, Engravers, Carvers, &c., &c., drawn and engraved by F. Delamotte, fifth edition, with additions, royal 8vo, oblong, cloth, 4s.

'We can very heartily commend it to the attention of those whom it has been especially intended by its ingenious collector designer, Mr. F. Delamotte."—*Sun.*

ARCHITECT & SURVEYORS' HANDBOOK.

A handbook for Architectural Surveyors and others engaged in building, by J. T. Hurst, C.E., containing formulæ useful in designing Builders' work, tables of the weights of the materials used in Building, memoranda connected with builders, work, mensuration, the practice of builders, measurement, constants of labour, valuation of property, summary of the practice in delapidations, and a scale of professional charges for Architectural surveyors, &c., &c., royal 32mo, roan, 5s.

BERNAN (W.)
History and Art of Warming and Ventilating Rooms and Buildings by Open Fires, Hypocausts, German, Dutch, Russian, and Swedish Stoves, Steam, Hot Water, Heated Air, Heat of Animals, and other Methods, &c., by W. Bernan, 240 *engravings*, 2 vols in 1, 12mo, cloth, 1s. 6d.

BIRT (W. R.)
The Manifestation and Operation of Volcanic Forces in modifying the Moon's surface, by W. R. Birt, F.R.A.S., 12mo, sewed, 6d.

BREWING.
Instructions for making Ale or Beer in all temperatures, especially adapted for Tropical Climates, by John Beadel, on a sheet, 6d.

CHANNEL RAILWAY (The).
Connecting England and France, by James Chalmers, *plates*, royal 8vo, cloth, 3s. 6d.

COTTAGES.
Designs for Schools, Cottages, and Parsonage Houses for Rural Districts, by H. Weaver, folio, half bound, 7s. 6d.

CHOCOLATE AND COCOA.
Cocoa; its growth and Culture, Manufacture, and Modes of Preparation for the Table, Illustrated with engravings, accompanied by easy methods of analysis, whereby its purity may be ascertained, by Charles Hewett, post 8vo, price 1s.

COFFEE AND CHICORY.
Coffee and Chicory; their culture, chemical composition, preparation for market, and consumption, with simple tests for detecting adulteration, and practical hints for the producer and consumer, by P. L. Simmons, F.S.S., Aut' of "The Commercial Products of the Vegetable Kingdom," "Dictionary of Trade Products, &c." &c., &c., post 8vo, sewed, 1s.

E. & F. N. SPON, 16, BUCKLERSBURY, LONDON.

COTTON CULTIVATION.
Cotton Cultivation in its various details, the Barrage of Great Rivers, and Instructions for Irrigating, Embanking, Draining, and Tilling Land in Tropical and other Countries possessing high thermometric temperatures, especially adapted to the improvements of the cultural soils of India, by Joseph Gibbs, Member Institute Civil Engineers, *with 5 plates*, crown 8vo, cloth, 7s. 6d.

COTTON SUPPLY.
Considerations relative to Cotton Supply, as *it* was, as it is, and as it might be, by Joseph Gibbs, Member Institute Civil Engineers, 8vo, sewed, 1s.

EARTHWORK TABLES.
A general sheet Table for facilitating the Calculation of Earthworks for Railways, Canals, &c., by F. Bashworth, M.A., on a large sheet, 6d.

EARTHWORK TABLES.
A general Table for facilitating the Calculation of Earthworks for Railways, Canals, &c., with a Table of Proportional Parts, by Francis Bashforth, M.A., Fellow of St. John's College, Cambridge, in 8vo, cloth, with mahogany slide, 4s.

"This little volume should become the hand-book of every person whose duties require even occasional calculations of this nature; were it only that it is more extensively applicable than any other in existence, we could cordially recommend it to our readers, but when they learn that the use of it involves only half the labour of all other Tables constituted for the same purpose, we offer the strongest of all recommendations, that founded on the value of time."—*Mechanics' Magazine*.

ELECTRICITY.
A Treatise on the Principles of Electrical Accumulation and Conduction, by F. C. Webb, Associate Institute Civil Engineers, part I., crown 8vo, cloth, 3s. 6d.

ELECTRO-METALLURGY.
Contributions towards a History of Electro-Metallurgy, establishing the Origin of the Art, by Henry Dircks, crown 8vo, cloth, 4s.

ENGINEERS' POCKET BOOK.

A Pocket Book of useful Formulæ and Memoranda for Civil and Mechanical Engineers, by Guildford L. Molesworth, Member Institute Civil Engineers, Chief Resident Engineer Ceylon Railway, seventh edition, revised and improved, 32mo, roan, 4s. 6d.

"Mr. Molesworth has done the profession a considerable and lasting benefit by publishing his very excellent Pocket Book of Engineering Formulæ. What strikes us first, is, the very convenient size and form of the book adopted by the author, and next in glancing over its contents we are pleased to find many really useful things not found elsewhere in any Engineering Pocket Book. Mr. Molesworth's treatment of Hydraulics and Hydro-Dynamics, and Motive Power, generally, is excellent. To the latter branch of his subject, Mr. Molesworth has evidently devoted considerable attention, and his collection of formulæ will be found most useful. But to stop to detail everything that is good and useful in this book would be nearly equal to reprinting a list of its contents."—*Artizan*, April, 1863.

ENGINEERS' PRICE BOOK.

Appleby's Illustrated Handbook and Prices current of Machinery and Iron Work, with various useful Tables of Reference, compiled for the use of Engineers, Contractors, Builders, British and Foreign Merchants, &c., 8vo, cloth, 2s. 6d.

FRENCH CATHEDRALS.

French Cathedrals, by B. Winkles, from drawings taken on the spot, by R. Garland, Architect, with an historical and descriptive account, 50 *plates*, 4to, cloth, 18s.

GLACIERS.

Expeditions on the Glaciers, including an ascent of Mont Blanc, Monte Rosa, Col du Géant, and Mont Buét, by a Private of the 38th Artists, and Member of the Alpine Club, post 8vo, sewed, 2s.

GOLD-BEARING STRATA.

On the Gold-bearing Strata of Merionethshire, by T. A. Readwin, F.G.S., 8vo, sewed, 6d.

HEAT.

An enquiry into the Nature of Heat, and into its Mode of Action in the Phænomena of Combustion, Vaporisation, &c., by Zerah Colburn, 8vo, boards, 2s.

HYDRAULICS.

Tredgold's Tracts on Hydraulics, containing Smeaton's experimental Papers on the Power of Water and Wind to turn Mills, &c., &c., Venturi's Experiments on the Motion of Fluids, and Dr. Young's Summary of Practical Hydraulics, *plates*, royal 8vo, boards, reduced to 6s.

ILLUMINATION.

A Primer of the Art of Illumination, for the use of beginners, with a rudimentary treatise on the art, practical directions for its exercise, and examples taken from Illuminated MSS. in gold and colours, by F. Delamotte, small 4to, cloth gilt, 9s.

"Modestly called a Primer, this little book has a good title to be esteemed a manual and guide-book in the study and practice of the different styles of ornamental lettering used by the artistic transcribers of past centuries. . . . An amateur may, with this silent preceptor, learn the whole art and mystery of illumination."—*Spectator*.

ILLUMINATION INITIALS.

Mediæval Alphabets and Initials for Illuminators, by F. G. Delamotte, with an Introduction by J. Willis Brooks, printed in gold and colours, small 4to, cloth gilt, 6s.

IRON BRIDGES.

A complete Treatise on Cast and Wrought Iron Bridge Construction, including Iron Foundations, in three parts, theoretical, practical, and descriptive, by William Humber, Associate Institute Civil Engineers, and Member of the Institution of Mechanical Engineers, 2 vols, imperial 4to, containing 80 double plates and 200 pages of text, an entirely new work, £6. 16s. 6d.

IRON BRIDGES.
Diagrams to facilitate the Calculation of Iron Bridges, by Francis Campin, C.E., folded in 4to, wrapper, 2s. 6d.

IRON BRIDGES.
A practical Treatise on Cast and Wrought Iron Bridges and Girders as applied to Railway Structures and to Buildings generally, with numerous examples drawn to a large scale, selected from the Public Works of the most eminent Engineers, *with 58 full page plates,* by William Humber, Associate Institute Civil Engineers, and Member of the Institution of Mechanical Engineers, imperial 4to, half bound in morocco, £1. 16s.

"Mr. Humber's admirable work on Iron Bridges."—*The Times.*

IRON (APPLICATION OF).
Two Lectures on Iron, and its application to the manufacture of Steam Engines, Millwork, and Machinery, by William Fairbairn, C.E., F.R.S., demy 8vo, sewed, 1s.

IRON MANUFACTURE.
The Iron Manufacture of Great Britain, Theoretically and Practically Considered; including Descriptive Details of the Ores, Fuels, and Fluxes employed; the Preliminary Operation of Calcination; the Blast, Refining, and Puddling Furnaces; Engines and Machinery; and the various Processes in Union, &c., by William Truran, C.E., Formerly Engineer at the Dowlais Iron Works, under the late Sir John Guest, Bart., subsequently at the Hirwain and Forest Works, under Mr. Crawshay, second edition, revised from the manuscript of the late Mr. Truran, by J. Arthur Phillips, Author of "A Manual of Metallurgy," "Records of Mining," &c., and W. H. Dorman, C.E., royal 4to, cloth, *illustrated by 84 plates of Furnaces and Machinery,* £3. 10s.

"Mr. Truran's work is really the only one deserving the name of a treatise upon and text-book of the Iron Manufacture of the Kingdom. It gives a most comprehensive and minute exposition of present practice, if the term may be applied to Iron Manufacture as distinguished from strictly professional subjects. The author does not go out of his way to theorise upon how Iron should or may be made, but he describes how it is made in all the Iron Districts of the Kingdom."—*Engineer*, December 26, 1862.

"It has seldom fallen to our lot to introduce to the notice of the scientific public a more valuable work than this. It is evidently the result of long, careful, and practical observation, and it forms at once a glorious monument to the memory of its author, and an excellent guide to those who are directly or indirectly interested in the great subject of which it treats."—*Mechanics' Magazine*, Sept. 26, 1862.

JONATHAN HULLS.

A description and draught of a new invented Machine for carrying Vessels or Ships out of or into any Harbour, Port, or River, against Wind and Tide, or in a calm, by Jonathan Hulls, 1737, reprint in fac-simile, 12mo, half morocco, reduced to 2s. sewed 1s.

LIFE CONTINGENCIES.

A brief View of the Works of the earlier eminent writers on the doctrine of Life Contingencies, by Thomas Carr, 8vo, sewed, 1s.

LOCKS AND SAFES.

A Treatise on Fire and Thief-proof Depositories, and Locks and Keys, by George Price, in one large vol. (916 pages), *with numerous wood engravings*, 8vo, cloth gilt, 5s.

LOCKS AND SAFES.

A Treatise on Gunpowder-proof Locks, Gunpowder-proof Lock Chambers, Drill-proof Safes, Burglars' methods of opening Iron Safes, and the various methods adopted to prevent them; why one maker's safes are better than another's; the Burnley Test, its history and results, by George Price, author of "A Treatise on Fire and Thief-proof Depositories and Locks and Keys," demy 8vo, cloth, *with 46 wood engravings*, 1s.

MARINE STEAM ENGINE.

A Catechism of the Marine Steam Engine, for the use of young Naval Officers and others, by Thomas Miller, Captain, R.N., F.R.G.S., F.S.A., 12mo, cloth, 2s.

LIST OF BOOKS PUBLISHED BY

MECHANICAL DRAWING.

An elementary Treatise on Orthographic Projection, being a new method of teaching the Science of Mechanical and Engineering Drawing, intended for the instruction of Engineers, Architects, Builders, Smiths, Masons, and Bricklayers, and for the use of Schools, *with numerous illustrations on wood and steel*, by William Binns, Associate Institute Civil Engineers, late Master of the Mechanical Drawing Class at the Department of Science and Art, and at the School of Mines, formerly Professor of Applied Mechanics at the College for Civil Engineers, &c., third edition, 8vo, cloth, 9s. Mr. Binns' system of Mechanical Drawing is in successful operation in all the Art Schools of the United Kingdom.

"Mr. Binns has treated his subject in a practical and masterly manner, avoiding theoretical disquisitions on the art, and giving direct and applicable examples, advancing progressively from the correct orthographic projection of the most simple to the most complex forms, thus clearing away the mist from the mind of the student, and leading him gradually to a correct and thorough appreciation of what he has undertaken, and to that which it is his desire to attain."—*The Artizan.*

MEMOIRS OF SCIENTIFIC MEN.

Memoirs of the Distinguished Men of Science of Great Britain, living A.D. 1807-8, by W. Walker, Jun., with an Introduction by Robert Hunt, F.R.S. second edition, revised and enlarged, containing the Lives of Watt, Rennie, Telford, Mylne, Jessop, Chapman, Murdock, the first to introduce gas into practical use; Rumford, Huddart, Boulton, Brunel, Watson, Bentham, Maudslay, Dalton, Cavendish, Sir Humphry Davy, Wollaston, Hatchet, Henry, Allen, Howard, Smith, the father of English Geology; Crompton, inventor of the Spinning Mule; Cartwright, Tennant, Ronalds, the first to successfully pass an electric telegraph message through a long distance; Charles Earl Stanhope, Trevithick, Nasmyth, Miller, of Dalswinton, and Symington, the inventors and constructors of the first practical Steam Boat; Professor Thomson, of Glasgow; Troughton, Donkin, Congreve, Herschel, Maske-

E. & F. N. SPON, 16, BUCKLERSBURY, LONDON.

lyne, Baily, Frodsham, Leslie, Playfair, Rutherford, Dollond, Brown the Botanist; Gilbert and Banks, the Presidents of the Royal Society at that epoch of time; Captain Kater, celebrated for his pendulum experiments; Dr. Thomas Young and Jenner, the benefactor of mankind; Jas. Ivory, Dr. Priestly, and Cort, the Father of the Iron Trade, post 8vo, cloth, 3s. 6d.

MINING.
A Practical Treatise on Mine Engineering, by G. C. Greewell, 61 *plates*, royal 4to, half bound, £2. 15s.

MINING.
Records of Mining and Metallurgy, or Facts and Memoranda for the use of the Mine Agent and Smelter, by J. Arthur Phillips and John Darlington, in crown 8vo, cloth, *illustrated by wood engravings*, by F. Delamotte, reduced to 4s., in boards, 3s.

MINING.
A Treatise on the Ventilation of Coal Mines, together with a Narrative of Scenes and Incidents in the Life of a Working Miner, by Robert Scott, 8vo, sewed, 1s.

MODERN ALPHABETS.
Examples of Modern Alphabets, plain and ornamental, including German, Old English, Saxon, Italic, Perspective, Greek, Hebrew, Court Hand, Engrossing, Tuscan, Riband, Gothic, Rustic, and Arabesque, with several original designs, and an analysis of the Roman and Old English Alphabets, for the use of Draughtsmen, Masons, Decorative Painters, Lithographers, Engravers, Carvers, Schools, &c., collected and engraved by F. Delamotte, royal 8vo, oblong, cloth, 4s.

"To artists of all classes, but more especially to architects and engravers, this very handsome book will be invaluable."—*Standard*.

List of Books Published by

MODERN ENGINEERING.

A Record of the progress of Modern Engineering, comprising Civil, Mechanical, Marine, Hydraulic, Railway Bridge, and other Engineering Works, with Essays and Reviews, edited by W. Humber, Associate Institute Civil Engineers, and Member of the Institution of Mechanical Engineers; the vol. for 1863 is now ready, imperial 4to, half morocco, £3. 3s.

OBLIQUE BRIDGES.

A practical Treatise on the Construction of Oblique Bridges with spiral and with equilibrated courses, *with* 12 *plates*, containing 100 figures, by Francis Bashforth, M.A., Fellow of St. John's College, Cambridge, 8vo, cloth, 6s.

ORNAMENT.

The book of Ornaments of every style, applicable to Art and Industry, for the use of Lithographers, Engravers, Silversmiths. Decorators, and other Art Workmen, by Jos. Scheidel, 5 numbers at 1s. 6d. each.

ORNAMENT.

Gleanings from Ornamental Art of every style, drawn from examples in the British, South Kensington, Indian, Crystal Palace, and other Museums, the Exhibitions of 1851 and 1862, and the best English and Foreign Works, *in a series of* 100 *plates*, containing many hundred examples, by R. Newberry, 4to, cloth, 30s.

PERPETUAL MOTION.

Perpetuum Mobile, or Search for Self-motive power during the 17th, 18th, and 19th Centuries, illustrated from various authentic sources in papers, essays, letters, paragraphs, and numerous patent specifications, with an introductory essay by Henry Dircks, C.E., *with numerous engravings of machines*, crown 8vo, cloth, 10s. 6d.

"A curious and interesting work. Mr. Dircks' chief purpose was to collect together all the materials requisite to form a record of what has been done, or attempted, rather in this curious branch of *quasi* science, and most instructive in one sense it is. Mr. Dircks' volume is well worth looking into; it contains a vast deal of entertaining matter."—*Builder*.

E. & F. N. Spon, 16, Bucklersbury, London.

RAILWAYS.

Railway Practice, a collection of working plans and practical details of construction in the Public Works of the most celebrated Engineers, comprising Roads, Tramroads and Railways, Bridges, Aqueducts, Viaducts, Wharfs, Warehouses, Roofs and Sheds, Canals, Locks, Sluices, and the various Piers and Jetties, Tunnels, Cuttings, and Embankments, Works connected with the Drainage of Marshes, Marine Sands, and the Irrigation of Land, Water Works, Gas Works, Water Wheels, Mills, Engines, &c., by S. C. Brees, C.E., Text in 4to, *with 279 plates in folio*, together 2 vols, half bound morocco, £3. 10s.

RAILWAY MASONRY.

The Guide to Railway Masonry, containing a complete Treatise on the Oblique Arch, by Peter Nicholson, third edition, revised by R. Cowen, C.E., *with 42 plates*, 8vo, cloth, 9s.

ROPEMAKING.

A Treatise on Ropemaking as practised in public and private Rope-yards, with a description of the manufacture, rules, tables of weights, &c., adapted to the Trade, Shipping, Mining, Railways, Builders, &c., by R. Chapman, formerly foreman to Messrs. Huddart and Co., Limehouse, and late Master Rope Maker of H.M. Dockyard, Deptford, 18mo, cloth, 2s.

SCREW CUTTING.

Screw Cutting Tables for the use of Mechanical Engineers, showing the proper arrangement of Wheels for cuttings the threads of screws of any required pitch, with a Table for making the Universal Gas Pipe Threads and Taps, by W. A. Martin, Engineer, royal 8vo, oblong, cloth, 1s., sewed, 6d.

SCREW PROPELLER.

The Screw Propeller, what it is, and what it ought to be, by R. Griffith, 8vo, sewed, 6d.

SURVEYING.
A practical Treatise on the science of Land and Engineering Surveying, Levelling, estimating quantities, &c., with a general description of the several Instruments required for Surveying, Levelling, Plotting, &c., and Illustrations and Tables, by H. S. Merrett, royal 8vo, cloth, 16s.

TRADE OF NEWCASTLE-ON-TYNE.
History of the Trade and Manufactures of the Tyne, Wear, and Tees, comprising the papers prepared under the auspices of a Committee of Local Industry, and other documents of a similar character, read at the second meeting in Newcastle-on-Tyne of the British Association for the advancement of Science, revised and corrected by the writers, second edition, 8vo, boards, 3s. 6d.

TURBINE.
A practical Treatise on the construction of the Turbine or Horizontal Water-wheel, with seven plates specially designed for the use of operative Mechanics, by William Cullen, Millwright and Engineer, 4to, sewed, 6s.

TURNING.
Turners' and Fitters' Pocket-Book for calculating the change wheels for screws on a Turning Lathe, and for a Wheel-cutting Machine, by J. La Nicca, 18mo, sewed, 6d.

TURNING.
The practice of Hand-turning in Wood, Ivory, Shell, &c., with Instructions for turning such works in Metal, as may be required in the practice of Turning in Wood, Ivory, &c., also an Appendix on Ornamental Turning, by Francis Campin, *with wood engravings*, crown 8vo, cloth, 6s.

WAGE TABLE.
Delany and Okes' Wage Table for Engineers, Shipbuilders, Contractors, Builders, &c., from one-quarter of an hour in regular progression to nine and three-quarter hours, from one day to ten days, at one shilling to eight shillings per day, on one sheet, 1s.

E. & F. N. Spon, 16, Bucklersbury, London.

EXPERIMENTAL RESEARCHES
IN
STEAM ENGINEERING,
By B. F. ISHERWOOD,
Chief Engineer U.S. Navy, Chief of the Bureau of Steam Engineering Navy Department,

Made principally to aid in ascertaining the Comparative Economic Efficiency of Steam used with different measures of Expansion, and the Absolute Cost of the Power obtained therefrom in Weights of Fuel and Steam; the Causes and Quantities of the Condensations in the Cylinder; the Economic Effect of Steam Jacketing, and Steam Superheating and of various proportions of Cylinder Capacity for the same weight of Steam used per stroke of Piston; the Economic and Absolute Evaporative Efficiencies of Boilers of different types and proportions; the Comparative Calorific Values of different Coals as Steam Generators; the Performances of United States' War Screw Steamers, &c., &c., the whole being original matter composed of extensive Experiments made by the U. S. Navy Department.

Vol. 1 (all published) 4to, half morocco neat, £2. 5s.

In 2 vols., royal 8vo, half morocco, neat, price £2 10s.

APPLETON'S
DICTIONARY OF MACHINES,
MECHANICS, ENGINE-WORK, & ENGINEERING,
WITH
4000 ENGRAVINGS ON WOOD, AND MANY STEEL PLATES.

EDITED BY OLIVER BYRNE.
SECOND EDITION.

London: E. & F. N. Spon, 16, Bucklersbury.

Just Published, Elephant Folio, Cloth, Price £2 2s.
PRACTICAL ILLUSTRATIONS OF

LAND AND MARINE ENGINES, shewing in detail the Modern Improvements in High and Low Pressure, Surface Condensation, Superheating, together with Land and Marine Boilers. By N. P. BURGH, Engineer.

LIST OF PLATES.

Plate 1. High Pressure Steam Engine, 12 H.P.; Scale 1½-in. =1 foot; 3 Views.

Plate 2. Details of High Pressure Engine, 12 H.P.; Scale 3-in. =1 foot. Cylinder, Piston, Slide Casing, Slide Valve and Rod, Connecting Rod, Piston Rod and Guide Block, Eccentric and Band, Slide Connecting Rod, Disengaging Socket, Eccentric Rod, Weigh Shaft, Lever Stud Bracket, Slide and Pump Levers, Main Lever, Starting Handle, Ball Governor, in detail, Governor Standard and Pully.

Plate 3. Details of High Pressure Engine, 12 H.P.; Scale 3 in. =1 foot. Main Framing, Fly-Wheel, Crank and Shaft, Feed Pump, Disengaging Socket, Link and Pin, Governor, Mitre Gear, Holding down Bolts, Studs, Plates, &c., &c.

Plate 4. Details of High Pressure Engine, 12 H.P.; Half-size. Feed Pump, Valves and Box, Relief Valve, Safety Valve, Starting and Governor Valves, Engine Feed Cock, Boiler Front Doors, Fire Bars, and Supports.

Plate 5. Boiler and Settings, 12 H.P.; Scale ¾-in. =1 foot; 4 Views.

Plate 6. Patent Antifriction Trunk Engine, 6 H.P. Invented by the Author, Burgh and Cowan's Patent. Arrangement, 4 Views; Scale 1½-in. =1 foot; Details—Scale, 3-in. = 1 foot. Cylinder, Slide Valve and Casing, Piston Covers and Trunks, Piston Rod and Guide Rod, Connecting Rod, Main Framing, Fly-Wheel, Governor and Levers, Eccentric Rods and Strap, Shaft and Discs, Starting Handle, Feed Pump, and Plunger.

MARINE ENGINES.

Plate 7. Marine Engine, Direct Acting for the Screw Propeller, 400 H.P. Collectively; Scale ¾-in. 1 foot; 7 Views.

Plate 8. Details of One Marine Engine, 200 H.P.; Condenser and Air Pump, Feed and Bilge Pumps, Cylinder, Equilibrium Slide Valve and Casing, Main Frame, Connecting Rod,—Scale 2-in. =1 foot; Guide Block and Cross-head—Scale 2-in. =1 foot; Discharge and Suction Valves for Air Pump, 3-in. =1 foot.

Plate 9. Details of One Marine Engine, 200 H.P. Eccentrics and Straps, Solid Valve Link and Block, Slide Valve Rod and Guide, Blow Through Valve, Shifting Valve, Relief Valve, Bilge and Feed Pump Valves, Spur Wheel for Expansion Gear, Kingston and Injection Valves,—Scale 3-in. = 1 foot; Crank Shaft—Scale 1½-in. = 1 foot.

Plate 10. Details of One Marine Engine, 200 H.P.; Scale 3-in. = 1 foot. Air Valves for Air Pumps, Steam Piston, Injection Pipe, Air Pump Plunger, Air, Feed, and Bilge Pump Rods, Blow Through Valve for Condenser, Bracket for Reversing Gear, Drain Cock and Handle for Condenser.

Plate 11. Scale 3-in = 1 foot; Expansion Valve Gear, Throttle Valve, and end of Thrust Shaft for Marine Engine, 200 H.P.

Plate 12.—Oscillating Engines for the Paddle Wheel, 150 H.P. Collectively; Scale 1-in.=1 foot; 7 Views.

Plate 13. Paddle Feathering Wheel, 75 H.P.—Scale 1-in. =1 foot; 2 Views.

Plate 14. Details of Paddle Wheel, 75 H.P. Paddle Centre, Plummer Block, Eccentric Shaft and Bracket Lever Arms, Rings, Stays, Rods, Bolts and Pins, Float Clamps, Arm Stays, and Floats, —Scale 3-in. = 1 foot.

Plate 15. Griffith Patent Screw Propeller, with Lifting Frame. Scale 1½-in. =1 foot; 5 Views.

Plate 16. Arrangement of a Pair of Marine Steam Engines of 900 H.P., for the Imperial Ottoman Iron-Clad Frigate, "Sultan Mahmoud," constructed by Ravenhill, Salkeld, & Co., London, 1864. Scale ½-in. =1 foot.

Plate 17. Marine Boiler, with Superheating Tubes, Scale 1-in. = 1 foot, 6 Views.

Plate 18. Ordinary Condenser and Air Pump for Screw Marine Engine, 200 H.P. and Oscillating Paddle Engine, 75 H.P.; 8 Views.

Plate 19. Surface Condenser, 200 H.P. — Scale 1½-in. =1 foot; 4 Views.

Plate 20. General Arrangement of Engines, Boilers, Shafting and Screw for a Despatch Boat, 100 H.P. Scale ½-in. =1 foot; 5 Views.

N.B.—The Detailed Plates have the dimensions fully given.

Also by the same Author, Royal 32mo, roan, price 4s. 6d.
RULES FOR DESIGNING, CONSTRUCTING, AND ERECTING LAND AND MARINE ENGINES, AND BOILERS.

London: E. & F. N. SPON, 16, Bucklersbury.

www.ingramcontent.com/pod-product-compliance
Lightning Source LLC
Chambersburg PA
CBHW020526300426
44111CB00008B/559